PRINCIPLES
FOR A
CATHOLIC MORALITY

REVISED EDITION

PRINCIPLES FOR A CATHOLIC MORALITY

REVISED EDITION

Timothy E. O'Connell

HarperSanFrancisco

A Division of HarperCollins*Publishers*

Library of Congress Cataloging-in-Publication Data

O'Connell, Timothy E.
    Principles for a Catholic morality / Timothy E. O'Connell.—Rev. ed.
      p. cm.
    Includes bibliographical references.
    ISBN 0-06-254865-4
    1. Christian ethics—Catholic authors.   I. Title.
BJ1249.026 1990   89-45553
241'.042—dc20   CIP

90 91 92 93 94 BANTA 10 9 8 7 6 5 4 3 2

To my colleagues,
faculty, staff, and students,
at the
Institute of Pastoral Studies,
Loyola University Chicago.

The journey is better with friends.

ACKNOWLEDGMENTS

The author gratefully acknowledges permission to use material on which the following hold copyright:

Chicago Studies, for the bulk of chapter 9, which originally appeared as "The Theology of Conscience," (Vol. 14 [1976], 149–166); for portions of chapters 7 and 8, which originally appeared as "A Theology of Sin," (Vol. 21 [1982], 277–292); for portions of chapter 17, which originally appeared as "Moral Method and Healthcare Ethics," (Vol. 27 [1988], 241–256).

Liturgy Training Program of the Archdiocese of Chicago for portions of chapters 2 and 12, which originally appeared as a pamphlet entitled, "Identification of Sin," *Reconciliation Background Papers* (1976).

Confraternity of Christian Doctrine for all scriptural quotations that are taken from the *New American Bible*.

CONTENTS

FIRST EDITION

In the autumn of 1973 I began to teach a course in principles of Catholic morality. And as I began to develop this course, I soon became aware of a major obstacle: the lack of appropriate resources.

It was not that I had no idea of what I wanted to do. Having previously studied the development of one of the major moral theologians of our time, I was conscious of the basic shape of moral theology today. On certain ideas that remain controversial, I had been following and participating in the dialogue in the theological community. And it was certainly not that there was no literature available. If anything, recent years have witnessed a superabundance of writing on the issues in this field. So if one wanted simply to distribute articles to students, there were plenty of articles to choose from.

But articles do not necessarily make an appropriate resource, and that was the problem. The writing that was available to me was episodic and incoherent. On some topics it was extremely repetitive while on others it left many questions unanswered. Different authors used different vocabularies to say the same thing and similar terms with different meanings. In a word, it was the sort of literature that is both interesting and useful *after* one has a general understanding, but is a poor tool for the achievement of that understanding.

What I was looking for was a statement of Christian moral principles that would have three qualities. It would be moderately resonant with contemporary human experience, speaking to the real lives of Christians today and making sense to them. It would be internally consistent, not contradicting itself or presenting its various ideas in a disintegrated way. It would at least attempt to be comprehensive, trying to ask all the important questions and to formulate all the necessary answers. That is what I was looking for. And it did not exist.

This book was conceived, therefore, in the autumn of 1973. As I have continued to teach the course on principles of morality, as I have devel-

oped my own ideas on the various topics, and as I have shared my conclusions and dialogued about them with audiences of clergy and laity,
Catholics and Protestants, teachers and college students, as all this has
taken place, this book has moved slowly toward birth. It has now
arrived, and a few introductory comments are in order.

First of all, while the book clearly exists within the context of contemporary Catholic moral theology, it is a personal synthesis. It is true that
many of the insights developed here are derivative, and I have tried to
give credit to all those thinkers on whom I depend. But at the same
time, the structure and organization of the synthesis as well as a number
of the assertions are purely my own. They must therefore stand or fall
on their own merits.

Secondly, and following from the above, as a personal synthesis the
book tries to blend the worlds of ordinary living and scholarly reflection. It is forthrightly scholarly in the sense that it attempts to deal with
and make use of the best work being done today in the science of moral
theology. But at the same time, it also attempts to speak plainly and
directly about a topic which is, after all, our own lives as we live them.
So for the most part, the intramural debates of scholars are relegated to
the footnotes. The text itself simply takes a position and seeks to present
it clearly and meaningfully.

Thirdly, this direct style is intended to make the book useful to a relatively wide audience. Its ideas are addressed not only to students of theology or to clergy, but also to anyone interested in understanding the
living of the Christian life. Just as the ideas of this book have already
been presented to widely divergent audiences and have been found
helpful, so I hope that offering them in written form will also provide a
service.

Fourthly, while it is hoped that this book is an appropriate resource
for the academic study of moral theology, it cannot pretend to be an
exhaustive resource. Much has been written on the various questions
that challenge moral theology today, and many worthwhile and enriching nuances have been developed by various authors. Within the limits
of this book it has been impossible to give extended attention to all of
these. So again I have had to settle for the modest indications that can
be given in footnotes. Many of the notes function as doorways to further
study, indicating some of the more important available resources which
the reader may wish to investigate, some of the participants in and locations of the ongoing discussions of the various issues we will consider.

Finally, the book deals with principles of *Catholic* morality. And that
needs a bit of explaining. I do not mean to adopt a sectarian stance that
would make the discussion meaningful only to Catholics. Quite the contrary, when I have shared these ideas with those who are not Catholic,

they have found them helpful. I hope that the book will have some ecumenical import, too. But at the same time, we all think about life in ways that are influenced by our traditions, by the perspectives we habitually adopt, by the questions we have learned to deem most important. So it seems only fair to acknowledge that in the case of this book the fundamental commitments that color the way our topic is handled are those of a Roman Catholic. This may mean that some issues are pursued which are of little interest to non-Catholic readers, but it should also mean that such a reader has here an opportunity to discover the style and content of Catholic moral theology today.

Among the many debts I owe for the development of this book, at least a few must be enumerated. First in importance and appreciation are my colleagues on the faculty of St. Mary of the Lake Seminary. Their vision of the intimate link between theology and ministry, and of the accountability of each to the other, has permanently shaped the perspective out of which I work. Of those colleagues, Rev. Michael Place has earned my particular gratitude for his support, challenge and continuing theological dialogue. I am grateful, too, to my students, who endured reading earlier drafts of most of these chapters, whose suggestions were always helpful, and whose occasional frank admissions of total confusion sent me back to the typewriter anew. My thanks to Mr. Michael Leach and Mr. Frank Oveis of The Seabury Press, who have been both conscientious and kind in facilitating the publication of this book. Finally, I am indebted to Mrs. Dorothy Hatton, whose skillful and efficient secretarial assistance greatly expedited this project.

Preface

SECOND EDITION

Five years in the composition, ten years in the revision! An interesting proportion. The fact that a decade had passed since the publication of *Principles for a Catholic Morality* at least explains the immediate push to complete this revision. It was the mobilizing of three reasons for a revision.

First, the mere passage of time meant that many of the citations were out of date. Significant new literature had appeared. And even if it did not have the effect of materially changing the synthesis presented in the book, these contributions deserved to be noted. So an updating of the citations seemed increasingly called for.

Second, there were any number of topics regarding which I was increasingly discontent with my presentation in the book. It was not so much that my theological position had changed, but rather that I had discovered more effective and more illuminating ways of expressing those matters. Once, after a lecture, a member of the audience approached me and said, "It must have taken you a long time to make it that simple." I was stunned by the insight – and, as I reflected on it, the accuracy – of her comment. More and more, as the years passed, I was embarrassed at the ungainly manner of presentation to which some key theological ideas were subjected. So I yearned to integrate into the book these later, more felicitous articulations.

Third, there were a few points on which my theological position had, indeed, changed. This is not surprising, of course, given the ferment of theological discussion in the area of Christian ethics in our time. But it is also not insignificant. And it could not be ignored. The first edition was blessed with a number of insightful reviews at the time of its publication. As the years passed, its theological positions received commentary in various forums. I am most grateful for all these contributions. I have, without exception, given them serious and respectful attention. And, as you will see, in several cases I have been convinced of the wisdom of the reflections offered. This development, then, made me increasingly interested in preparing a revision that would more comprehensively express the current state of my thought on these important questions and would locate this development in the latest stage of the ongoing theological conversation.

This second edition, then, meets a need for updating, clarifying, and modifying the presentations that appeared earlier.

As always, this effort has been supported by many. First, I must acknowledge the generous support of Loyola University of Chicago. The revision was begun during a research leave that I was granted for the spring semester, 1988. Without that time for sustained research and reflection, the project would not have been possible. I particularly wish to thank Dean Francis Catania, of Loyola, who assisted me in organizing my duties in the succeeding months so that I could continue and complete the task.

I have already mentioned my appreciation for the attention that the first edition received from my theological colleagues. I want all of them to know that I mean that most sincerely. But I must also single out Edward Vacek, who engaged me in ongoing dialogue, reviewed and commented on drafts of the revision, and offered an extraordinary array of helpful suggestions. His generosity made a great difference.

I wish to offer a special word of thanks to my colleagues at Loyola. I received generous staff assistance from Scott Theisen, Kathy Cunningham, and, preeminently, Rachel Gibbons. I am also grateful for the patience and support of the faculty and staff of the Institute of Pastoral Studies. Their conviction that this revision was a worthy project made it possible; their interest and enthusiasm made it less burdensome; and their abiding commitment to the project of ministerial education made it important.

PART I

Introductory Essays

Chapter 1

THE MEANING OF
MORAL THEOLOGY

As the title of this book indicates, our topic is Catholic morality. And since the reflections that we shall pursue will seek to be systematic and intelligent, we will actually be involved in moral philosophy; or, since they will be the reflections of believers based on a fundamental religious commitment, in moral theology.

But to call this project a presentation of moral theology perhaps raises more questions than it answers. For both theology in general and moral theology in particular are understood in many different ways today. By some people they are not understood at all. So the starting point of this book must include some account of what we mean, and do not mean, by these terms. This, in turn, will lead to a clearer definition of the project of this book.

Theology's Task

This is certainly not the place for a full-scale treatise on the science of theology. Whole books have been written on the subject.[1] But perhaps a few brief remarks will be helpful.

Theologian Jean Daniélou has observed that Christians often confuse the two terms "religion" and "revelation."[2] Religion is the term we use to denote all those efforts of human beings to touch the transcendent, to contact and appease the divinity. Revelation, on the other hand, indicates divine initiative, the actions by which God approaches and touches us. Thus understood, says Daniélou, Christianity is not so much a religion as a revelation. It proclaims not human searching but divine salvation, not human effort but divine gift. And it celebrates that ongoing revelation-presence of God.

But if Christianity is essentially revelation, God's action and not ours, it is not solely revelation. There remains the need for human involvement, and in that sense Christianity is also, though subsequently, a religion. Indeed, inasmuch as revelation was humanly articulated from the beginning, and inasmuch as it must be humanly rearticulated as time goes on, the human contribution – the religious component – is utterly essential. And this for several reasons.

First, revelation was humanly articulated from the beginning. If we understand the primeval revelation of God to be Jesus himself, then we must take seriously the fact that Jesus came among us humanly. That means concretely, specifically, with all the particularities of time, place, and situation. Jesus was not "man" in some general and undifferentiated sense. Indeed, to give him only this vague and unspecified sort of humanity is to deny him any humanity at all. The flesh of human living exists only in concreteness and particularity; it exists only here or there, now or then, in this way or in that.

Thus, if we are truly to understand the Jesus of revelation, we must pursue the human task of understanding, in all its specificity, the cultural and personal situation in which he lived. And if we understand revelation to be the words of Scripture, then it is even more apparent that a human, cultural task of understanding will be required. Indeed, the whole science of biblical exegesis is premised on the fact that we can only understand the texts of Scripture if we understand the language in which they were written, the cultural and historical context, the philosophical and religious presuppositions of their human authors, the current literary conventions, the prevailing metaphors and symbol systems, and so on. If the Scriptures are God's revelation, still they are that revelation as humanly articulated. And thus the human task of discernment cannot be avoided.

Second, a human contribution is demanded by the need to humanly transmit and rearticulate revelation as time goes on. In either of the conceptions of revelation just mentioned, Jesus himself or the Scriptures, it is clear that we are dealing with a culture different from our own. And just as Jesus could not be "man" in some general and undifferentiated sense, just as the words of Scripture could not speak their truth in some unenculturated and universal language, so also we cannot share the Good News of revelation with our time and our place in that vague form. Rather, we must deal with the concreteness of the present as well as the concreteness of the past. Thus the believing human community stands forever charged with the duty of translating the truth of revelation into new languages, new symbol systems, images, and metaphors.

Third, we human persons are "verbal animals." This means that, in a very profound sense, we do not understand things until we put them into words. It is not as if we have clear ideas and then, in a second operation, enflesh those ideas in words. Rather, it is in the process of communication that we come to understand. Thus the process of rearticulation is itself central to the experience of God in our lives. The experience of revelation that is only expressed in someone else's language is not just a deprived experience, it is a radically ineffectual, even ephemeral experience. So articulation and rearticulation are not only a service to others, they are also functions essential to the self.

This task of translation, of reconstituting the inner meaning of revelation for successive audiences, belongs to theology. In fact, Christian theology can be defined as the science that seeks to understand and forever to rearticulate the life-giving Good News of God in Christ Jesus. And that is the definition that will be presupposed in this book. But if we accept that definition, several things follow.

Consequences

First, it is obvious that theology is an essential function within the Church. For the Church to fulfill its mandate to "proclaim the good news to all creation" (Mk 16:15), it must continually restate that Good News. That is, it must "do" theology. Therefore, the ministry of theology and of the theologian is a service the Church cannot do without. St. Paul declared that "God has set up in the church first apostles, second prophets, third teachers" (1 Cor 12:28). And history has borne him out. The pastoral leadership in the Church, the college of bishops in union with the bishop of Rome, comes first. But it is not sufficient. There is need also for those especially trained in the human understanding and translation of the Good News. There is need for teachers, for theologians, to serve the Church.[3]

Second, it follows from our definition of theology that all Christian believers are, in some sense, theologians. Inasmuch as all the members of the Church must, of human necessity, express to themselves the meaning of their inner experience of faith, they are involved in the theological enterprise. One sometimes hears a dichotomized description of Christian experience: that theology is somehow peripheral and that "we will avoid theology and simply speak the truths of revelation." But of course that cannot be. To "speak" revelation is to "do" theology; that is, it is to make use of language, cultural vision, and so on. Therefore, all the words of faith that are spoken within the Church are theological words. Whether they are the finely tuned words of a papal proclamation or an episcopal speech, whether they are the homespun prayers of a mother with her child, whether they are the groping articulations of a parish discussion group, the words that are spoken are theology.

The difference, then, between other members of the Church and theologians is a difference in degree and not in kind. It is a matter of scientific sophistication and not of fundamentally different tasks. Still, that difference is important. One could say that all persons are psychologists, since all can (perhaps must) develop a vision of how human persons function. But there remain better and worse ways of describing that functioning. And some ways are simply erroneous. Similarly, there are better and worse ways of expressing the faith, and some ways are simply erroneous. It is the task of the professional theologian to bring scholarship to the project of articulating the faith of the Christian community and thereby, as far as possible, to find better, more transparent ways of articulating that faith.

Third, our definition makes clear that theology is a sort of bridge between revelation and culture. In pursuing its objective of translation, then, theology must constantly seek to be faithful to both, to remain fully established on both shores. To lose touch with the ground of revelation experienced in faith is to have nothing to say or, even worse, to misguide the listener with that which is false. Equally true, to lose touch with the canons of the culture is not to be heard or, even worse, to be misunderstood. The challenge of theology, therefore, and of all Christians insofar as they "speak" theology, is to speak both from deep faith and from broad cultural sensitivity.[4]

Fourth, defining theology as the science of understanding and rearticulating makes clear that there is no such thing as a "perennial theology." To be sure, the central faith experiences that theology seeks to express are perennial. But inasmuch as theological expressions are culturally derived and directed, they are subject to all the laws of life and death that are the fate of human cultures. Theologies, like societies, are born, they live, and they die. As people change, so theology must change. Thus, what is perennial about theology is not its formulations, but rather its critically important task.

Finally, and following from all that has been said thus far, our definition suggests that the precise goal of theology, its most specific objective in all that it does, is not truth but meaning. It is not truth as if truth could be achieved once and for all, as if truth could be grasped and articulated in a way that transcends all the limitations of time and culture. Rather, it is meaning, truth as apprehended, truth as germane, truth as effectively communicated, truth not only as sincerely given but also as successfully received. The goal of theology is meaning: not some cheap relevance that is achieved at the price of falsehood, of course, but that real meaning which is the appropriate incarnation of the perennial experience of faith in the passing flesh of particular cultures.

Theology's Divisions

As theology has pursued this task over the centuries, however, it has demonstrated a perduring concern with two different agendas. On the one hand, it has attempted to discern the meaning of the gift of God that is the Good News of revelation. And on the other hand, it has sought to discover what this gift means for the conduct of our daily lives. To put this another way, theology has reflected on revelation both as a gift to and a challenge for the human person.

This double understanding of revelation is not surprising. Even human experiences of self-revelation always include these two moments: on the one hand, an offer of the self to another and, on the other hand, an implicit call for response, for acceptance and appreciation and reciprocity. So if it is true that the God of revelation is also the God who created this human world, it is not surprising that a similar dialectic should be discerned in divine revelation as well.

Be that as it may, it is a fact that theology has always had this twin focus. And in more recent centuries it has even consciously structured itself along these lines, dividing itself into dogmatic theology and moral theology, or systematic theology and Christian ethics.[5] These two sub-sciences have related in different ways at different times, as we shall see in the next chapter.[6] But they have always existed in some form or other, and they have always related in some fashion or other.[7]

Moral Theology

Moral theology, then, is that portion of the theological enterprise which attempts to discern the implications of revelation for human behavior, to answer the question: "How ought we, who have been gifted by God, to live?" In answering this question, moral theology has itself discovered a double focus. On the one hand, there are questions about the general shape of the Christian life. What does it mean to live as a Christian? How shall we understand all the moral terms we use: right and wrong, good and evil, sin and virtue? What is an appropriate strategy for responding to the divine challenge? And on the other hand, there are any number of questions about specific areas of living. What is appropriate behavior for the Christian in such areas as justice, respect for life, truth telling, property rights, sexuality?

From the beginning, then, moral theology has included concerns both general and concrete. Indeed, in the course of Catholic tradition, these two concerns evolved into two treatises, General Moral Theology (*De principiis*) and Special Moral Theology (*De preceptis*). And although these two need to be continually and carefully related, they are at least logically distinct projects. This book will concern itself only with the first of these categories. That is, it will be concerned with the principles of Christian morality, as developed within the Catholic tradition.

But even General Moral Theology implicitly contains two different agendas. And it is important to note these agendas, because they will dictate the shape and order of the chapters to follow.

In seeking to understand the basic shape of the Christian moral life, one can direct one's attention either inward or outward. One can ask questions about the moral agent or about moral action. On the one hand, one can inquire about who we are when we seek to respond to the Good News. What really constitutes that authentic response? What is the significance of human knowledge and freedom? How do we go about choosing our response? How does the reality of conscience fit into all this? What is the real meaning of sin and virtue? In a word, who is the moral person? And on the other hand, one can investigate the outer world of moral behavior with an eye to discerning its general characteristics and dynamics. What makes an action right or wrong? What is the place of law in a Christian ethic? What of moral values and norms? Are they real? Objective? Unchanging? What of all the human laws that confront us? In a word, what is the moral world?

Resources

These are the two agendas that will occupy our attention in these pages. And as we deal with each in turn, we shall make use of a number of resources.

It is important to proclaim that the primary resource for this study will be the experience of believers. Since theology is, in the end, nothing else than the externalization of the faith experience, its primary source and benchmark is that experience. So, it must be acknowledged that a central source for this project will be its author's experience. Not that the result can be allowed to be idiosyncratic. Quite the contrary, it will need to be rooted in, and responsive to, the experience of the faith community. Still, there is no denying that one must start with oneself. Nothing dare be included here that does not "make sense" to the author. (And conversely, all that is said here will need to be tested against the reader's own experience.)

But, as just mentioned, one avoids distortion by testing one's experience against others. So the experience that is the primary source for this study includes the experience of many. But how do we incorporate that experience? Through a variety of other sources, which should be specifically identified here.

For example, our immediate sources in many cases will be the insights of today's Christian community, as these are communicated through official church statements and the writings of contemporary theologians. We will report these sources. But more important, we will seek to understand them. Since, in a genuine sense, it is wisdom that is our source, we will search for the content of these documents in order to appropriate their wisdom, to embrace the meaning that illumines – and tests – our experience. An attempt will be made to integrate all the ideas we discover, to produce a coherent whole that at the same time speaks to the contemporary experience of responding to the Lord.

Also important as a resource will be the insights of scholars in other fields of study. At times, for example, we will be interested in the data of the social sciences. For if the resonance of our synthesis with the experience of people will be a benchmark of our success, so also the shape of their experience will be a guide for our reflections. Interpretations of experience by theoretical social scientists and philosophers will also play a significant role. For they will reveal to us the self-understanding of contemporary humankind, an understanding that cannot just be uncritically accepted but that cannot be ignored, either. Finally, even the data and theories of the physical sciences will occasionally be of use.

But wisdom and insight are by no means the sole possession of our age or of those individuals most like ourselves. So, as we proceed, we shall also give considerable attention to our past as a Christian community. And we shall try to do so in a way that avoids a narrowly sectarian outlook in these pages. Much wisdom is to be found in the past and present of all the Christian communions, and we will try to make use of it all. We will try to listen to the convictions and values of past ages of disciples of the Lord, to discern their significance for our time, and to incorporate them into a contemporary statement. In so doing, we will try to accept the warning that those who do not learn from history are doomed to repeat it. And, of course, given the perspective of our study, we will be especially concerned to listen to the statements of the Roman Catholic magisterium and of that Church's theologians through the centuries.

Yet another resource for our project will be the Scriptures. The Bible is the charter document of the Church, after all. As inspired, it is a sort of privileged theology that puts us in especially close contact with the truth of revelation. So we shall be quite concerned to listen to its moral proclamations, to try to understand them, and to translate them for our time. Indeed, so central is the biblical witness to our project that at several points in the book we shall pause to give its proclamations direct and extended attention. It is, after all, unthinkable that one could construct a Christian ethic that is not centrally a biblical ethic.

Finally, moral theology always remains rooted in dogmatic theology.

Just as our vision of revelation made clear that the task is always grounded in the gift, so these two branches of theology must always be related. Although the limits of this current project will not allow the development of a comprehensive dogmatic theory, we will draw on dogmatics as we pursue our own objectives.[8]

Structure of the Book

On the basis of everything said thus far, we can now state clearly the way in which this presentation of principles for a Catholic morality will be developed.

The three last-named resources, history, Scripture, and dogmatics, will play a role throughout these pages. But they surely deserve more than passing attention. What is more, their contribution to our project is not only in content but also in context. So the remainder of part I will look to each of these resources in turn. What can they tell us that will help to specify our task and guide the direction of our reflections?

In part II we shall give our concentrated attention to the moral person. And in part III we shall turn outward to consider the shape and dynamics of the moral world. Finally, a number of conclusions will be offered in part IV.

As we pursue each of these topics, we shall have in mind that the goal and criterion of theology is meaning. Indeed, if meaning is central to theology in general, it is even more so in the case of moral theology. For in talking about the moral person, we are talking about ourselves; in seeking to understand the moral world, we are attending to our world. So, surely, the ultimate test of our discussions will be whether they are meaningful, in the best sense of the word. Do they seem faithful to our experience of revelation, of God gifting and challenging us in our lives? Do they speak in terms that resonate with our human experience, with our own particular cultural presuppositions and perspectives?

This book is ultimately about us. Thus, only if these questions can be answered in the affirmative will we really have achieved principles for a Catholic morality.

Chapter 2

THE HISTORY OF
MORAL THEOLOGY

Children have always asked the question: "Where did I come from?" As they have begun to experience themselves as persons, they have realized that their roots are part of their identity. Of course, the issue of one's roots can be addressed at various levels and in various ways; a child's question is quite different from an adult's. But one way or another, to one degree or another, the question always seems to present itself.

The matter of one's history is also relevant to the transpersonal world of ideas and cultures and institutions. Where did we come from? Where did these ways of understanding, of living and functioning, come from? Why are we the way we are today? And just as the personal question cannot be avoided, neither can this corporate questioning.

At least it can be avoided only at high cost. For to the extent that we do not understand our past, we really do not understand our present, and we are less prepared intelligently to construct our future. So the purpose of this chapter is to sketch the broad outlines of our ethical history. We want to try to understand the historical reasons for the way Catholic moral theology has developed and for the way it expresses itself today. We want to see, at least in a general way, the path by which we have come to the present. We want to recognize that foundation on which, of necessity, our future must somehow be constructed.[1]

Patristic Era

The writing on moral topics in the first five hundred years of the Church's history is fascinating, both because it represents the initial understandings of Christian theology and because it bears so many similarities to the reflections of our own time. From the very beginning, a concern with the behavioral implications of the Gospel proclamation manifested itself. The Didache (ca. A.D. 75) begins with a portrayal of the "two ways," the way of virtue and the way of evil, and challenges the listener to a deep conversion.

But this ethical concern did not result in any comprehensive moral systems, let alone any single, universally accepted system. Indeed, the writing of the period was not even the product of "theologians" in a professional sense. Rather, it was produced by pastors and monks, by individuals who used it as part of their ministry, either to serve a local church or as counsel to disciples in the mystical journey. As such, the writing was characterized by a desire to respond to the concrete needs of the community in a way that was still authentic to the core of the Christian faith.

What is more, this dialectic of faith and experience was differently handled by various authors. Clement of Alexandria (d. 216), for example, exhibited a rather optimistic vision of life, a willingness to integrate the Gospel truth with the insights of the pagan world. He viewed pagan wisdom as "so many seeds strewn by the Logos"[2] and thus expected a fundamental continuity between experience and revelation. Clement was not above dealing with concrete issues; at one point he described in detail the typical day of the Christian with its various ethical challenges. But even in such discussions he revealed a humanistic and optimistic perspective. In contrast, Origen (d. 253) was quite negative. It is true that he was an educated man, in touch with pagan knowledge and willing to make use of it. Indeed, it was Origen who first used the classic concept of the cardinal virtues in Christian theology. But even so, one discerns in his discussions of sin, of human freedom, and of the meaning of salvation a relatively pessimistic view of human life. As a representative in theology of the burgeoning monastic movement, of the concern for "white martyrdom," Origen was much more inclined to dichotomize the life of Christian faith and the life of the world.[3]

A century later, a landmark book was written by Ambrose, the bishop of Milan (d. 397). His De officiis followed the lead of Cicero in both title and area of concern. Though contextualizing his reflections with the vision of Christian faith and doctrine, Ambrose addressed himself to the myriad "duties" of the believer. And he sought to articulate these moral responsibilities in a concrete way that presaged the works of casuistry that would flourish 1,300 years later. Perhaps we might call Ambrose the first of the Christian casuists.

Most notable of the patristic figures, however, is Ambrose's disciple, Augustine of Hippo (d. 430). Augustine is a compelling, and at the same time rather confusing, representative of the early Church. Some have called him one of the greatest moral theologians of all time.[4] Others note the negative influence of his rigorist, perhaps subtly Manichean perspective on later Church teaching.[5] All these points are debated despite the fact that Augustine never attempted to develop a coherent and inclusive system of moral theory. Instead, his style (and it is a characteristic one of his era) was to range far and wide across the spectrum of theological concepts and human concerns. Augustine sketched his personal theological vision in his *Confessions*, he developed his understanding of the world in *City of God*, and he wrote shorter works on such diverse ethical topics as lying, widowhood, and especially sexual ethics.

If Augustine does not demand our attention because of his systematic approach, he does because of the shape of his thought. He addressed himself to the perennial underlying issues of ethics: the relationship of faith and works, of grace and freedom, of sin and virtue. He focused on the centrality of love in the Christian life. He utilized a rather psychological, introspective, and inductive approach to the development of ethical insight. And in all these ways he revealed himself as a fundamentally modern Christian thinker.[6]

Sixth Century

In the history of Christian theology the sixth century marks an important watershed. The Christian faith had emerged from its minority status and had become the commitment of the masses. It had become the officially espoused religion of the state, and its theological vision and pastoral approach had to be appropriately adjusted.

One of the more significant elements of that adjustment was the change in practice as regards the Sacrament of Reconciliation. During the Patristic era this sacrament had been relatively rare. Its use was limited to the confession of truly major sins, lengthy penances were required before absolution, and the penitent was not allowed to return to the sacrament with any frequency. In effect, it functioned as a liturgy of reconciliation with the community, within the context of a church discipline that included excommunication for those guilty of behaviors that were highly threatening to the community.

During the sixth century, however, this practice changed. Particularly in Ireland and through the ministry of the Celtic monks, the confession of sin became more private and more frequent, a much more comprehensive variety of sins were submitted to the confessor, and penances began to be fulfilled after absolution. In a word, auricular confession, as we know it, entered the life of the Church, and the Sacrament of Reconciliation became much more an ongoing component of the Christian life.

This innovation, however, had immediate implications for moral theology, for it was presumed that the penances should fit the particularities of the sins confessed. Therefore, some systematic reflection on the nature of sin, its varieties, and on the demands of retributive justice was required. Moreover, at this time the level of clerical education was notably low, with the result that priests could not generally be trusted to make unguided judgments in these matters. As a result, there emerged at this time a series of compendiums known as Penitential Books.

These were not really works of theology. Even less were they descriptions of the ideals to be sought in the Christian life. Rather, they were simply lists of typical sins along with an indication of the appropriate penance in each case. But despite their modest intent, these books exercised a far-reaching influence on the nature of moral theology.

For one thing, the Penitential Books were addressed to priest-confessors. Thus began the rather unhealthy identification of moral theology both with the Sacrament of Penance and with priests. This presumption that moral theology is primarily for priests has survived to our own time, and only recently has it been challenged.[7] Second, the very specific purpose of these books inevitably led to the association of moral theology with Christian minimalism. That is, the very existence of lists such as those in the Penitential Books tempted the Christian world to conclude that virtuous and faithful living consisted in the avoidance of the sins mentioned therein and that successful avoidance of these sins justified confidence in one's moral righteousness. There was, or appeared to be, no reason to "walk the extra mile." Third, the specific association of penance with sin encouraged an approach to Christian forgiveness that emphasized not mercy but justice. Absolution became more a matter of retribution. And thus the focus on the loving kindness of God, though never lost, was quite overshadowed.

Finally, the Penitential Books contributed to an emphasis on the importance of the individual act, an emphasis that remains today. We shall consider this emphasis in great detail in this book, and we shall attempt to downplay it by locating the act in its broader context. But before any of that, it is important to note how this act orientation, the urge to fragment the Christian life into its smallest possible components, developed. And the Penitential Books played a significant role in that development.

Eleventh to Thirteenth Centuries

Shortly after the passing of the first millennium, the character of European culture underwent a significant change, and that change had considerable influence on the progress of moral theology. This was the era of the rise of the great European universities. Centers of learning in widely dispersed locations were founded over an amazingly short period of time. And these were entirely new sorts of learning centers: not monastic schools, not even the educational programs of the cathedral canons, but relatively autonomous institutions whose utter *raison d'être* was the pursuit and communication of knowledge.

It was still Catholic Europe, of course, and thus the study of God held a central place in these new universities. Thus, for the first time it is appropriate to speak of the *science* of theology in something like the sense we use today. But if theology influenced the academic scene, it is also true that the academic world influenced theology.

Systematic thought was the order of the day; the urge was to integrate, summarize, and articulate logically. This approach became the approach of theology as well. It was the era of the "Summas," those great constructs of systematic theology, those attempts to proclaim the Gospel in a philosophically consistent and logically compelling manner. And among the thinkers who contributed to this development, two in particular deserve our attention.

One was the Franciscan, Bonaventure (d. 1274), whose fundamental commitment was still to the Platonic tradition that had prevailed in the centuries before. Out of that perspective he developed a brilliant synthesis of Christian theology and morality. For Bonaventure, the central characteristic of people was their will, their power to decide and to act. The intellect, though extremely important, was a tool to be used for action. Indeed, Bonaventure declared that the purpose of all theology was "not merely to serve contemplation, but also to make us holy. In fact its first purpose is to make us holy."[8] And even in his discussion of the intellect he emphasized the "practical intellect" as our highest achievement.

Bonaventure had no separate presentation of moral theology; that was not the style in the age of the Summas. But for the reasons mentioned, his theological synthesis was an amiable contribution to later reflections on that reality.

The other figure was Thomas Aquinas (d. 1274). Aquinas, the Dominican, holds unparalleled fame in Catholic theology, and for many wise reasons. In his time the writings of Aristotle were being rediscovered, and Aquinas especially demonstrated the aptness of that philosophy for the articulation of Christian theology. For Aquinas, as for Aristotle, humans were preeminently intellectual beings, rational animals. And their highest achievement was precisely that contemplation which Bonaventure played down. Theology was for understanding; it was a pure science in the service of pure truth. It is clear, then, that Aquinas would have no place for a separate science of moral theology. The isolation of behavior from truth was precisely what he opposed. But to say this is not to say that he was disinterested in ethical questions. By no means.

On the one hand, the method espoused by Aquinas led surely to an attempt to understand the Christian life; our understanding of ourselves and of our behavior was an important component of our attempt to understand God. And, on the other hand, once the Gospel was heard and understood, it was clear that a responsive lifestyle was demanded. So Aquinas was more than willing to discuss the specifics of that lifestyle. Indeed, the whole *pars secunda* of his *Summa Theologiae* is a sort of treatise on moral theology, dealing first with general concepts (I-II) and then with specific ethical topics (II-II). But for our purposes the important point is that these ethical discussions were incorporated into the overall synthesis of Christian theology and not isolated in any way.

To a certain extent, this integration of dogmatics and ethics characteristic of both Aquinas and Bonaventure is also characteristic of the whole of the High Middle Ages. There was no compartmentalizing of theological components, no isolating of faith and action, no dichotomizing of grace and nature. Reality was viewed holistically, theology was developed holistically. And in writings such as the Summas, this integrating perspective yielded a rich and clearly contextualized moral theology.

Fourteenth to Sixteenth Centuries

Shortly after the deaths of Aquinas and Bonaventure, there began a process of change and development that can hardly be overestimated in its influence on moral theology. The first step in the process was marked by two highly significant changes in the theological situation.

On the one hand, the philosophical context shifted substantially. The high Scholasticism of the thirteenth century devolved, in the fourteenth, into a nominalistic vision of reality. The conviction that the human person was capable of distilling concepts, universal notions that capture and represent the real essence of things, was replaced by a skepticism on this matter. Philosophers such as William of Ockham (d. 1349) became convinced that there were no such essences, that the human person did not achieve universal concepts. Rather, the object of human intellectual attention was the uniqueness of each existing thing. The only way in which one could move beyond the unique existent was by a somewhat arbitrary process of "collection." Nominalists willingly conceded that it was common practice to grant various groupings of objects a general and inclusive name. But in their judgment these names were simply that and nothing more. There is no essence or nature "tree." We simply group various unique existing things and call them "trees." For nominalists, reality is fundamentally discontinuous.

This philosophical development was ethically important because it rendered useless the attempt to discuss the nature of the Christian life and to predict intrinsically good or intrinsically bad acts. Where there is utter uniqueness, there is no tool of predictability. And where that tool is lacking, there can ultimately be no useful objective component to ethical decision making. In fact, the consequence of a nominalist epistemology is complete ethical individualism. My situation is utterly unique, and I am an utterly unique person. Hence only I can judge what I must do; and even I can only judge in the midst of the experience.

If society finds itself threatened by this individualism — as it surely must, since such individualism invites a chaotic narcissism — it has only one alternative: the arbitrary imposition of law. Society cannot attempt to impose demonstrably rational guides for action, for these presume the existence of universals and essences. So it can only have recourse to power, to the naked demand for conformity. Thus, if the immediate consequence of nominalism is individualism with its potential for social chaos, its eventual consequence is tyranny, the imposition of order through dominative power.[9]

The other highly significant change in the theological situation of the time was economic. This was the period in which medieval feudalism was beginning to give way to an emerging structure of middle-class commerce. The exchange of goods and services greatly increased, individual mobility became more common, and thus a quantity and variety of relationships among strangers became necessary. In this situation, it was no longer sufficient to appeal to the duties of fraternity to justify correct behavior. Instead, it became necessary to articulate the precise demands of justice, to specify with great accuracy just what was due one. As a result, traditional Christian virtues such as love, fidelity, and piety came to be neglected as justice and equity were emphasized. And a certain moral minimalism was inevitable.

These two developments, the philosophical and the commercial, combined to give fifteenth-century morality a peculiar flavor. Law was celebrated as central to moral thinking and living and was seen as a tool for expressing the necessary minimum, for establishing rights and duties in such a way as to regulate the rapidly multiplying relationships within the European community. There was a pragmatic and utilitarian tone that, though somehow surprising, is in retrospect completely understandable.

Into this situation, then, came one of the most influential figures in the history of Christendom: Martin Luther (1483–1546). Luther the monk, Luther the Christian tortured by personal feelings of inadequacy and sinfulness, Luther the student of St. Paul. This Martin Luther entered a Christian situation that was far removed from the Gospel ideal. The situation emphasized justice, and Luther was convinced that no one is just. The situation emphasized the law, and Luther shared

Paul's distrust of law. The situation focused on minimums, and Luther felt driven to perfection. The situation cherished good works, and Luther placed his trust in faith.

We are, of course, sketching with a broad brush events that included innumerable subtleties. But for our purposes it may suffice to become conscious of the polarities, for they indicate the shape of the response to Luther. When the Church finally formulated its Counter-Reformation in the Council of Trent (1545–1563), it was faced with a full-scale rebellion. Much of Europe had been lost to the Church, and the first priority was to establish the lines of demarcation with clarity. Unlike many, if not most, of the councils in the history of the Church, the Council of Trent did not have reconciliation as its goal. Rather, its purpose was protection, the isolation of the rebels, the clear delineation of the boundaries of the Church, crisis management of a certain sort. This strategy had many effects, but not the least was the imposition on moral theology of a definition and an approach that have lasted into our own time.

In a situation of such total conflict the council, and the Church, may be forgiven for an overwhelming emphasis on the practicalities of behavior. This was not the time for leisurely theological or philosophical discussions; like any period of war, it left little time for speculation. Action was required, unanimity and uniformity were necessities, and thus the response of the council had those characteristics.

For one thing, seminaries were established. For the first time in the history of the Church, a clear and formal system for the education of clergy was developed. Clergy were to be isolated from the crises and turbulence of the day, placed in safe, protected environments, in intellectual greenhouses, as it were. (This, after all, is a literal translation of the Latin *seminarium*, from *semen*, seed.) They were to be provided with clear and concise directions for their ministry. They were to be inculcated with loyalty and a willingness to obey.

For another thing, the kind of education provided seminarians was to emphasize the behavior necessary for the Catholic. It was important to know what to do, and those areas of theology that indicated the proper action were to be highlighted. And thus, again for the first time in the history of the Church, a separate science of moral theology emerged. No longer was it merely a matter of reflecting on the truths of the faith and, in the course of this reflection, taking note of their behavioral implications. Now it was a matter of an isolated conversation aimed only at a specific and detailed presentation of the requirements of the Christian life.

For a third thing, when this separate moral theology emerged, it took on a specific character. It, too, was expected to emphasize the concrete, the objective, the necessary and required. And thus, as moral theology became separated from its roots in dogmatic theology, it became affiliated with that other science dedicated to these qualities, namely, canon law. The law indicated most clearly what one must do; and so it was completely reasonable to graft moral theology onto law, to give them the intimacy of sister sciences. This integration was done so completely and so successfully that, even to our day, textbooks of Christian ethics have often borne the title *Theologia moralis ad normam juris canonici* (moral theology according to the norm of canon law).[10]

Seventeenth and Eighteenth Centuries

The consolidation of the post-Reformation period did not, of course, bring to an end the questioning that has always characterized moral theology. But it did establish the terms in which that questioning took place. Throughout the centuries after Luther, the issue was predominantly one of the precise meaning of the law. What, exactly, is the right thing to do? What is the minimum expected of the Catholic Christian? How can one permit a certain amount of legitimate Christian freedom while at the same time protecting the supremacy of objective moral demand? What is the proper response to a situation in which the demands of the law are in doubt?

Questions such as these were hotly debated by moralists. At the one extreme, a Jansenist rigorism was proposed; at the other (and partly in reaction to Jansenism), a laxist preoccupation with freedom. And all these debates eventually led to the development of a variety of moral systems for the responsible resolution of ethical doubts. Of these systems, perhaps the best known today is "probabilism," the system that held that when there is a genuine division of expert opinion on a specific moral issue – and therefore two probable (reasonable) opinions – one may feel free to follow the more lenient opinion. And this even if the lenient opinion is held only by a minority of the experts.

One of the major figures in the debates of the time was Alphonsus Liguori (1696–1787). Alphonsus is notable in the history of moral theology not precisely because he was creative or innovative, but rather because he was a prudent man, able to formulate balanced, reasonable, and humane opinions. In the midst of a morass of disagreements, with zealots on all questions, Alphonsus was a beacon of reason, of common sense, in the eighteenth century. Although he actually supported "equiprobabilism," a slightly more strict alternative to probabilism, his commitment to prudent moderation made him a model for moral theology up until the very recent past.

Alphonsus is also significant because his moral method, noting the various opinions and then seeking to walk a prudent middle course, modeled an ethical style that has perdured. That style is exemplified in the "manuals," textbooks that summarize the prudent and reasonable position on the various issues of the time. Manuals were largely designed for the use of seminarians, and they were clearly oriented toward the application of moral theology in the confessional. But although they were in some ways conservative documents, greatly dependent on arguments from authority, they were also somehow pastoral. For given the legalistic premise that prevailed, there was a great tendency to multiply laws to the point of completely eliminating the reality of Christian freedom. In this context, manuals often functioned as voices of reason, guiding the confessor away from the extremes and toward the moderate position. They prevented the priests of the day from arbitrarily imposing unreasonable demands on their people and instead protected a certain gentle and patient spirit in moral theology.

Still, one could hardly celebrate the manuals as paradigms of profound moral theology. They were simply too much creatures of their own philosophical, theological, and cultural milieu to be that. And so eventually a move away from the manuals was to be expected, a fundamental renewal of moral theology was required.

Nineteenth and Twentieth Centuries

When that renewal of moral theology began, one of its earliest manifestations was at the University of Tübingen, in Germany. Perhaps the first significant figure in the renewal at that school was John Michael Sailer, bishop of Ratisbon (1750–1832). He was soon followed by John Baptist Hirscher (1788–1865). These two men, and the school they represented, were greatly influenced by the revival of scriptural studies in Germany. And in light of those new scriptural insights they began to question not specific moral teachings, but rather the whole style of moral theology. They issued a call for a more kerygmatic moral teaching, with emphasis on the inner realities of conversion and discipleship. They pointed out the essential link between Christian morality and Christian spirituality. They participated in the revival of interest in the Fathers of the Church, and particularly Augustine. Noticing patristic themes that resonated with the science of psychology developing in northern Europe, they called for increased psychological sensitivity in moral theology. Finally, and perhaps most importantly, they demanded a reunification of moral theology and dogmatic theology; they sought to reestablish the truly theological roots of Christian ethics.

This renewal did not achieve hegemony with any speed. Such political realities as the First Vatican Council, the Syllabus of Errors, and the mood of suspicion that separated Italians and Germans made this impossible. But it did continue, and at a slow and painful rate it developed. In the early years of this century, theologians continued to develop their ideas of moral theology. Such individuals as Joseph Mausbach (1861–1931) and Theodore Steinbuchel (1888–1949) made significant contributions. And when German theologians Bernard Häring (1912–) and Josef Fuchs (1912–) assumed their posts at two Roman universities (the Alphonsianum and the Gregorian, respectively), the widespread dissemination of these ideas was assured.[11]

Conclusion

To say this, however, is not to say that the renewal of moral theology has been completed. Quite the contrary – if anything, it has just begun. Perhaps it is because institutions are, by instinct, more conservative about behavior than about intellectual doctrines. Or maybe it is because a renewed moral theology must depend on (and await) renewals in scriptural and dogmatic studies. But the fact is that Christian ethics continues to lag behind the other theological disciplines in renewal and renovation.

In large part, the fundamental renewal of scriptural sciences took place in the early part of this century. Even the development of dogmatic theology was well advanced before the Second Vatican Council. Indeed, in many ways the council was the ratification and implementation of that development in terms of the theology of revelation, Church, culture, and liturgy. But in the area of moral theology this is not the case. The council said very little about moral theology; and when it did speak, its words had much more the tone of a call for renewal to come than of a ratification of tasks completed. Consider these words that, significantly, appear in the Decree on Priestly Formation:

Special attention needs to be given to the development of moral theology. Its scientific exposition should be more thoroughly nourished by scriptural teaching. It should show the nobility of the Christian vocation of the faithful, and their obligation to bring forth fruit in charity for the life of the world. (art. 16)

And the twenty-odd years since the close of the Second Vatican Council have not fundamentally changed the intellectual situation. There has been a major reconsideration of many of the themes of moral theology. Indeed, the possibility of this book, as well as both the possibility and the necessity for a second revised edition, bespeak the ferment of the time. But it remains true that the Church today finds itself "between the times." It is clear that the ethical vision of the nineteenth and early twentieth century, with its reliance on unjustified arguments from authority and its tendency toward naive positivism, is inadequate. There is, by the grace of God, no going back to that perspective. At the same time, no new intellectual synthesis has captured the imagination and satisfied the searchings of the whole Church. Instead, there is a situation of disagreement and, to a certain, unavoidable extent, confusion. A feeling of historic transition prevails.

Hence the moment at which we find ourselves in moral theology, the moment when this volume was first composed and the moment when it is being revised, remains a moment of beginning. It is not the time for complete new systems. Even less is it a time for the repetition of old formulas. It is a time to mine the past for useful and helpful insights. And it is a time to begin to reformulate and rearticulate the perennial truths of the Christian life. It is a time to ask hard questions, and it is a time to attempt tentative but internally coherent answers to those questions.

And that, of course, is the goal of this book.

Chapter 3

CHRIST AND MORAL THEOLOGY

We have established the basic understanding of theology that will ground this book. We have recapitulated the history of moral theology. Before we begin our methodical reflections on the nature and content of Christian ethics, moral theology, one further task remains. That is to indicate the way in which moral theology is rooted in the theology, and reality, of Christ. This project will occupy us in the next two chapters.

> We conclude our remarks on Paul's ethical teaching in general by insisting on its Christocentrism. As Christ was the "image of God," so man in his earthly existence is to be the "image of the heavenly man." It is growth in Christ that Paul recommends to his readers, contemporary and modern. In this way the Christian lives his life "for God."[1]

These words of Joseph Fitzmyer indicate one of the reasons for these chapters. Seeking a Christian morality inevitably leads us to meditation on the person of Jesus himself. Discipleship is an ethical dictate, but discipleship requires that we know the teacher well.

There is another reason for these chapters. Contemporary theology has become increasingly conscious of the central role in all theology held by Christ. Christ is not one of the important aspects of Christian belief; he is not one of the truths espoused by Christian faith; he is not one of the realities proclaimed in Christian revelation. No, Christ is the summary of all those things. He is the way, truth and life. He is the revelation of God to humankind. When Edward Schillebeeckx wishes to develop the theology of the seven sacraments, he begins by asserting that his study is really an aspect of Christology. Indeed, Christ is the "sacrament of the encounter with God."[2] All grace is grace of Christ; the only church worthy of the name is the church of Christ; the kingdom to come is the kingdom of Christ. When Jesus says that "he who sees me sees the Father," he is not merely making a statement. He is making *the* statement, summarizing all that he was to say and do in his earthly life. And so we are Christians in a most profound sense. We are Christ-people. We pray to the Father only "through Christ our Lord," as the liturgy says.

Therefore, to establish the ideas that will certify this book as Christian ethics, as moral *theology*, we must root them in Christ himself. And on the other hand, as we shall see, to root our ideas in the person and mission of Christ is to begin to discover the particular shape that ethics must take in our time. It is to discover that moral theology is a very specific thing, a discipline that possesses very specific characteristics.

The prolegomenon to our Christian ethics, then, is a series of reflections on the mystery of Christ, an explicit consideration of the relationship of Christ and morality.

One further note. It must not be forgotten that theology is in pursuit of meanings, not proofs. In this discussion, therefore, we will not be attempting to prove anything. We will not justify our assertions on the ground that they are irrefutable. Rather, we will present an understanding of Christ that is common in contemporary theology, that is rich in meaning and implication, and that resonates with common experience. The test of these reflections, then, will not be their syllogistic logic. Rather, it will be their internal coherence and their external adequacy. The test will be the fact that they make sense and nourish our Christian lives.[3]

Christ and Creation

"In the beginning was the Word." These words open the Gospel of John (1:1). And they open our reflections as well. Indeed, as we proceed, we shall repeatedly return to John's proclamation for insight and support. But we begin with this very simple statement. Jesus the Christ is the Logos, the Word of God. But if this is so, if we know this about Jesus, then we know much more as well. For we know about "words." They are part of our experience, of our everyday lives. That experience may help us to grasp the mystery that is Jesus Christ.

Words. Tools of communication. Means of human interchange. Very common things: intuitive, immediate, universal. But at the same time very specific, particular things. Human communication has quite particular characteristics, and these are worth noting here.

First, where there is communication, there are always two persons: a speaker and a listener. These two persons are united by means of a word, a symbol of some sort. And this word is what causes the communication to take place. Second, for real communication to occur, not just any word will do. On the one hand, it is not possible to achieve communication unless the word really represents the person who speaks it. It must manifest his or her mind, judgment, question. On the other hand, the word must be aptly proportioned to the listener. That is, it must be in a language she or he understands, and it must use images and concepts that are familiar. Thus the essence of communication in our human experience is two persons sharing a word that is representative of the speaker and proportioned to the listener.

If this is true of human experience, however, and if St. John is correct in saying, "In the beginning was the Word," then we can expect to find in God's actions some of these same characteristics.

We have a speaker, the Father himself (to use Jesus' own word for God). Indeed, the Father is a speaker, a producer of words, a creative, fruitful, fertile being. That is what follows from John's simple assertion. God is not some static and sterile being. God is a font of energy, dynamic and, quite literally, expressive. The Nicene Creed asserts that God is "creator of heaven and earth." But now, reflecting on John's words, we realize that God the Father is much more. God is creator of this world because God is a creative being – indeed, an infinitely creative being. Should not such a being also be creative within the self, be the producer of the infinite interior Word? Or, to say this another way: Would the Father even be able to create those finite words that comprise our world if he were not also and preeminently the source of an internal and infinite Word, if God were not by nature creative and fertile and dynamic? These are mere speculations, of course. We cannot presume to dictate what God can or cannot do. But they are reasonable speculations. If it is not logically compelling, it is nonetheless quite plausible to hold with Karl Rahner that "the immanent self-utterance of God in his eternal fullness [the Word] is the condition of the self-utterance of God outside himself [human persons and their world]."[4]

All of this is supported elsewhere by St. John when he proclaims that "God is love" (1 Jn 4:8). Love, that most fertile, most unitive and creative of realities! God not only has love, God is love. God is fertility, energy, creativity itself. So we are very close to the mystery of God's own self when we notice (without really understanding, to be sure) that God is a speaker, a producer and proclaimer of words.

"In the beginning was the Word." John invites us to set up the analogy to the human experience of communication. We do so, and we discover that with God, as with that human experience, we have a speaker. We also have listeners. We have the human community, those whom Jesus was to save, those whom God loves. We have the person who "hears my words and puts them into practice" (Mt 7:24). And, of course, we have the Word itself.

This Word, moreover, is representative of the speaker. As we have already intimated, it is an infinite Word. As it comes from an infinite speaker, unlimited in creativity, so it is infinite and unlimited. This

Word does not have only that "representative" existence of our human communications. It does not merely point to the existence of the speaker. It participates in that existence. The Word is so representative of the speaker that it shares the speaker's life. It is a person as the speaker is a person; it is eternal as the speaker is eternal. This Word is consubstantial with the Father. It has real existence. It shares in the very Godhead of the speaker. And thus we are not at all surprised when John goes on to declare that "the Word was in God's presence and the Word was God" (Jn 1:1).

This Word is proportioned to the listeners, too. Here is a point that we often overlook. God is a speaker interested in genuine, successful communication. And so God's Word is adjusted to the capacities of the listeners. "The Word was made flesh, he lived among us." That is what John says (1:14). The Word took on human proportions, became humanly present, became palpable and thus able to be humanly experienced. And thus communication of a most important sort took place.

Revelation occurred, and revelation's name was Jesus, the Christ, the Word of God. This, of course, we know not *a priori* but *a posteriori*. We know it not because some logic drives us to it; we know it because it happened. As Christians we believe that the Father revealed himself in Christ. We believe that revelation took place and was incarnated in Jesus. And thus we conclude, on the basis of the historical evidence that we choose to understand in a particular way, that the Word of God is both representative of the speaker and proportioned to the listeners.

"All things were made through him, and without him was made nothing that has been made." These words of John (1:3) give us another angle. They make us reconsider the foregoing argument, at least in one particular. For we realize that divine communication is not, after all, exactly like human communication. In God there is a power that is beyond time, that somehow stands outside time and makes time be. God is not only the Speaker of Words, God is also the creator of the world, of the listeners. In God, the Word preexists the listeners; it is an eternal Word bestowed on temporal, finite listeners. So in this case it is simply impossible to proportion the Word to the listener. In this unique, divine case the listener must be proportioned to the Word.

"All things were made through him," because all things were made for him. The world was created, was shaped, as a readiness for God's Word, as a place apt to receive the Word that God would share. It was, quite literally, proportioned to the Word. We are, in Karl Rahner's phrase, "hearers of the Word." Hearing the Word of God is not just something we can do and may do. It is something we are created in order to do. Under the light of faith we discover that the very essence of humankind is this capacity to receive the Word of God, to give it flesh and make it present.

In scholastic terminology, Christ was the Exemplary Cause of creation. He is the model, the pattern according to which we and our world were created. He is the paradigm in terms of which creation was accomplished. Thus, when in due time the Word does become flesh in Jesus Christ, it can honestly be said that "he came unto his own." The entry of the Word into creation is not some frightful coincidence of opposites. It is not the magic of God making the impossible happen. It is not, if you will forgive the metaphor, like a dozen circus clowns somehow fitting into a tiny automobile. Quite the contrary. When the Word becomes flesh, humanity fits him like a glove. Humanity was made to order for this event, it was shaped as a ready receptacle for divinity. In Rahner's terms, humanity is "that which ensues when God's self-utterance, his Word, is given out lovingly into the void of god-less nothing."[5]

Christ is the exemplary cause of creation. Creation is shaped in terms of the Word of God, is proportioned to that Word. And the result of this is that incarnation is able to occur. Communication is able to take place. God the speaker is able to share divine life with us, the listeners. God is able to communicate a divine Word. And the act in which this communication preeminently, irrevocably, takes place is the Incarnation. In Jesus of Nazareth the "Word became flesh and dwelt among us."

Implications

Now, from this understanding of Christ in relationship to creation, a number of important implications may be drawn.

First, it follows from what has been said thus far that Christ is the forethought of the Father's creative action, not its afterthought. So often Christians seem to assert that creation and incarnation bear no relationship to each other, that the world was created as it was for no particular reason and that the idea of incarnation came to God "late in the game." We're speaking anthropomorphically, of course; Christian theology cannot altogether avoid doing so. But at least we should take care that our anthropomorphisms are attuned to the truths of our faith. In this case we have an anthropomorphism that utterly betrays our faith.

To assert, then, that the very idea of incarnation, the possibility of that joining of God and humankind, enters into our salvation history only after creation is complete, and in a way that is irrelevant to creation itself, is to distort the Christian faith. It is to divide the God of creation from the God of redemption in a most unacceptable way. And most certainly it is to stand apart from the brilliant, inspired insight of St. John. No, the God of redemption *is* the God of creation. This world is created *in view of* the incarnation. Even if we do not wish to hold that the Father made a commitment to incarnation in creating this world, still we must hold that the potential for incarnation was there. If the human race was not shaped as it was in view of a *necessary* self-utterance of God in incarnation, still it was so shaped in view of a *possible* self-utterance. Thus, in some sense the incarnation stands at the head of creation, as its presupposition and guiding principle. The incarnation, at least as a possibility, is the blueprint for all that God does in our regard.

It follows from this, in the second place, that the incarnation of God's Word in Jesus Christ makes sense with or without the reality of original sin (about which we will say much more, later in this volume). Once again, we have here the response to a common misunderstanding of our faith. There is no doubt that the reality of sinful alienation is present when the incarnation takes place. It is also true that the life, death, and resurrection of Jesus succeed in overcoming that reality and reuniting us with God. But it does not follow from this that original sin is the necessary prerequisite for incarnation, that apart from original sin incarnation would be meaningless and absurd.

It is debated in theology whether incarnation *would* have taken place apart from the "mystery of iniquity." Both those who say yes and those who say no are well within the bounds of Christian orthodoxy. What must not be debated is the fact that incarnation *could* have taken place apart from original sin. Inasmuch as this world was created as a potential receptacle for the divinity of God's Word, incarnation was possible from the first moment of creation. Therefore, even if the function of incarnation was (at least in part) the rectification of the evil situation of humankind, such was not the essence of incarnation. No, the essence of incarnation was simply the self-gift of God to the human family, the union of God, through this Word, with that good world which had come from the divine creative hand. If the function of the incarnation was to transform the world from evil to good, still the essence of incarnation involved an affirmation of the preexisting goodness of the world that was entered. Or to put this one last way, the most fundamental premise of incarnation was not, as is often implied, the evilness of the world, but rather its goodness. If sin makes incarnation necessary, sanctity yet makes it possible.

Consequently, and in the third place, the entrance of God's Word into this world is not to be likened to the surreptitious entry of a guerrilla warrior into enemy territory. It is not to be described as the entrance of an envoy from the kingdom of heaven into the midst of the kingdom of the demon. Indeed, if one speaks in this way (and people do speak in this way, in Christian preaching if not in Christian theology), one espouses a profoundly un-Christian dualism. No, St. John says that the Word "came unto his own," and he means precisely that. God is "at home" in this world; this world is God's kingdom. In some very real sense (and in view of God's preparation in the act of creation), the incarnation represents the "coming home" of God's Word to this world. It is a matter of the Word finally taking possession of the "kingdom prepared for you since the foundation of the world" (Mt 25:34), as Scripture says in another context.

Thus, if the incarnation in some way constitutes the first act of redemption (as it surely does), nonetheless it also constitutes the "eighth day of creation." It is the completion of creation, the fulfillment of the promise that lies within the very fiber of creation itself. There is, then, a sense in which creation itself is not complete until the moment of incarnation. Even if God was not compelled to complete creation in the gift of incarnation, still, since God chose to do so, we ought to be conscious of the "rightness" of the act. It did, indeed, complete the process of communication that began at the first moment of creation. It brought to magnificent fullness the ancient promise that "I will be your God and you will be my people."

Finally, this understanding of Christ and creation makes us appreciate with unparalleled richness the potential of this human world. It is a world filled with hints of the incarnation for which it is prepared. It is modeled on the Word, it is designed as his potential receptacle. It possesses the Word already before the act of incarnation as its exemplary cause. Thus this world is always and everywhere a certain revelation of God the Father.

How often people will exclaim that a particular human experience makes them feel very close to God. It may be the beauty of nature, the wonders of technology, the excitements of art and music, the intimacy of another human person. Whatever it may be, it gifts the recipient with an experience of closeness to God. We see now that this is no accident; it is not an illusion. All of creation contains hints of God. All of it speaks of God the way clothes speak of their wearer, the way a room speaks of its inhabitant, the way these pages speak of their author's beliefs. Everything in our experience is revelation; everything is words of God, words modeled on the Word. The fertility of God is thus expressed and communicated in the fertility of creation. All that is is a vehicle of God, able to transmit God's love. All that is, all that we encounter in the process of human life, is a matter of whispers preparing for the great shout of God's Word. And that shout, that final, irrevocable, unsurpassable shout, is incarnation.

Christian ethics must therefore take this world seriously. It is God's world – and God's words. It is a gift from God to us, and it is part of our way to God. It holds a wonderful place in the process of God's self-revelation to creation. It must also hold a prominent place in our efforts to respond to that revelation by Christian living. Christian ethics is humanistic ethics, and for deeply theological reasons.

Christ and Redemption

We have referred in the preceding pages to the redemptive function of the incarnation. We have acknowledged that function, but we have not emphasized it. Now we must give it our direct attention.

Given the fact that God's Word entered this world in Jesus Christ, what was he up to? What did he do in this world? It is the common conviction of Christians (and a central tenet of their faith) that he saved humankind. He overcame the alienation of sin, he reunited us with God, and he established the new covenant in his blood by which we are all made one.

This is true. Indeed, it is more than true. Not only did Jesus bring about this union, not only did he effect it, he also constituted it. Jesus Christ was (and is) the union of God and humanity. Throughout the early centuries of the Church great battles were fought over various ways of understanding the person of Jesus. And in spite of various heretical adversaries, the Church always remained faithful to its central conviction: Jesus is divine and human, both. Right in his very personhood is the reunion of humanity with God accomplished. If Jesus is the Redeemer, he is all the more redemption itself. If he is the Savior, yet he is more profoundly salvation itself. The deeds of Jesus are important primarily because they express and manifest his personhood. They are the result of what occurs when the promised reunion comes to pass. The Christian church throughout its history, therefore, celebrates the personhood, the salvific and redemptive personhood, of that Jesus who is the Christ.

Still, to say all this is not to say that the deeds of Jesus were unimportant. Quite the contrary. To the extent that we discover how the Word-made-flesh comported himself in this world, to that extent we have the possibility of discovering how we should live as well. So, although this project will occupy us in the next chapter as well, even in this present context it is worth taking note of what the New Testament reveals about the lifestyle of Jesus Christ.

The first thing to be noticed in pursuing this investigation is the strong emphasis on the humanity of Jesus. Unlike some of the apocryphal writings of early Christianity, the Gospels present us less with a divine wonder-worker and more with a preeminently human person. We notice his solicitude at the marriage at Cana. We are repeatedly reminded of his need for solitude and reflection. We are allowed to view his tears before the grave of Lazarus. And, although we tend to take the force out of the words, we are clearly informed that his ministry began and ended with "temptations." He loudly proclaimed that "as often as you did it for one of my least brothers, you did it for me" (Mt 25:40), and he lived that style himself. He fed the hungry, gave sight to the blind, cured the sick.

He worked miracles, so we are told, out of solicitude for the people and that faith might be strengthened. But as best we can tell from the scriptural testimony, Jesus never worked a miracle for himself. Indeed, he refused to do so. "Do you not suppose I can call on my Father to provide at a moment's notice more than twelve legions of angels?" (Mt 26:53). Do you not know that I can appeal beyond this human world, can claim power and privilege that is far above human rights? But I will not do so. God has become human, and will be faithful to that humanity.

That is the essence of what Jesus did: He was human. He lived the human life that he had embraced. And he lived it faithfully, unstintingly, and without exception. Indeed, he lived it to the end. Sometimes one has the impression that Christians believe that Jesus came only to die, that it was his death alone that gave us the gift of salvation. But that seems to be a distortion. Better to say that life, authentic and faithful human life, was his purpose. And inasmuch as that life leads to death, for him as for us all, the death of Jesus was the outcome, the inevitable completion of his commitment to human life. Christ "humbled himself," humbled himself to his heavenly Father but also to his human vocation, "obediently accepting even death, death on a cross." Therefore, because of that fidelity and love, "God highly exalted him" (Phil 2:8f).

This, then, is the redemptive mystery espoused by the Christian faith. The incarnation is the embrace of humanity by God; in that embrace is its fulfillment and salvation. God becomes human, and in so doing he divinizes humanity. It is the personhood of Jesus Christ, both God and human, that unites God and all of us in a finally salvific way. And precisely because of this salvation in his person, Jesus lives his human life; he lives it completely, in love and fidelity and generosity. He lives it even when it leads to the ignominy of murder at the hand of his Father's creatures.

Implications

This doctrinal statement, then, also leads us to a number of implications. And these have great import for the task of moral theology.

First, it is clear from all the foregoing that this human world is not only fertile with hints of God (as we saw before), it is also truly salvific.

It is precisely the place where salvation takes place. It is where God meets humankind and transforms it into a community of sons and daughters. As we might express it colloquially, God does this saving thing "on our turf." God's commitment to the reality of communication, God's desire to proportion a divine Word to human listeners is so deep that we can declare quite literally that salvation is a human event. Thus the dignity of this world, which we perceived in the previous section of this chapter, is now seen to be totally beyond what we might have imagined.

It follows from this, in the second place, that we human persons are not only permitted to appreciate this world, we are commanded to do so. For this world is where God is to be found.

For thousands of years our religious instincts have led us to desire union with God. This desire has, in turn, led to religious behavior. A common characteristic of that behavior has been to set aside some quantity of "sacred space," some place within this world that is viewed as "outside" this world, a bit of heaven on earth. As religious people, then, we become one with God by leaving "this world," by going to that place where God is. We find God "on God's turf," or we do not find God at all.

The Christian faith, we now see, is quite otherwise. If we leave "this world," go beyond the world in the search for God, we will miss God. For God is here. To attempt to enter the domain of God is not only ludicrous; for the Christian it is also futile. We will simply pass God on the way. And it is also unnecessary. God is to be found in the fabric of human life, in the midst of those tasks and projects that constitute the human experience. God does this saving thing "on our turf." It is here that we encounter God; it is here that we receive the redemptive gift.

This insight has, of course, all sorts of consequences for Christian theology. It explains why the Church (*ekklesia*) is not really a place, a building, or an institution. It is the community itself. For it is in the Church, in the community, that God is found. It explains why Christians do not really have "sacred space," in the theological sense. We do not have temples, necessary for the encounter with God. We have gathering places for the community Church, nothing more.[6] This insight also explains the high importance of sacraments. We do not apologize for the apparent outrage of saying that God can be encountered and experienced in oil and water, bread and wine. Indeed, God can be met in all of creation. But God's presence is particularly promised in these peak moments of the human experience.

Finally, this insight explains why the Church-as-institution is both the minister of God's gifts and a merely human reality. Perhaps of all Christians, Catholics are particularly tempted to expect of the Church a wisdom and virtue that are superhuman. They can be angered by the frailty of the Church, by its failures, its errors, its infidelities. But to expect more than this of the Church is unfair. The Church is human, genuinely and truly so. It may also be a place of grace, a place where love beyond human hopes can be mediated. But for all that, the Church never ceases to be fundamentally human. Indeed, it is precisely by struggling with this humanness that the Church succeeds in proclaiming the Gospel and sharing the gift of salvation. As we shall repeatedly see in the pages of this book, the human vocation of the Church, grounded in the human vocation of God's Word in Jesus, is a privilege and a burden. But in any case, we must be careful to ask no more than the Church can give. As Jesus refused for himself those legions of angels, so he refuses them for his Church. And that is the mystery of our faith.

All of this leads to the third implication, namely, that the fundamental ethical command imposed on the Christian is precisely to be what he or she is: "Be human." That is what God asks of us, no more and no less. Imitate Christ, and do this by seeking to be as faithful to the human vocation as he was. Love your neighbor as yourself. Do unto others as you would have them do unto you. Christian ethics, viewed from the perspective of its goal, is human ethics, no more and no less.

This is a most important point. There is, often enough, an implicit gnosticism in the way people talk about the ethical life of Christians. One has the impression that they view moral theology as some sort of arcane science, some body of wisdom from another world. In principle, though, Christian ethics knows nothing that all people cannot know. It reflects on human experience, it searches for the human good. It attempts to articulate, in a way that is helpful, the demands of human living. For right human living is precisely what is demanded of the Christian.

Or again, some people will describe Christian moral demands as if they were constituted by a body of arbitrary and extrinsic divine commands. It is as if one thought God had created an intrinsically amoral world and then, after the fact, added a few rules. It is as if one believed God to have said: "My people, there's really nothing wrong with murder. But I do want to test you. So as one of my regulations I insist that you refrain from murder. It is only my command that makes murder wrong."

What a travesty this sort of legalism is! And yet it is not uncommon. It can be heard regularly in the pulpits of Christian churches. Perhaps it is not expressed so clearly, but it is there. "God's law," the "will of God," "it is wrong because it violates the Ten Commandments": Phrases like these are heard often. As we can see, they are insidious. Christian ethics is not arbitrary, it is not a form of religious legalism. It is the faithful articulation of the meaning of Jesus' call that we should "be what we are." And if there is a place for moral laws (as there surely is), that place can be justified only by the fact that the laws helpfully express what it means to live the human life with fidelity and generosity. Christian ethics is human ethics. Christians are unconditionally humanists; that is our pride and our privileged vocation.

A fourth and final implication follows from this line of thought. By reflecting on the way of life that Jesus shared, we are eventually led to a quite particular strategy for Christian ethics. And that strategy will comprise our methodology in this book.

Christian ethics, like all of the Christian faith, is essentially and profoundly human. It is a human task seeking human wisdom about the human conduct of human affairs. It develops its understanding of the human and its strategy of love on the basis of the world vision of Jesus, of course, on that revelation of the deepest meanings of life. And that makes a critical difference. Still, moral theology is not "sectarian." It is not an isolated enterprise. Quite the contrary. With its Jesus-inspired commitment to the human it is, in a certain sense, moral philosophy pursued by persons who are believers. It speaks in the midst of the human community and attempts to speak for and to that whole community.

Of course, this does not mean that we shall go to the other extreme, adopting an utterly secular approach to the ethical process. Quite the contrary, we shall be pursuing moral theology. But by that term we mean something quite specific.

We mean, first, that these will be the reflections of believers, developed in the midst of the Christian community. Indeed, as we shall see, it is an important premise of our approach that ethics is always an intrinsically communal product. Since our ethics will be the sort generated within the Christian community, we will be proud to call it moral theology. Second, we use this term because, as believers, we shall confidently expect to find applicable and valuable insights in our tradition. We have already given our attention to the resources of Scripture, dogmatic tradition, and theological reflection, and we shall continue to do so. These resources will, it is true, have to be tested against our personal and communal experience; that is what it means to say that our ethics is human. But they will nonetheless be highly useful.[7] Third, our enterprise deserves the name of moral theology because our very starting point, indicated to some extent in this chapter, is a fundamentally Christian vision of human beings and their world. This is our perspective. And as it is unique, so the resulting ethic will in some ways be unique.

Conclusion

St. Paul called Christ

the image of the Invisible God, the first-born of all creatures. In him everything in heaven and on earth was created . . . all were created through him and for him. He is before all else that is. In him everything continues in being. (Col 1:15–17)

This is a description of cosmic Christology, of the relationship of Christ and creation. And in essence it proclaims to us that we may be human. It is permitted to be human, Christ himself permits it. And Paul continues that Christ is

the first-born of the dead, so that primacy may be his in everything . . . and, by means of him, to reconcile everything in his person . . . making peace through the blood of his cross. (Col 1:18–20)

In these words he summarizes historical Christology, the relationship of Christ and redemption. In this we discover that we must be human.

Be human! No more and no less! Christ permits it, and Christ demands it. That is the central conviction of the Christian faith. And it is the fundamental premise of the following principles of Christian ethics.

Chapter 4

JESUS AND MORAL LIVING

Having explored the relationship of Christ and moral theology and having discovered the sense in which Christian morality is a consciously humanistic morality, something else still remains to be said. For the simple fact is that Christians do not extend themselves in love of their neighbor for purely humanistic reasons. Rather, they are motivated by a profound devotion to Jesus and his way of life. That is, within the events of their lives, and decisively motivating them, is a *spirituality* that is centered on Jesus. And that spirituality makes all the difference.[1]

This chapter, then, balances the one preceding by focusing on the person of Jesus as it grounds the living of the Christian life.[2] But to do this is not easy. For the honest truth is that every generation of Christians claims from the life of Jesus the message and the vision they need. There is not just one Christian spirituality; rather, there are many. Indeed, to some extent each person's spirituality is unique. Beyond the critical feature: that the person of Jesus plays a central role in one's interpretation of life and in the motivation of one's deeds, there is little that is universal. For some it is a gentle Jesus, for others a prophetic revolutionary; for some a Jesus of fidelity and long suffering, for others an impatient activist; for some a Jesus ever faithful to the traditions of his people, for others a critic who carefully assesses all that is handed down. And, in the end, the Jesus who serves as this central life figure is not precisely the Jesus of history at all, but rather the Jesus whom the individual has met in personal and incommunicable encounter.

Still, if we cannot describe that Jesus who is so significant for each Christian person, we can at least explore a bit the same Jesus as he emerges in the Scriptures. After all, the Jesus of personal encounter is, in the end, to be tested for authenticity precisely through comparison with the Jesus of the Bible. So to consider some biblical themes, particularly those pertinent to ethics, seems a worthy project.

But that is not easy. For one thing, the sheer quantity of biblical materials pertinent to moral living is overwhelming. Questions of behavior, and the issues of ethical and religious vision that underlie them, arise continually in the pages of Scripture.[3] Volumes have been written analyzing this material, and thus any attempt at exhaustive treatment here is doomed to failure.

For another thing, it is axiomatic that the Bible does not provide us with any one ethical system. The ethical ideas to be found in sacred Scripture are not comprehensive and integral, as those of a philosophical system might be. Nor are they even consistent. One might possibly be able to speak of the "ethics of" Hosea or Jeremiah, Luke or Paul. But as soon as one moves beyond generalities, it is clear that one cannot speak of the "ethics of" the Bible. So in pursuing these reflections we most certainly have no pretensions of developing a "biblical morality" or even a "biblical spirituality of moral living." Such a goal is not possible.

Still, as one reviews the history of the Christian people, it becomes clear that certain themes, intimately identified with the person and mission of Jesus, do perdure. Certain ideas, rooted in the Scriptures themselves, are hallmarks of a Christian spirituality as they were hallmarks of Jesus' spirituality. As such, they are cherished by the whole family of Christian people. We should take the time to note these perennial themes.[4] In light of this modest goal, then, we will select only the more obvious themes in the biblical materials, those that scripture scholars themselves most commonly highlight. And even among these themes, we will focus on those that are most deeply related to the person and ministry of Jesus.

By considering them, we will attempt to delineate at least the broad outlines of a Jesus-way-of-living, however it may be detailed in one era or another. More deeply, we will try to enrich our picture of the moral vision that was Jesus' own and that was presented in his preaching. But most deeply, we shall seek to encounter Jesus himself, or to put words to the encounter we have had. For only in this way can we develop some sense of the way in which this deeply human morality of ours is nonetheless centered on that Jesus who changes lives forever.[5]

Covenant

Jesus was, of course, a Jew. And thus, to understand him, to enter into his vision of morality, to chisel out the shape of this spirituality, we must become sensitive to the categories of Jewish thought. For that purpose, no theme is more significant than that of "covenant." In some ways, it is the axis for the entire story of ancient Israel.[6] From the first bond between Yahweh and Abraham (Gn 15:18) through the time of Moses and the Sinai experience (Ex 34:10) and on into the era of the prophets, the mystery of covenant was a recurring theme – not some cold-blooded contract, but an intimate and very personal reality. For the Israelite, to covenant with another party was, in some ways, to join families. Indeed, one's obligations to a covenant partner were second only to the responsibilities of immediate family life. Covenant did not mean that one agreed to do this thing for or with another; it meant that one agreed to be responsible for the person himself or herself in this and any other context.

All of this is exemplified in one of the classic formulations of the Israelite covenant with Yahweh: "They shall be my people and I will be their God" (Jer 24:7; Ez 11:20; cf., also, Jer 7:23, 11:4; Ez 14:11; Hos 2:25). Scholars tell us that this formulation was nothing more than an adaptation of a common text of the marriage vow: "She is my wife and I am her husband this day and forever." The reality of this covenant was that Yahweh was marrying the people, assuming that kind of responsibility for them and expecting that kind of fidelity in return. It was not a relationship of convenience or efficiency; it was a relationship of intimate and genuine love.

Indeed, the emphasis on intimacy and inner authenticity grew in the writings of the prophets. Jeremiah declared: "The days are coming . . . when I will make a new covenant. . . . I will place my law within them, and write it upon their hearts; I will be their God, and they shall be my people" (Jer 31:31ff). And Ezekiel proclaimed: "I will give you a new heart taking from your bodies your stony hearts and giving you natural hearts. . . . You shall live in the land I gave your fathers; you shall be my people, and I will be your God" (Ez 36:26ff).

And finally we should note that the idea of covenant continued to be important in much of the New Testament writing. All four of the Last Supper narratives, though they varied in other ways, were one in pointing out the function of "new covenant" (Mt 26; Mk 14; Lk 22; 1 Cor 11), whereas John seems to have "rescheduled" his passion narrative to make the death of Jesus coincide with the moment of the Passover covenant sacrifices.[7]

Kingdom

Jesus, for his part, does not seem to have laid primary emphasis on the idea of covenant. Instead, as Rudolf Schnackenburg points out, the central focus of Jesus' preaching seems to have been the "kingdom."[8] Indeed, inasmuch as this term is very common in the Synoptics and yet is quite rare in the other books of the New Testament, there can be little doubt that it goes back to Jesus himself. And so, when we are considering moral themes of the New Testament, the idea of kingdom must surely come first.

But we must be clear about the meaning of the term. The Greek word is *basileia*, which is better translated as "reign." The emphasis is not on a place, like the "kingdom of England." Rather, the term speaks of a situation, a state of being where the Lord rules and with loving power holds sway. And this nuance makes important differences in a number of familiar texts. For example, the Lord's prayer: "Our Father, who art in heaven . . . may your reign come!" (cf. Mt 6:9). Or the request of the good thief: "Remember me when you come in your kingly power" (Lk 23:12 RSV). Or again, the powerful words of Jesus: "You cannot tell by careful watching when the reign of God will come. . . . The reign of God is already in your midst" (Lk 17:20f). God does not primarily rule with signs of outward power. God's power is the power of love; it rules through and in the hearts of human persons.

But if the idea of kingdom, of the reign of God, is central to Jesus, still it is not alone. A number of other themes connected to the idea of kingdom are also prominent. And they contribute greatly to a Christian spirituality of moral living.

Repentance

First, there is what may be called the "prerequisite for the kingdom." At the very beginning of the Synoptics comes the call of John the Baptist challenging his listeners to repentance. He describes the baptism to which he invites them as a "baptism of repentance" (Mt 3:2–11; Mk 1:4–6; Lk 3: 1–14). And this for a very special reason: the kingdom. "When John the Baptizer made his appearance as a preacher in the desert of Judea, this was his theme: 'Reform your lives! The reign of God is at hand'" (Mt 3:1–2).

But what is this repentance? It is not merely a change of behavior. Indeed, the Greek *metanoia* actually means "change of mind." It suggests a total reversal of lifestyle, a turning round of one's whole being, a personal moral revolution.[9] Jesus himself compared it to becoming like a little child (Mt 18:31). Paul described it as putting on "the new man," as dying to sin (Rom 6:11). And Nicodemus was warned: "No one can see the reign of God unless he is begotten from above" (Jn 3:3). (It is interesting that because John's Gospel was addressed to believers, he never actually used the word "repentance.")

This focus on repentance is no small thing. It was not a new concept in Israel; the prophets had repeatedly issued the same call. But Jesus and John the Baptist did not live in the age of the prophets. And the Jewish leaders may well have considered themselves and their people as much better than their ancestors who were the objects of the prophetic condemnation. So when John the Baptist, and then Jesus, spoke in these terms, they were making a highly volatile political statement. Their listeners knew the word, knew its association with an unfaithful Israel. There must have been a stinging, humiliating pain in having those words addressed to them.

But addressed they were. And inasmuch as this theme of repentance is much more prominent in the Synoptic Gospels than in the other books of the New Testament, there is a strong likelihood that it really belongs to the message preached by Jesus himself.

Discipleship

A number of other themes are associated with the idea of repentance in one way or another. Among these are faith, baptism, and the good works that should exemplify the new life now lived. But perhaps the most powerful of these themes is that of discipleship.[10] Indeed, one could argue that Christian living is nothing else than the attempt to make discipleship one's whole way of life. For if repentance is the prerequisite for the kingdom, discipleship represents "membership in the kingdom."

It was not uncommon in Israel for rabbis to gather around themselves a body of disciples. They were to be learners (*matheiteis*), followers ready and willing to learn from the teacher. They were to follow him, remain with him, become loyal to him. And because this practice was somewhat common, it is not surprising that Jesus acquired and encouraged disciples also. But in his case, the notion of discipleship took on several interesting nuances.

First, discipleship meant the simple fact of following after the Lord. One statement, at least part of which appears in each of the Synoptics, proclaimed:

If anyone comes to me without turning his back on his father and mother, his wife and his children, his brothers and sisters, indeed his very self, he cannot be my follower. Anyone who does not take up his cross and follow me cannot be my disciple. (Lk 14:26f; cf. Mt 10:37f and Mk 8:34)

Or again, Jesus advised the rich young man: "There is one thing more you must do. Go and sell what you have and give to the poor; you will then have treasure in heaven. After that, come and follow me" (Mk 10:21). Indeed, this quotation is representative of the total commitment that Jesus demanded of his disciples. To follow after him meant leaving everything else behind (Lk 5:11), giving up family (Lk 1-1:26), money and wealth (Mk 10:21), former occupations (Mk 2:14), and, indeed, all economic security (Lk 9:58).

This notion of following after Jesus, demanding though it was, still remained within the Jewish tradition. What was much less traditional was a second meaning that discipleship had for Jesus: the idea that the disciple was to replace Jesus, act on his behalf, take on a mission for the sake of the Lord. Indeed, the entire "apostolic discourse" in Matthew's Gospel (chap. 10) was premised on this idea. To be a disciple of Jesus was, sooner or later, to be sent. It did not involve remaining forever at the side of the rabbi; on the contrary, it involved going forth to do his work, "To another he said, 'Come after me.' The man replied, 'Let me bury my father first.' Jesus said to him, 'Let the dead bury their dead; come away and proclaim the kingdom of God'" (Lk 9:59f; note the connection to kingdom).

Finally, discipleship to Jesus even went beyond this call to mission. To follow the Lord ultimately meant to share in his very destiny. "No pupil outranks his teacher, no slave his master. The pupil should be glad to become like his teacher, the slave like his master" (Mt 10:24f). "If anyone would serve me, let him follow me; where I am, there will my servant be" (Jn 12:26). Indeed this participation would include the specific rhythms of Jesus' life. There would be the victimhood of suffering:

If a man wishes to come after me, he must deny his very self, take up his cross, and follow in my steps. Whoever would preserve his life will lose it, but whoever loses his life for my sake and the gospel's will preserve it. (Mk 8:34f)

And there would also be the gift of ultimate victory:

You are the ones who have stood loyally by me in my temptations. I for my part assign to you the dominion my father has assigned to me. . . . You will sit on thrones judging the twelve tribes of Israel. (Lk 22:28ff)

Law

The theme of discipleship reveals that membership in the kingdom of Jesus was a rigorous and demanding thing. It included obligations, or at least the reality of being obligated. This aspect of obligation we may consider under the rubric of law, the "rule of the kingdom." Since we shall return to the topic of law in chapter 12 and examine it in detail, however, only some brief comments will be included here.

Law, of course, was a concept with a powerful and pivotal history in Israel. And Jesus, as a Jew, saw himself as being in continuity with that past.[11] At the same time, as we shall see, at least part of Jesus' mission was to free his followers from the negative aspects of law. But that call to freedom did not mean there were no expectations placed on them. Quite the contrary.

"Let the dead bury their dead; come away and proclaim the kingdom of God. . . . Whoever puts his hand to the plow but keeps looking back is unfit for the reign of God" (Lk 9:60, 62). No, the kingdom to which Jesus dedicated himself required a singlemindedness. It demanded fidelity and commitment of a very personal, authentic sort. "What emerges from within a man, that and nothing else is what makes him impure. . . . All these evils come from within and render a man impure" (Mk 7:20, 23). It demanded a position of priority in one's life, and a willingness to trust the Lord.

Stop worrying, then, over questions like, "What are we to eat?" . . . Your heavenly Father knows all that you need. Seek first his kingship over you, his way of holiness, and all these things will be given you besides. (Mt 6:31ff)

So if anything, the "law" of Jesus was more demanding than the law of Israel's history. But it also seems to have been more discriminating. Granted that the evidence from the Gospels is not completely consistent, that at some times Jesus evidences great reverence for the law, still in matters of ritual and ceremonial laws he often appears to consider himself quite free.[12] One might even say that he was quick to reject that sort of "legalism" which would use the law as an excuse. For example, he would cure whether it was the Sabbath or not (e.g., Lk 14:1-6). He was undisturbed that his disciples should pick grain to eat on the Sabbath (Mt 12:1-8). But at the same time, where the law expressed the requirements of genuine and generous living he could be amazingly rigorous. "Anyone who looks lustfully at a woman has already committed adultery with her in his thoughts" (Mt 5:28). And his expectations of marital fidelity went beyond those of the Mosaic tradition (Mt 5:31f).

As Rudolph Bultmann declares, for Jesus

one decisive demand shines out. The good that it is a question of doing must be done totally. Anyone who does it a little lazily, with reservations, just so that at a pinch the outward precept is fulfilled, has not really done it at all.[13]

Thus, if law is understood as demand, it is a concept very central to the message of Jesus. But the demand had a very different flavor. With the proclamation of law by Jesus there was a distinct and decisive turn to the interior. The reality of surface appearance was relativized, whereas the reality of inner authenticity was absolutized. It is the quality of one's heart, the mystery of intention, that is truly central.

Love

This increasing emphasis on interiority is nowhere more manifest than in the New Testament considerations of the theme of love.[14] We will postpone consideration of one aspect of this theme, the two great commandments of love, until chapter 12. But several other aspects demand immediate attention. So we move now to reflect on love, the "life of the kingdom."

But what do we mean by love? Psychologists sometimes say that only one who has been loved is capable of love. If this is true, then love can be defined simply by looking to its source. And in this respect the New Testament offers a very special insight. "I give you a new commandment: Love one another. Such as my love has been for you, so must your love be for each other" (Jn 13:34). "This is my commandment: love one another as I have loved you" (Jn 15:12). "Love, then, consists in this: not that we have loved God, but that he has loved us and has sent his Son as an offering for our sins" (1 Jn 4:10).

So the school of love, especially as this is envisioned by John, is God's own self, and that Jesus whom God has sent. The starting point for the ethic of love is not the Golden Rule of self-love but the astonishing faith-truth of God's love for us. In this love we are taught love, and according to its measure is our own love to take shape. And as that love of ours takes shape, it points in two different directions.

First there is the love of *koinonia* (community, fellowship). This theme is developed particularly by John. Indeed, some scholars accuse John of an elitism by which the love command is restricted to those within the community. They argue that John is concerned only that Christians love "one another" (see the quotations just given), and not that they strive to love the more general "neighbor."[15] Be that as it may, there is no doubt that the love of fellowship is a theme dear to the Johannine vision. Jesus proclaims it at length in his final discourse. He exemplifies it in the powerful symbol of washing his disciples' feet. And he lives it in his own self-sacrifice: "The way we came to understand love was that he laid down his life for us; we too must lay down our lives for our brothers" (1 Jn 3:16). It is total love, therefore, that ought to characterize the Christian community, a love that is willing to sacrifice to the point of death. "If God has loved us so, we must have the same love for one another" (1 Jn 4:11).

There is also another kind of love, however, the love of *diakonia* (service). There is the charity that reaches out to all people in need to care for them and raise them up. As we have suggested, the degree to which John envisioned this love of general service is debated by scholars. But there is no doubt that Paul is concerned about it (as well as about the love of fellowship).

Owe no debt to anyone except the debt that binds us to love one another. He who loves his neighbor has fulfilled the law. The commandments, "You shall not commit adultery" ... and any other commandment there may be are all summed up in this, "You shall love your neighbor as yourself." Love never wrongs the neighbor, hence love is the fulfillment of the law. (Rom 13:8ff)

And this love has several specific characteristics. It is universal in its scope; we are expected to show love "for all" (1 Thes 3:12; cf. 1 Thes 5:15). It calls for humility and a spirit of self-sacrifice that are rooted in Christ.

Though he was in the form of God, he did not deem equality with God something to be grasped at. Rather, he emptied himself and took the form of a slave, being born in the likeness of men. (Phil 2:6-7; cf. 2 Cor 8:8f).

It constitutes the sum and substance of all Christian moral demands. For love "binds the rest together and makes them perfect" (Col 3:12-14). It is therefore by love that we "fulfill the law of Christ" (Gal 6:2).

All of this is gloriously summarized in Paul's great hymn to love (1 Cor 13). He begins by stipulating the absolute necessity of love: if I "do not have love, I am a noisy gong." Then he goes on to be thoroughly concrete about the love he has in mind. Not some vague feeling of affection. No, the love of concrete service, the very mundane struggle to be "patient . . . kind . . . not jealous . . . not snobbish." And he concludes by proclaiming the permanence of love's centrality:

Love never fails. . . . My knowledge is imperfect now; then I shall know even as I am known. There are in the end three things that last: faith, hope, and love, and the greatest of these is love. (1 Cor 13:8, 12f)

Beatitudes

We continue this series of scriptural reflections with some comments on the Beatitudes. For if repentance is the prerequisite for the kingdom, if discipleship represents membership in the kingdom, if law speaks the rule of the kingdom, and if love is the life of the kingdom, the Beatitudes can with justice be described as the "proclamation of the kingdom."

To say this may seem strange. The Beatitudes are more commonly viewed as new and challenging requirements, as part of the "law of the kingdom." But that is a misunderstanding. Note that the text in both Matthew (5:3-12) and Luke (6:20-23) is not a series of imperatives; it is a series of indicatives. It makes statements, it proclaims facts. The significance of the Beatitudes is not that they announce something to be done; no, they announce something that is. In the kingdom life is ordered differently than it is in the human world. Human priorities –

money, power, comfort, joviality – do not pertain. In the kingdom the priority is love.

Thus Jesus announced with great solemnity: Even if you are poor, nonetheless in the kingdom you will be happy (blessed). Even if you suffer or hunger, nonetheless God's gift of joy will be yours. There is no doubt that these experiences are evil. No one seeks suffering or persecution or the pain of death's separation. But they will nonetheless come. When they do, you must not despair. Their supremacy is not final. Do not grieve if you appear to be a loser in the categories of the world. In the kingdom those categories will be toppled. Naively immediate human values will be disposed of; they will be supplanted by the inner values of the Lord. So all people, no matter what their human situation, if they share in the kingdom of the Lord, have good reason to rejoice and forever to be glad.

The Beatitudes can thus be called a proclamation. They are Good News. They are an instrument of liberation and exaltation. They are Gospel in the fullest and richest of senses.

Eschatology

Thus far we have considered a series of themes – and terms – that are explicitly present in the biblical texts, and particularly in the New Testament. There remains one theme that deserves our attention. It is, however, a bit different. For the term "eschatology" is not biblical. Rather, this theme is in some ways the distillation of, and a summary of, everything that has been said thus far.

By "eschatology" we mean a focus on the end of time, the "last things," the promise and the reality of our judgment and hoped-for union with God. An eschatological vision was present in the Old Testament. But more significant for us is the central role that vision played in the preaching of Jesus and, subsequently, in the New Testament texts. As Thomas Ogletree has pointed out,

The New Testament writings continue a version of the historical contextualism found in the pentateuchal traditions and the prophetic literature. However, the sense of history present in these writings is profoundly marked by a distinctive eschatology: a conviction that the new age has already dawned.[16]

"If eschatology is an important qualifying theme in some Old Testament literature, it is the decisive feature in much New Testament thought."[17]

This conviction that the end is coming helps explain the intensity of the themes we have already considered. The kingdom, we now see, is not simply a future reality. It is somehow already present. Repentance is critical because there is a need to live this new time, to cut one's connections not only to old ways but even to the old world. Discipleship represents the nonnegotiable challenge to "enter" the kingdom by one's way of life or, more precisely, to imitate Jesus in the living of that life. The heightened demands of the interior law and the relative decentralizing of external observance make sense in this context. So also does the attention to love and the truly radical vision of the Beatitudes.

Of course, the focus on a fairly literal, immanent *eschaton* changed in the early years of the Church. Even within the New Testament writing, particularly in Luke-Acts, there was the need to make sense of the "postponement" and to develop an ethic of ongoing life. But, if Ogletree is correct, even the way in which this delay was understood involved a focus on eschatology.

In one sense eschatology has for Luke been dissolved into the church's missionary expansion. Thus, the book of Acts concludes not with a community awaiting Jesus' coming in power and glory, but with Paul preaching the kingdom of God in Rome. . . . In another sense, the epoch of the church is itself eschatological. It is the age of the Spirit.[18]

So, in summarizing the many ethically pertinent themes in the New Testament, it seems fair to say the linchpin is the conviction that the end of the old is on us, that the time has come for something new. There is, then, an urgency to the ethics of the New Testament, an urgency rooted not in idle opinion or in arbitrary command, but in truths, seen in faith, about the human situation.

Conclusion

This, then, leads us to a conclusion that is significant for our purposes. We have been considering themes that are morally relevant, that define the shape of Christian morality. We have seen that the Christian life is not a matter of conforming to abstract ethical principles, it is a matter of responding with fidelity to the God of the *covenant*. We have seen that the Christian life is a wholly new life, a life of the *kingdom* where the Lord reigns supreme. It is a life turned completely around by *repentance* and focused on the Lord in *discipleship*. It is a life that accepts the new *law* of total, demanding commitment. And it is a life generated from and expressed in *love*.

Even more deeply, in seeing these themes developing, we have been experiencing the Jesus who preached them and who modeled them in his life. And in doing that we have been remembering that, for Christians as they actually live, the Christian life is most profoundly a following of Jesus himself. It is the encounter with the Jesus of these themes that initiates a true Christian life, and it is the attempt to be faithful to the loving, graceful gifts of that Jesus that comprises its ongoing conduct. As much as the goal of Christian life remains the achievement of full humanity for oneself and for the world, the dynamic thrust of that life is to be found in the reality of a person decisively transformed by the presence of the Holy One of Bethlehem.

But as these themes – and Jesus himself – are morally relevant, so are the "indicatives" of the Beatitudes and of the proclamation of the *eschaton* that we were last considering. But the moral relevance of these themes lies precisely in their relativizing of the entire moral enterprise. Even as the immanence of the end lends an urgency to the ethical challenge, it also highlights divine initiative, bringing the divine will to fulfillment in love. And thus, from this perspective, morality, whether viewed as an intellectual science or as the practice of personal living, is not of preeminent importance. What is most significant, in the end, is in no way the mundane facts of our decisions and actions. What is most significant is the transcending fact of God's decisions and actions in Jesus.

We speak of Christianity as a "religion." The word is very significant. It comes from the Latin *religare*, which means "to bind together." The axis around which all of Christian living and all of Christian teaching revolve is this mystery of being bound together with and in the Lord. And this binding, we know, is not something we do at all; it is something God does. That is what the Beatitudes represent, that is what the proclamation of the *eschaton* implies: the final, irrevocable, infinitely loving act of God. In the end, the really significant thing is not the way we live in Jesus. It is the power for living that is Jesus living in us as he continues his living for us forever.

Only in the context of an awareness of this divine initiative can any consideration of a Catholic morality be worthy. Only after one has acknowledged the fact that human actions are not initiatives but responses to the empowering call of the Lord, only then can one truly understand the reality of Christian ethics. And only when one has grasped the peculiar quality of the divine initiative, that it is an inner reality, a matter of the heart, only then can one comfortably accept and confidently live the fact that even morality is primarily a matter of interiority. It is not appearances, not even the shape of our behavior, that ultimately counts. It is the mystery of intention. And this because that mystery somehow participates in the primeval interior intention of God's own self.

This balance between exterior and interior, between human and divine, is well captured in the words of Rudolf Schnackenburg. And even though there is so much more that could be said about the message of Scripture and about the Jesus that Scripture presents, we will conclude our reflections by quoting them.

Jesus' preaching was both a proclamation and a warning, an announcement of a divine act and a demand for a response to it from mankind. Everywhere in the New Testament we find that the acts of God are a call to men; the summons arises from the message. The sequence is invariable too. God acts first, and his act lays responsibility on men. Nowhere in the New Testament do we find a mere morality, a mere ethical system, but neither do we find a piety that imposes no obligations and is divorced from moral behaviour.[19]

PART II

The Moral Person

Chapter 5

HUMAN ACTION

"We are not just animals. We may share much with the animal kingdom; our prehistoric roots may be theirs. But we are more. Indeed, in some ways we are ultimately, radically different than animals."

Words like these represent the common-sense wisdom of most human beings. More than that, they represent the conclusion reached by most serious thinkers through the centuries. Of course, if we are to understand ourselves accurately as human beings, it is necessary to take seriously our connections with the animal world. But it is equally necessary to notice and take into account those things that make us different. To neglect either of these emphases is to distort the reality that we find ourselves to be.

It is true that during the past century human distinctiveness has come under attack from several quarters. It has been suggested that human persons are not really free. Rather, they are determined by biological drives (psychoanalytic psychology) and cultural influences (behavioristic psychology). What is more, said some, the human ability to find and know the truth is largely self-deception (Marx). Persons do not see reality as it is but as they would like it to be. Consequently, one should not speak of knowledge at all, but rather of self-serving ideology.

These critiques of human distinctiveness have much to commend them. Past theories may well have been characterized by a naive humanism that failed to take into account the myriad sources of, and influences on, human behavior. As we continue with this study, we shall often have occasion to utilize the insights of these recent thinkers. But we will not adopt their conclusions uncritically; nor, in the end, will we accept the fundamental perspective of their thought. And this for a number of reasons.

For one thing, the thoroughgoing affirmation of a deterministic and ideological vision leads one to the strange contradiction that even this affirmation is intrinsically unreliable. Indeed, the only really consistent response to this antihuman vision is silence, no response at all. For another thing, many thinkers, even in the fields of psychology and sociology, no longer give complete allegiance to the vision we have described. In addition to the perspectives of psychoanalysis and behaviorism, one also finds psychologists today proposing a number of theories that take far more seriously the distinctively human characteristics of persons: existentialism, transactional analysis, and reality therapy, to name just a few. Similarly, the Marxist theory of ideology has, in recent decades, been nuanced by the still developing field of the sociology of knowledge.[1]

In the following chapters, then, we will attempt to sketch out an understanding of human persons that takes due account of both what unites them to, and what differentiates them from, the animal kingdom. We will do this by utilizing and uniting three distinctive sources of insight. For one thing, we will employ a number of categories from the heritage of Roman Catholic moral theology. For another, we will introduce various insights from contemporary thought. And third, we will test all of these ideas against the benchmark of our own human experience. For in the last analysis, to describe the human person is to describe ourselves. And thus we have the right to expect from any theoretical analysis a synthesis that is true to our own experience and that contributes to our own self-understanding.

To begin, the present chapter will establish a basis for our synthesis by presenting a number of assertions from traditional moral theology.

The Human Act

Scholastic manuals of moral theology often began their discussion of human beings and their behavior by introducing a fundamental distinction between an "act of man" and a "human act." Indeed, it is not unusual for this distinction to be employed as the starting point for the entire discussion of moral theology.[2] This is a reasonable decision, since the distinction is truly fundamental. At the same time, as we shall see, it is a decision that led to some undesirable consequences. For us, in the end, another starting point may prove more helpful. Nonetheless, it will be best to begin by gaining clarity about the difference between these two terms.

A human act (*actus humanus*) describes an action performed by a human being and, what is more, performed in a truly human way. That is, a human act is an action done with at least a modicum of awareness and free choice. The act of reading this book, or of choosing to read it, the planning of a day's activity, the purchase of a new set of clothes, the pursuit of a pleasant conversation: All these are human acts. They are actions done by us as human persons, and they are actions done through and with the human capacities for knowledge and freedom.

An act of man (*actus hominis*), on the other hand, describes a piece of behavior arising through human agency, but without that same knowledge or freedom. I am driving my car when suddenly one of the tires hits a nail and goes flat. I lose control of the car, swerve across the road, and collide with another car, injuring its driver. I may grieve over this event. I may feel tremendous sorrow because of the harm that has been done. Very likely I will even feel an obligation to make some recompense for the evil that has befallen my fellow human. But I will not judge myself to be guilty of any moral fault, any true irresponsibility or sin, in this situation. The "accident" (the term itself is significant) is not something that I did; it is something that happened to me. It was not truly a human act, but rather merely an act of man. Indeed, our daily lives are full of acts of man, and examples could be multiplied. Sleepwalking, actions following unintentional intoxication, the reflex response of a person being attacked: All these actions take place in the human world. But they are no more than acts of man.[3]

So, some actions are merely acts of man whereas other actions are genuinely human acts. And it is human acts that are the focus of attention in moral theology – or at least in that part of moral theology which is our focus in these chapters. For one can only be morally responsible when one has knowledge and freedom, when one is truly in control of the events that transpire.

This traditional distinction, then, commends itself in that it resonates with our common experience. But in that it does not fully resonate with that experience, some additional nuancing remains necessary. For the fact of the matter is that only rarely does a human action fall clearly and completely into one category or the other. Behavior grounded in comprehensive awareness and thoroughgoing freedom is really uncommon in our daily lives. So on further reflection, it becomes clear that the categories human act and act of man represent not so much two mutually exclusive alternatives as rather two extremes on a continuum of human experience. Most of our behavior falls somewhere between those extremes, neither totally unfree nor totally free, neither totally ignorant nor totally aware. Most of our human actions do not deserve the title "human act" in any full and unequivocal sense. Rather, they can only be accurately described as limited, partial, incomplete examples of the reality denoted by the traditional term.

Impediments

In the manuals of moral theology, the notion of "impediments" embraces those factors that limit and inhibit the humanity of human acts. Far from being rejected today, this notion has become more prominent. For, as was intimated earlier, the insights of the social sciences have lately made us more and more aware of the numerous factors that can oppose and inhibit truly human behavior. Consequently, even though we shall need to return to the notion of impediments and to consider it far more deeply later on, it may well merit a brief discussion now. For a standard scholastic list of common impediments to human acts, summarizing our ordinary experience as it does, can serve to illuminate that sense of inner unfreedom that we have.

Ignorance is a very common impediment. Indeed, as was already suggested, total ignorance has the effect of completely "dehumanizing" a human act. But a much more common experience is that of partial ignorance, the situation where I know what I am doing but do not appreciate the implications and consequences of my actions. Consider our previous example of an automobile accident, and now add the factor that I was driving in excess of the posted speed limit. I knew that I was taking a risk, but to the best of my knowledge it was a reasonable risk. I was late and trying to make up time. Inasmuch as I was not driving in a completely responsible manner, I consider myself to be a real cause of that accident and to be morally responsible for it. But inasmuch as I did not know about the road hazard that caused my flat tire and, in fact, did not even consider the possibility of that happening, I consider myself much more a victim of fate than a creator of my own destiny. Ignorance did not completely eliminate my personal responsibility. For, in the last analysis, I probably should have considered all those possible factors. But it did function as at least a partial impediment, blocking the full expression of a truly human act.

Another impediment is passion. Indeed, to be an adult is to be aware of the extent to which anger, envy, sexual desire, and other emotions can limit one's freedom of choice – even while, from another point of view, they are the fuel of energetic moral action.[4] Is a person completely absolved of responsibility for actions that follow on these emotions? Very likely not. But by the same token, he or she is not completely responsible, either. Such actions fall in the grey area between acts of man and human acts; that is our experience. And the traditional moral theology simply ratifies that experience in its analysis of the moral life.

A third impediment found in traditional lists is fear. In this case the older wisdom is even more strongly urged today as a result of the input of the social sciences. Psychologist Abraham H. Maslow distinguishes people motivated by a desire to eliminate "deficiencies" in their life situation from persons generally motivated by an open-ended desire for a fuller experience of "being" (D-people and B-people).[5] In Maslow's perspective, the latter goals, though ideal, cannot be pursued until the former have been duly addressed. For the anxiety generated by deficiencies in one's life makes a decision for fuller being difficult, if not impossible. Other psychologists may analyze the situation a bit differently, but their ultimate conclusions are remarkably similar. Fear and anxiety are the enemies of full human life and genuinely human decision. They are, in the traditional terminology, impediments to human acts.

Finally, the presence of external violent force, or the threat of such force, stands in obvious opposition to the exercise of the human act. Whether the case be that of a "shotgun wedding," the dire threats of a rapist, or the more subtle pressures of the corporate supervisor against a needy employee, the underlying reality is the same. The presence of force (and the fear it engenders) inhibits and at least partially prevents the clear thinking and free choosing that comprise a really human act.

Now, one might argue that these factors do not really prevent moral choice but are the very objects of that choice. To be moral is to withstand temptation in spite of fear or force. This understanding of impediments, therefore, really constitutes a rationalization of moral irresponsibility. The response to this objection is very simple. If the facts of the case are as the objection suggests, if I really have the power within me to withstand this pressure and don't use it, then of course I am morally responsible. But is it not possible that the facts are otherwise? Is it not possible that these pressures truly have robbed me of the power to resist? And if that is so, then the reduced responsibility suggested by this theory of impediments cannot help but make sense. In other words, the notion of impediments is not intended to prejudge the facts of the case. It is only intended to explain what may very well be the facts of the case. As always, the actual data of our personal experience are the benchmark against which moral theory must be measured.

The four types of impediments just mentioned share one thing in common: They all tend to be associated with specific actions or moments. They tend to be passing things, more associated with the situation than with the person. Because of this connection with specific acts, such impediments have traditionally been known as "actual." In contrast with these, there is another sort of impediment that is more intrinsic to the person. It constitutes an aspect of a person's individuality and is carried from situation to situation. This type of impediment, because of its continuous aspect, is termed "habitual." A few examples of habitual impediments may be helpful to our reflections.

The first and most obvious habitual impediment is the simple fact of the individual person's personality structure. It is a commonplace of experience that some people are "morning persons" and other people are "night persons." Whether an individual is one or the other is beyond free choice. It just happens to be so. But this fact still has very real implications for the exercise of human life. When am I most able to make really human decisions? To think clearly? To decide freely? It may be early in the day or it may be toward evening. But in any case the ideal moment is not always the same. At some time or other in my day, the very structure of my personality stands as an impediment to the exercise of fully human acts.

And not only my personality. Habits, particular ways of doing things that have, over time, become relatively automatic, can also serve as impediments. They were not always so, of course. For habits are, by definition, aspects of the human person that have been developed over a period of time. Nor are habits necessarily bad.[6] No human person could sustain the tension of making new and conscious decisions about every detail of daily life. It may very well be in people's best interests that their procedure for washing and dressing in the morning, the route by which they drive to work, the choice of a time to eat should remain on the level of an act of man. All we are saying is that at the present moment such automatic ways of operating are, in fact, habits, and that such habits eliminate from activity the freedom required for a fully human act.

A third habitual impediment is particularly relevant in contemporary society. Traditionally this impediment went by the name of "false opinion." But for our purposes it can be well understood as prejudice. Prejudice distorts the way people see things. It blinds them to certain facts and encourages them to see what is not there. It consequently results in ignorance – and a particularly pernicious sort of ignorance, at that. Inasmuch as prejudice is a habitual and perduring sort of ignorance, it is especially difficult to remedy. Prejudice is not the simple fact of ignorance in an individual and unique situation. Rather, it is one person's way of "mis-seeing" a whole range of experiences over a lifetime. In any case, prejudice has the effect of generating actions that lack either the knowledge or the freedom to be considered really human.

The way a racially prejudiced person, for example, behaves is surely evil. But objective evil and moral culpability are not at all the same, as we shall have occasion to see in great depth later in this book. A fervent desire to remedy the objective injustices caused by a prejudiced person should not blind us to those factors that really render her or him unfree. Good people, with good intentions, often do evil deeds. And the habitual impediment of prejudice is one reason for this.

Finally, mental illness can also function as a habitual impediment. It is clear that the psychotic, during the periods when the psychosis is active, is so lacking in awareness and freedom that the behavior can only be termed acts of man. What is not always so clear, but what is surely true, is that neurotic anxieties, obsessions, and feelings of guilt can also have somewhat the same effect. Homeowners may know they ought to forego house-cleaning to deal with community needs. But they "cannot stand" a dirty house. A Roman Catholic may have a perfectly good excuse for not attending Sunday Mass but "just wouldn't feel right" about it. Despite repeated attempts to change, a businessman besieged by his own insecurity continues to indulge in harmful gossip about his coworkers. In many ways (and psychology is making us aware just how many), the neuroses that affect us all inhibit the freedom necessary for a fully human act. A desire to change may be morally demanded. A willingness to accept help may be expected. But for the present, the simple fact is that such neuroses place many human actions in the grey world between the act of man and the human act.

The twin categories of actual and habitual impediments, with the various subdivisions within each, all serve to articulate a very simple insight. There are moments in human life when a person is totally ignorant or totally unfree; there are such things as acts of man. There also are, or seem to be, moments in life when one substantially succeeds in mobilizing one's capabilities for human acts. But the vast majority of life lies somewhere between. We are somewhat aware, somewhat free, somewhat human. And moral theology must take account of that fact.

Freedom

In our initial discussion of human acts, it was stated that such acts are characterized by freedom and awareness. We then proceeded to consider in detail the impediments that stand in the way of either freedom or awareness. It now remains to go into greater depth regarding those two central ideas. What does it mean to be free? To be aware? What sort of liberty and knowledge is required? These are the questions we must now consider. We will discuss freedom first.

What do we really mean when we say that freedom is a prerequisite for a human act? Isn't it true that in a very common-sense sort of way we mean that the agent has some choices available, some options at his or her disposal? A common characteristic of several of the impediments we considered earlier was that they robbed the agent of options. They certainly limited and inhibited the options available, and in some cases they totally eliminated all the options but one. So to be free, in the sense in which it is being used here, means to have options, to have choices.

In some deeper philosophical sense, freedom may be a separate reality, a capacity of humans, a general state of being. But in any ordinary sense of the word, freedom must be more than this. It must be a concrete state of being, a state of being-in-this-situation. This freedom, then, is what St. Augustine meant by his term *liberum arbitrium*. Indeed, that phrase is accurately translated as "freedom of choice." And it designates the sort of freedom that exists where an agent has more than one alternative: the alternative of doing this or that, the alternative of doing or not doing a particular action. In any case, the agent is in a situation of alternatives that are really there and really available to her or him.

Knowledge

What of knowledge? Is there anything to be said about the kind of knowledge necessary for a really human act? Indeed there is. In fact, in developing a response to this question we will be presenting one of the central insights of this entire book, an understanding that is pivotal to all the strategies of Christian ethics that will emerge later on.

To state the point very baldly (before developing it in detail), many psychologists as well as theologians distinguish between quite different ways of knowing: what may be called "speculative knowledge" on the one hand and "evaluative knowledge" on the other. And in the last analysis, only evaluative knowledge can serve as the required prerequisite for a genuinely human act.[7] But before we can see why this is so, we must develop a much fuller understanding of these two sorts of knowledge. We begin with a sketch of speculative knowledge.

In a very gross sense, speculative knowledge can be viewed as the knowledge of science, whereas evaluative knowledge is the knowledge of art. This is not altogether accurate, as we shall see. But it does give us a place to start. Speculative knowledge is intellectual knowledge, as we ordinarily speak of it. It has a certain objectivity, a certain independence from the knower. The fact that two plus two is four is not particularly associated with me as knower. Rather, it stands apart from me. It is something I just happen to know. What is more, precisely because of this objectivity, speculative knowledge is easily communicable. It can be passed from person to person, it can easily be shared. It is universal in its character, prescinding from individual circumstances and differences. Speculative knowledge is, therefore, in a certain sense essential knowledge. It deals with the essence of things, that which both is and must be. Or at least it deals with that which happens to be and has the potential for always happening to be.

Speculative knowledge is fact oriented. Because speculative knowledge has this factual, objective, essentialist character, the knowledge of the physical scientist can, as we suggested, be taken as a prime example. Similarly, the scientific method can be viewed as a paradigm for dealing with all speculative knowledge. Just as we expect experimental scientists to maintain a certain disinterest in their research, a distance from their materials that allows them to search for the truth and not for their own desires, so all speculative knowledge has the characteristic of disinterestedness. Speculative knowledge, like scientific knowledge, is provable. And what is more, it ought to be proved. We do not admire people who quote facts to us without any attempt to prove or ground or justify those facts. We want to know why something is so, or at least how the speaker knows it to be so. Speculative knowledge can be taught, because it is objective and independent. But if we are willing to be taught, we also expect to be taught responsibly. Thus the demand for proof is considered thoroughly appropriate in the case of speculative knowledge.

Finally, speculative knowledge is, in a certain sense, subservient to the knower. We use such knowledge. After a period of serious study, we are proud that we have "mastered the facts." Though we feel obligated to have respect for the truth, in the case of speculative knowledge that respect is grounded in our own needs, and not in the reality of the facts. In other words, we respect the facts because we need the facts in order to achieve our goals. We respect the facts the way a carpenter respects tools, as the means that are necessary and thus must be carefully used.

Evaluative knowledge is quite otherwise. It has to do with quality rather than quantity. It deals with the goodness or beauty of a thing, with its value. And inasmuch as value does not exist "out in space," by itself, evaluative knowledge is not universal but intensely concrete. Evaluative knowledge is a particular way of knowing the individual existing thing. It deals, therefore, not with essences but with existence. We stand before a concrete thing, a specific experience, and interact with it. We find it to be good or bad, beautiful or ugly, and we appreciate it (ad pretium = toward value). In the case of evaluative knowledge, we "understand" (stand under) it. We go out of ourselves and attach ourselves to the value that we find in the object. Indeed, in an ultimate experience of evaluative knowledge, we may achieve a sort of ecstasy (ekstasis = standing outside).

Evaluative knowledge, then, is in a certain sense not subservient to the knower, but rather superior to him or her. The knower serves this knowledge, going out to embrace and accept and appreciate the value that is found. The knower finds the self confronted by a beautiful sunset, a magnificent piece of music, an awe-inspiring work of technology, the mystery of a human person. She or he cannot remain detached in the face of this knowledge. Rather, it calls for, it demands, commitment. Evaluative knowledge is involving knowledge. It is knowledge that is at the same time a command. Consequently, evaluative knowledge is intensely personal. It is not subjective in the sense of being fabricated by the knower. Quite the contrary, it is in a certain sense the most objective of all knowledge. For in evaluative knowledge the knower is presented with something that transcends the self, that he or she didn't ask for, may not even have wanted, but that is nonetheless there and must be accepted. At the same time, though, evaluative knowledge is deeply personal. It results from the unique interaction of a unique subject and a unique object. And thus it cannot be shared, at least in its entirety.

I can try to tell you of the beauty I found in the Grand Canyon. I may even succeed in sharing a partial understanding of that experience. But I can never fully express or communicate the knowledge that is mine as a result of that experience. Similarly, precisely because evaluative knowledge is so personal, it cannot really be taught. Rather, the process of sharing evaluative knowledge, to the extent that this can occur at all, is a process of education (*e-ducere* = to draw out), where a similar experience is occasioned and encouraged in another person, where the knowledge is quite literally drawn out of the other. For example, the briefest presentation of definitions would have been sufficient to give the reader of this chapter a speculative knowledge of the difference between speculative and evaluative knowledge. But we are hoping for more. Through this long discussion of the two sorts of knowing, through the use of many evocative words and images, through the introduction of a number of examples, our hope is to call forth from the reader a genuine appreciation of that difference. We hope, quite literally, to evoke an evaluative knowledge of evaluative knowledge!

Two further points need to be made on this topic. The first is to nuance our opening statement on the relationship of speculative and evaluative knowledge, pairing the two with science and art, respectively. We said at the beginning that this was imprecise, and we can now see why. The two terms, speculative and evaluative, refer not to two objects of knowledge but rather to two ways of knowing. In technical language, the difference lies not in the *material object*, in what is known, but in the *formal object*, in the way it is known. Thus, it is actually likely that a person dedicating her or his life to the pursuit of science does so precisely because of a deep evaluative knowledge of the wonders of the natural universe. And contrariwise, who has not been bored by an academic course in art, where all that was shared was the most speculative and technical explanation of the artistic medium? So anything in the world can be known both speculatively and evaluatively. What makes the difference is the way it is experienced by the knower.

The second point has to do with the importance of this distinction. Insofar as contemporary culture is highly technological in character, emphasizing scientific objectivity, efficiency, a "businesslike" approach, we are confronted with a certain bias in favor of speculative knowledge. Indeed, one can often find discussions of evaluative knowledge in which the propriety of the term "knowledge" is itself denied. Such people prefer to view evaluative knowledge as intuition or feeling, taken in a pejorative way. The real knowledge, they say, is the knowledge of the disinterested scientist. The knowledge of the poet, of the artist, of the lover is not knowledge at all. Such an approach, however, has the effect of greatly cheapening human life. And in some cases it can be positively destructive.

Two young newlyweds, for example, may boldly proclaim their confidence in each other's love. And they are right; they know their love without proof or technical analysis. But as time passes, that confidence may pass as well. Under the pressure of the American technological bias (as well as their own insecurity), they may attempt to prove their love. Indeed, like good scientists, they may demand such proof. So signs of love are tendered by the other party. Gifts are given. But do they constitute the required proof? Of course not. Each gift can be variously interpreted; it could be sincere or it could be a lie. Professions of love are distrusted, gestures of love are overlooked, and the uncertainty does nothing but grow. Why? The answer lies in the difference between speculative and evaluative knowledge. The knowledge of love cannot be proved, for it is not grounded in quantifiable facts but in qualitative realities that must be directly perceived. The nervous lover has attempted the impossible. He or she has attempted to make evaluative knowledge follow the rules of speculative knowledge. And what is really insidious is that the lover has been encouraged to do precisely this by the technological, speculative bias of our culture. The lover is told in a thousand different ways that what is not provable is not real, that objective is best. And thus she or he attempts to make the experience of personal love fit that model.

It cannot be done. What is more, with a reasonable understanding of the unique differences between speculative and evaluative knowledge, it need not be done. As many contemporary Americans are realizing, both sorts of knowledge are needed and both sorts of knowledge are valuable. But each must be allowed to follow its own laws. There is a place for mysticism, for poetry, for the beauty of a simpler lifestyle, for rich and varied human relationships, for meditation and quiet reflection. And our culture must make room for these kinds of knowledge as much as for the knowledge of science and industry.

Evaluative Knowledge and Moral Theology

The distinction between speculative and evaluative knowledge, then, is of pivotal importance for the understanding of the human act, and therefore for moral theology. As human persons we cannot build a life or make a real decision on the basis of some bare fact flatly transmitted in a didactic and noninvolving way. When the exercise of *liberum arbitrium* brings us to the moment of decision, we are not deciding among facts. We are deciding among values. We are choosing good over bad, or good over less good, trying to respond to reality as we find it. Therefore, the only kind of knowledge that can genuinely fund and prompt the decision of a human act is truly evaluative knowledge.

The implications of this truth for moral theology are many. Before concluding this chapter, we should develop some of them, at least briefly. In particular, we should note its significance for the whole project of moral education, understood in the broadest, most life-long sense. In doing this, we will be bringing to bear some wondrously helpful contemporary research into the reality of evaluative knowledge.

We can enter this conversation through a key question: If evaluative knowledge has this, quite different character, how is it communicated? We know how speculative knowledge is communicated: by the simple articulation of terms. "Two and two are four." There! Now you have the information! But how is a genuine appreciation communicated—or better, elicited? Several points will help to answer this question.[8]

First, evaluative knowledge is rooted in experience.[9] I appreciate things only after I have actually encountered them. Different persons have different sensibilities, are attentive to different values, primarily because of their different life experience. Thus, to communicate evaluative knowledge, the key strategy is to occasion an experience. If I want students to appreciate the problem of hunger in America – appreciate it to the point where it will "make a difference to them"– I will do well not only to discuss the subject in class but also to arrange for them to work in a soup kitchen for an evening. Such a direct experience is more likely to facilitate true evaluative knowledge than abstract discussion.

Second, this experience that engenders evaluative knowledge is communal as well as individual. Human persons are not isolated individuals. They exist in community, in family, neighborhood, friendship group, church, and many more. All these groups have experiences. Indeed, because of their prior experiences they attend to different values and pursue different experiences and thus achieve increasingly diverse constellations of evaluative knowledge.

Third, experiences can take place not only in the "real world," but also in fantasy.[10] And to a fascinating, frightening extent, the latter is just as likely to stimulate evaluative knowledge. We all know about "self-fulfilling prophecies," those times when imagining something increases the likelihood of its happening. The ability of fantasy to genuinely change persons is widely noted. Consider the strategies of leaders as different as spiritual directors and athletic coaches. The spiritual director may well encourage the client to practice Ignatian contemplation, a form of prayer where one seeks to imagine in vivid detail the setting of, for example, a miracle of Jesus, tries to "be there" and even to participate imaginatively in the event. Generations of Christians have found this to be a powerful and transforming way of prayer. The athletic coach, meanwhile, urges the team to practice "creative visualization," to climb in bed and, last thing at night, imaginatively take a hundred jump shots, "seeing" the ball move from their hands to the hoop. And it works! An appreciation and, it seems, even a skill can be honed through the medium of "imaginary experience." Imagination can create an inner world of experience that can ground true evaluative knowledge.

Fourth, the way in which human persons contact and guide the fantasies of one another is *story*. We tell stories not to transmit information but to share experiences. When I tell you the story, I allow you to be present in fantasy to my experience. In this way it becomes your experience, an opportunity for evaluative knowledge for you. Through story, then, human persons can expand their horizons of experience, transcending space and time and developing a true appreciation of things that are "yet unseen." Such stories come in many types. They can be the simple recounting of personal experiences. They can be the artistic creations of novelists, playwrights, and poets, sharing experiences that are truer than true.[11] They can be the ancient stories of children's fairy tales, epic poems, national myths. And, of special importance for us, they can be the biblical and historical stories of a faith community.

And thus, fifth, story, narrative, is central to the identity of the Christian community and to the strategy of moral education.[12] For through story the formative experiences of the community are relived. And through that reliving successive generations of disciples are provided the basis for a life-changing evaluative knowledge of the truths of the gospel message. It is no coincidence that biblical authors recorded not only what Jesus did, but also the stories he told. It is similarly no accident that we continue to recount both, the parables of Jesus and his deeds, when we gather in worship and prayer. In the words of Stanley Hauerwas, the church is a "story-formed community."[13]

Conclusion

What does the reality of evaluative knowledge mean for moral education? There are several answers to this question. And they should all be obvious.

For one thing, an appreciation of evaluative knowledge would seem to demand considerable revision in the style of moral education for children. It is not sufficient to pass on to the next generation the objective facts of what we find to be good and bad. Much more is required by way of occasioning and encouraging in the children a growing appreciation of those values. We must provide the experiences and tell the stories that will incorporate them into the world of true Christian experience. For only in this way can children be provided with a true basis for concrete behavioral decisions.

Another implication of this analysis of evaluative knowledge pertains to the communication of moral values among adults. Just as a speculative style of teaching will not satisfy the needs of children, neither will it satisfy the needs of adults. Church leaders or ethical teachers cannot acquit themselves of their duties by edict. What is required is education, in the fullest sense of that word. And moral education has much more in common with homiletics than it does with didactics.[14]

A third implication, which we will have occasion to discuss again, has to do with the function of moral norms and rules. All too often such norms have been analyzed and used as "fact purveyors." In many cases, however, moral norms function preeminently (and importantly) as evokers of value appreciation. They are the way in which communities articulate and seek to share the value insights that have emerged from their experience. As such, though, the norms are always accountable to the experiences. And for successful transmission of the value commitments, it will often be necessary to do more than restate the norm. It will be necessary to reappropriate the commitment by recreating the experience. For it is only on the basis of shared experiences that shared norms can hope to survive.

Other implications may become clear as this study continues. For the present, this discussion of evaluative knowledge must be allowed to conclude our consideration of the human act. We must go deeper now and consider the place where the human act resides: the human person.

Chapter 6

THE HUMAN PERSON

In the previous chapter, we attempted to understand ourselves. We took as our starting point the idea with which the scholastic
manuals of moral theology ordinarily begin: the human act. Then,
finding that bare concept somewhat inadequate, we began a process of
nuancing. We enriched our reflections by adding a strong emphasis on
the impediments to full human action. We clarified our understanding
by bringing the concepts of knowledge and freedom into clearer focus.
And, in particular, we came to realize the central importance of evaluative knowledge as a basis for moral knowledge, decision, and action. As
a result, we achieved a fair approximation of our own experience. The
description of the human act distilled from the tradition of Catholic theology and elaborated in the light of the social sciences eventually found
a strong resonance with life as we live it every day.

Still, it was only an approximation. It did not fully coincide with
experience. Why was that? The answer can be found in the twin concepts of permanence and accumulation. Starting with the idea of the
human act, as the manuals of moral theology did, has many advantages.
But it also has one disadvantage, one deficiency, that must now be reme-
died. Human acts are, by definition, passing things. They happen, and
once they have happened they are gone. But human beings are not passing things. They continue. They change, they grow or deteriorate; but
they continue nonetheless. And the scholastic understanding, beginning with the human act, failed to take due note of that perduring,
developing aspect. So it is interesting that the flaw in the previous presentation, the inadequacy that we sense, was not the result of some middle step in our reasoning. Nor was it the result of some factor
accidentally excluded from our calculus. Rather, it was the result of the
starting point itself. What was said in the previous chapter needed to be
said. But now we must say more. Without denying the truth found in
our reflections on the human act, we must now consider the continuing,
perduring, developing reality of the human person.

Third Dimension

What do we mean by human person? That question is not as easy to answer as it would seem. For in fact we never see "person" in its bare reality. What we see, what we experience in ourselves and in others, is person-clothed-in-action. Or more precisely, we experience actions that, we realize, do not stand by themselves, but rather reveal and manifest and express a person that lies beneath. Let us consider our own experience.

I am a person: I find myself to be a person. Why is that? First, I assert my own personhood because I experience myself as being more than my actions. I am never apart from action, of course. I am never "doing nothing." The "being" and the "doing" of my life are never separated, but rather always coexist. Still, I sense that to view myself as nothing more than the sum total of my activities is to reduce myself, cheapen myself, make myself less than I really am. "People are known by their actions." That is true, but it is not altogether true. If you could make a comprehensive list of all the things I do, all the deeds I perform, all the thoughts I think, all the feelings I possess, you would still not have captured the being that I am. Or so my experience tells me. There is a "moreness" to life, something that is not adequately accounted for in the passing reality of events and actions and experiences. To account for that moreness, we must posit another reality beyond the human act. And that reality is the human person.

But there is another reason for asserting the notion of person. Namely, it is personhood that gives actions their human importance. When I make the statement, "I am cold," I am really asserting two things. First, I am asserting the experience of coldness. But I am also asserting the presence of person. Coldness in itself is unimportant; what is important is that it is mine. The localization, the grounding, the rootedness of the experience or the event ultimately gives it its value. How different it is to say, "Someone died," and, on the other hand, "I killed someone." But what is the difference? The difference is personhood. Killing didn't just happen, it was not merely a human act that came and went. Rather, it was the action of a person, of a reality that remained. In fact, just as a garden plant can live only because its roots lie deep in the soil, so these human acts have life only in and because of the person in whom they are rooted.

A third reason for our assertion of human personhood follows from what has been said. If moral theology means anything, it means that human beings are responsible for their behavior. But whence comes that responsibility? It comes from personhood. We are not merely the sum total of an infinity of actions laid end to end, so to speak. And we do not totally mutate from moment to moment, moving from identity to identity as we move from place to place. If we were thus, we could not be held responsible for our actions. "That was yesterday's human act," we would say. "Today I am someone different." But we reject that. The actions pass, but the agent remains. And thus we are responsible, whether we admit it or not. In the last analysis, then, human beings are morally responsible precisely because (and only inasmuch as) they are persons.

The vision presented by the previous chapter, then, must be complemented by this new insight. The people we met in the previous chapter, we might say, were two dimensional. They had length and width. They had various different actions, various different experiences. They moved from place to place, from event to event, from feeling to thought to conviction. But there was a flatness to them; they were no more than two dimensional. Now, however, the people we see are three dimensional (indeed, as we shall see, four dimensional). They still have those two dimensions of the previous chapter, but more than that, they have a certain depth. And that depth is personhood. Beneath and within human actions, the depth of person resides. And that third dimension ultimately grounds and generates action, gives action its importance, and continues to survive when the action passes.[1]

In an appropriate if homely image, then, people might be compared to onions. Like onions, they are comprised of myriad layers beginning at the surface and moving to the center. None of these layers can stand by itself, yet each has its own identity. At the outermost layer, as it were, we find their environment, their world, the things they own. Moving inward we find their actions, their behavior, the things they do. And then the body, that which is the "belonging" of a person and yet also is the person. Going deeper, we discover moods, emotions, feelings. Deeper still are the convictions by which they define themselves. And at the very center, in that dimensionless pinpoint around which everything else revolves, is the person himself or herself—the I.

This, then, is the understanding of that person we most centrally are. But there is one paradox to this understanding, and we must now highlight it. Although we are driven to assert the existence of the human person within activity for all the reasons that have already been adduced, nonetheless it remains true that personhood is the one thing about human beings that we cannot actually see. In a process of reflection I seek to discover myself. I hold up to the eye of my mind the experiences that I have. But who looks at those experiences? I do, the person that I am. So I look deeper, at my emotions, my feelings, my attitudes. I reflect on those things that characterize the way I live. But who does the looking? I do, the person that I am. I go deeper, ever deeper, lifting up from within myself my most central convictions, my deepest identity. Repeatedly I attempt to gaze on the very center of myself. But I always fail. For the real person that I am always remains the viewer and can never become the viewed. As a person, I am a subject. And I cannot become an object, even to myself.

So I do not assert my personhood, and the personhood of all human beings, because I can see that personhood. No, that personhood is subject, not object to be seen. Rather, I assert the existence of personhood because I am aware that it is the subject implied by and experienced in the contemplation of all objects. In the terminology of Karl Rahner, personhood is not something we consider; rather, it is the "condition of the possibility" of all things that we consider. And thus we can see why, even in the process of introducing and analyzing the nature of the human person, we did not reject or deny anything that had already been said about the nature of the human act. For to do this would not only be to give personhood more credit than it deserves, it would also destroy the very reality that reveals personhood to us.

Person and Agent

With all these nuances, distinctions, and warnings said, we can now proceed to clarify the differences between the human person and the human act. Or more precisely, we can highlight the various characteristics of these two aspects of that being we find ourselves to be. We can be viewed as agents, as doers of human acts. But we can also be viewed as persons, as beings who precede, ground, and transcend those actions. We can be viewed on the surface of our day-to-day lives or, through more subtle considerations, we can be viewed in the depths of our own reality. The listing, then, of a number of these characteristics should serve to clarify what has already been said.

First, humans-as-agent, human beings as they were especially viewed by the Scholastics, are objects. Humans-as-person, on the contrary, are subjects. And precisely this nonobjective status makes human persons unique in the world. It follows from this, second, that humans-as-agent are able to be analyzed. In fact, inasmuch as they are objects, they are the perfect focus for human knowing. Not so with humans-as-person. Persons are simply there, self-aware and implied in activity. But as subjects they are never the direct object of knowledge. Third, agents, by definition, are changeable beings. As actions change, so the doers of actions change. Persons, however, perdure beyond the life span of any individual action. It follows from this, then, that agents are preeminently "do-ers," whereas persons are more clearly understood as "be-ers." Human beings, inasmuch as they are agents, exercise their existence through action. But humans-as-person exercise their reality precisely by being. Another way to say the same thing is to assert that inasmuch as human beings are agents, they are little more than particular instances of "humanity." I can make a given decision, perform a given deed. But you are capable of making the same decision, performing the same deed. We are both agents, and both of our actions, as actions, can be really the same. But humans-as-person are far more than mere instances of human nature. They are also unique. The "being" that comprises them as persons is at least partly unique being, never before real and never to be reduplicated.

Knowledge

But if all these characteristics differentiate humans-as-person from humans-as-agent, by far the clearest way of distinguishing them is through the realities of knowledge and freedom. In the last chapter we considered these two realities in the context of our overall discussion of the human act. But now we must reconsider them, adding the new, deeper vision of the human person that we have achieved.

Inasmuch as we are human agents, performers of human acts, we exercise a very real sort of knowledge. What sort of knowledge? Our response was: evaluative knowledge. Without denying that, we must now add a new term and a new understanding. The sort of knowledge involved in human acts is "reflex knowledge." What does that mean? When you and I say that we know something, we are really saying two things. First, we are saying that we know the object of our attention. We know that the house is green, that the plain is vast, that murder is wrong. But we also know that very knowledge of ours. As the Scholastics said, we "know that we know." We are able to hold the very knowledge that we have up to the eye of our mind. We are able to make it the object of our attention. We are able to reflect, as in a mirror, on the knowledge that is ours. Thus we can term our original knowledge of the house, the plain, the act of murder reflex knowledge. It is knowledge that is or can be the object of its own reflection within our minds.

But when, in this chapter, we considered ourselves under the aspect of our personhood, we came on a different sort of knowledge. We discovered that our personhood could not be "reflected on." It could not be the direct object of our attention. Person could not be held up to the mirror of the mind for the very simple reason that person (as subject) would always be viewing that mirror image. We do have a certain awareness of ourselves. We have a sense of our own identity. But that awareness, that sense, is not available as a direct object of reflection. Thus we find ourselves forced to assert a second sort of human knowledge, non-reflex knowledge. The knowledge of the human act is reflex knowledge. The knowledge of our core human person, however, is nonreflex.

Freedom

And then there is freedom. Once again, in the previous chapter we discovered that freedom is an essential component of a genuinely human act. But what sort of freedom? Our answer, you will recall, was *liberum arbitrium*, freedom of choice. It was the freedom made possible by the presence of a number of options, multiple possibilities. And it was the freedom exercised in the selection among those options and possibilities. In our present context, however, let us pursue this line of thought a little more deeply. The freedom of the human act, of human-as-agent, is a dividing freedom. It is a freedom that takes the experience of life and separates it, divides it into alternatives. It organizes life into categories and then selects from among those categories. In a paradoxical way, the freedom of the human act is a limiting freedom, for it takes one from the situation in which all options are open to the situation in which all options but one are foreclosed. What is more, this selectivity of the freedom of the human act reveals itself from the very beginning. It is, no doubt, a human act to prepare the menu for a dinner. But to be involved in that human act precisely means that the agent is involved in no other act. To focus one's attention on, and to exercise one's freedom within, the category of food is to not do an infinite number of other possible things at this moment.[2] Thus, because the freedom associated with the human act both operates in the context of categories and exercises itself by the selection of categories, that freedom can accurately be termed "categorical freedom."

The freedom of the human act is categorical, however, only because it is the freedom associated with "doing." At the deeper level of "being," of personhood, things are quite otherwise. We experience ourselves as men and women who are free not only as agents but also as persons. But that does not mean that the freedom associated with these two levels of our reality is the same. No, the freedom associated with our core, our personhood, is a quite different sort. Only objects can be categorized, and my personhood is not an object. It is a subject. From the perspective of my central personhood, the focus for free decision is not one category of objects or another. Rather, it is all objects taken together. Inasmuch as I am a "being," really the only free decision to be made is the decision "to be or not to be." It is the decision to accept or reject reality as I find it. The central core of myself, the "I" that is my personhood, is confronted with a reality that transcends all categories. It is confronted with the reality of my world, my situation, my body, my feelings, my attitudes and prejudices. In fact, it is confronted even by the condition of the possibility of that reality, namely, God. And from the perspective of my own core, the subjectivity that I am, this cosmically inclusive objectivity presents itself for decision. A simple, singular decision: yes or no. The freedom of the human person, then, is not categorical freedom at all. Rather, it is a freedom that transcends all categories, it is "transcendental freedom."

This is not a freedom that determines and limits my range of life. Rather, it is a freedom that opens up life. For if through some perversity I were to respond to the cosmic choice presented to my core with the word "no," I would be saying no not only to my world, but also to myself. I would be rejecting my opportunities for action, the possibilities of my own being. I would, in a word, be denying and destroying myself. If, on the other hand, my response to this cosmic query is yes, then I am in a very real sense bringing myself into being. I am freeing myself, liberating myself for action and for fuller reality. Thus, it is true that the decision of transcendental freedom, like the exercise of any freedom, defines me. But in the case of transcendental freedom I am doing a "de-fining" in the root sense of that word; I am de-limiting myself, going beyond my limits, making something exist that did not exist before.

So there are two sorts of freedoms. There is the categorical freedom of human-as-agent, the freedom associated with human action. And there is transcendental freedom, the freedom of human-as-person, the freedom associated with perduring being.

One thing remains to be said. And it is merely an extension of a point made previously. To assert the existence of human-as-person in addition to human-as-agent is not to assert that person ever exists apart from agency and action. I am never, quite literally, doing nothing. Rather, it is through and in my action that my personhood is expressed and realized. But if this is true of our basic understanding of person and action, it must also be true of the new understanding of knowledge and freedom we have just achieved. The self-awareness characteristic of human-as-person is an awareness that arises in the very midst of the actions with which we fill our day. And similarly the cosmic exercise of transcendental freedom occurs only in and through the exercises of categorical freedom with which we are so familiar.

If it could be determined that in the last twenty-four hours I have made a hundred categorical decisions, human acts, and if through some omniscience I were able also to know clearly and be certain that in that same period of time I have exercised my deep-down freedom to define and establish myself as person, how many decisions did I make? A hundred and one? No. Rather I made a hundred decisions, some one of which, in addition to being a decision about this or that action, also functioned as a decision about me myself. The exercise of transcendental freedom, then, does not stand apart from categorical freedom. The action by which I establish, create, and define myself does not stand apart from the actions by which I direct the events of my life. Rather, transcendental freedom – transcendental, self-defining decision – occurs within and through those day-to-day categorical choices.

So here is the key point: The level of the human being that we have named "personal" is not asserted because we see it clearly or because it stands clearly apart. It is only asserted because if it were not, the reality that we find ourselves to be would be cheapened and aborted. And similarly, the realities of nonreflex knowledge and transcendental freedom are asserted not because they stand apart or by themselves, but rather because without them the reality of ourselves that we experience day in and day out would not be adequately accounted for.

Human Identity

If there is anything characteristic of adulthood, it is the fact of having a personal identity. Men and women are admired for being adults precisely because they have such an identity. They are not totally subject to the manipulations of the outer world or to the whims of their own desires. They do not live spineless, directionless lives. Rather, they have taken charge of themselves. They stand in some particular way toward the world. Beneath all the actions that they do, and revealing itself through those actions, is a "fundamental stance." And it is that stance which gives their lives direction, significance, and definition. It is, in a very real sense, that fundamental stance which makes their lives human. For it affirms and expresses, as it also creates and effects, the person that they have chosen to be.

That fundamental stance, however, did not always exist. Just as such a stance is characteristic of adulthood, so the lack of it is characteristic of childhood. To be a child is to be subject to manipulation and whim. It is to be without particular direction. It is to be a being without a stance toward the world. But if that is true, then it follows that at some point or another we, as persons, assumed the stance that we now hold. There must, logically, have been a moment at which we chose that stance, a moment at which we exercised that transcending kind of freedom in order to define ourselves as persons. And if the stance we now possess is a fundamental stance, then we can appropriately term that moment of decision a "fundamental option."[3]

This notion of fundamental option is, of course, a concept often discussed in contemporary theology.[4] So, since we have introduced the term here, it might be well to add a few comments immediately. First, it was most important that we approach the concept in this rather circuitous way. For the fact of the matter is that the fundamental option is only of secondary importance. What is really important is a person's fundamental stance. Fundamental option is nothing more than the name we give to the moment in which the stance is assumed or emphatically renewed. Fundamental option is the name for any exercise of transcendental freedom. Thus, just as all freedoms are subservient to the action or being they direct, so the fundamental option is subservient to the definition and identity it brings about: the fundamental stance.

Second, as is clear from the way we described it, a fundamental option does not exist all by itself. A fundamental option is not a particular decision standing next to all the other categorical decisions of life. Rather, it is the deeper meaning and significance of some of the decisions of our lives. Indeed, like all the other aspects of human-as-person, the fundamental option is not something we can directly see or consciously analyze. At most, it is something of which we can be nonreflexly aware.[5]

Third, a fundamental option is not a once-and-for-all reality. True, it is a decision about the sort of person one chooses to be. It is an inner act of self-definition. But it is not irrevocable, not final or definitive. As one author expresses it, the fundamental option is a decision about the person *totus sed non totaliter* (as a whole person but not totally).[6] Our experience tells us that we retain the capacity to reverse even our basic approach to life. Indeed, even if we would like it otherwise, life periodically presents us with critical turning points, moments in which the making of a categorical behavioral choice also challenges us to elect once again the person we wish to be. The option may be a reaffirmation of a stance already adopted, or it may involve a reversal. But in either case it is a new, still not definitive but yet fundamental, election of the self.

Let us summarize. When we attempt to observe the life that we live, we discover that there are two distinct types of behavior. We have termed these types of behavior "act of man" and "human act." On further reflection, however, we have concluded that not all human acts are alike. Some are human acts pure and simple, focusing our attention in decision on a particular categorical object. Others, however, are more than that. They are actions that arise from the very core of ourselves as persons. They are actions in which and through which we are choosing not only a particular categorical object, but also a transcendental subject for ourselves.

Within some of our human acts a human person is being born, or being recreated and reaffirmed. Not all our actions, to be sure; but some of them express and define us as persons. They are, in a very real sense, sacraments of the person that we are. These human acts are rich symbols of the person we are choosing to become, and like all sacraments they tend to effect that which they symbolize. Thus, in these most richly human acts, these acts that carry and include a fundamental option, we as beings of depth, as persons, create ourselves.

The human person that we sense ourselves to be does not stand apart from the actions we do. So also the nonreflex knowledge and the transcendental freedom that we find ourselves to have do not stand apart from the reflex knowledge and categorical freedom of our daily lives. The fundamental stance that gives us the identity we so highly treasure is not to be found in a vacuum but rather is to be found incarnated in the behavior by which we build our lives. And finally the fundamental option we have just been considering is not really something that we "do" at all, but is rather the term we use to describe what is "really going on" within the rich activity that we perform.

We are, then, three-dimensional beings. We are beings of depth. But this depth does not stand apart, it stands within. It is perceived, not next to the surface layers of human action but through those layers. Thus we should not be at all surprised if, like most realities perceived through covering veils, our understanding of our central personhood never ceases being somewhat opaque. It has often been said that the most important things in life are ultimately mysteries. Our analysis of the human person – of the being that constitutes our human acts, lies within those acts, and goes beyond those acts – does nothing to deny that thesis.[7]

Fourth Dimension

Still, something more remains to be said. If this three-dimensional vision of the human person is accurate, it is nonetheless not altogether accurate. For if the picture is relatively rich, still it is also static. It does not change. It does not include the reality of time. It does not acknowledge that human life truly is a vocation: a call-ing, a do-ing, a be-ing and a becom-ing – a verb far more than a noun. It does not advert to the fact that we all stand within a process of living, a process that is ongoing and not yet at all complete. If the vision notices that life is not lived in a single act, still it does not sufficiently notice that life is also not lived in a single moment.

So to the three dimensions of length, width, and breadth we must now add the so-called fourth dimension: time. In a sense, the picture we have developed to this point has been a sort of snapshot of the human being (or perhaps a hologram, to keep the three-dimensional focus).

But including the reality of time makes us realize that we have actually been viewing a single frame of a motion picture. We have been "stopping the action" in order to understand the actors. But to understand them more completely, we must also watch them move. Human life is temporal life, changing life. There is a past and a future, and they are at least as important as the present.[8]

This notion of time implies another idea: that of growth. For the change we have been noticing is not merely change on the same level. Rather, it is cumulative. Life is not only a process, it is also progress. As we live our individual lives, we inevitably grow. We develop. We evolve in our consciousness of the issues of life and in our responsibility in dealing with them. We become progressively more free, but at the same time we also become progressively more accountable. Our lives are cumulative, with each new moment standing on the shoulders of all that has preceded.

This is not, of course, to say that we necessarily become better persons as we grow older. We always remain able to choose evil as well as good. But it is to say that the depth with which we choose increases with time and age. As our lives proceed and as we grow, we take hold of ourselves more and more. For better or for worse, the various components of our lives increasingly cohere. We know more, we feel more, we perceive and experience more. Consequently, the profundity with which we choose at the present moment surpasses whatever we may have done before. So, paradoxically, we become increasingly capable of both good and evil as the years go by.

At the transcendental level, this growth means that our fundamental stance is progressively deepened as we take hold of our lives and increasingly affirm them. Indeed, even the reversals of that stance are not mere shifts of direction. Rather, they are increasingly deep appropriations of one's life, in either the positive or negative direction. Where a positive fundamental stance, for example, is reaffirmed in a new option, this deepening is obvious. But it is equally true that a person who once lived a life of virtue, then turned to evil, and now has returned to a virtuous commitment, has "grown" through the experience. The positive stance of the present is not the same as that of the past. It is deeper, more mature, more emphatic.

So true is this that, in the end, we might more accurately describe the human person if we spoke not of fundamental stance at all, but rather of fundamental direction. After all, for the human person who lives in a four-dimensional world, perhaps the most significant factor is the direction that the life process is taking.

At the categorical level, the law of growth means that we develop styles of life and skills of living that increasingly manifest themselves as time goes on. For the process of life involves a reciprocal causality, where the agent shapes his or her acts and the acts shape the agent. In a certain sense, life is like playing tennis, performing a job, or loving a spouse; it is a matter not just of decision, but also of facility. There is skill involved, a growing fluidity and spontaneity that actually leaves one increasingly free while also more immediate. Thus, in the process of life we develop "habits," in the richest Thomistic sense of that word. We develop a progressively integrated identity, a constellation of virtues or vices that represent our chosen selves. We develop character: "the qualification of man's self-agency through his beliefs, intentions, and actions, by which a man acquires a moral history befitting his nature as a self-determining being."[9]

Conclusion

Now, at last, we have a relatively comprehensive vision of the individual human person. We have noted the characteristics and patterns of human acts. We have acknowledged the blocks to human activity known as impediments. And we have focused on evaluative knowledge, that sort of knowing which is involved in fully human action. We have looked at the mysterious reality of human personhood, a third dimension located within and constantly implied by human activity. And we have tried to describe it through the notions of transcendental and categorical freedom. Finally, we have expanded this view by attending to the fourth dimension, time, and by reminding ourselves that persons are in process, that lives are both temporal and cumulative.

Throughout the course of this description, we have intentionally limited ourselves to speaking of the *human* person, without reference to religious dimensions. But human persons, simply as such and without further delineation, do not exist. Persons are male or female, old or young, a member of this ethnic group or that. And they may well be Christian. This specificity of human persons was, indeed, starting to reveal itself in our final comments: on the reality of human character.

So now it is time to get much more specific, to talk about Christian persons, and, indeed, to bring the lens of religious reflection to this project of self-understanding. Now it is time to talk about Christian life, about moral life as understood within the Christian vision. To do all this, we shall see, is to talk about sin and sanctity.

Chapter 7

THE THEOLOGY OF SIN

Until now, our discussions have maintained a relatively neutral tone. It is true that we considered the mechanism by which we perceive and appreciate value. And our description of the yes and no that constitute fundamental option could certainly be taken to imply some sort of personal obligation. But inasmuch as we have consistently focused on human acts and the human person as facts, we have avoided any blatant value judgments of our own. That objectivity, that neutrality, now ends. To be human is to be responsible for oneself. And to be responsible is, in some sense, to be obligated. So, whereas we have thus far attempted to understand ourselves as beings who are free, we must now discuss ourselves as beings who are obligated.

But to talk about ourselves as obligated, whether to ourselves or to God, is to talk about morality. Indeed, the term "morality" is nothing but a sort of shorthand by which we refer to the whole realm of obligation and human responsibility. To say that I am a moral being is to say nothing else than that I am a being responsible and accountable, and therefore obligated. But to discuss morality within a religious frame of reference is inevitably to introduce the notions of sin and sanctity. Therefore, in this chapter our task will be to reconsider the human persons we have come to know and to attempt to analyze them precisely from the perspective of human and religious obligation, from the perspective of morality. In the process of doing this, we shall largely direct ourselves to the term "sin" as this has been understood in Christian tradition and as it can well be understood today. But as a sort of preamble to these systematic reflections, we shall begin with a consideration of the notion of sin as that reality is presented in the pages of sacred Scripture.

Scriptural Sin

Throughout the pages of the Jewish and Christian Scriptures references to the reality of sin, and uses of the term itself, abound. Indeed, one could make a good case for the assertion that the entire Bible is "about" sin and what God has done about sin. There are, of course, a number of different nuances that the word takes in various contexts. Still, the fundamental meaning of sin in the pages of the Bible has a remarkable consistency.

Sin is, first and foremost, a religious reality. For biblical authors, sin makes no sense apart from the presence of God and of our obligation to God.[1] Why is that? The God of the Bible is the God of the Covenant, the God who has made a commitment to us and who expects our commitment in return: "I will be your God, and you will be my people." This covenantal relationship, even when it is not the primary focus, stands as a perduring backdrop. Covenant is the horizon within which the biblical world is understood and the biblical life lived. Covenant is, therefore, also the context within which the biblical notion of sin makes itself evident. Sin is infidelity to that covenant, our failure to live up to our part of the bargain.

In some of the earliest strata of the biblical material, sin means nothing more than "missing the mark," making a mistake. Even unintentional mistakes could be considered sins, since they, too, are not in accord with God's will for the world. But since the human challenge to free response is so central to the theology of covenant, to the self-understanding that Israel had, it was not long before the idea of sin was further nuanced. "Sin" came to be understood as a free offense against God, a free refusal to be and do what God wants us to be and do.

Sin is our failure to accept the claims of the God of revelation on ourselves. It is the substitution of some other reality for God, the placing of oneself or some created thing where God alone should stand. Thus, for biblical authors, sin, in an ultimate paradigmatic sense, is idolatry. Indeed, in the last analysis, all sin is but a form of idolatry. Sometimes the idolatry is blatant, as in the construction of the golden calf by the Israelite people at Sinai (Ex 32:1–6; Deut 9:7–21). At other times it is more subtle. In fact, one gets the impression that straightforward construction of worship objects is not, for the biblical authors, the most pernicious form of idolatry. Rather, idolatry at its worst is idolatry of self. Self-sufficiency is the greatest sin. From the story of Adam and Eve in Genesis to the era of the prophets, the people are most forcefully condemned and most strongly rebuked for daring to "go it alone" (e.g., Deut 32:18; Is 10:13–19; Ez 28:2). It is their pride that Yahweh finds most offensive. They fail to love God, to serve God. They seek to make themselves God and to take divine prerogatives to themselves. They are, therefore, "a people of unclean lips" (Is 6:5). They have sinned, and must repent (e.g., Hos 14:2–4).

This religious emphasis is so thoroughgoing that even offenses against the neighbor find their malice in the betrayal of God. We may say that David sinned against Bathsheba by his lust, or that he sinned against Uriah by sending him into the battlefront. But David says, "I have sinned against Yahweh" (2 Sam 12:13). It is true that one's love of God is to manifest itself in love of neighbor (e.g., Lev 19:9–18; Is 1:23–25). But the same logic led the scriptural authors to assert that the deepest malice of the offense against the neighbor is precisely that it implies a rejection of God (e.g., Ez 18:3–32).

In the Gospels, too, the religious dimension of social sin is emphasized. When the prodigal son finally repents and returns to his ancestral home, he confesses: "Father, I have sinned against God and against you" (Lk 15:21). Not one or the other; both have been offended by his action. And the two great commandments of love from the Old Testament, love for God (Deut 6:5) and love for neighbor (Lev 19:18), are expressed in a way that irrevocably unites them (Mt 22:34–40; Mk 12:28–31; Lk 10:25–37).[2]

In the biblical understanding, then, the reality of sin is not directly connected to any particular action in itself. Rather, the focus of attention with regard to sin is the meaning of the action, the significance of the action for God and persons, and the effect of that action on their relationship. Sin is the failure to love God and to serve God. No matter how it happens to manifest itself, its reality remains the same.

Moreover, inasmuch as the failure to love can perdure and become a state of being, sin itself can also be viewed as a state. Sin is the state of alleged independence, of imagined self-sufficiency. Sin is that "hardness of heart" that lasts, the ears that will not hear and the eyes that will not see (Is 6:9). Sin is the situation of Israel, and humankind, when they refuse to acknowledge the claims and prerogatives of God. Indeed, it does not constitute an undue projection of our own perspectives on the Bible to assert that "acts" of sin assume major significance only because of their effect on the "state" of sin. Such typically biblical images as "stubbornness," "obstinacy," "refusal to listen and repent," as well as "divine readiness to forgive any number of offenses"– all this suggests as much (Is 65). And as time went on, the relationship between act and state became more nuanced. By the time of the composition of John's Gospel, indeed, this relationship had become so central that the Baptist says, "There is the lamb of God who takes away the sin of the world" (Jn 1:29). Note here that it is sin in the singular, the state of sin: not individual errors or acts of malice but rather the cosmic situation of alienation, of fractured relationships between God and the people. It is this state of sin, this posture of proud self-sufficiency, this self-destructive illusion, that Jesus has come to change. And thus, for example, Jesus willingly associates with "sinners." It is only the proud ones, the arrogant ones, the Pharisees, that he continually condemns.

In the end, then, the sinful, fractured, alienated state of the whole world takes center stage. It becomes the symbol for all the individual sinful acts that we are wont to do. And it explains why these acts are, indeed, of ultimately religious and not merely ethical import.

These, then, are some aspects of the scriptural vision of sin. Much more could be said. We have, for example, emphasized the roots of the understanding of sin in the Jewish Scriptures. It would be interesting to indicate the developments to be found in the Synoptics and Paul. In fact, we shall return to some of these ideas later. But what has been presented is sufficient for our purposes here. Now we must go on. After all, even the most complete elucidation of a scriptural theology of sin would be insufficient for our time. We must expand our sights in order to develop an understanding attuned to our own culture, and our own needs. Using these scriptural themes as a backdrop, a benchmark against which to measure our own reflections, we must attempt to develop a contemporary theology of sin. But to do this, we must first consider some theological themes in the tradition.

Traditional Vision

Through the centuries of Christian tradition, the idea of sin has supported a variety of theological conceptions. Given the rich variety that we found in the Scriptures, this is not surprising. All the more is this to be expected when we focus on the fact that "sin" is the believer's word for things not right in our world. As our vision of the world changes, as our presumption of how things should be changes, and most of all as our understanding of ourselves as human persons changes, so our understanding of sin will change.

Thus, in reviewing some traditional visions of sin, we will be trying to understand why these visions were formulated and what perspective on life and humanity they presumed. This will lead us simultaneously to a respect for that tradition and to an awareness of its ultimate inadequacy. And it will provide us with a basis for a renewed, enriched, and illuminating understanding for our own time.

Essentially, we want to suggest that the word "sin" can point to three different realities. What is characteristic of the traditional understanding, the understanding that the church lived out for centuries, was not that the three realities were affirmed. (We, too, will wish to affirm them.) Rather, it was the way in which those realities were organized, the way they were related to each other. (And what has changed, as we shall see, is the way in which those three realities are related today.)

What is "sin"? "A sin is an action by which I refuse to do what I believe God wants me to do, and thereby injure my neighbor." This definition seems fairly reasonable. It is the kind of definition that could be encountered almost anywhere. But did you notice the way in which the answer modified the question? The question asked about "sin." The answer described "a sin." That is, the answer understood sin not as a reality but as an event, an act. And typically so. In the traditional Catholic view, the root understanding of sin, the very paradigm of sin, was that it is an act. Sin was something people do.

At times, this act was understood very trivially, as if sins could be committed by accident. At other times, it was understood with considerable sophistication, when attention was paid to the impediments to human freedom, the requirements of a genuine evaluative understanding, and the mystery of genuine human decision. Religious educators, for example, have contributed greatly when they describe sin in terms such as, "the moments when we refuse to accept the Lord's challenge in our lives." Still, in all these cases sin was understood as an act. Indeed, the tradition could speak of "actual sins."

The tradition did not limit its understanding of sin to actual sin, however. It did affirm the existence of a quite different reality, original sin. Let us call that "sin as a fact," sin not as something we do, but as something we are subject to.

But how was original sin understood? At least in the popular mind, original sin could be defined as "exactly like actual sin, only you didn't do it. But you might as well have, for you are guilty just the same!" That is, original sin was understood as a variation on the paradigm of actual sin. Original sin was somehow both like and unlike – but understood in terms of – actual sin.

And precisely because original sin was so understood, most Catholics today find it an embarrassment. They either do not believe in original sin, or they choose to avoid the question. Not only do they view the biblical images of apple, tree, serpent, and garden as quaint, they regard the entire concept of original sin as ridiculous. They can accept the reality of actual sin because they accept the truth of human responsibility, but they cannot accept the fact that we should be punished for the actual sins of another. That is unjust; and if that is what original sin is, then they cannot accept original sin.

In the tradition, there was yet a third type of sin. It spoke of the "state of mortal sin," that situation which arises from the act of mortal sin. It described a situation in which a person is abidingly cut off from God, out of the state of grace, and liable to hell. It described sin as the quality of a person in that situation, so that the person could be described as being "in sin."

But this understanding of sin, too, was viewed as derivative, not basic. It depended on the concept of actual sin for its meaning. After all, the Council of Trent specifically taught that Catholics must confess their mortal sins by species and number. It was insufficient for Catholics to announce: "Bless me, Father, I am a sinner." They must go on to describe the actual sins from which this situation arose. This is very curious! It is as if one announced that a friend was dead, only to be questioned about the precise location of the bullet holes. What is more important: being dead or how one got there? The tradition seemed to suggest that the acts were more important than the resulting state. And how can one meaningfully speak of numbers of sin? How much deader than dead can one be? The tradition seemed to suggest that one could be multiply dead – and that, if so, this was a very significant piece of information.

In summary, then, Catholic tradition asserted three meanings for the word "sin." We call them sin as a fact, sin as an act, and sin as a state. What is really significant is that the overall understanding was constructed around the second of those realities. It was sin as an act that was taken as the paradigm. Sin as a fact and sin as a state were defined in terms of, and made dependent on, sin as an act. And, as we have implied in this description, that had regrettable effects. The overall view of the Catholic tradition can therefore be conceived in the following way:

$$\text{FACT} \longleftarrow \text{ACT} \longrightarrow \text{STATE}$$

Two Dimensions – Or Four?

Much of that has changed. But what has changed? The understanding of sin, to be sure. But as we saw earlier, our understanding of sin is really a function of our understanding of ourselves as human persons and believers. It is that self-understanding which has changed.

In medieval philosophy, which produced the synthesis we considered in chapter 5, the description of the human person was premised on the fact that the human person is an *agent*. The human act was the fundamental category in terms of which the overall anthropology was developed. Human beings were identified with their acts in such a way that total description of human actions equaled description of the human person. It was an anthropology that we described as "two dimensional." Just as a piece of paper, having length and width but not depth, presents itself to us as immediate, evident, transparent, and obvious, so this traditional anthropology described human beings in such terms.

Note that it was medieval philosophy that described the human person in this way. That description was not an article of faith, it was not intrinsic to the Christian gospel. And yet since our theology of sin is rooted in our understanding of ourselves, that anthropology could not avoid being absorbed in its weakness as well as in its strength. And so that perspective served to structure the theology of sin. But that philosophical perspective has changed, as we have seen. It has been enriched by focus on the third dimension, depth, and the fourth dimension, time, as we noted in chapter 6. It follows, then, that we must be true to the deepest instincts of the tradition and seek to rearticulate the theology of sin in our own, four-dimensional view of the human. That is our next task.

Sin Today: A Fact

We return to the three traditional meanings of sin—fact, act, and state. And we start with sin as a fact. Why? We start with sin as a fact because our *experience* of sin starts with sin as a fact. Picture the moment of birth. The physician or midwife holds up the newborn baby, slaps it smartly on the behind. And in response the baby gives forth a cry. What a powerfully symbolic exchange! The baby enters the human world, and what is its first experience? It is harassed! It is treated roughly, insensitively, almost brutally![3] Of course, we know that this action is in the baby's best interest. Still, the gesture is far from affectionate. And how does the baby respond? It protests. It screams out its displeasure, its anger, its fear, its surprise. And in so doing, it begins to breathe. Indeed, it is as if the baby finally, as a result of this outside interference, becomes angry enough to survive in this world of ours, as if rage is the radical life-giving emotion!

And perhaps it is. The baby has reason to be angry, after all. And least of all for the harassing gesture. Much more profoundly, it could be argued that the baby is angered by its discovery that it has been "delivered to the wrong address." Like all of us, the baby has an unending lust for perfection, for happiness, for tranquility and excitement—in a word, for heaven. But this is not heaven! This is not the kingdom. This is not a place where all is well. And having discovered that, the baby gives forth a cry, a protest.

As time goes on, the same insight is re-encountered, and in much more profound ways. Over and over again, expectations are disappointed, plans are unfulfilled, desires are contradicted. The infant makes a sound by which it announces its hunger – and its diaper is changed. The three-year-old cries out in the terror of a nightmare – and the babysitter has the TV turned too loud to hear. The first grader attempts to share the experience of starting school – and is not understood. The teenager falls in love – and the love is unrequited. The adult fails to meet career objectives. And through it all this person observes the world around: Good people become ill, mean-spirited people succeed, and, most profoundly, in the end we all die. Over and over again, the person discovers that this is not the best of all possible worlds. It is not the world we would like to inhabit. And, if God is indeed good, this is not the world we were meant to inhabit.

It is a sinful world. The baby does not yet know whose fault this sin is – if, indeed, it is anybody's fault. But that does not make it any less real. The sin is a fact, and the baby is its victim. Sin here is not something the baby does; it is something the baby discovers, experiences, encounters. But it is sin. Indeed, it is original, the *original* sin. It is sin in its most basic and elemental sense, sin as a situation, sin as a reality, sin as a curse under which we all stand.

But is this tragic dimension of life really sin? After all, we defined "sin" as a religious concept, as a term meaningful only to believers. And all human persons, believer and unbeliever alike, encounter the tragic. So how can the two be the same?

It is true that all human beings experience this dark side of life, but it is also true that all human cultures have found this dark side sufficiently perplexing to deserve an explanation. The ancient Persians, for example, explained it by positing the existence of two gods, one good and the other evil. The two gods are in mortal combat, with neither clearly the victor. We are simply caught in the middle, experiencing sometimes good and other times ill. Not an unreasonable explanation! Existentialist thinkers found an explanation in the assertion that the world is absurd, that the world is intrinsically evil, and that part of its evil is to have the sometimes appearance of good. For them the only logical response to life is suicide, and therefore they propose survival as a final frantic act of human independence.[4]

The Judaeo-Christian tradition likewise experiences the evil of life and feels the need to provide an explanation. Characteristically, it proposes an explanation in the form of a story.

Once upon a time, it says, there was a man and a woman, intensely happy, utterly at peace. They lived in a place where all their needs were met and all their desires satisfied. So comfortable was their setting, both physically and emotionally, that they did not even experience the need for clothing.

In this veritable garden of delight, there was, however, one tree whose fruit they were not to taste. (If you ask why this tree was forbidden, the storyteller will quite rightly tell you not to interrupt the tale. After all, no story is perfect!) But they disobeyed and ate the fruit. Admittedly, it was not altogether their fault; they were tempted by some otherworldly force that took the form of a snake. And even though it was less the fault of the man (for whom the storyteller evidently has special sympathy), he did eat the fruit. Both he and the woman violated the order that had constituted and supported their paradise. They disrupted that order. (Note that "order" means both command and structure.) Obviously they know it now and are not proud of themselves. Suddenly they feel a need to hide, from God behind the trees and from each other behind clothes. They have made their world one of dis-order, a place of subterfuge and deception, a place of domination and dissimulation. They have made it a place where things are not right. They have made it a place of sin. And that is why things do not go well for the baby, indeed, do not go well for any of us. That, in the end, is why we must die.

What is the point of the story, then? It is very simple. We do not really know why things are often so bad in our world. We do not have any "scientific" explanation. No item of history will explain our predicament. Still, we believe in God. Almost against the data of our experience, we believe in God.[5] And so we will not blame God. If blame must be placed somewhere, we will place it on ourselves. We will accept responsibility for the darkness that inhabits our world. We will accept the guilt. And since the tragic has always been part of our experience, since it does not really look as if the trouble is your fault or mine, we will assert and presume that the first disruptive act occurred at the very beginning of our human history. None of us is guiltless. All of us – and not God – are responsible for the mess we are in. In yet another sense, this sin is original, for it comes from the very beginning.[6]

So evil is a fact. That is a sad truth, and it must surely cause us all pain. But at the same time, it is a somehow dignified truth. We are sin's victims, and our pain is not our fault. If we must suffer, then at least we can enjoy the compensation of appropriate self-pity. That is, if sin is merely a fact . . .

An Act

But it is not. Granted that Adam and Eve did the destructive disobedient deed, so have you and so have I. Granted that they said no to life – so have we. Granted that they indulged in self-serving deception – so have we. Granted that they tried to dominate life when they ought to have harmonized with it – so have we. Granted that they introduced sin into the world, so indeed have we.

Above and beyond sin as a fact, there also exists sin as an act. The deeds we have done, the acts we have perpetrated are usually not grand acts, they are often small and trivial. Still, we in our own unique ways have made things worse. If sin is a fact today, it is partly our fault, too. And not just today, in the full bloom of our adulthood: We did such deeds as we moved out of our childhood. Perhaps even beginning at the age of nine or ten, at the very "age of reason," we knowingly did what we knew would make it worse. In a simple and childish way, of course, but little by little we grasped the fact that our behavior could make it better or worse. And at times, from selfishness or fear or anger or spite or fatigue, we chose to make it worse. In that moment, we encountered and experienced and indeed perpetrated sin as an act. It was a secondary and derivative reality, of course. But it did occur. No longer was it sufficient to say, "It's a shame and I need help." Now it became necessary to say, "I was wrong and I need forgiveness."

A Direction

As we moved into adulthood, however, we passed another turning point. It is difficult to say just when or how, but we discovered the mystery of our freedom. Allow me to phrase this in a personal manner.

I can remember, as a college student, staring into the mirror, looking into my own eyes, sensing the depths and the mysteries that lay behind those strange organs. For the first time I realized in a genuine and convincing way that I was free. I was not on a leash; no one controlled me. I had the power to say yes or no, to affirm or reject whatever was presented. I was not a dog or cat. I was a human person, and I was free. That freedom was a frightening thing. I almost wished it didn't exist. But it did, and that made all the difference.

I had the power to choose how I would stand toward life. I had the power to choose the posture I would assume, the attitude I would enflesh, the direction I would take. I had the power to choose to stand on the side of good, to resist evil, to combat the fact of sin, to struggle that life might be better and not worse. Or I had the power to stand on the side of sin, to accept it and embrace it, to let the fact of sin define my life and shape it, to let go of the dream of a better world and settle for a cozy spot in the broken world that we know, to take sin as given and let it shape my life. Far more frightening than any simple act of sin, I had the power to make sin my very state of life. And so, in that awesome moment when I discovered the full meaning of human freedom, I also discovered the possibility – and therefore, in some sense, the reality – of the state of sin.

Or perhaps the word "state" sounds too definitive. Perhaps it suggests more clarity and finality than we actually experience in life. For we do live in a four-dimensional world where we are much more becoming than being. So perhaps the word should be "direction." I discovered that sin could be the direction of my life, that my path could be away from the dream as well as toward it, that ambiguity could be allowed to deepen progressively into death as well as to move toward the clarity of new life. I discovered that I could shape the direction of my life: That is a human insight. And I understood the alternative directions as sanctity and sin, union with God and isolation from God, fidelity and idolatry: That is the conviction of Christian faith.

What is sin, then? It is all three of these: a fact, an act, and a direction. But it is all three precisely in that order. We begin with original sin, the most basic and fundamental meaning of the word. We grow into the possibility and the reality of actual sin, an expression of our human freedom of choice. And we finally face the possibility of a sinful life direction, sin in its ultimate most profound and fearsome, most characteristically human form. In the end, the deepest question each of us adults faces is the question of where we will point our lives, the question of direction. In some sense everything else leads up to this and is important because of how it relates to this. Sin as a direction possibility and its blessed alternative, a direction pointed toward God: These two are, in the end, what life is all about.

So what does "sin" mean? It means three things. And they should be ordered as follows:

$$\text{FACT} \longrightarrow \text{ACT} \longrightarrow \text{DIRECTION}$$

Conclusion

In this diagram, then, we have a theology of sin that rearticulates the ancient Christian convictions in the vocabulary of our own four-dimensional world. It is, in that sense, a profoundly Catholic, profoundly traditional vision. But that does not mean it is sufficient.[7]

The traditional two-dimensional theology was part of the heritage for such a long time that it developed a wide range of related terminology. There was a whole way of speaking about sin that was part of Catholic life, a way of speaking that was based on the two-dimensional theology but that also expressed a collection of important, related truths. What are we to do with that terminology? It may be that it can be retained in this theology of sin. It may be that it must be disposed of, on the grounds that it only makes sense in the older perspective. But the one thing we cannot do is simply ignore it.

Hence the next chapter will be devoted to exploring the implications of this four-dimensional theology of sin, with its use of original sin as the starting point, for a number of traditional insights and expressions. And as a central element of that traditional structure, the notions of mortal and venial sin will be considered.

Chapter 8

SIN: MORTAL AND VENIAL

When we consider the four-dimensional theology of sin developed in the last chapter, one difficulty certainly presents itself: It seems quite different than the understanding of sin with which many Christians have been raised. Therefore, in this chapter we should take the time to connect this vision to the tradition, to indicate the ways in which it is profoundly faithful to the tradition, and to explain how — and, more important, why — it diverges from that tradition.

In religious conversations over the centuries, sin was often discussed in the language of "mortal" and "venial." Those terms have not yet appeared in these pages. How do they fit? Do they have meaning any more? Are they useful or appropriate?

It is obvious that these words were formerly employed in a way that focused almost exclusively on individual acts. But that is not surprising, given that the entire understanding of sin had a similar focus. But must they have this focus? Or can they be reconceived in such a way as to be helpful and meaningful in a four-dimensional world?

Let us start with the terms themselves. Take the word "mortal." What does it mean? Deadly, utterly destructive, producing annihilation. Apart from the world of religion, in ordinary conversation we may speak of a "mortal blow," "the curse of mortality," "wounds that turned out to be mortal," and so on. And take the word "venial." What does it mean? In both religious and legal contexts, it refers to things that are pardonable, light, ordinary, and so on. Current usage does not often employ this word in nonmoral contexts. But even apart from the religious focus on God, one can speak of a "venial fault," and "venial matter," and the like.

With these understandings, then, we can return to our vision of sin and sense the connection. After all, we view sin as something awry with our world and with our relationship with God. But how bad is our situation? Is it hopeless (mortal) or resolvable (venial)? What about our relationship with God? Is it, like a marriage that has been abused too often, simply hopeless and dead? Or is it wounded but still alive, needing remedial attention but still capable of responding to that attention? What about our actions? Are they deadly in their effects (mortal)? Or are they simply ordinary (venial) faults? Would our destructive deeds be better described as deadly or daily? Mortal or venial? Put more profoundly, are these deeds expressive of a fundamental life direction that is self-destructive? Are they indicative of a person who has lost hope, who no longer seeks the "kingdom" of justice, peace, and love? Are we dealing here with a person who has settled into the sinful, death-dealing situation and made it her or his own? Or, on the contrary, are we dealing with a person who remains a seeker, attempting to journey toward that kingdom while nonetheless failing in this or that particular?

Mortal Sin—The Act

Let us say more. Let us give specific attention to the notion of mortal actual sin, of human acts that have this sort of deadly effect. For that, after all, is how the term has been used most commonly in recent tradition.

And with some justice. "Was it a mortal sin?" That is, after all, a meaningful question. It asks whether an act or series of acts has been hopelessly destructive. And some acts do have that effect. Relationships are killed, blessings are thrown away, things of beauty are destroyed. And sometimes there is nothing the agent can do to restore the previous state of things. Perhaps an undeserved gift can inject hope into the situation; perhaps a grace can come. But nothing else will do the trick. So it is meaningful to speak of "mortal sin." But notice that what makes the sin mortal is not some arbitrary stipulation of a human authority—or even of divine authority. Rather, what makes it so is the objective and intrinsic fact that the sin is mortal! That is, its intrinsic destructiveness is what makes a sin mortal. The deed either was hopelessly destructive or it was not. If so, it can be rightly termed "mortal." If not, then it was in fact "venial." And what sort of destructiveness are we talking about? Self-destructiveness, of course. For although the term "mortal sin" was often used in a colloquial sense to describe deeds that have great potential to cause destructive effects in the wider world, its true meaning was always understood to refer to the effect of the deed on the one who acts. Mortal sins are so called precisely because they are death dealing for the very one who performs them. And for human persons, such self-destructive behavior is quite conceivable.

So the term is rightly used—indeed, more than rightly used. Thomas Aquinas states in his *Summa Theologiae* that only mortal sin truly deserves the name "sin" (I-II, 88, 1). Any other event or reality that we may name sin deserves that name only in an analogous sense. This we can now very well understand. For, as we saw in chapter 6, we only become fully human by the exercise of basic, transcendental freedom, and not any other sort. Sin (and beatitude, its opposite) are characteristically human realities. Even sin as a fact only makes sense in a human world, since it makes sense only in light of the human person's kingdom destiny. All the more so, sin as a direction only arises when we live our humanity in the fullest, most complete way. And that complete exercise of humanity only occurs in the fundamental direction arising through a fundamental option.

Thus, as we have seen, the reality we have previously termed fundamental direction is nothing but a philosophic synonym for the religious realities of sin and beatitude, or, if you like, the "state of sin" and the "state of grace." But there is also place for acts of sin and acts of virtue. For we also asserted in chapter 6 that the concept of fundamental option, though not of primary importance, was still logically required. If to be adult means to have a fundamental direction, to become adult means to assume that direction by means of a fundamental option. Similarly, to remain adult, and to exercise that adulthood, means periodically to review or change that fundamental direction by means of additional fundamental options. This series of ideas, we now add, can also be articulated in religious language. Mortal sin as an act is nothing else than a synonym for fundamental option. A mortal sin (or a mortal act of virtue – it is interesting that the Christian tradition has never generated a clear vocabulary for positive acts) is that act by which we substantially reject God and assume instead a posture apart from, and in alienation from, God. Mortal sin is the moment in which we deny the God who calls us through and in creation and thus, paradoxically, deny our own deepest selves. Mortal sin is the act of sin by which we take on ourselves the state of sin.

But if mortal sin is nothing else than a negative fundamental option, it follows that, like that option, it is a transcendental act. That is, mortal sin is not precisely the doing of any one categorical act. Rather, it is the act of self-disposition occurring through and in that concrete categorical act. The "things" that in the past we had been inclined to call mortal sins are more precisely symbols of sin, the sacraments of sin. In a very real sense, those objective acts are "occasions of sin." But if all this is true, it is also true that, like the fundamental option, mortal sin never occurs apart from objective acts. Just as all transcendental acts occur in conjunction with (and are expressed through) categorical acts, so, too, mortal sin occurs in connection with the doing of specific deeds. Still, mortal sin and the deeds that we do are not precisely identical. And for reasons that will become apparent further on, that is a very important point to make. But before we can proceed, certain implications of our identification of mortal sin and fundamental option must be highlighted.

Mortal Sin: Fundamental Option

First, it should be clear that according to this understanding mortal sin is a relatively rare phenomenon.[1] We do not assert that mortal sin never occurs; far from it. But we do assert that it is a genuinely serious event. It is an event whose importance, moreover, is not the result of some extrinsic rule but rather is intrinsic to the reality. The act by which we place ourselves in alienation from God, our world, and ourselves is not something that is done casually, flippantly, or in a moment of distraction. It most certainly is not something done by accident. Rather, as the most serious act that we can perform, mortal sin or mortal act of virtue (conversion) must be something that occurs relatively infrequently, in a sort of peak moment of human experience.

Second, it follows from our equation of mortal sin and fundamental option that we lack any clear reflex knowledge of our prevailing moral state. Because fundamental option occurs at the core of the person, where the person is totally subject and not at all object, we are intrinsically incapable of reflecting either on that option or on the direction that it produces. In religious language we can therefore say that we are equally incapable of knowing, in a reflex way, whether a given action truly involved a basic decision to reject world and self or not, whether we are truly in the state of grace or in the state of sin. We have a nonreflex awareness of our decisions and state, of course. Also, by honest observation of our categorical behavior, we are able to posit a reasonable conjecture about our situation. But we can never know in a definitive, irrefutable, proof-oriented way how we ultimately stand with God.

Given the understanding of sin that has often been taught to Christian people, and especially Catholics, this may seem a rather radical idea. But in point of fact it is a thoroughly traditional and orthodox Christian understanding. Consider, for example, these words of St. Paul, in which he seems to be referring to this same sense of ultimate moral uncertainty:

The first requirement of an administrator is that he prove trustworthy. It matters little to me whether you or any human court pass judgment on me. I do not even pass judgment on myself. Mind you, I have nothing on my conscience. But that does not mean that I am declaring myself innocent. *The Lord is the one to judge me,* so stop passing judgment before the time of his return. He will bring to light what is hidden in darkness and manifest the intentions of hearts. (1 Cor 4:2f; emphasis added)

What does it mean to say that the Lord will "bring to light what is hidden"? Does it mean that he will illuminate the state of my soul *for you*? At least that. But it can also mean that he will light up *for me* the secrets of my own heart. He will finally make me transparent to myself, finally remove the darkness that I find in the center of my own person. Thus when Paul insists that there should be no "premature judgment," he is referring not only to our penchant for judging others. He is also insisting that we must not pretend to be able to judge ourselves adequately and finally.

If this is what Paul is saying, it is also what theologians through the centuries have said. Even official Church teaching, in the Council of Trent, spoke to the issue of certitude when it declared:

Whoever reflects on himself, his personal weakness, and his affective disposition may fear and tremble about his own grace, since no one can know with a certitude of faith which cannot admit any error, that he has obtained God's grace. (DS 1534)

Moreover, we may reflect that this sense of human unclarity about one's stance before God is the very reality to which the Christian virtue of hope responds. Hope, as distinguished from presumption on the one hand and despair on the other, prompts Christians to trust in God despite their own lack of subjective certitude. We have only a certain sense of our relatedness to God, we have only a nonreflex awareness. Although our observations regarding our categorical behavior may generate a certain prudent confidence, we are nonetheless aware of our own capacity for self-deception. Therefore, the Christian truly has no alternative except to hope; there is no place for "premature judgment."[2]

Our identification of mortal sin with fundamental option, finally, reminds us that acts of mortal sin and virtue can occur in a person who already holds a direction against or for God, as the case may be. That is, the fundamental acts of sin and virtue do not only occur in the moment when we reverse the direction of our lives; they can also occur in the moment in which we ratify and reassert that direction. Sinners are capable of redeclaring the choice for alienation in a new fundamental option (that is, a new mortal sin). Similarly, persons of virtue are capable of deepening their positive fundamental direction by means of a new act of virtue, a new positive fundamental option. Sin and conversion, then, are seen to be complex terms, referring as they do both to the moment of reversal in life and to the moment of ratification.[3]

Impediments Revisited

Everything that has been said thus far in this chapter may serve to explain the religious notion of mortal sin in a helpful way. But it does not succeed in explaining our experience totally. For the fact is that, in our everyday experience, we often choose to do things that are wrong without thereby redefining ourselves as total persons. In the vocabulary of chapter 6, we find ourselves performing human acts that are merely that, and nothing more, acts that are not "fully human" in the way that fundamental options are. And of course our attempt to find a parallel in the language of religion for this natural experience is not difficult. Catholic theology has for centuries spoken of venial sin. But before we can establish the identity between venial sin and "merely human acts," we must answer a previous question: How is such a merely human act possible at all for the human person? Why does not every decision of the human person constitute a self-definition from the core of that person? Or, to put this another way, why is not every human act a fundamental option?

The answer to this question lies in a deeper and fuller consideration of the reality called "impediments." We have already discussed impediments in the context of distinguishing human acts from acts of man. In that context we defined them as realities that affect either the knowledge or the freedom necessary to a human act, and thereby rob that act of at least some of the human force it should contain. But now we are in a position to broaden and deepen that definition.

As we saw in chapter 5, our experience reveals that our categorical acts, our decisions to do this or that concrete deed, are often flawed by the presence of impediments. We may lack the proper knowledge or the totality of categorical freedom necessary for a genuinely human act. And thus we saw that the actions in which we are really involved in our day-to-day lives lie somewhere on the continuum between human acts and acts of man. But since we articulated the reality of impediments in that way, we have come to appreciate the deeper dimensions of human beings. In chapter 6 we came to see that we are not merely our actions, nor are we merely agents. We now understand that we are more deeply persons and that we are characterized by transcendental levels of being. With that new knowledge, then, we can return to our experience. And what do we find? We find that the forces of division, of disunity, of disintegration run deeper than we had ever expected. In addition to the flaws within our activity at the categorical level, there are deep flaws that mar the connection between the categorical and transcendental levels of human beings.

How do we know this? The answer is very simple: We know it because our categorical behavior is a strange and contradictory collection. We do good things, and we do bad. That is clearly our experience. But what can this experience mean? If I hold a fundamental direction, and if the deeds I perform at the categorical level are symbols and sacraments of that direction, then it should follow that my behavior displays a consistency and continuity symptomatic of that direction. There should be a pattern to my everyday behavior, and more than a pattern. There should be an absolute homogeneity; everything that I do should be good or bad. And this is clearly not the case. The fact is that my lifestyle is a combination of good and bad, of virtue and vice. Indeed, that very ambiguity lying within my behavior makes it impossible for me to draw sure conclusions about my fundamental direction.

But if that ambiguity, that lack of consistency, is visible in my behavior, then it follows that at least some of that behavior must be at variance with my fundamental direction. Perhaps I am fundamentally an evil and self-seeking person, and my occasional acts of kindness, of generosity, of honor, do not truly represent the person I have chosen to be. Or perhaps the opposite is the case: I am in fact a person of love, and this love somehow strangely coexists with selfish and unloving acts. But no matter which of these two alternatives is the case, the central fact remains. Some of my behavior does not coincide with the basic self-identity that I have assumed. Some of my actions, it is true, are symbols and sacraments of my fundamental direction. But by the same token, some of my actions are veils of that direction. They hide my direction both from others and from myself.

How can this be? Only one answer is possible. This type of contradiction is possible only on condition that we suffer from a strange sort of disunity within ourselves. The connections that link our inner core with the more superficial levels of our behavior are fragile connections. They are connections that are sometimes broken, sometimes missing. If, as we have suggested, the human person can be imaged as an onion, then we are now claiming that certain intermediate layers of that onion are flawed. We are not, after all, thoroughly integral persons. Quite the contrary, we are "untogether."

What shall we say of this lack of inner integration? Is it the right and normal status of the human person? Is it, as viewed by the person of faith, the way the God wishes things to be? The way that the human person is intended to be? The Christian religious tradition responds to these questions very firmly. This is *not* the way things are meant to be. The human person is meant to be integrated and whole, transparent and consistent, able to express the self in appropriate action and, indeed, incapable of doing otherwise.

But if that is true, if this situation of ours is not what should be, what God wishes to be, what shall we call it? Of course, the answer is clear. The traditional word for things about this world that are not as they should be is "sin." And since the sin of which we now speak is radical sin, experienced as woven into every fiber of our experience in this human world, it is rightly termed "original sin."

Actually, the tradition spoke of this situation as "effects of original sin." In traditional Catholic theology the focus was on original *actual* sin, that primeval action by which our forebears were understood to choose to stand apart from God and to be alienated from God. And this original sin was understood to have certain effects in the human world and the human person. Chief among these effects was "darkening of the intellect" and "concupiscence."

But what are these effects if not the very things that we have called impediments? So it is because of these effects of original sin – which in a deeper and more profoundly theological sense are original sin themselves – that we find it so difficult to perform a genuinely human act even on the categorical level.

In contemporary theology, with its enriched understanding of the depth of the human person, this same concept has been expanded. There are, indeed, effects of original sin. And those effects make us beings who are out of sorts, beings working somehow at cross-purposes with ourselves, beings divided and divided again. So, just as traditional Catholic theology asserted that even with the "remission" of original sin the effects remain, we assert the same. No matter that individual human persons have opted in a fundamentally positive way for God and the world and themselves. No matter that their stance in life is virtuous. The integration that ought ideally to be theirs is not forthcoming. We are not transparent; we are not consistent. Our behavior can reveal our inner direction, but it can also hide that direction. Similarly, no matter how genuinely meant the direction that a person has adopted, the integration of the whole manifold of categorical behavior in it, the rendering of behavior consistent with it, remains a long and arduous task, a project yet to be completed.[4] Indeed, so true is this incompleteness that, in the end, we might better speak of our "dominant fundamental direction," to include an honest admission of the continuing presence of contradictory behavior.

To say this, of course, is to do nothing more than describe our experience. What is often overlooked, however, is the fact that this insight has long been part of the Christian experience as well. As just one example, consider these powerful words of St. Paul:

We know that the law is spiritual, whereas I am weak flesh sold into the slavery of sin. I cannot even understand my own actions. I do not do what I want to do but what I hate . . . the desire to do right is there but not the power. What happens is that I do, not the good I will to do, but the evil I do not intend. But if I do what is against my will, it is not I who do it, but sin which dwells in me. (Rom 7:13, 18–20)

The "sin which dwells in" Paul is original sin, that fact of sin, that situation of alienation and brokenness which is presently a part of the human condition. And as that sin lived in Paul, so it lives in us all, with the result that our fundamental direction never succeeds in expressing itself fully and unequivocally in behavior.

Venial Sin

Now, at last, we are in a position to understand the reality of venial sin. Venial sin (or virtue) is purely and simply a human act that is not fully so, that does not come from the core of the human person and that does not involve a fundamental option. It is, we say, a human act. It does involve freedom and knowledge. But it is not a fully human act, a fundamental option. It does not engage the transcendental freedom of our deepest level. In venial sin there is a genuine decision to do this or that action. But there is no decision to become this or that sort of person.

The difference between venial and mortal sin, then, is nothing other than the degree of personal penetration, personal involvement in the act. In the former there is no deep core involvement, whereas in the latter there is. In the case of mortal sin, the person, deciding to do this deed, is also deciding to be a particular sort of person, to reject God and world and, paradoxically, self. In the case of venial sin, however, this is not the case. The person is rather choosing to do this deed while also more deeply choosing to be the sort of person who stands opposed to this deed. Every act of venial sin, then, contains an inner contradiction. And such an act would be simply impossible for us were it not for the inner divisions that separate us from ourselves. Or to put this another way, venial sin would be impossible were it not for impediments, the effects of original sin.

But problems yet remain. To explain in a theoretical way the intrinsic difference between venial and mortal sin is not to explain how we can concretely identify these two, how we can accurately distinguish them from each other in real life. Two possible answers to this problem immediately suggest themselves, although both must ultimately be rejected.

First, it was often suggested in the past that one could distinguish venial sin from mortal sin by the "gravity of the matter." That is, one could simply consider the deed that had been done, evaluate its objective and intrinsic significance, and conclude that if it was a seriously evil act, then a serious and central decision must have been made. In other words, the older view suggested that every commission of a seriously wrong act involved a fundamental option. The insights of modern psychology, however, force us to reject this position. It is clear that for a variety of reasons (impediments, once again) we do things that are seriously wrong without in fact making such a personal decision. And we know this because of the rapidity with which we do such deeds and repent of them. It is inconceivable that a person could define himself or herself, repudiate that definition, and then reassert it in a matter of hours or days.[5] Indeed, to suggest that this could happen is to undermine our very dignity and to cheapen us as persons. So even though lists of objectively grave matter may serve a useful function (as we shall see), they do not provide us with an infallible list by which to judge whether a particular action involved venial or mortal sin.

A second alternative suggests itself. We could simply invite agents to look within, to reflect on their motivations and desires. And we could ask them to tell us if, by this action, they intended to define themselves as persons. This, too, however, will not do. For as we have repeatedly seen, the self-awareness characteristic of our core being is a nonreflex awareness. We simply do not have that sort of clarity about ourselves and our own identity. We cannot hold our innermost being up to the mirror of our mind; we cannot make our subjectivity into objectivity. Thus we cannot establish with absolute certitude the depth from which our moral decision came.

We are forced back, then, to a conclusion we saw earlier, a painful but realistic conclusion. Just as we cannot be certain of what our fundamental direction is in life – whether we are in the state of sin or the state of grace – so we cannot be certain about the import of our individual actions. We can have in this case, as in the other, a conjectural certitude, an awareness or sense of the truth. But we cannot establish unequivocally and certainly that a particular deed was or was not a fundamental option. Therefore, we are forced to locate the line between venial sin and mortal sin in the mystery that is the human person. That both sorts of sin are real is a datum of experience. That both sorts of sin have occurred in our experience is a greater or lesser possibility. But that any particular act was one or the other is a question mark.

Once again, we are driven to the virtue of hope as the only reasonable (and Christian) way to deal with ourselves. Just as God is ultimately a mystery, impervious to our rational efforts, so God's creation, the human person, is a mystery. And there is no avoiding that fact.

Two Formulations

We can conclude this chapter by isolating two elements of traditional moral theology, two ways of speaking that are very common in the Catholic world. This we ought to do in order to make perfectly clear that we no longer support these particular formulations, at least as commonly understood.

The first formulation has to do with the so-called "fonts of morality." Briefly, it asserts that a moral act has three elements, all of which must be considered in order to judge that act accurately. First is the deed itself, what is to be done. Second are the various circumstances that can alter or modify the value of that deed. For example, if I tell you that I gave my neighbor a ride in my automobile but fail to mention that I did so holding a gun to his head, I have clearly ignored an important element of the situation. And third is the motive for the deed. The reason I forced my neighbor into the car was that he was gravely injured and, in his hysteria, was refusing treatment.

Now, it is clear that this principle, focusing on the action itself as it does, is primarily concerned with objective morality. And as such, it pertains more directly to the considerations that will comprise the second half of this book. We shall discuss this principle again in chapter 16, but inasmuch as the principle includes the notion of motive, some comments will be useful now. For "motive" is really a term describing the meaning that an action has for its agent. And as such, it is a term that summarizes everything that we have been discussing in the last several chapters. It is very much part of the vision of subjective morality that we have been pursuing and, indeed, stands as a sort of symbol of that vision.

And here, precisely, is the problem. By grouping together deed, circumstance, and motive, the three-font principle brings together both subjective and objective morality. It unites these two, which is admirable since they are existentially united in the lives we lead. But it also confuses the two, which is something we must avoid in the extreme. How is there confusion?

Manuals of moral theology often raised the question: Which of the three fonts is the primary determinant of the morality of any one action? And the usual response was that the deed itself made an act moral or immoral. But is that the case? If by "moral" one means to refer to objective morality, to the actual goodness or badness of the action, then the statement is somewhat true. (It is not altogether accurate, as we shall see in chapter 16.) But by the same token, if one is discussing objective morality, then motive is not at all germane. For actions as such do not have motives; they only have ends or results. Agents have motives; human persons, human subjects, have motives.

Thus, if one really wants to include the element of motive, then one must talk about subjective morality, about the sinfulness or saintliness of an action. And once we assume this perspective, then it is clear that the motive is the primary determinant of the morality. Indeed, motive is the only determinant of the morality. For morality, in this subjective sense in which we have understood it in these pages, is not a quality of

deeds but a quality of persons. It is a term describing the sense of obligation, the accountability, that is characteristic of persons. To be moral, in
this sense, then, is to be authentic, to be honest, to be seeking to do what
is really good. And, in the same way, to be immoral is to refuse to do so.

Thus, the three-font principle might best be altogether avoided. For
in uniting objective and subjective morality, it continually runs the high
risk of confusing these two spheres. And that confusion can have disastrous effects.

Indeed, these disastrous effects are clear in the second topic we must
now consider. For based on the assertion that the deed was the primary
font of morality, the manuals of moral theology often asked a second
question: What, then, distinguishes mortal from venial sin? And the
only logically appropriate answer was given: the gravity of the deed or,
as it was more often called, the "gravity of the matter." If the matter, the
substantial reality of the deed, was the primary source of morality, then
it must follow that the gravity of that matter would be the primary
source of the grave moral act (that is, the mortal sin). Similarly, where
that gravity was lacking, the morality would be light (that is, venial sin).
Indeed, it was often said that for any sin there must be knowledge and
freedom, and that for mortal sin there must be knowledge, freedom,
and grave matter.

This, of course, we must altogether reject. It is not the gravity of the
matter that makes a sin mortal, but rather the degree of personal
involvement in the decision to act. And it is not the lightness of the matter that makes a sin venial, but rather the absence of such involvement.
One is either involved in the decision in fact, or one is not. Our transcendental freedom is either part of what we are doing, or it is not. We
are either choosing the sort of person we will be in this action, or we are
not. And if we are not, then the fact that the matter is in and of itself
grave will change nothing. In that case we simply have a person who has
committed a venial sin in the course of doing something that, objectively speaking, is gravely wrong. Indeed, as we suggested earlier in this
chapter, that is precisely what happens in many cases.[6]

What, then, shall we say of all the lists of "mortal sins" and "venial
sins" that have been developed over the years? Are they completely useless? No, indeed. It is not accurate to describe those lists precisely as
mortal and venial sins, but it is certainly appropriate to formulate such
lists of grave and light matter.[7] Once this is done, such lists have several valid uses. For one thing, they are helpful information to those who
are seeking genuinely and objectively to care for their neighbor. They
instruct such persons as to what will or will not be truly in the best
interests of their neighbor. Thus they have a noble role to fill in the task
of moral catechesis.

In addition, such lists may, within limits, assist in the evaluation of one's past actions. We have repeatedly insisted that our transcendental level of being does not exist apart from our categorical level of action. We have warned that the link between these two levels is not perfect, because of the impediments, the effects of original sin. But by the same token we have been careful to deny that the two levels are totally separated. This being the case, it follows that individual human persons are much more likely to exercise their transcendental freedom, to perform fundamental options, and therefore to affect their fundamental stance in an action that is, in and of itself, grave matter. Thus there is a certain presumption, a prevailing likelihood, that a person who performs a deed that is gravely wrong of itself, and who does so with apparent freedom and awareness, may also have performed a fundamental option in that action. There is not, of course, certitude. But there is a certain likelihood. Thus, given the mystery of human persons, to which we have alluded several times, it is more than appropriate that whatever wisdom we have regarding the objective value of acts be formulated into lists such as those the moral manuals often possessed.

Again, such lists provide useful guidelines for the administration of the Sacrament of Penance. If it is true that we are and remain a mystery to ourselves, it is to be expected that the Sacrament of Penance, focusing on the encounter of human mystery with divine, will reveal a certain ambiguity. For one thing, penitents approaching the sacrament often have doubts about the deep personal meaning of the actions they have performed. Was that really a moment of fundamental option against God? I am not sure. Indeed, there is no way to eliminate that doubt utterly. For another thing, it is often the case in practical experience that such people approach the sacrament precisely because of a feeling of repentance (that is to say, because they have already converted). But that means they have either made or reaffirmed a positive fundamental option. Therefore, even if the past action had the worst possible personal meaning, it is a distinct possibility that freedom, new grace, and conversion precede the moment of the sacramental act. But all this does not eliminate the meaning of the sacrament, and here is where those lists serve their purpose.

Christians who truly believe, who hope, and who experience repentance will not be unduly concerned about isolating the moral significance of their past acts. Nor will they be turned away from the sacrament by the possibility that God's gift of grace has already been bestowed on them. No, they will approach the sacrament in a straightforward way, declaring the deed they have done and reaffirming their desire for the forgiving love of Christ. Were such a person a moral theologian(!), he or she might very well speak words somewhat like the following: "Father, this is what I have done. I don't know for sure if it was a fully human act, a fundamental option. I cannot even be certain that it was a human act, totally devoid of those impediments that affect the mind and will. But I know what I did, and I know that it was gravely harmful to my neighbor. I repent it. And I want the forgiveness of Christ, which may already have been given to me and which I may already have accepted, to be incarnated and renewed in this sacrament."

Conclusion

Sin, then, is not only a religious concept, it is a deeply theological concept. As such, it participates deeply in the mystery of God and the human person. But for all that mysterious ambiguity, it cannot be ignored. Just as we assert the preeminence of the moral person over the moral act despite the fact that we cannot clearly articulate or see that person, so also we assert the preeminence of sin and virtue over the objective realities of value and disvalue. For in the last analysis, Christians who are called to covenantal relationship with their God live a life that cannot be measured by deeds. They live a life that can only be measured by love, the love that God puts in them, which is the love that is God's own self.[8]

Chapter 9

CONSCIENCE

There can be little doubt that any discussion of morality must include a major consideration of conscience. Indeed, in the popular mind, conscience is often taken to be a synonym for morality itself. The rights of conscience, the duty of conscience, what conscience demands or permits, all these phrases are taken to be summaries of the human moral enterprise.

In point of fact, the matter is considerably more complicated than such colloquialisms might lead us to believe. But the popular understanding is at least correct inasmuch as it insists on a central role for the reality of conscience. Thus, having considered what it means to be a human agent and a human person, and having sought to analyze the moral implications of that agency and that personhood, we now turn to a particular aspect of the human person: conscience.

In the course of this chapter we will consider a number of separate though related topics. First we present a psychological discussion. Then we summarize the scriptural input. Third, we present an overall understanding of conscience expressed in useful contemporary vocabulary. And fourth, we confront directly the very real question of the relationship between the personal conscience and Church authority.

Guilt Feelings

In the course of this chapter we shall find that the term "conscience" has a number of legitimate meanings. In order to keep them straight, and to appreciate the legitimate insight of each, we will need to make some distinctions. One hopes, though, that these will not be idle distinctions. Rather, they should represent a helpful ordering of our own human ethical experience.

When the word "conscience" is used in ordinary conversation, it is often presented in the following ways: "My conscience is bothering me."

"I have a guilty conscience." "My conscience tells me what I did was wrong." The common denominator in these statements is that they point to a human experience that comes *after* an act has been performed. They understand conscience as an aspect of the human person that is activated by certain sorts of behavior and provides a sort of gut-level evaluation of that behavior. Let us call this *posterior* conscience, since it makes its presence known after (*post*) the action.

Curiously enough, when the Catholic tradition talks about conscience, it is *not* talking about posterior conscience. The use of the term in this way is a peculiarly modern phenomenon. The tradition, for its part, uses the term to point at *anterior* conscience, conscience before (*ante*) the act. And that reality, therefore, will be the major focus of our attention for the rest of this chapter. For that very reason, then, let us begin with a few comments about posterior conscience.

What shall we say about posterior conscience? The first thing to note is that in describing this experience of conscience we are, in reality, describing the human experience of guilt. Indeed, we are acknowledging the painful reality of these negative feelings, we are locating them, and we are affirming their function in human life. So let us talk about these feelings of guilt.

One of the more significant contributions of contemporary psychology to the moral enterprise has been that discipline's emphasis on the strange ways in which our feeling systems operate. Feelings are very real, and it has been the desire of psychology to emphasize the importance of dealing with them. But in the process of calling for increased understanding of feelings and respect for them, psychology has also brought us to a greater appreciation of the nonrational and noncontrollable ways of feelings. What is the genesis of the feelings we have? Where do they come from? That question is, often enough, impossible to answer fully. But one thing is clear: They come from experiences and not from intellectual reflection.[1]

Indeed, it is interesting to note that no matter how far various schools of psychology diverge from one another, on this point they share a common understanding. Freud speaks of the superego, that font of taboo and stricture, that policeman of the personal life, that agent of enforced socialization. Just as the id is prepersonal and prerational, the same is true for the superego. And it is precisely the function of the ego to mediate those prerational demands of the other two realities. Practitioners of Transactional Analysis make statements analogous to those of Freud: They describe the "tape recordings" that every human person makes early in life and that continue to exercise influence into the adult years. In particular, they emphasize "Not OK Child" tapes, with their tendency to continue to generate feelings of guilt when guilt is no longer appropriate. And for behaviorists, guilt feelings, like all aspects of the human person, are not rationally generated but rather are culturally conditioned.

The united voice of these diverse psychologists, then, is that feelings of guilt to a significant degree stand apart from human freedom and human rationality. If this is true, it must also be true that such feelings are morally ambiguous. It may happen that guilt feelings will call our attention to a situation or an action for which we are and ought to be truly guilty. And if so, they are to be cherished as helpful guides for human living. But the exact opposite may also be the case. For whatever reason, I may very well feel guilty about something that I should in no way repent.

Consider the case of the compulsive worker who leaves a task half completed in order to help a needy neighbor. Such a person, despite the realization that he or she has done the correct thing, is quite likely to feel guilty about the abiding disarray. Are such feelings an accurate barometer of his or her moral situation? By no means. They are purely and simply the result of some quirk of personality or accident of personal history, nothing more. Thus, in and of themselves those feelings are morally neutral. And as regards their usefulness in moral decision making, they are decisively undependable.

Opposite examples would be equally valid and perhaps even more disturbing. The equanimity with which contemporary culture accepts the phenomenon of widespread nontherapeutic abortion suggests that many people feel no guilt whatsoever about a situation that is morally reprehensible. Once again, feelings are seen to sometimes be undependable guides to moral judgment. If and when such feelings coincide with the actual moral facts of the case, that is certainly a wonderful thing. In that sense, of course, feelings are friendly, helpful, useful contributors to the moral enterprise. But when they are not, and to the extent that they are not, the moral project will be significantly complicated. For in that case we will have a further task: to assess and deal with these distorted feelings of guilt so that we may move beyond them to good judgment.

So posterior conscience is real; who, after all, could deny its occasionally cutting presence! But it is an ambiguous reality, sometimes helpful, sometimes troubling. And, in any case, as a reality of human experience it represents only one of the dimensions of what the Catholic tradition has meant by conscience.[2] So let us proceed now to that larger consideration.

Conscience in Scripture

The idea of conscience, if not the term, receives generous attention in the pages of sacred Scripture. And it will assist our subsequent reflections if we summarize now the data from that source.

The data from the Jewish Scriptures are both interesting and illuminating, for the Hebrew language simply has no word for conscience. Indeed, even in Greek and Latin the specific words for conscience (*syneidesis* and *conscientia*) are fairly late developments. But that fact is actually helpful to us. For research into Greek and Latin literature has revealed that before the emergence of the technical term those languages ordinarily expressed the idea of conscience by the word "heart" (*kardia* and *cor*). And even the most cursory look at Scripture makes clear that "heart" is a most common word. Indeed, there is even one case (Job 27:6) where the Septuagint translates Hebrew "heart" (*leb*) with Greek "conscience" (*syneidesis*). So it will illuminate our understanding of conscience for our time if we search the Jewish Scriptures a bit for its major references to "heart."

The psalmist urges us: "O, that today you would hear his voice: harden not your hearts" (Ps 95:7f). Repeatedly we are told that "God probes the heart" (e.g., Jer 11:20, 17:10; Prov 21:2; Ps 26:2). Twice in the Book of Samuel, King David is described as a man whose "heart misgave him" (1 Sam 24:6; 2 Sam 24:10). The Book of Ecclesiastes (7:22) justifies an assertion by declaring that "you know in your heart." (This example is interesting because the Vulgate in this case renders *leb* with the Latin *conscientia*.) And Proverbs often urges us to "take it to heart" (e.g., 2:1; 3:1; 4:10; 4:21; 7:3).

In the Book of Job, the beleaguered hero responds to his critics with the simple statement, "My heart does not reproach me" (27:6). Indeed, one could reasonably assert that fidelity to conscience, clearness of conscience, constitutes the very theme of the Book of Job. Similar calls for inner authenticity can also be found in the prophets, particularly Ezekiel (11:14–21) and Jeremiah (31:31–34).

The Christian Scriptures also offer a number of interesting examples. Consider the Gospel of Matthew, where Jesus condemns the righteous Pharisees by quoting Isaiah, "This people honors me with their lips, but their heart is far from me." Asked by his disciples for an explanation, Jesus proceeds to expand this critique by declaring:

It is not what goes into a man's mouth that makes him impure: it is what comes out of his mouth. Do you not see that everything that enters the mouth passes into the stomach and is discharged into the latrine, but what comes out of the mouth originates in the mind? It is things like these that make a man impure. (Mt 15:11,17f)

And this understanding of conscience/heart greatly illuminates the Beatitude: "Blest are the single-hearted for they shall see God" (Mt 5:8). Indeed, this example is particularly interesting inasmuch as the more primitive and more socially oriented Lukan version lacks this Beatitude. It appears that Matthew presents a subsequent revision, a turning from the social to the personal level. We may be justified, then, in surmising that to the extent that Christianity emphasizes the inner realities of personal commitment, some reference to conscience is demanded.

And then there is a classic description of conscience (*kardia*) provided by John. He declares:

> This is our way of knowing we are committed to the truth and are at peace before him no matter what our consciences may charge us with; for God is greater than our hearts and all is known to him. Beloved, if our consciences have nothing to charge us with, we can be sure that God is with us. (1 John 3:19–21)

Conscience in Paul

But it is to Paul that we must particularly direct our attention in this context. For on the topic of conscience Paul introduced something genuinely new, something truly creative in the history of Christian theology. The Greek word for conscience, *syneidesis*, was not in common use much before the time of Christ. Indeed, the Septuagint, the Greek translation of the Jewish Scriptures, used the word only twice. By contrast, Paul used it thirty times in his letters and discourses in the Acts of the Apostles. As we shall see, he used it in a number of different contexts that illuminate various meanings of the word. But before we spell out these details, we may appropriately ask why it is that Paul introduced this new emphasis. There appear to be a number of reasons.

First, the word *syneidesis* was common in the secular literature of Paul's time, and, as we know, Paul was a well-educated man. He was an urban man, a cosmopolitan man. It is therefore to be expected that he was in touch with that literature. Indeed, as a child of the cosmopolitan city of Tarsus, Paul was very probably part of the great philosophic discussions of his time. Second, we must be aware that Paul was often writing to educated people. In his letter to Rome he would have been conscious that those people were familiar with the writings of Cicero and Seneca, replete with their discussions of conscience. And the highly philosophic tone of the letters to Corinth makes clear that Paul was acutely aware of the educated status of his readers. So for these reasons, among others, it appears that Paul took a common secular term, united it with a traditional Jewish notion, and forged a new and exciting insight for the Christian faith. He developed with considerable precision an aspect of the human person that had heretofore not been highlighted. But what was that insight? A consideration of a few selections from Paul's writings will answer that question.

"Gentiles . . . show that the demands of the law are written in their hearts [*kardias*]. Their conscience [*syneidesis*] bears witness together with that law" (Rom 2:15). Here we see Paul explicitly connecting the Jewish notion of heart with his own understanding of conscience. Conscience is what bears witness to and illuminates; conscience judges that inner awareness, evaluating it in an impartial and unbiased way (cf. also Rom 9:1; 2 Cor 1:12f). But conscience is not an exterior judge; it is an aspect of the self. And thus understood, it can have several different qualities of its own.

Conscience can be bad, denying the realities of the moral life. Thus the Christian is challenged to "draw near, . . . our hearts sprinkled clean from the evil which lay on our conscience" (Heb 10:22). Or conscience can be just the opposite. Paul declares that "I always strive to keep my conscience clear before God and man" (Acts 24:16). Second, conscience can function as an infallible guide to action. Paul commands his disciple Timothy to "fight the good fight and hold fast to faith and a good conscience. Some men, by rejecting the guidance of conscience, have made shipwreck of their faith" (1 Tim 1:19f). But in this case, too, the opposite is just as possible. Paul tells his disciples that it is perfectly acceptable to eat food sacrificed to idols. But then he warns them, "Not all, of course, possess this 'knowledge.' Because some . . . eat meat, fully aware that it has been sacrificed, and because their conscience is weak, it is defiled by the eating" (1 Cor 8:7). And this possibility, says Paul, must moderate his disciples' behavior.

If someone sees you, with your "knowledge," reclining at table in the temple of an idol, may not his conscience in its weak state be influenced to the point that he eats the idol-offering? . . . When you sin thus against your brothers and wound their weak consciences, you are sinning against Christ. (1 Cor 8:10–12)

So consciences can be weak; they can be erroneous. And to the extent that this is true, they demand the charity of the brethren, fraternal solicitude.

A number of these nuances are brought together in a classic statement on the topic of clean and unclean foods. Paul says this:

"All things are lawful," but not all are advantageous. . . . If an unbeliever invites you to his table and you want to go, eat whatever is placed before you, without raising any question of conscience. But if someone should say to you, "This was offered in idol worship," do not eat it, both for the sake of the one who called attention to it and on account of the conscience issue – not your own conscience but your neighbor's. (1 Cor 10:23, 27–29)

In all these citations, then, we find a surprising variety of understandings of the word. Conscience is infallible, yet it is fallible. Conscience is a value, a good thing, and yet it is also a bad thing. Conscience is dependable, and it is undependable. Conscience is a person's heart, and it is something that criticizes that heart. Conscience is the person himself, yet conscience is a subservient part of the person. All these definitions find some support in the writings of Paul. And all resonate to some degree or other with our own experience. But how shall we put all this in order? The purpose of the next part of this chapter will be to organize these ideas and to develop an overall understanding of conscience.

An Understanding of Conscience

Traditional moral theology habitually distinguished three different meanings for the word "conscience." And these it delineated by the use of three different terms: *synderesis*, moral science, and *syneidesis*.[3] Moreover, the tradition contended that the first and last of these terms, and the ideas they represented, were to be found in the twin fonts of Scripture and tradition. In our own presentation we will begin with a few brief remarks regarding that last assertion, the genesis of those two terms. After that we will proceed to a presentation that will not greatly diverge from that of traditional theology. But we will abstain from using any of the three terms. For, in this writer's experience, they are never particularly helpful and, indeed, often distract from the matter at hand. We will substitute for them, therefore, some terms of our own.

As we indicated, traditional moral theology distinguished between *synderesis* and *syneidesis*, claiming that these two terms and ideas were to be found in Scripture itself. By *synderesis* they understood the habit of conscience, the basic sense of responsibility that characterizes the human person. And by *syneidesis* they understood the act of conscience, the judgment by which we evaluate a particular action. We have already seen that the term *syneidesis* is clearly present in Scripture. But what of *synderesis*? The simple and embarrassing fact is that this term does not appear in Scripture. Indeed, there is no such word in the Greek language. Rather, it appears that this entire theological tradition is the result of a massive error.

As nearly as we can tell, it was St. Jerome who first alleged the existence of these two different words for conscience. In preparing the first Latin text of the Bible, Jerome was apparently working from a Greek manuscript that was not altogether legible. He had to deal with selections where the topic was clearly conscience but the word did not appear to be "syneidesis" but rather "synderesis." Jerome studied the text and thought he detected differing nuances when one or the other word was used. Thus he concluded that the latter must simply be a Greek word with which he was unfamiliar, a word being used to make a very specific point. But recent scholarship has made clear that Jerome was wrong.

There are not two words in Greek for conscience, but only one. The distinction between the two concepts may very well be useful, and indeed we shall find it so. But in making that distinction, we must be clear that it is ours, not the Bible's.

What, then, can we say of conscience? We shall assert that the word "conscience," as it is generally used both in theology and in those ordinary conversational usages that refer to *anterior* conscience, points at one or another of three quite different ideas, that there are three distinct *facets* of this reality of anterior conscience. And for purposes of simplicity, we shall refer to these as conscience/1, conscience/2, and conscience/3.

To begin, we speak of conscience/1. Here we are referring to conscience as an abiding human *characteristic*, to a general sense of value, an awareness of personal responsibility, that is utterly emblematic of the human person. Repeatedly through the chapters of this book we have seen that to be human is to be accountable. It is to be a being in charge of one's life. This human capacity for self-direction equally implies a human responsibility for good direction. Indeed, so much is this true that we question the "humanity" of anyone who lacks an awareness of value. Psychologists speak of sociopaths and psychopaths, of people devoid of any sense of right and wrong. And they consider such people sick. The courts of law regularly ask the question: "Was this person aware of what he or she was doing, and of the wrongness of it?" If that question is answered negatively, the court will not bring such a person to trial. For he or she is in a very real sense not "human" and is not accountable at the bar of human law. But apart from such bizarre aberrations, all human persons share a sense of the goodness and badness of their deeds and of their accountability for these deeds.

It is true, of course, that the contemporary period is replete with examples of moral disagreement. Lively moral debate is a sign of the times. What is more, there is tremendous disparity among various cultures in their judgment of what is right and what is wrong. But far from refuting this first understanding of the word "conscience," that debate and disagreement proves its existence. It is only because we agree that there are such things as right and wrong, and that we ought to do the right and avoid the wrong, that the conversation even begins. We can have varying opinions about what is right or wrong only because we share the common realization that it makes a difference *whether* a thing is right or wrong. Thus every discussion of moral values, every consideration of moral questions, has as its presupposition the existence of conscience/1. The human person has such a conscience, and only because of that fact is the person genuinely and truly human.

But the existence of conscience/1 does not mean that we "rest on our laurels." Quite the contrary, conscience/1 forces individual human persons to search out the objective moral values of their situation. They feel obliged to analyze their behavior and their world, to seek to discover what is the really right thing and what is not. This search, this exercise of moral reasoning, can be termed conscience/2. "I wonder what I ought to do? I wonder if the action I contemplate is right or wrong?" Here we understand conscience/2. For if conscience/1 is a characteristic, conscience/2 is the *process* which that characteristic demands. Conscience/2 deals with the effort to achieve a specific perception of values, concrete individual values. It is the ongoing process of reflection, discernment, discussion, and analysis in which human beings have always engaged.

It is here, in the functioning of conscience/2, that we start to experience difference and disagreement. Some may find it right to withhold taxes used to wage war, others will find it wrong. Some may condemn horse racing, others will praise it. Some may judge our culture to be morally depraved, others will consider it an advance over previous ages. People disagree, and that is characteristic of conscience/2.

Indeed, as we reflect on these examples and on many others that might come to mind, it becomes clear that conscience/2 permits not only disagreement but also error. We seek to find and understand the concrete moral values of our situation, but we may fail. We are capable of blindness as well as insight, of distraction as well as attention, of misunderstanding as well as understanding. In fact, whole societies can fail in this way. Consider the nation of Germany in the 1930s. What shall we say of their moral sensitivity? Were they all sinners, refusing to do what they knew to be right? By no means. What must be said (and it is a universal, often tragic human weakness) is that, by and large, the people of Germany were guilty of a moral blind spot, of an inability to see and appreciate the evil of their situation. One could well assert that our own culture is equally guilty of blindness in the areas of respect for human life and human sexuality.

So when we speak of conscience/2, we are speaking of a fragile reality. We are speaking of an aspect of humankind that needs all the help it can get. It needs to be educated. Individual persons are not always able to "see what's there." They need assistance. And if they are sincere persons, if they have accepted the fundamental responsibility implied by conscience/1, then they will seek that assistance. They will turn to their friends, their colleagues, their peers, and seek to benefit from their insights. They will listen to the larger culture, to the wisdom of previous generations, and they will listen to voices from other situations, more objective voices, as these help them to interpret their situation.

In a word, the sincere person will engage in the process known as "formation of conscience." For that, indeed, is a mark of conscience/2: It needs to be formed. It needs to be guided, directed, and illuminated. It needs to be assisted in a multitude of ways. Conscience/2, then, is quite distinct from conscience/1. It is not universal, at least in its conclusions and judgments. And it most certainly is not infallible. Quite the contrary, conscience/2 possesses a sort of humility, an emptiness that needs to be filled by the facts. Conscience/2 is not an arrogant thing, it is not proud. Rather, we might say that it kneels before the truth. In the realm of conscience/2, truth is supreme; truth is the object that is sought. And conscience/2 sincerely and docilely undertakes the task of finding and respecting that truth.

It should be clear from what has been said that the Church has its greatest role in the realm of conscience/2. For the Church is, among other things, a teacher of moral values. Even viewed simply as a human institution, the Church deserves to be heard. And when one adds the belief of faith that the Holy Spirit somehow guides the Church, not protecting its every word from error but nonetheless providing it with some illumination and guidance, it stands to reason that the prudent person will listen to its declarations. But note that conscience/2 is not directly accountable to the Church. No, it is accountable to the truth and nothing else. In its search for truth, conscience/2 makes use of sources of wisdom wherever they may be found. And major among those sources is the Church, the religious community.

But we, as human persons, are not only thinkers, analyzers of facts. We are also doers of deeds. Indeed, it has been the wise insight of philosophy in our century that our highest achievement is not contemplation (as Aristotle said) but rather intelligent action. And so we may not settle at the level of conscience/2. We cannot be perennial observers, commentators on the current scene. No, we must act. We must make a decision, we must judge our own behavior. At some point we must finally declare: "It is theoretically possible that I may be wrong, but it seems to me that I ought to do *this*." This final declaration, this judgment, likewise deserves the name conscience: conscience/3.

If conscience/1 is a characteristic and conscience/2 is a process, conscience/3 is an *event*. And as such, conscience/3 is consummately concrete. It is the concrete judgment of a specific person pertaining to her or his own immediate action. But for all that concreteness, the judgment of conscience/3 is also supremely powerful. For it constitutes the final norm by which a person's action must be guided. Indeed, by the personal decision either to accept or to refuse the demand of conscience/3, the moral agent engages either in an act of sanctity or in actual sin. Why is that? The answer lies in the unique conjunction of conscience/1 and conscience/2.

It was conscience/2 that led us to analyze and understand our situation in a particular (fallible) way. But we also have conscience/1. And that aspect of conscience demands, insists, requires (nonnegotiably) that we seek to do good and avoid evil. Thus, because the nonnegotiable obligation of conscience/1 permeates and fertilizes the fallible judgments of conscience/2, we find ourselves in the moment of action with a tentative yet absolute guide for our own actions. Is it possible that in following that conscience we may do that which is (objectively) wrong? Most certainly. Are we thus justified in saying that in doing so we have acted in a (morally) wrong way? By no means. It is the quintessence of human morality that we should do what we *believe* to be right, and avoid what we *believe* to be wrong. The fallibility of our objective judgment (conscience/2) in no way obviates that fundamental moral obligation.

Therefore, if it was accurate to say that conscience/2 kneels before the altar of truth, it is equally accurate to say that we kneel before the altar of conscience/3. If I genuinely believe that I should do something, it is not only accurate to say that I may do it. More than that, I should do it. Indeed, I must do it, and this for all the reasons that have been presented here.

Implications

A few comments about this presentation are now in order. First, it should be noted that this strong distinction between conscience/2 and conscience/3 would go a long way toward eliminating much contemporary confusion. Consider the endless debates over the maxim, "One must always follow one's conscience." It seems that arguments regarding the validity of this maxim result precisely from an unclarity about whether one means conscience/2 or conscience/3. One does not follow conscience/2; rather, conscience/2 follows the truth – and, indeed, does not always do that very well. But one must surely follow conscience/3 For in the last analysis that is the only possible guide for action by a free and knowing human person. This is precisely what Bernard Häring means when he declares: "Everyone, of course, must ultimately follow his conscience; this means he must do right as he sees the right [conscience/3] with desire and effort to find and do what is right [conscience/2]."[4]

A second observation has to do with the "orthodoxy" of this presentation, and particularly of the notion of ultimately absolute conscience. It is no doubt true that in recent years many Catholics have been led to believe that conscience is the enemy of the true moral life They have been told that in any situation of conflict between conscience and Church authority, they ought always to follow authority. We shall go into the role of Church authority in further detail shortly. But in the present context it still ought to be pointed out that this understanding is not the authentic tradition of the Catholic church.

Even Thomas Aquinas strongly supported the rights of conscience. His view, as summarized by theologian Josef Rudin, is that

anyone upon whom the ecclesiastical authority, in ignorance of the true facts, imposes a demand that offends against his clear conscience, should perish in excommunication rather than violate his conscience.[5]

The American bishops, in responding to the encyclical *Humanae Vitae*, made a similar point. It was, of course, the bishops' primary purpose to support the pope's teaching and to encourage Catholics to accept it in a spirit of cooperation. And so they did not particularly emphasize the rights of conscience. But they did affirm those rights. For example, they asserted that "we recognize the role of conscience as a 'practical dictate,' not a teacher of doctrine."[6] If that sentence had been phrased, "Even though we do not recognize conscience as a teacher of doctrine, we do recognize it as a practical dictate," the emphasis would have been quite different, but the basic affirmation would have been the same. And as if this were not enough, the bishops proceeded to a lengthy quotation from Cardinal John Henry Newman, one of recent history's more forceful spokespersons for the centrality of conscience:

When I speak of conscience, I mean conscience truly so-called. . . . If in a particular case it is to be taken as a sacred and sovereign monitor, its dictates, in order to prevail against the voice of the Pope, must follow upon serious thought, prayer, and all available means of arriving at a right judgement on the matter in question [7]

To say this is simply to say that conscience/3, to deserve its name, can only follow on the responsible exercise of conscience/2.

And one final quotation, this from contemporary moralist Josef Fuchs, who admirably unites the understandings of conscience/2 and conscience/3 that we have developed.

The dictate of conscience [3] . . . enjoys absolute certainty. For it dictates that the person acting ought to act according to the personal judgement which he has concerning the act [conscience/2]. . . In a word, the judgment [of conscience/3] . . . is not only infallibly true but is also absolutely certain.[8]

Conscience and Church Authority

Throughout this chapter we have made reference to the role of the Church as it relates to conscience and to the limits of that role. Before concluding, however, we should make explicit what has already been implied, and develop somewhat these reflections. But the reader should note that inasmuch as we have already indicated the unique personal character and inviolability of conscience/1 and conscience/3, we are here discussing the relationship between conscience/2 and the Church.

The first point to be made is very simple. It is that the Church, and particularly the hierarchical magisterium, has a very positive and very important role to play in the illumination of conscience. Why is this? There are a number of reasons.

First is the fact of human need. As we have seen, human persons, in the exercise of conscience/2, are not immediately in possession of the truth. And yet they must always seek the truth. The values for which they search are fragile and ambiguous. Consequently, these persons are genuinely needy, requiring all the assistance they can find. What is more, when we move beyond the individual case and view the culture as a whole, the same reality becomes increasingly evident. There is an overwhelming need for moral leadership in our world. Consequently, if the Church can fill that role, it will perform a genuinely valuable service.

A second reason that the Church should be viewed positively derives from its credentials in human history. There is no doubt that the Church has not always spoken unequivocally on behalf of moral values. There have been times when its behavior and its words betrayed those values. But the fact is that it often has been a force for the improvement of the human situation and for the protection of human dignity.[9] Perhaps this has been so precisely because of the shape of the Church. To the extent that it is a cross-cultural institution, it is perhaps more likely to overcome the biases and blindnesses that can afflict the consciences of people within a given cultural context. To the extent that the Church is the beneficiary of centuries of tradition, of the accumulated wisdom that is part of its temporal longevity, it is perhaps in a specially good position to provide an objective evaluation of the trends and tastes of the moment.

Or at least this can be the case. And often enough, the human community finds it to be the case. When men and women around the world turn out to cheer the man dressed in the odd white robe who has come to visit, often the reason is not because they are members of the Catholic church. It is not because they are believers, either. It is because they recognize in this man the symbol of an institution whose contribution to culture and civilization they admire. It is because they not only acknowledge the need for moral leadership in our time, but also celebrate the role the Church plays in providing that leadership. We, too, should celebrate that role.

A third reason that the Church should be viewed positively derives from Christian faith. For Catholics sincerely believe that the Holy Spirit inhabits the Church and, at least to some extent, guides and illuminates its actions. We do not arrogantly assert that the Church is identical with the kingdom of Christ; we are more than willing also to recognize the presence of the Spirit in other individuals and institutions (as the Second Vatican Council strongly affirmed). But we do assert that the Church is part of the kingdom, and that the Spirit is to be found here. Similarly, we do not profess that the Catholic church is the "unblemished bride" of Christ. No, inasmuch as the Church is a human institution, composed of human sinful people, it may sometimes be more appropriately viewed as the "whore of Babylon." But ever since the prophet Hosea, it has been part of the Judaeo-Christian tradition that God forgives the infidelities of the beloved, that God remains faithful even when we are unfaithful, and thus that God's faithful presence is a permanent and irrevocable promise.

It follows from this, then, that when conscience/2 sets out on its journey searching for the truth, it will take the time to listen respectfully to the insights of the Church. It will not listen in a way that makes it deaf to all other insights. But it will listen, and this because such listening is a dictate of common sense and a consequence of deeply held faith.[10] But if this is true, there is another truth as well. For the Church's role in moral reflection has distinct limits. And these ought also to be honestly acknowledged.

First, we should be aware of the fact that the Church never has issued an infallible pronouncement on a moral question. The First Vatican Council asserted the right of the pope (and by implication the Church) to speak in such a manner. But in fact that right has never been exercised. Therefore, all existing moral teachings of the Church fall in the realm of "ordinary magisterium." And although the category of "infallible teaching by way of ordinary magisterium" also belongs to Catholic theology, it seems as well to be a "species with no members," as the logicians say.[11] So what we have are teachings that, although assisted by the Spirit, are nonetheless susceptible to error and therefore fallible. Thus the possibility of error constitutes one limit to the Church's role as that is ordinarily exercised.

The danger of incompleteness constitutes a second limit. Morality has to do with concrete life, with infinitely variable confluences of action and circumstance. In the traditional vocabulary, it has to do with contingent things, things liable to variety and to multiplicity. As a result, the Church in its teaching will never be able to speak to the totality of the concrete situation in which any person finds himself or herself. The most that the Church can hope to do is address particularly important values that are part of that situation. Thus the teaching of the Church in moral matters is liable to a certain incompleteness, a certain partiality.

Individual moral agents will still be obligated to decide for themselves whether the instruction of the Church truly applies to their specific situation, and if so how. They will need to clarify, to apply, and to nuance that teaching for their own use.

Third, the Church's role in moral matters is limited by the possibility of inadequacy. Conscience/1 demands that human persons seek to do the really, objectively good thing in life. But persons are temporal beings subject over time to evolution and change. It is distinctly possible that what once was good, truly helpful to persons, truly serving their humanization and spiritualization, may someday become the opposite. Thus, even though a Church teaching may well have been both adequate and accurate at one time, it does not follow that it will always be so. On the contrary, there may well be need for revision and rearticulation.[12] What was once adequate teaching can become inadequate. And we ought not to be surprised.

The Church therefore has an important and responsible role in the process of moral education. But it is a limited role. It is limited by the possibility of error, the possibility of incompleteness, and the possibility of inadequacy. The prudent person acknowledges this, yet seeks from the Church whatever wisdom it is able to give her or him.

Conclusion

We can put all this one last way. The Catholic church claims the right to teach in matters of faith and morals. And we affirm that right. But in so doing we also acknowledge that faith and morals are quite different realities.[13] The truths asserted in the realm of faith are perduring truths, touchstones of unchanging belief. To the extent that they capture the reality of our unchanging God, they constitute unchanging and perennially true statements. The truths asserted in the realm of morals are quite different. They do not describe an unchanging reality such as God is, but rather the consummately changing reality of the human world. They are tools for the illumination of contingent realities. Thus they hold within themselves the potential for that mutability which is the destiny of all contingent things. To say that the Church was correct in asserting that Jesus is both divine and human is to say that Jesus always will be both divine and human. But to say that the Church was correct in asserting the immorality of charging interest on a loan is simply to say that this practice was once, in a particular context, immoral.[14]

In a fundamental way, then, the Church finds itself in the same situation as the individual moral person. Just as the individual's conscience/2 must search for the truth of its situation and, once having found it, must kneel before that truth, so must the "conscience" of the Church. We look to that ecclesial conscience with a certain confidence and trust, but we do not ask of it what it cannot give Throughout the whole exercise of conscience/2, as we maturely and prudently listen for whatever wisdom we can receive, we never forget that we are looking, not for the "approved," not for the "permitted," but for the "good." We and the Church together search for the true values of our situation; and once we find those values, we accept them as challenges for our own lives. It is that truth, that goodness, which is supreme; and to that both Church and moral agent must bow.

In the final analysis, then, the wisdom and the judgment of the Church are important, but they are not supremely important. Therefore, the genuinely important role of Church teaching must never be allowed to deteriorate into a "loyalty test" for Catholics. Is a Catholic who finds himself or herself able to agree with the judgment of the Church a better Catholic than one who cannot? We must never say so. For just as to use Church teaching properly is to celebrate it, to ask it to be more than it is is to destroy it. And to make of that valuable and cherished source of moral wisdom a tool for ecclesiastical discipline or a measure of religious fidelity is to betray it. Indeed, to see the moral teaching of the Church as a test of Catholic loyalty is ultimately to violate the nature of the Church, the nature of humanity, and surely the nature of conscience.[15]

Chapter 10

THE CHRISTIAN VOCATION

As we saw early in this book, the notion of covenant is one of the primary images for understanding the way people should live in the Judaeo-Christian tradition. For this idea highlights the dialogical character of that living; it focuses on the dynamic dialectic of call and response. But to say that as Christian people we have been called, that we have a calling, is literally to say that we all have a vocation (*vocare* – to call). So we will conclude this analysis of the Christian person by several reflections on the Christian vocation.

This use of the term "vocation" may at first seem strange. For some time it has had only a limited meaning, being identified with the entrance of individuals into the clerical state or religious communities. But the fact is that every Christian does have a calling, an invitation to enter into relationship with God, to respond by authentic living, and to adopt a lifestyle of fidelity and sincere generosity. Thus it is worthwhile to rehabilitate the idea of vocation, to free it from the tragedy of past limitations and to return it to its place of ethical and religious centrality.

So we reflect on the meaning of the Christian vocation, and in so doing we highlight three themes that complement and complete the Christian anthropology we have developed so far. We find that the Christian life is unique, communal, and graced. Let us attend to each of these themes in turn.

Unique

In seeking to understand the Christian life as vocation, we must acknowledge the high degree to which each one of us is unique. Granted that we have much in common with our sisters and brothers in the human community (a commonality that will be our primary focus in part III of this book); granted that we are rooted in our family, our nation, our culture; granted that the members of the human family constantly interact and influence one another, it still remains true that each of us is unique. Indeed, even as we participate in community, we each do so in a personal and unique way.

This fact is extremely important to our reflections. For it suggests an added dimension to the pursuit of the Christian moral life, a dimension too often overlooked. So often discussions of morality develop an almost exclusive focus on the common elements, on actions that all persons should do, postures that all should adopt. Even the understanding of fundamental option and fundamental direction that were developed here had a certain common focus. And, of course, that is not entirely avoidable. On the one hand, there is indeed much that is common in all human beings; such a thing as human nature does exist, and it does generate a certain number of universal moral obligations. On the other hand, if we are going to go to the effort of sharing ideas with one another, we will tend to emphasize those ideas that will be applicable to all. So a certain emphasis on commonality is probably inevitable. But that does not mean it is exhaustive. Quite the contrary.

Early in these pages, we contrasted the human act with the human person, and we saw personhood as a principle of continuity in the individual life, as an ongoing font of self-consciousness that directs behavior and assumes responsibility. By doing so, we implied already that each human person is to some extent unique. But it must be granted that we did not emphasize this uniqueness. Rather, we suggested a basic similarity among all human persons. By noting a number of transcendental characteristics of human personhood, we suggested that persons are fundamentally similar. In saying this, we came close to implying that persons are nothing more than individual instances of human nature, that they are mathematically disparate but essentially identical. And this implication we must now reject.

As persons we are not mere instances. We are also at least partly unique. The dynamics by which we guide and shape our lives through self-consciousness, the Christian character we develop over time, all this conjoins to differentiate us from one another and to highlight our utter particularity. We are not totally interchangeable with one another, totalitarian ideologies notwithstanding. We are from the beginning special and different, and over time our uniqueness becomes increasingly apparent.

But if this is true, and if it is also true that the call of God is addressed to the human person, that it is an interpersonal call to interpersonal relationship, then it follows that at least some moral demands may also be unique. After all, in the process of making a fundamental option a person does not merely say yes to life in general. He or she says yes to the concrete, specific, and therefore partly unique reality of this life. Thus, inasmuch as one's relationship to God is dependent on the response of the fundamental option, it is quite possible that one's salvation may be mysteriously worked out in terms of some action that would have no moral import at all to someone else.

Take, for example, the selection of a profession, a lifestyle, or a spouse. It has often been asserted that such selections are not the stuff of moral obligation, that they are free choices, that (to use an often cited instance) one is never obligated to become a priest, a member of a religious community or a pastoral minister. Now, this sort of position makes considerable sense from the perspective of human nature, of what is common to all human persons. For about a matter so personal it would be highly inappropriate to formulate moral norms of one kind or another. It would be completely out of line to attempt to say, in some general formulation, what people should or should not do.

But not so from the perspective of the unique human person. Is it not possible that I, being who I am, could not reject a felt impulse to ministry without at the same time rejecting the God-present-in-life that I encounter? Is it not possible that the uniqueness of myself, with talents and liabilities, with inclinations and attractions, might not also present itself to me as obligation? Is it not possible that in experiencing myself in this way, I am quite correct, quite in touch with the reality, that I am not a victim of some neurotic scrupulosity, but rather a healthy respondent to the prophetic dimension that must always remain part of the Christian life? Therefore, is it not possible that in articulating the challenge to "be what you are" we are actually summarizing the most profound and far-reaching dictate of Christian morality?

From the perspective of Christian vocation it is indeed possible. For we are at least partly unique; our vocation is at least partly specific to our personhood. And even if such obligations will never be able to be formulated, at least for anyone other than oneself, in any helpful way, that does not mean they are any less real.[1]

Communal

> No man is an island, entire of itself;
> Every man is a piece of the continent, a part of the main.

These words of John Donne poetically articulate a truism of human experience. We are all shaped by our experiences within the human community, we are radically social beings. And that sociality, if it does not entirely constitute our particular human lives, nonetheless profoundly and extensively affects them. Thus, to assess the meaning of the Christian vocation accurately, we must look not only to the individual, in his or her progressive Christian life, but also to the group, with all its myriad influences.

Indeed, so true is this need that the communal reality of the human vocation deserves a place of special attention at the end of the discussion of the human person comprising part II of this book. For if there is a danger in the forces of totalitarianism, a danger that swallows the individual spirit in the force of collectivity, there is equally – and perhaps more so in our day – a danger in individualism, a danger that condemns the individual to the meaninglessness of an unconnected, unrooted existence. As human persons we are connected, rooted, social beings. And only as such, paradoxically, can our individuality truly flourish.[2]

A precise delineation of the social dynamics of human experience is, of course, far beyond what can be attempted here. But it is interesting at least to note the greatly increased attention they are receiving in theology today. Catholic scholarship, from the Marxist liberation theologies of Latin America to the sociotheology of Canadian Gregory Baum,[3] is giving more and more attention to the social factors in Christian life. Protestant theology, in a reversal of its historic tendency toward individualism, is attempting to develop a positive theology of ecclesial community.[4] And on the other hand, the social sciences themselves are devoting considerable attention on religious phenomena.[5] Even psychology, a science traditionally oriented toward the individual, is becoming increasingly sensitive to these social realities.[6] Such pivotal works as *Habits of the Heart* are challenging Americans to attend to the dangers of individualism and to the radically social fabric of human fulfillment.[7]

And from the vantage point of the understanding of the human person developed in these pages, we can see that this is as it should be. Our line of argument in the previous chapters of this book did build out from a focus on the individual. For each of us does root our conscious journey of life-understanding in the "inner point" of self-awareness. But the argument quickly identified the many-layered relational fabric that constitutes that individual life. The Christian life, as we saw, is dialogical. And the dialogue between God and the human person is primarily transcendental, taking place through the mediation of creation's sacramentality.

Thus it is no surprise that the pursuit of the ethical life involves a pivotally important human dialogue as well. Whether the dialogue is between two individuals, between the individual and the group, or between various groups, the result is a process of growth or decline that is tremendously significant. Indeed, this author would wonder whether "morality" is even a meaningful term apart from the social situation. If there is no "other" in my life, no person who is important to me and to whom I am important, does it really make any difference how I behave? Would there, if we can put it this way, be any such thing as morality if I were the only human being on a desert island? Or would my action truly have no value? Is there, in other words, any such thing as "responsibility"? Or is it rather always a matter of "responsibility to/for another"?

It is true, of course, that God can function as an "other" in my life. Indeed, God is the ultimate "other." But as we have seen, God enters my life most profoundly and effectively not as a single categorical object next to other objects, but rather as the transcendental "within" of all the objects that I confront. Indeed, God enters my life in the deepest way as the within of the various other subjects in my life, of the human persons whom I encounter in a really human, interpersonal way. Thus it is at least dubious whether there would be any such thing as morality apart from this interpersonal, thoroughly social context.

This essential communality of the Christian vocation has, of course, immense implications for pastoral practice. It suggests that the promotion of a genuine Christian community in the parochial setting is a necessity. The protection and nurturing of healthy family life, in a modified form if the times truly demand it, must become a priority. Concern for individual morality must be matched by attention to the overall moral flavor of the society. It may be difficult to assess this moral fiber, and the effort may be open to all sorts of hypocritical abuses. But the task can be avoided only at the price of moral, and therefore existential, injury to the individuals who dwell there. And, in general, the Church must incarnate in its pastoral practice this central insight: that for people to realize their own potential, they must be rooted in a community where support and challenge make clear the significance of their behavior and the importance of their growth. For moral behavior apart from this community becomes at least difficult, and perhaps truly meaningless.

We, too, must remain conscious of this insight. And in the awareness of it we must modify and complement all that has already been said in these pages. Our vision of the Christian life is inadequate if it is seen as a "snapshot"; it is also inadequate if it is seen to include only a single person. Rather, our vision, inasmuch as it truly perceives the reality of the Christian vocation, is a "motion picture" involving many people. In some sense, together they live only a single Christian life. In large measure the individuals who comprise this community grow or decline together; they find the strength to affirm the goodness of life and the loving presence of God, or they capitulate to suspicion and distrust and fear, together. Although it is no doubt somehow true that the individual always retains ultimate control of the fundamental stance that shapes his or her life, still it is also somehow true that the corporate life exerts tremendous, often immeasurable, perhaps decisive influence in that process. So we must ask not only, "Where are you going?" and, "Who are you becoming?" but also, "Who are you with?"

Graced

"And where do you find the strength to do it?" Now, that is a different sort of question. It is not a question of analysis, it is a question of empowerment. It is not a question of theory, it is a question of life.

But this entire discussion of the Christian person has, so we claim, been a discussion about life. So it is appropriate that, as our last point, we incorporate the profound and perennial Christian conviction: "Things that are impossible for men are possible for God" (Lk 18:27). It is appropriate to talk of grace.

But to sketch out an authentically Catholic understanding of grace is no small thing. For, in the first place, the central idea is profoundly paradoxical. It asserts that the achievement of human hopes and dreams, of the deepest yearnings of the human soul, is something we are radically unable to effect. It is something we can only receive and accept as gift. But at the same time this achievement is also something we must participate in. It demands our active and free cooperation. Or, to put this another way, the doctrine of grace asserts that the arrival of humankind at its ultimate goal is completely the result of a divine, unmerited initiative. But at the same time it is also the result of a genuinely free human response.

What is this ultimate human goal? It goes by many names: fullness of life, the overcoming of isolation and alienation and the achievement of union with God and reality, personal and complete fulfillment, happiness, heaven, immortality. But no matter what the term used, the central assertion is the same: It comes to us only as gift (*charis*, the Greek word that is translated as grace), and still this giftedness does not compromise the reality of human freedom.

And this twin assertion is surely paradoxical, which is our first difficulty in articulating the Catholic theology of grace. A second difficulty arises from the fact that the Catholic doctrine of grace was largely developed in response to various heresies. The positions of Pelagius (b. 354) and his followers were viewed as overly biased toward human freedom. So in a series of documents in the fifth century, a "strong" view of grace was proclaimed by the Church. On the other hand, the positions of Luther (1483–1546), Baius (ca. 1513–1589), Jansen (1585–1638), and Quesnel (1634–1719) were seen as involving an excessive protection of divine initiative and a pessimistic vision of humanity. Thus, the Church responded by emphasizing human goodness and the reality of freedom at the Council of Trent and in subsequent documents. But the systematic integration of these two emphases, the achievement of some synthesis without loss of the necessary tension, was left to theologians through the centuries.

A third reason for our difficulty lies in the related questions that present themselves. Does not God's goodness necessarily imply a desire for the salvation of all? That is, is there not a "universal salvific will"? And if this is so, and if God's power is preeminent, then are we not confronted with "positive predestination"? If some human beings are actually not saved, does this not lead us to assert "negative predestination" as well? And if so, how can this be squared with divine goodness? With human freedom? Finally, can this whole line of thinking be synthesized with the doctrinal assertion that salvation comes also as a result of "human merit"? How can merit be conceived so as to avoid Pelagianism?

All these difficulties complicate our efforts to articulate the basic but paradoxical reality of grace. But the attempt must nevertheless be made. For apart from grace everything we have said throughout these pages is no more than partially true. So even though we cannot deal here with all the many questions that have been raised, some general comments must be offered.

Catholic theology has traditionally used several distinctions in discussing grace. And we should take note of these. First, it distinguished actual and habitual grace. Actual grace is that divine gift which empowers the human person for specific acts. Habitual (or sanctifying) grace is the person's ongoing state of "giftedness." Second, habitual grace was itself distinguished into uncreated grace, which is the Trinity itself as present to us, and created grace, which is the resulting (or prerequisite) modification within the human person.

Articulated this way, however, these traditional distinctions seem arid. How can they be understood? If it is true, as St. John said, that God is love, then perhaps the human reality of love can give us a way to understand them. For love, too, is always a gift.[8]

The notion of required or coerced love is a contradiction in terms. I can make you treat me well, but I cannot make you really love me. On the other hand, even if I can only accept your love as gift, still I must at least accept it. That is, I retain some freedom, for I can always reject your gift. I can actively close myself to your gift, turning away from its message of union and favoring the proud foolishness of isolation.

Still, I clearly should accept your gift, for my own sake as well as yours. And if I do, then several things immediately begin to take place. First, you become present to me in an entirely new and far richer way.

You become part of my world of meaning; you become important to and for me. You move from the status of an object occupying the physical space of the world to the status of a fellow subject now inhabiting also my own personal world of existence. Second, this presence makes a difference. It changes me, transforms me, calls forth from me powers of love and concern and generosity I didn't know I had (and indeed did not have before your love). You make me able to respond in love, both to you and to the others who also touch my life. You act, for me, as a "life giver." My oneness with you makes me somehow also one with all creation. And the "intercourse" of our love gift generates the pulse of life far beyond our exclusive relationship.

The implications of this informal phenomenology of love for the theology of grace should be obvious. God offers the gift of love, the gift of self. Nothing we do can require that gift. The most we can do is accept it. And accept it we must, for our freedom always permits us to reject it. If we accept this God-gift, then God becomes present to us (uncreated grace) and transforms our very being (created grace). We are new, with a new being and new powers of life. We become sanctified, made holy, and that holiness moves through us into all our world.

Our resultant state of being, then, is one of union: union with God, with our world, and somehow even with ourselves. It is one of affirmation, of acceptance, of embrace. As such, it is life giving. But to say all this is obviously to speak much as we did when we analyzed the notion of fundamental option. And that is no accident. For the relevance of the theology of grace to our project in this book occurs especially at that point.[9] A positive fundamental direction, and the positive fundamental option by which that direction comes into being, are only possible through grace, through gift. Only the free self-offer of God can render us capable of responding affirmatively to all of life as it confronts us. Only God's self-gift can transform us into the positive beings, the fulfilled and ultimately happy beings, we yearn to be. And only this free divine initiative can lead us to accept the presence of God in our own personal world not as some categorical "object," but rather as the transcendental Thou who is truly a partner in love.

Since this is so, it is of profound importance that we nuance everything that has been said in the previous chapters by this consideration of grace. The fundamental direction, if it be positive, is only possible through grace. The fundamental direction, if it be negative, can truly be called sin because it involves (indeed is constituted by) a rejection of grace. Consequently, among those human persons who are truly "adult," who have in fact made their first fundamental option, there are none who are "merely human." All adult human persons are either more or less than human. Either they are more than human because they have accepted that self-gift of God which is utterly "supernatural" in the sense that no human could demand or expect it, or they are less than human because they have rejected that love relationship which alone can lead to the fulfillment of their deepest human dreams. In frustrating the love initiative of God, they have ultimately chosen to frustrate even themselves.

This, then, is the vision of grace that must be integrated into our understanding of the human and Christian person. But before we conclude, one final question must be asked: How can all this be applied to those who have never heard the Gospel message? How can we conceive of grace operating in their lives? And here we recall the vision of Christ that was developed in chapter 3.

For God does not approach us directly, in some reflexive or even merely categorical manner. Rather, God approaches us through that world which is, most profoundly, a sacrament of God's own self. Inasmuch as everything in the world speaks God's Word, everything likewise is a potential opportunity for response to God's gift of love. And thus, without in any way compromising our dogmatic commitment to the gratuity of grace, we can still repeat what was said earlier: All who say yes from the depths of their being to anything also say yes to everything. All who accept reality as a sacrament of love accept the Being of love who is signed and sacramented through that reality. All who are gifted by the invitation to loving response, as all people surely are, and also accept that gift as they experience it within the categorical realities of their life, also live no longer just their own lives, but also the life of Christ in them, the life of God's own self. They are truly gifted (graced) persons. In the deepest sense of the word, they have been saved.

Conclusion

We bring these reflections on Christian anthropology to a close, then, on this challenging and inspirational note. Christian persons are persons called by God to relationship through and in this world they inhabit. They are called to live the Christian life. But this life is really a vocation. That means it is also unique, communal, and graced. It is dynamic and profound. And it is ultimately mysterious.

And rightly so. For the person whom we have been studying is ultimately mysterious.

The urge we feel to understand the human person, to comprehend the person by our best efforts of thought and conversation — surely this is a right and proper urge. It is, after all, part of the human vocation to know. But more than comprehension, it is contemplation that is our destiny. And so we must understand the limits of our understanding and gently supplant curiosity with awe.

And perhaps even with something more than awe. We do seek a thoroughly adequate, thoroughly comprehensive word. That is the human condition. But perhaps the message of the Christian gospel is that the word we seek is the Word himself. No other word will satisfy. And if that is true, then our final posture is clear: not merely to comprehend, nor even to contemplate – not, finally, to hold in awe. We are called, in the end, to adore.

That is the challenge. That is the vocation which – together – we must pursue in our lives. And that, surely, is mystery without end.

PART III

The Moral World

Chapter 11

AN INTRODUCTION TO OBJECTIVE MORALITY

The German philosopher Martin Heidegger captured a profound insight in his famous definition of the person as *Dasein*. The human person is not simply being (understood either as a noun or as a verb), but located being, limited, circumscribed, contextualized being. The human person is *Da-sein* ("being-there"), being-in-the-world.[1] And if it was important to spend the first half of this book looking inward, as it were, in order to understand the operative dynamics within the human person, it is equally necessary to look outward, to analyze the context within which the person exists and by which the person is somehow constituted.

Indeed, we acknowledged as much in chapter 9 when we noted that the inner sense of responsibility that is conscience/1 inevitably drives the moral agent out into the world of values in the search that is conscience/2. For the most part, however, the first half of this book was concerned with conscience/1 (and with the equally personal judgment that is conscience/3) and with the person as characterized by that sensibility. Now, however, we must try to grasp what it is that persons seek when they pursue the search for moral values.

For there is a real world out there. There is a world that is somehow radically independent of human intention. There is a world that quite literally exists whether we like it or not. We did not create it and we cannot make it not be. Just as denying the reality of gravity will not make us fly, so also ignoring the world of objective morality will not make it disappear.

Objectivity

But what do we mean by objective morality? Philosopher Dietrich von Hildebrand offers a helpful response to that question. In his *Ethics*

von Hildebrand pursues a phenomenology of human living, a nonjudg-
mental attempt merely to describe how we experience the various
aspects of our lives.[2] In so doing, he begins from the notion of
"importance."

To be human is, in fact, to find some things important and some
things not. What is more, we do not find all things important for the
same reason. Some of the things we cherish are important to us simply
because they are subjectively satisfying. They feel good, and therefore
we like them. Other aspects of life, however, we consider important
because of their utility. They are objectively good for us. Visits to the
dentist, the pursuit of an education, or regular exercise may or may
not be fun. But most people consider them somehow important
nonetheless.

These two categories of importance, however, do not, in von Hildebrand's judgment, exhaust our experience. On the contrary, he finds
that members of the human community consider some things important simply because they are good in themselves. They have a kind of
life of their own, independent of both our wishes and our needs, and
human persons cherish them for what they are. Truth, for example, may
be mightily inconvenient. It may even oppose my best interests, at least
in the short term. But try as I may, I cannot bring myself to consider it
unimportant. And the same can be said for beauty. I may personally be
bored by a Beethoven symphony, I may not be in the mood to contemplate a golden sunset, I may rarely take time to read a novel. But I would
consider it tragic if the world were purged of these realities. They are
important, apart from me, and they should in all events survive.

So also with ethical goodness. Honesty is important. So are fairness,
compassion, chastity, justice, and all those realities we have traditionally named "virtues." I may not always succeed in embodying them; I
may not even particularly want to. But that does not mean I really consider them unimportant. No, they are important and, in fact, important
in themselves.

To these realities that fall into this category of independent importance von Hildebrand gives the name "values." Whether they be
intellectual, aesthetic, or moral, values have this common characteristic
of independent importance. Values are there, present in our experience,
whether we like it or not. But that does not mean that all values are the
same. Von Hildebrand notes that if certain people lack the ability to discern the truth, we merely call them poor scholars. If they fail to
appreciate a work of art, we consider them uncultured, perhaps even
boorish. But if they have no sensitivity to the importance of justice or
fidelity, we consider them poor human beings. They are failures not
only in a certain respect, but also in the central meaning of their

humanity. So of all values, moral values are by far the most important, not because we say so, or even because we wish it so, but simply because phenomenologically we find it so.

So it is not sufficient to say that the human person is *Dasein*, located being. It is not sufficient to note that we exist "within a world." We must also note, with von Hildebrand, that our world has a certain objectivity, a certain intransigence. It has a certain quality of self-existence that we cannot dominate. Instead, it demands our acceptance and affirmation and, indeed, appreciation.[3]

To speak of these moral values as having importance in themselves is not necessarily to say that they would exist apart from the existence of human persons. To question whether this would be so is like questioning whether a falling tree in an unpeopled forest makes a noise. It all depends on how the question is understood. And there is no doubt that the moral values we have listed indicate modes of human living. Dogs and cats, after all, cannot really be "honest." But the point is that despite the fact that these values are part of the human world, they are not human constructs. Such values are not created by us, they are found by us. And having been found, they must be respected if we are to be our best selves.

At the same time, everything that has been said thus far also does not answer the many questions about the nature of these values, their specific characteristics, and how they are to be concretely lived out. Indeed, these sorts of questions will be our concern in the coming chapters. But the vision of scholars such as Heidegger and von Hildebrand does at least establish the context for our investigation. Our interest is the world in which human beings live. In particular, we wish to see it as a moral world, as a world of responsibility and accountability, a world of obligation and duty, a world of challenge and opportunity, a world of values. And we wish to discover precisely what all this means.

For if the insights of these philosophers tell us anything, they tell us that the world is there. Whether we like it or not it is there. And it will not go away.

Scholastic Vision

It has been our practice in this book to link our contemporary reflections to the traditions of Catholic moral theology. And that practice should be maintained in this present context. For Catholic moral theology has given tremendous attention to the reality of objective morality–indeed, some might maintain that it has focused on objectivity to the neglect of subjective factors. Inasmuch as we began with the subjective, we cannot be accused of this neglect. Now, we must not neglect the objective. For what we discovered in the first half of this book is that a proper appreciation of the subjective itself functions as a challenge to move outward. In the very moment that we discovered the preeminent importance of being sincere, we also discovered that sincerity demands a concern for finding the good. And this search for the good is what now claims our attention.

So once again we begin with a brief summary of the scholastic tradition. We do this not because this tradition will answer all our questions; rather, we do it because it will provide us with a very helpful perspective, and because it includes a number of insights that will greatly enrich our own reflections as we proceed.[4]

The starting point in the well-ordered universe of the Scholastics was God. And since God is the source of all reality, it follows that God is also the source of our moral obligations, of the moral "ought" or "law" that exists in our experience. What is more, the various names that we give God in theology (e.g., creator, omniscient, omnipotent, *Esse*, etc.) never really capture the mystery of divine being. Rather, they simply describe aspects of God as these aspects pertain to us. Since this is the case, there is no reason why we cannot create also a name for God-as-source-of-moral-law. And this the Scholastics did. Their starting point in objective morality, then, was the "eternal law." But as we have intimated, this law is not law at all. It is God, inasmuch as God is the source of moral law and obligation in our world.

Natural Law

God is the creator of the world, the source of all its being. And so, as God brings about the human world and human nature, so the eternal law brings about "natural law." Or to put this another way, as the eternal law is God under the aspect of lawgiver, natural law is human nature under the aspect of its inherent obligations. Natural law is that reality of our situation whereby things are, in fact, good or bad, right or wrong. In von Hildebrand's terms, natural law is the reality of moral values as these impinge on our consciousness. Natural law is not arbitrary; or at least it is no more arbitrary than creation itself. Natural law, in fact, is not anything at all added on to creation. Rather, it is creation itself as obligating and obligatory. It is coexistent and coextensive with creation.

But this general definition of natural law raised several questions that were typically addressed in the manuals.[5] For one thing, it prompted the question of whether the natural law is really law at all. Their answer was: "Yes and no!" Inasmuch as the natural law is a source of true obligation, inasmuch as it somehow stands outside persons and pronounces judgment on them, it can rightly be described as law. The natural law does involve demand; consequently, it can be experienced as a coercive force. And again, in this regard it is truly law. But inasmuch as the natural law is not a written law, does not exist in books or in official pronouncements, but rather is "written in their hearts" (Rom 2:15), it is not aptly termed "law." The natural law can, of course, be formulated, though the degree to which it can be summarized with real accuracy is a question to which we will have to return. But it does not primarily exist in such formulations. Rather, the natural law is the demand of creation, experienced in the lives of human persons and promulgated through the light of human reason. So although it is a law, it is a law of a special sort.

A second question was this: The natural law is rooted in the eternal law, that is, in the very being of God. But if we were to try to specify this grounding further, would we be more correct in locating the source of the natural law in the divine intellect or the divine will? Now, to a certain extent this is a strange and useless question. But it is significant for us in that the answer given tended to reveal the overall philosophical bias of the respondent. These biases will demand a good deal of our attention later on. Some authors, working from the analogy of human legislation and noticing the fact that in medieval life the existence of specific laws depended on the will of the monarch, concluded that the natural law, too, is an exercise of will. They judged that we should obey the natural law, as found in creation through the use of right reason, because that law reveals to us the will of God. Other authors, however, noted that the whole content of the natural law is oriented toward the fulfillment of creation as it exists – that is, that God's creation ought to achieve the fullness of being toward which it is pointed. Thus the existence of the natural law is nothing else than one aspect of that exercise of divine wisdom which is the shape of creation itself. It is thus an exercise of divine intellect with which we are expected to cooperate.[6]

A third question investigated whether the natural law ever changes. Or is it rather universally applicable to all humankind and permanently unchanging throughout history? Obviously the first answer to this question is that the natural law is just as static as creation, no more and no less. Well, then, is creation static? Here the manualists answered with a qualified affirmative. But let us note their qualifications.

First, the Scholastics acknowledged that human nature has been substantially changed in some ways by the theological situation of the human race. That is, human nature in the present fallen-redeemed situation is different than human nature before the fall (prelapsarian man), than human nature fallen and still unredeemed, and than fully blessed human nature in the next life. The result of these differences is that moral obligations change. Thus, for example, many Scholastics asserted that the natural right to private property exists only because of our fallenness. Otherwise it would be unnecessary, if not undesirable. Then again, perhaps the right under the natural law of governments to coerce their citizens into socially acceptable behavior likewise is premised on the reality of sin. So for the Scholastics there was at least this slight element of change in the situation of human nature and, consequently, of natural law.

Second, the authors of the manuals willingly acknowledged that the more concrete and technical questions of ethics require considerable skill to judge. They distinguished three levels of natural law norms: universal principles, immediate conclusions, and concrete applications. Universal principles, such as, "Do good and avoid evil," are known and appreciated by all human beings. Indeed, principles such as this are self-evident in the practical realm in the same way that the principle of contradiction is self-evident in the speculative realm. Immediate conclusions, such as the norms articulated in the Ten Commandments, were also considered easy to apprehend. Only a perverse stubbornness can prevent an individual from appreciating the correctness of these moral laws.

But in the case of concrete obligations, the Scholastics were willing to grant that the correct action is often difficult to discern. Some one course of behavior is objectively correct, of course, and others are wrong. But the clear perception of this right behavior is not easy. Given the intricacy and ambiguity of human life, to say nothing of the "darkness of intellect" that follows from original sin, moral agents often err in their judgments. And where experts have, through subtle reasoning and high intelligence, come to see what should be done, their conclusions will often be difficult to communicate in a convincing and self-evident manner. So the natural law, as it is known by us, will doubtless change.[7]

Third, the manualists also affirmed "change" in the natural law in the sense that different objective situations may ground different moral obligations. The Christian is always obligated to do what is right. But that rightness is rooted not only in the general nature of human persons but also in the objective but concrete details of the specific situation. To put this another way, obligation can arise not only from human nature as such, but also from one's "state in life." Thus correct sexual behavior will be quite different for married and unmarried persons. The right handling of money will be different for the banker and the laborer, for the wealthy bachelor and the poor father of several children. So, at the level of concrete applications, different moral obligations may sometimes apply.

In this limited sense, then, even the moral theology of the manuals can be aptly termed a "situation ethic." But notwithstanding these details, there is no doubt that the manualist tradition generally emphasized the universal and unchanging character of natural law. They might briefly grant a certain amount of existential diversity and a considerable amount of epistemological difficulty, but the weight of their argument always returned to the permanent and the absolute.

Positive Law

It is clear, however, that the natural law by itself is insufficient for the ordering of human life. Given the obvious fact that we are social beings, beings who must coordinate with and relate to our fellows, it is obvious that there is also a need for a variety of regulations by which to organize common life. So, in accord with the data of experience, the manualists spoke of a third general category of law, "positive law." This term is ambiguous in contemporary English, but it was coined for the simple reason that such laws are "posited." They are the creations of human ingenuity, not given self-evidently by the fabric of creation like the natural law. Positive laws can be expressed in both affirmative and negative propositions (and hence are not necessarily "positive" in that sense of the word). But in either case they constitute the tools of the human enterprise of societal living.

Scholastics envisioned several subdivisions of positive law. First, they distinguished divine and human law, on the basis of the particular law's creator. Divine positive law is a category difficult to justify today; it largely resulted from naive scriptural exegesis. But from the manualists' point of view, it was clear that the Old Testament contained numerous ritual requirements that, though not at all derived from natural law, nonetheless appeared to be God's will. So they had no alternative but to view these as "rules made by God." What is more, the manualists sought to explain the demand of Christ that Christians make use of the sacraments by a similar construction. After all, there seems to be nothing in the nature of things that would make baptism truly necessary for salvation. We will leave to sacramental theologians to decide whether this way of expressing things is most appropriate; we simply report the historical fact that Scholastics had this understanding.

Human positive law is much easier to comprehend. In fact, its existence is both self-evident and self-justifying. But that did not prevent many of the manuals from pursuing an analysis that was tremendously lengthy and detailed. In part because of the intimate relationship between traditional moral theology and canon law, the introduction of the category of human positive law became the occasion for a lengthy excursion into the varieties of laws, the nature and characteristics of different jurisdictions, the obligations of good citizenship, and so on. They not only distinguished human positive law into civil and ecclesiastical, they also proceeded to subdivide each of these categories several more times. As a result, despite the clearly more central importance of natural law to the task of moral theology, many of the manuals spent exponentially more pages on their consideration of positive legislation.

Conclusion

We will attempt to avoid this distortion in our discussions here. On the contrary, we will try to make the issues of natural law our primary focus. We will consider the idea of natural law in the Scriptures in chapter 12. We will recapitulate the history of the idea of natural law in chapter 13. Then, on the basis of this data, we shall attempt in chapters 14 and 15 to develop a systematic understanding of natural law that will be appropriate to our contemporary situation. This understanding will force us to reconsider several common maxims of morality in chapter 16. The understanding will also force us, in chapter 17, to engage a very pointed contemporary debate about the natural law, to clarify the various current positions and to indicate how our position is justified in light of the different concerns. Finally, in chapter 18, we shall add a number of important related ideas having to do with the limits of our human ability to know the natural law.

Only after this entire investigation is completed will we return to the question of positive law. We will, of course, return to it (in chapter 19), for positive law inevitably plays a significant part in the conduct of our daily lives. But our consideration will attempt to make clear that, no matter how immediately relevant, the question of positive law is a subsidiary and tangential question at best. Even when we do pursue that consideration, our focus will still be that of moral theology. We shall not try to speak as lawyers. Instead, we shall try to develop some specifically theological insights into the nature, purposes, and limits of human positive law in a Christian and Catholic context.

In all this, generally, our abiding goal will be to understand the nature of objective morality, as viewed from the perspective of the Christian vision of life and within the flow of the Catholic tradition and heritage.

Chapter 12

MORAL LAW IN SCRIPTURE

$\mathbf{B}$efore we begin to develop a contemporary theory of natural law, or even to see if such is possible, we ought to be sure we are in contact with the insights of our tradition. Both the pages of sacred Scripture and the theological developments of the historical Church offer a richness of context we dare not overlook. In the next two chapters, therefore, we will attend to this context and try to penetrate those themes and developments that can serve us in our task.

In investigating the biblical source, however, we cannot limit ourselves to the precise term "natural law." To appreciate what the text has to offer, we must adopt a broader stance and think in terms of law in general. And this both because the more general term is logically previous to, far more common than, and quite pivotal to the biblical vision and because existing references to natural law, as we shall see, themselves relate it to law in general. Thus we will begin by asking about the notion of law in the Jewish Scriptures. This will lead to a detailed consideration of the Ten Commandments. Moving into the Christian Testament, we shall examine the two great commandments of Jesus. Paul's many discussions of law will follow, and then we will conclude with his comments precisely on natural law.

Law in The Jewish Scriptures

To understand the religious heritage of Israel, it is essential to understand the idea of law. For it is central, perhaps definitive of the Jewish experience. Nonetheless, at various times in the history of Israel, and in various strata of writing in the Jewish Scriptures, the term (*torah, nomos*) had somewhat different meanings. It could refer to individual moral precepts, to the Book of Deuteronomy, to all the sayings of Moses, or to the whole collectivity of obligations imposed by Yahweh. Ultimately, indeed, the entire scriptural library came to be summarized as the "Law and the Prophets." There were various types of law: moral demands, dictates of religious ritual, and legal stipulations for the conduct of social life.[1] And although references to law abounded throughout the Jewish Scriptures, there were several preeminent collections of laws: the Book of the Covenant (Ex 21-23), the entire Book of Deuteronomy, the Holiness Code (Lev 17-26), and what is known as the Priestly Code (Lev 1-7, 11-15; Num 28-29).

But no matter what the diversities of content, style, or context, the notion of law always had certain characteristics for Israel. Several of these features should be isolated. First, law was not a separate reality, but rather a consequence of *covenant*. Only because of the relationship between Israel and God were the various laws important, only because of Yahweh's commitment to the people were the laws given, and only because of their commitment to Yahweh were they observed. The laws were not symbols of some abstract moral order, nor were they the arbitrary demands of a cruel and distant deity. No, the laws (and the general reality of "law") were seen as symbols of the intimacy between God and the people. And obedient adherence to them was seen as an expression of that intimacy.[2]

Following from this, the second common characteristic of law, as that was described in the Scriptures, was that it was a manifestation of Israel's *election* by God. Inasmuch as the law followed on the divine initiative of the covenant, it was a point of pride for Israel. The giving of the law and their right and duty to accept it were privileges they cherished and celebrated. The unusually long text of Psalm 119 is a classic example of the "joy in the law" that was part of the Israelite heritage.

The emphasis on *obedience* was a third salient characteristic. In some ways, the entire religious life of Israel was conceived as an exercise in obedience – not blind obedience, to be sure, but a free and humble response to the love of God. This is why, as we have seen, the Jewish Scriptures always viewed sin as an offense against the Lord, not primarily as an offense against the injured party. The people were bonded to their God, and all the aspects of their lives were to express their singleminded obedience to God's demands.[3]

But to focus on obedience is not to imply that the laws were seen as empty rules. On the contrary, the law was seen as a divine gift, as a series of demands whose observance was in Israel's own best interests. As one author beautifully puts it:

God's election had, indeed, meant "political" freedom for the seminomadic tribes that came out of Egypt, and this liberation was deeply, ineradicably impressed upon Israel's historical memory. God had rescued them from servitude to men, and from the disaggregation and chaos of their life in Egypt; the law, by ordering their life, gave them justice and security, and by pre-empting their service for God, put a seal upon their freedom. The Decalogue was their "bill of rights."[4]

Saying this, of course, is much like saying that the law was a summary of some sort of natural law. And one might well argue, post factum, that this was the case. But we must be clear that this was not Israel's way of thinking. They simply acknowledged two central truths: that happiness and fulfillment were impossible apart from the Lord their God, and that God had enjoined these commandments on them. Thus for the pious Israelite, even if immediate prosperity and success were not forthcoming, the law remained the divine gift whose observance was, in some ultimate sense, in his or her own best interests. And this was precisely because it came from the hand of a near and loving Lord.

All this leads to a last characteristic of Old Testament law: It generated a strangely beautiful and compelling sort of *legalism*. This term, reserved as it usually is for empty and fear-motivated ritualism, is generally conceived negatively. And in our own systematic reflections here, we will often use it in that way. But we ought to acknowledge nonetheless that a different sort of legalism exists. There is a posture that primarily evaluates actions not in terms of their objective and immediate significance, but rather in terms of their potential as symbols of love, that sees behavior less as a tool for the accomplishment of tasks and more as a word speaking the language of love. For one who adopts this posture, even the most apparently empty of actions is full of devotional potential. Such a person is a legalist, but a legalist of a tremendously rich, poetic, and saintly sort. For the best of the Jewish tradition, this is precisely the significance that the law always had.[5]

Ten Commandments

But of all the laws in the pages of Scripture, perhaps those most celebrated are the laws of the Decalogue. To our own day the Ten Commandments remain an element near the center of the lived and celebrated faith. So we should give them some particular notice in this summary.

The first thing to be noted about the Decalogue is that it is not a single, tidy biblical statement. It appears in a quite complete form in two different passages in the Jewish Scriptures (Ex 20:1-17; Dt 5:6-21), and various portions can also be found elsewhere (e.g., Ex 12:15-17; Ex 21; Dt 27:15-26; Lev 19:11-18). What is more, there are several ways of dividing the text, with the result that even today three different enumerations are customary with various religious groups. Nonetheless, the basic structure and content of the commandments is sufficiently clear and well known to permit some further analysis. And this we do through a series of questions.

How old is the Decalogue? There was a time when scholars judged these commandments to be the product of late Israel. The argument was that they seemed to presume a settled agrarian society and to possess a subtlety that could only come after considerable development. Now, however, the weight of scholarly opinion seems to have gone the other way. It appears that at least significant parts of the Decalogue not only are not the product of a period after its alleged source at Sinai, they are actually the product of a period before Sinai. On this basis, then, the Decalogue continued to evolve through the periods of Israel's history.[6]

Was the Decalogue unique to Israel? No. At least the concrete requirements of the Fourth through Tenth Commandments can also be found in the Egyptian "Book of the Dead" and in Babylonian literature. It is true that there are no other lists exactly like the Ten Commandments. Most of the others are much longer. But they do include among the prohibited behaviors the same familiar items. Indeed, some are even more stringent. The Code of Hammurabi, for example, gives wives a number of rights that were not recognized in Israel. So the notion that the moral dictates of the Decalogue are either unique or particularly enlightened simply cannot be supported. (This suggests that it may be appropriate to view these moral demands as being, in fact, some sort of natural law.)

But does this mean there is nothing unique about the Ten Commandments? No. On the contrary, these statements are quite special in two ways: their context and their function. First, as regards context, it is very noteworthy that the Decalogue is not really a moral document; it is a religious document. The various moral strictures are placed, quite powerfully, in the context of covenant. They are justified by and related to the First Commandment: "I am the Lord your God." As some have put it, there is really only one commandment. And that commandment is followed by nine consequences.[7]

Second, the Decalogue is quite special because of its function. Scholars tell us that this text is far more liturgical than ethical. It was proclaimed at the Feast of Tabernacles as a way of expressing and celebrating the mystery of covenant. And this proclamation was part of a liturgy of rededication, by which the people recommitted themselves to the faithful Lord. The pivotal First Commandment was announced, the obvious consequent prohibition of idolatry was asserted ("no other gods before me"), and then some of the more obviously seductive "other gods" were specified. (You will recall that, in chapter 7, we noted that the biblical perspective saw all sin as reductively idolatry.)

These specifications were no surprise to the people; common sense would lead one to much the same conclusions. And the Israelites were under no illusion that these prohibitions might express the totality of their moral responsibilities. Clearly, the good person must do far more than is mentioned in this list. But the proclamation had a powerful effect nonetheless. No matter how much diversity there was among the people, no matter how widely dispersed across the countryside they might be, they were still one people. For they shared the one God to whom they were committed, and they shared a willingness to respond to that God through right living, some of the more obvious examples of which could quickly be outlined in a striking and poetic formulation.

To describe the Decalogue in this way, as a cultic text with some minimal ethical components, leads one to wonder about the specific prohibitions. Are they really so minimal? What, after all, was really prohibited? That is our next question.

Scholars tell us that the more concrete commandments were, indeed, minimalistic and that the texts had meanings quite different from those we naively presume. For example, the Fourth Commandment only forbade cursing one's parents (for to do so would, by implication, be to curse the source of one's own life, therefore oneself, and therefore the Lord who is Lord of life). The Fifth prohibited killing (whether intentional or accidental) within the community. Nothing was said about respecting the lives of foreigners. The Sixth Commandment really supported the "property rights" of a husband by forbidding sexual involvement with a married woman; liaisons with single women and recourse to prostitutes were unmentioned. The Seventh prohibited the kidnaping of Israelite freemen, and the Ninth and Tenth gave the same protection to the man's dependents (wives, children, slaves) and property. And the Eighth Commandment opposed only perjury in a court of law.

From all this, then, it is clear that the Decalogue did not present a particularly sensitive ethic, that the revelation of God's election of Israel neither included revelation of moral specifics nor guaranteed that the people would quickly perceive the ideal of human behavior. But, as we have indicated, this was not a cause for any special concern. For the Decalogue was never expected to express the ultimate in morality.

Indeed, a careful reading of the text makes clear that the Decalogue was not particularly concerned about individual morality in any form. Rather, its consistent focus was the needs of the community, and it prohibited those actions that might injure the community. It was the survival and flourishing of God's people as a group that was important, and this precisely because they were God's people. So the Decalogue was a tremendously important document – indeed, a primary statement of Israel's life. But its importance was not precisely ethical.[8]

Two Commandments

We now move to the Christian Scriptures. We have already seen, in chapter 4, the aspect of "demand" that was integral to Jesus' message, so there is no need to return to that more general theme.[9] But several ideas that immediately pertain to our search for natural law should now be pursued. We begin with Jesus' teaching of the two New Commandments (Mt 22:34–40; Mk 12:28–34; Lk 10:25–28) because these are so often contrasted with the Ten Commandments of the Old Law.

This opposition is, of course, a great exaggeration. For one thing, that posture of love which was summarized in the New Commandments was also a clearly central reality for the life of Israel. To understand the Decalogue in a way that makes love irrelevant is a travesty that only later generations of Christians would dare to think. For the people of Israel, the love intimacy of covenant was the only thing that gave meaning to their moral and religious lives. So for this reason it is an exaggeration to oppose the New and Old Commandments.

It is also an exaggeration for another reason. And that, simply, is the fact that the New Law was part of the Old: "You shall love the Lord, your God, with all your heart, and with all your soul, and with all your strength" (Dt 6:5). And "You shall love your neighbor as yourself" (Lev 19:18). What is more, the existence of these two commands, and their preeminence as a summary of the "whole law and the prophets," was well known in the time of Jesus. We can only presume that Jesus himself was well aware of them.

Consider, for example, the text in Mark (12:28–34). A scribe questions Jesus about the heart of the law. Jesus answers with the two commandments. And the scribe responds: "Excellent, Teacher! You are right." Now, if Jesus were really introducing some radically new concept (as people sometimes seem to suggest), the scribe's response would be either absurd or outrageous. But it is neither. In this episode he has been testing Jesus on his knowledge of legal scholarship. And Jesus has passed the test.

So the proclamation of the New Commandments does not represent the introduction of any radically new ideas. But to say this is not to say that Jesus made no contribution whatever in this teaching. Rudolf Schnackenburg, in a classic statement, makes clear that this is not the case. He says that Jesus'

action was threefold: he revealed the indisoluble interior bond between these two commandments; he showed clearly that the whole law could be reduced to this and only this chief and double commandment; and he reinterpreted "neighborly love" as "love of the nearest person," that is he interpreted it in an absolutely universal sense.[10]

So perhaps the most balanced conclusion would be that Jesus did not introduce an altogether new concept in his preaching of the dual commandment of love. But he did move the Jewish tradition ahead by a sort of quantum leap. He took the materials of his own heritage, he shaped them according to his own vision, and in so doing he produced a special focus and thrust for his own moral teaching. He produced a moral ideal that St. Augustine could summarize quite accurately in his famous dictum: "Love and do what you will."[11]

Paul on Law

One last series of reflections on the reality of law is required. And these revolve around Paul's thought. We will begin by noting the overall thrust of Paul's understanding of law, and then we will look at his specific references to natural law.

That Paul was in continuity with the Gospel tradition we have just considered (indeed, as we know, committed it to writing before the Gospels were finally formulated) is clear. In his letter to the Romans he declared that

the commandments . . . are all summed up in this, "You shall love your neighbor as yourself." Love never wrongs the neighbor, hence love is the fulfillment of the law. (13:9f)

But he did not merely mimic the teaching we find in the Synoptics and in John. Rather, Paul developed ideas particularly his own. And surely one of the most powerful of these is his conception of the opposition between the law and the Spirit.[12]

As is well known, Paul insisted on rejecting any myth of self-righteousness held by his readers. We do not save ourselves; neither ritual purity nor moral correctness can purchase the gift of divine grace and love. Therefore, to the extent that the law is a symbol of that presumptuous independence, the law must be rejected as well. We are saved not by the law but by the Spirit of God.

Now we have been released from the law – for we have died to what bound us – and we serve in the new spirit, not the antiquated letter. (Rom 7:6; cf. also Gal 3:13f)

This new life of the Spirit can, of course, be called a law. It does not represent a lifestyle of license; rather, it demands its own style of generous love. But it is a law in a very different sense.

The law of the spirit, the spirit of life in Christ Jesus, has freed you from the law of sin and death. (Rom 8:2)

My point is that you should live in accord with the spirit and you will not yield to the cravings of the flesh. . . . If you are guided by the spirit, you are not under the law . . . (Gal 5:16, 18)

The law of the Spirit, the law of the Christian's new being, is an inner law. It is not a law imposed by God on unwilling humankind. Rather, it is, if we may put it this way, the result of intimate communication between the heart of a loving God and the heart of the believing human person. Indeed, viewed most profoundly, this law is a kind of revelation, a gift of God, that far surpasses the revelation and gift of the Old Law. For this law of the Spirit is God's own self. Thus, in this law is found a very real and very profound sort of human freedom. "The Lord is the Spirit, and where the Spirit of the Lord is, there is freedom" (2 Cor. 3:17).

In a certain sense, then, Paul stands as a model of that process we noted in chapter 4, the move to the interior. Any taint of superficiality, of legalism or ritualism, must be rejected. The arena of God – the kingdom, call to conversion, discipleship, and law – is to be found in our hearts. The covenant between God and the people is a relationship, indeed. And like any genuine relationship it is primarily a matter of the heart, of the inner personal intention. Of course, this intention needs to be expressed in behavior. But this does not mean that behavior, by itself, can ever suffice. Behavior is at most the consequence. The core reality lies much deeper. It lies at the level of the Spirit.

Paul on Natural Law

This emphasis on interiority is evident in a special way in the first and second chapters of Paul's Letter to the Romans. For there he speaks of something very like our idea of natural law itself, the law that is not announced from the outside but that rather is heard and experienced in the depths of one's own heart. Let us begin by quoting the two salient texts in their entirety.

The wrath of God is being revealed from heaven against the irreligious and perverse spirit of men who, in this perversity of theirs, hinder the truth. In fact, whatever can be known about God is clear to them; he himself made it so. Since the creation of the world, invisible realities, God's eternal power and divinity, have become visible, recognized through the things he has made. Therefore these men are inexcusable. (Rom 1:18ff)

Sinners who do not have the law will perish without reference to it. . . . When Gentiles who do not have the law keep it as by instinct, these men although without the law serve as a law for themselves. They show that the demands of the law are written in their hearts. (Rom 2:12, 14f)

So here we find Paul making a number of related, and very significant, assertions. He claims that God's self-revelation to us is not only through direct intervention, but also through "the things he has made." From this we can presume that we are capable of knowing God in this natural way, too. Moreover, Paul believes that even those pagans who are not gifted with the Old Law know what they ought to do. For these moral demands are proclaimed not only by revelation but also by instinct. Similarly, the requirements of morality are heard not only by the ears but also by the heart/conscience.

Now, we must be clear that Paul is not "doing" philosophical ethics in these passages. He is neither proposing the concept of natural law nor supporting the somewhat optimistic view of the human person that goes with that concept. Indeed, his actual intent is quite the opposite. Paul's emphasis in this part of the Letter to the Romans is on the mystery of our salvation in Christ. And in the process of developing that theme he wishes to assert strongly the insufficiency of any other humanly accessible reality. Paul proves this assertion by the fact that "all have sinned." Those who possess the law are not thereby saved; for by highlighting their evilness the law has simply become an "occasion of sin." Indeed, "no one will be justified in God's sight through observance of the law; the law does nothing but point out what is sinful" (Rom 3:20). But this line of argument would seem to suggest that those under the law are worse off than others; knowing what is right only gives them more chances for failure. But Paul rejects this conclusion. No, he says, all people are equally burdened by sin. For what the Jew knows through the law, we all know in our consciences.

Thus Paul's proclamation of general moral knowledge is actually part of his proclamation of the general need for salvation. His reference to natural law is a symbol not of our right to be proud but of our need to be humble. But perhaps this Pauline emphasis only serves to make his texts more interesting. For we certainly would not claim that we are able to do the good consistently by our own power. Indeed, the Christian doctrine of grace proclaims just the opposite. So we have no quarrel with Paul on this account. But if, while maintaining this God focus, Paul nonetheless suggests that we can truly know the good and that this good is a human, this-worldly good, then he has said something very important. He has articulated a vision of reality into which a concept of natural law most surely fits. And he has given no small basis on which to build on our own reflections.[13]

Conclusion

We have seen that the notion of law meant many different things at various points in the development of Scripture. On rare occasions it seemed to mean something very like our idea of natural law. Much more commonly, it meant the Mosaic Law. But even these latter demands are, on examination, revealed to be quite human insights into the good that one must do. Indeed, they are found to be insights not unlike those of Israel's pagan neighbors. Thus they, too, though clearly expressive of a religious spirituality, can nonetheless somehow be understood as part of the natural law.

But to assert this is obviously to maintain a very colloquial understanding of the term "natural law." And for the overall purposes of this book, that will not suffice. The history of secular thought and the history of the Church's reflections on its own identity reveal considerable sophistication in the handling of that term. So the next step in our investigation will be to recapitulate some major intersections along the road of that extensive history.[14]

Chapter 13

THE HISTORY OF NATURAL LAW

We have seen the ways in which the notion of natural law, if not the term, was exploited in the pages of sacred Scripture. Now, before we synthesize an understanding for our own time, we ought to give explicit consideration to the wider history of the concept. The purpose of this chapter, then, is to provide a general outline of the evolution of the idea of natural law. It will be impossible to be complete, of course, but perhaps we can isolate certain highlights that will not betray the more subtle flows of history and will nonetheless suffice for our purposes.

Greeks

Probably one of the more amazing things about the notion of natural law is the fact of its early emergence in the history of humankind. Indeed, one could plausibly argue that some sense of moral accountability (what we earlier termed conscience/1) is absolutely coextensive with human existence as we know it. Be that as it may, the specific idea and term of natural law first emerged in the midst of Greek civilization. Whereas the earlier Greek tragedies, for example, had turned on the capricious will of the gods, the later plays seem to have grasped in a compelling way the unyielding reality of objective obligation. As has often been noted, it is precisely the disproportion between ill will and ill effects that provides the tragic experience in these plays. Morality, they seem to be saying, is not merely a matter of intention. It is also a matter of responding to life as it is. And failure to do so, even unintentional failure, wreaks havoc for those involved.

The notion of natural law was also considered by Greek philosophers, but to varying degrees and in varying ways. In a certain sense Aristotle's *Nichomachean Ethics* depends on some idea of natural law for its whole validity. Aristotle does use the term or some equivalent in a number of cases. But curiously enough, he does not develop a theory of natural law as such. On the contrary, it was left to the later Stoic philosophers to explicate these ideas. And for them natural law was precisely the objective demand placed on humankind to conform to the givenness of reality. We find ourselves in a cosmos that is fundamentally static, rigid, and unyielding. If we wish to survive, let alone to develop as we ought, we must accept these facts of life. We must learn to live with life, not resisting, not pretending to control it, not attempting to mold it to our will, but rather accepting its domination and demands.

Given the general Greek commitment to a cyclic view of history, of course, this understanding of natural law is not surprising. Even less is it surprising if we realize how much this vision resonated with their experience. In a world without easy access to heat and light, in a world where preservation of food was difficult at best, conformity to the demands of reality and cooperation with the rhythms of life were indeed the keys to survival. Thus, the extrapolation of this experience into a theory of natural law was an eminently reasonable project. In any case, this extrapolation is what occurred in Greek civilization.[1]

Romans

The Roman world, as is well known, was quite different in style from the Greek. If we may put it this way, the Romans were the activists of the ancient world. They were the conquerors, the pragmatic rulers, the politicians of a sort. Because of these "expansionist" commitments, they were also the lawyers. To this day, scholars revere Roman civilization for its gift to the Western world of an appreciation of law and of its development. Thus it is to be expected that the Romans would build on the Greeks, modify the earlier views, and greatly expand the understanding of natural law. In fact perhaps the Romans are the parents of natural law, if one puts the emphasis on the second term. For while the Greeks primarily reflected on the realities that confront us – human nature and the world – the Romans spotlighted the law of the natural order and human nature and, in fact, compared and contrasted that law with the other laws of their experience.

One can hear this Roman activism, this optimism toward life, in the way Cicero (d. 43 B.C.) emphasizes things when he speaks of "true law which is right reason in agreement with nature."[2] There is, indeed, something natural, to which we should conform ourselves. But what is natural is right reason, human intelligence, prudent and thoughtful action directed to humane ends. Here is no abject capitulation to the facts of life; instead, we find a willingness to take on life, to use common sense and intelligence to solve its riddles and control its caprices.

The legal philosopher Gaius (ca. A.D. 160) betrayed a similar vision. He distinguished *jus civile* (civil law) from *jus gentium* (law of the nations). He saw the former as including all those regulations and customs that are specific to a single group or society. *Jus gentium*, on the contrary, referred to laws that are, as experience shows, the common possession of all. They are rules of behavior that are pandemic and therefore provide the basis for the interaction of various cultures. But although Gaius noticed and acknowledged this sort of universal law, he did not emphasize its necessity. We do not hear him speaking in the passive, almost fatalistic terms of the Greeks. Rather, he simply acknowledged the empirical fact of these universal laws, these natural laws, and sought to appreciate their utility.

As Roman history proceeded, however, a certain amount of the Greek influence began to reemerge. (It would be fascinating to speculate on the relationship between this shift and the deterioration of Roman culture.) And it is well exemplified in the categories of Ulpian (d. 228). For although Ulpian accepted Gaius' terminology, he so modified its meaning and so added to it as to fundamentally shift the perspective. For Ulpian there were three sorts of law. *Jus civile* was for him, as for Gaius, the collectivity of specific laws devised by various communities for their own reasons and purposes. Ulpian also spoke of *jus gentium*. But for him this term referred to those somewhat arbitrary laws that nonetheless transcend the boundaries of particular societies. Ulpian's *jus gentium* was not unlike our contemporary notion of international law, clearly a human construct, going beyond self-evident moral demands and yet reasonable enough to justify general acceptance and appreciation.

But the real contribution of Ulpian was a third term that he added: *jus naturale* (natural law). He described this term as a "rule of action common to man and all the animals." Apparently Ulpian considered man far more like other animals than unlike them. He seemed to feel that what was fundamental was the brute facticity of our being-in-the-world. The givenness of reality impressed him. Thus he saw the natural law as the demand placed on human beings (as on all beings) to be what they are, to conform themselves to the facts of life, to accept themselves and their fate, to be docile fellow animals in the world.

Gone is Cicero's celebration of human reason. Gone is Gaius' vision of intelligent beings shaping the openness of the world to their own envisioned ends. For Ulpian, reason's only task is to discern the facts and laws that are then obeyed. It is true that we are different than other animals. But the difference lies, we might say, at the level of means and not ends, of method and not meaning. Whereas other animals know and pursue their natural functions by instinct, we must discover ours by intelligence. But having discovered them, the proper response is the same: obedience. That is the implication of Ulpian's understanding.

With the close of the Roman period we have the terms of a perennial debate well established. And before continuing, we should try to articulate it in a strong, concise form. Are we fundamentally identified with the animal kingdom, as the Greeks and Ulpian said? Are we basically beings who use our intellects to conform to the facticity of nature? Or are we primarily different, as Romans such as Cicero and Gaius said? Is our task to shape and control our world, to guide it to our own ends? Or again, looked at from the perspective of the world, do we live in a situation that is basically closed, predetermined, univocal in its meaning and possibilities? Or do we live in an open creation, filled with multiple possibilities, a creation possessed of multivalent and malleable meanings?

Granted that these alternatives are matters of emphasis. After all, in Heideggerian terms human persons are both "being" and "world-context." We are both creativity and facticity. Still, the emphasis that one elects is significant. And probably such an election cannot be avoided even in a definition that attempts to incorporate both the Greek and Roman visions. Shall we understand natural law as the "obligation (perceived by reason) to conform to nature"? Or shall we see it as the "obligation (built into nature) to use reason in moral judgment"?[3]

These are the questions we inherit from the Greeks and Romans. They are the questions to which succeeding cultures have repeatedly returned.[4]

Medievals

For example, Isadore of Seville (d. 636) reflected on these questions, and on the very terminology developed by Gaius and Ulpian, and sought to bridge them. Ostensibly he accepted Ulpian's tripartite conceptualization of law: *jus civile, jus gentium,* and *jus naturale.* But he modified the definition of the last term significantly. Isadore viewed the natural law as being the sum of laws shared by all cultures and societies everywhere. He easily granted Ulpian's idea that *jus naturale* is not a mere formulation of human conventions, a somewhat arbitrary solving of pragmatic problems; thus it is indeed quite different than *jus gentium.* But he rejected (or at least pointedly avoided) the description of natural law as "common to man and all the animals." Isadore seemed to view the *jus naturale* as a peculiarly human reality, a specifically human exercise of specifically human reason. Natural law is what distinguishes human beings from the animals.

Thus Isadore aligned himself to some extent with Cicero and Gaius. True, his adoption of the tripartite division of law gave him a superficial connection with Ulpian. And indeed it is possible that his emphasis on the difference between *jus gentium* and *jus naturale* may indicate some allegiance to a conception of a closed universe. But his celebration of human reason nonetheless established him as being also in continuity with the Roman approach.

Later history makes clear the importance of this commitment of Isadore's. For the early Scholastics, Alexander of Hales (d. 1245) and Albert the Great (d. 1280), present similar understandings. In fact, they acknowledge a debt to Isadore and forthrightly accept his theory as their own. Bonaventure (d. 1274), however, did not. The great Franciscan, whose Platonic perspective, behavioristic focus, and somewhat pessimistic flavor we have seen before, opted for Ulpian's point of view. But even he, in so doing, felt obliged to take account of Isadore and respond to him in the course of developing another understanding.

Thomas Aquinas

Among medievals, however, Thomas Aquinas (d. 1274) demands special attention, and not only because of his eminence in Catholic theology. On the question of natural law, Thomas is important also because of the enigmatic character of his loyalties. Study of the *Summa Theologiae* reveals a genuine ambivalence on Thomas's part. Sometimes he appears to support the open-ended vision of the Romans and Isadore. At other times, however, his loyalty to Ulpian and the Greeks manifests itself quite clearly.

For example, Thomas's general understanding of the human person as a rational creature, his commitment to human law as a "determination of reason" (to which we will return in chapter 19), even the appeal to reason implicit in the very style of his writings, would all support a Roman approach to natural law. Indeed, in his general discussion of natural law Aquinas asserts that "to the natural law belong those things to which a man is inclined naturally: and among these it is proper to man to be inclined to act according to reason" (I-II, 94, 4). And he goes on to say that "as to the proper conclusions of the practical reason [i.e., concrete moral judgments], neither is the truth or rectitude the same for all, nor, where it is the same, is it equally known by all." Thus, whereas Thomas admittedly holds a certain skepticism about the accuracy of human knowledge (his last point) that is Greek in flavor, he also asserts that the rectitude of specific actions may well vary according to the situation. And this position reflects a much more open, Roman perspective on life.

Still, it also remains true that in many places Aquinas appears to support Ulpian by referring to natural law as "common to all animals" (I-II, 95, 4), by including the demand to conform to animal facticity under the rubric of natural law (I-II, 94, 2), and by the way in which he deals with many concrete ethical questions. Thus it must be granted that

the Thomistic natural law concept vacillates at times between the order of nature and the order of reason. The general Thomistic thrust is toward the predominance of reason in natural law theory. However, there is in Thomas a definite tendency to identify the demands of natural law with physical and biological processes.[5]

This ambivalence about the natural law may be due to an ambivalence –or at least an ambiguity– about Thomas's definition of the human person.

A common philosophical definition proclaims that the human is a "rational animal." And although this definition remains open to a Roman perspective on natural law (since the inclusion of the idea of "rational" lets this perspective remain plausible), it probably encourages a Greek view. After all, a general philosophical principle is that beings are primarily defined by their genus and only nuanced by their species. So if the human person is an animal that is secondarily rational, then the expectation is that the natural law will be common to "man and all the animals," though enacted somewhat differently (i.e., through the use of reason) within the human community. The person is essentially and permanently a *rational* animal, of course; so this different mode of actuation is predictable. But the goal remains the goal of animal: eating, sleeping, propagating, and dying. Thus, embracing this definition of the human person predisposes one to a Greek understanding of the natural law. And it seems likely that in certain sections of the *Summa* this is the perspective that Aquinas embraces.

But there is another, equally defensible understanding of the human person. And according to philosopher Richard Westley, this second understanding is more characteristic of Aquinas.

Inasmuch as the soul is the form of the body (and thereby gives the body its "form" or identity) and the soul is spiritual (characterized by the activities of spirit, knowledge and love), it equally makes sense to define the human person as "enfleshed spirit." That is, the person is a spirit who secondarily but essentially is physical. But if this is true, then the central identity of the human person is the identity of spirits, which is self-transcendence, interpersonal intimacy, communion, and, in general, unity with other beings through knowledge and love.

Human persons are different than other spirits, of course. For human persons achieve the goal of spirit only through body, that is, through word and gesture. The human person, that is, is essentially and permanently an *enfleshed* spirit. The body is not the temporary locus of the soul or its prison. Indeed, the body is the soul's only means of achieving the goals of spirit. Apart from the body this specific sort of spirit, this human spirit, finds itself impoverished. But the goal remains the goal of spirit.

This understanding of the human person, however, puts quite a different light on the reality of the natural law. No doubt, a Greek vision of natural law remains plausible (since the human person is still truly body, as are the animals). But it is not hard to see that the perspective encourages a Roman vision. The human person, as spirit, must use right reason in the conduct of human affairs, must reasonably enact himself or herself so that, through word and gesture and all the enfleshed activities of this physical world, the goals of spirit – unity in knowledge and love – are achieved.[6]

Two views of the person, then, suggest two views of the natural law. Both understandings of the natural law are in Thomas, and now we can understand why. There is an ambiguity – perhaps an irreducible ambiguity – in the very being of the human person. And that radical ambiguity allows alternative interpretations of the natural law and, more profoundly and perennially, alternative judgments about the posture of the human person in encountering the world: passive and accepting (à la the Greeks, if the person is understood as "rational animal") or active and shaping (à la the Romans, if the person is understood as "enfleshed spirit").

Later Scholastic Synthesis

Our general survey of the history of moral theology (chapter 2) dwelt at length on the nominalist movement of the fourteenth and fifteenth centuries. We also noted the behavioristic shape taken by moral theology when it emerged as a separate discipline after the Council of Trent. So rather than belaboring the obvious, let us simply summarize this period by saying that the perspective of the Greeks and of Ulpian almost completely dominated the scene. Indeed, it is saying the best one can of this period to assert that it adopted the more restrictive elements of the Thomistic vision of natural law. In many cases, it even forsook that degree of rationality in favor of a voluntaristic and positivistic conception. Human law often became the paradigm, and natural law was seen simply as "rules made by God." But as we will have occasion to see again, this kind of formulation does not deserve to be called natural law at all.

In any case, the final outcome of the debates of these centuries was the scholastic synthesis in the manuals of the late nineteenth and early twentieth centuries. And the kind of understanding that was theirs we have seen in chapter 11. Indeed, in sketching out in that chapter the manualist vision of natural law we were viewing the final stage in the history of the theory that has been our concern here. There is no need, therefore, to repeat all of those details.

But just because we have completed our overview of the understandings of natural law found in Catholic theology up until recently, it does not follow that everything important has been said. On the contrary, at least one other line of thought demands our attention: the developments outside theology that have influenced recent reconsideration of natural law. For especially in the last two centuries, a number of insights from various other disciplines have been highly influential. Let us pause before concluding this chapter to take note of these related developments.

Attacks on Natural Law

In the last century or so, Western civilization has experienced a number of intellectual events that summarily constituted a substantial attack on the notion of natural law – not just an attack on some particular theory of natural law; rather, a much more thoroughgoing attack on the ideas of the human person and human nature that underlie all such theories. Perhaps these attacks were a necessary reaction to the excesses of the Enlightenment, with its naive optimism about the human race. Perhaps they were the inevitable concomitant of the scientific advances of this era. But whatever the explanation, the simple fact is that natural law was rather completely discredited. And this occurred as a result of attacks on human freedom or intelligence or both.

Three attacks in particular should be noted. And they are associated with three major figures in modern thought: Sigmund Freud (1856-1939), Karl Marx (1818-1883), and Charles Darwin (1807-1882). Each of these men was, of course, brilliant in his own way, and we do not wish to denigrate their importance. But whether appropriately or not, their contributions did function as sources for a popular rejection of natural law and human nature. This fact should not be overlooked.

So we begin with the Freudian attack. Freud's typology of the human person as composed of id, ego, and superego is well known. For our purposes the really significant point is the emphasis on the id. This cauldron of libidinal energy, this source of life force, was viewed as the central reality of our existence. The id may be controlled by the superego; its energies may be channeled by the ego; but it cannot be denied. Our image of ourselves as free of these drives, or as masters of them, is illusion. In fact, true freedom resides precisely in coming to know these forces that cannot be controlled. We are the victims of our own being, and it is naive to pretend otherwise. Our unconscious rules our life.

In the Marxist vision, the human person is similarly unfree. But here the source of the unfreedom is not the depths of the inner person but the forces of surrounding society. Because of ideology (which we will discuss again in chapter 18), we see life not as it is but as we wish it to be. We are betrayed by our situation, deceived by its shared and supported untruths. Thus, even though we may pretend to rule our life by intelligence and reason (because it suits our purposes to so pretend), in reality we are victims to the core.

Charles Darwin's discoveries likewise contributed to a disinterest in natural law. But in this case the reason for the disinterest was the simple realization that we are not only like the animals (as Ulpian might assert), we are animals. The continuity of human evolution with animal evolution is so thoroughgoing that the correct categories with which to understand and deal with the human person are the categories of zoology and related sciences. The Darwinian thesis, of course, offers a felicitous basis for the psychological theories of B. F. Skinner and other behaviorists. A common theme of their writings is that our notions of freedom and dignity must be recognized and accepted as illusions. We are beings who can be trained, but not truly educated; we are beings who can be manipulated, but not respected. We use each other, not because of nastiness but simply because there is no alternative. The admirable human creature envisioned by even the most conservative of natural law theorists does not exist, and there is no use pretending it does.

Thus the doubtlessly correct scientific discoveries of these men and their followers led, by immediate implication, to the undermining of one or another of the premises of natural law. They either denied our ability to know and understand ourselves or they rejected the reality of that freedom which alone can justify the call to ethical responsibility.

More recent developments, particularly in psychology, cultural anthropology, and the social sciences, have continued to reinforce these ideas. So have many schools of philosophy: One thinks of the British empiricists. The assertion that only what is measurable is real clearly makes any discussion of ethics and value difficult, if not impossible. The even more pessimistic premises of linguistic analysis – that we never really achieve contact with "underlying reality," that the proper task of philosophy is not the myth of metaphysics but only the phenomenological consideration of how we express ourselves – all this had an immediate adverse effect on natural law theory. Even the American pragmatism of John Dewey and others had that effect: It discouraged the kind of long-range reflection characteristic of moral theology. It asked about what "works," it celebrated the "technological criterion," and it attempted to avoid tarrying over the abstractions of evaluation. Or at least, that was the effect of this philosophy in the popular mind.

Indeed, in all these cases we are focusing more on the actual impact of the theories than on the subtleties of their originators. For subtleties have a way of not surviving the process of idea dissemination. And there is little doubt that the result of these various innovations was a modern cultural climate in which natural law theory, no matter what its stripe, was not well received. Indeed, until quite recently it exercised almost no influence whatsoever.

Rebirth of Natural Law

We say "until quite recently," for recent years have been characterized by an astonishing rebirth of interest in natural law, a renewed respect for the objective reality of human nature, a reawakened appreciation for the limits of our malleability on the one hand and for the possibilities of our power for self-direction on the other.[7] Let us note just a few examples of this phenomenon.

Given the widespread influence of the psychological theories of the Freudians and the behaviorists, it is of more than passing interest that a number of developmental psychologists have claimed to isolate patterns of personal growth that transcend geographical and social boundaries. One thinks of Jean Piaget, Erik Erikson, Lawrence Kohlberg, Eric Berne and, perhaps most obviously, Carl Jung. There is tremendous variety in the approaches and conclusions of these men, but there is also something they share in common: the fact that they assert the existence of patterns. Not culturally derived patterns, not patterns by which we are victimized. Rather, patterns that seem intrinsic to the human constitution and that are both a challenge to human intelligence and freedom and an opportunity for those faculties to realize their potential. No doubt these psychologists would hesitate to view themselves as proponents of some sort of natural law theory. But it is not altogether inappropriate to describe them in just this way.[8]

Other sciences also provide examples of this shift in approach. In cultural anthropology – a field long dominated by relativistic schemas and by the conviction that one must study each culture only on its own terms and without any attempt to make comparisons between cultures – there is a new interest in the "universal" in human behavior. Indeed, structural anthropologist Claude Lévi-Strauss has spent most of his career studying precisely this sort of general dynamic. And in the related discipline of linguistics, the radical innovations of Noam Chomsky have been highly influential. Chomsky's thesis – that there are underlying ways of human thinking and speaking that are neither relative to culture nor malleable by human intervention but are or appear to be intrinsic to the constitution of the human person – is as strong an assertion of human nature as one could fairly expect. And this thesis is not without its own potential for interesting extension. Musician Leonard Bernstein has used Chomsky as a starting point for his own investigation of the nature of music.[9]

So, in a number of areas developments have taken place that have significantly altered the state of the question regarding the existence and relevance of natural law. The posture for the last century or so was one of relativism and pessimism. Relativism, in that many sciences held the view that human beings were infinitely malleable, without any inner constitution to set limits on their potential or to preestablish the direction in which their most rewarding growth would occur. And, paradoxically, pessimism in that scientific views often held that people were not truly in control of their own fate. Intelligence and/or freedom are myths, it was said. The human person is perhaps a machine, perhaps a mere animal, and most certainly not the rational and free being that classic philosophy envisioned.

But both those perspectives have changed. In the work of people like those discussed here relativism has itself been relativized. The realization has emerged that the human is some particular sort of being. We possess a nature that is both characteristic of us, wherever and whenever we may live, and distinguishably ours, setting us apart from other creatures of this planet. This commitment to a substance lying beneath all the relativities of culture has generated a certain sort of pessimism of its own. Or at least it has led to a new realism. We cannot (or should not) become just anything. There are laws of nature, whether we like it or not, in terms of which the future must be shaped. But this new understanding has also rejected that other sort of pessimism. If our possibilities are now seen to be limited, they are nonetheless real. We are in charge of this nature that is ours; if we cannot do everything, we can do something. We are free; our intelligence is real. And that, after all, is no small thing.[10]

Conclusion

At the end of this thumbnail history of the concepts of human nature and natural law, we are left with a certain irony. For in the flow of theological and Christian-philosophical thought we saw a movement toward a rigid conception of natural law. It was a conception that felt very much at home in the rationalistic context of the Enlightenment, perhaps too much so. For at the end of that era secular culture strongly rebeled against what was seen as a prevailing naivete. And as the various fields of science and art moved away from natural law and toward the pessimistic and relativistic conceptions that we have discussed, the manuals remained locked into their traditional formulations.

But then came the new period. On the side of theology, we have the strong conciliar call to renewal that was highlighted at the end of chapter 2. And on the side of the secular sciences we have a new interest in these traditional themes. There is no doubt that the old formulations will not satisfy the cravings of today's thinkers. But it just may be a special moment in which to rethink the ethical notion of natural law. Perhaps we can tap into the openness of our culture and attempt to offer a theological vision of the human person, a concept of human nature and of its ethical aspect, natural law, that will speak to thinking people today.

Perhaps there is a way of extrapolating from the best of our tradition those ideas that appear to have abiding validity and of complementing them with ideas derived from the long road traveled by the history of thought. Perhaps this is just the right moment to once again, in a new context, ask the old question: What is the nature of natural law? At least one can try to formulate a contemporary answer to that question. The next chapter is dedicated to this task.

Chapter 14

A VISION OF NATURAL LAW

In this chapter we wish to provide a basic vision of the natural law, of a Catholic understanding of objective morality. At the same time, we wish to articulate this vision in a way that is useful today. We want our language, our examples, our order of presentation, and our focus to respond to the experience and needs of Christian disciples at the conclusion of the twentieth century.

To meet this goal, however, means that some questions will be ignored, some details eliminated, some debates overlooked, and some historical perspectives neglected. But these other concerns are also important, so they will be addressed in the next three chapters. Chapter 15 will add to this basic vision an explanation of the technical jargon used by theologians today. Chapter 16 will set this contemporary vision in its historical context by looking back at the way in which Catholic moral theology has addressed these concerns in the past. And chapter 17 will give direct attention to a serious debate that continues today within the ranks of those who seek to serve the Church through the discipline of moral philosophy and theology.

But before these details must come the basic vision. That is the goal of this chapter.

Let us take as our starting point an actual moral decision – any decision. We ask you, the reader of this chapter, to put in your mind a choice you have recently been forced to make: whether to give money to charity, whether to discipline your child, whether to become sexually intimate with someone, whether to reveal a confidence, whether to join a community group. As we proceed, keep this moral choice of yours in your mind, check the ideas presented and see if they are verified in your case.

To begin, note that we are dealing with something *important* here. Not all decisions are equally important, of course. But inasmuch as they are decisions about our lives and the lives of others, our moral decisions have an intrinsic significance. This is not silliness, not meaningless game playing. This is *valuable*. In the language of von Hildebrand, we are dealing here with *values*, things that are important in themselves. Not things that we *make* important by our attention; rather, things we *find* to be important and therefore give attention.

What else can be said about these values? We will claim that there are four qualities that the values – those qualities found in the case you are keeping in mind – have in common.

Real

First, the values are real[1] – that is, they are not figments of our imagination. They are part of the real world to which we are ultimately accountable.[2]

In claiming that these values are *real*, we are rejecting two counterfeit visions of morality. Explaining these counterfeits will help to highlight the importance of saying that the values are real.

Relativism

The first counterfeit vision is known as *relativism*.[3] Relativism is an ethical approach asserting that what is important is the sincerity of our decision, nothing else. As long as you mean well, it's okay. If you're sincere, that's all that counts. The only important thing is that you follow your conscience.

Obviously, we consider it important – indeed, essential – that one follow one's conscience. But it is not the *only* important thing. Rather, the very reason why we are obligated to follow our consciences is because the conscience is our only way to come in contact with the reality of objective morality. It is, after all, only through our personal capacity for moral consciousness (conscience/1), our individual efforts out of docility and toward truth (conscience/2), and our personal judgment about moral value (conscience/3) that we can realize the good. So if the immediate moral challenge is to follow the conscience, it is because the ultimate moral challenge is to do what is truly, objectively right. Relativism is the ethical approach that gets things backward, that asserts sincerity/conscience, and nothing more.

Described this way, the error of relativism probably looks obvious.

I know you're considering putting a bomb on an airplane. I want you to know that the only important thing, as far as I'm concerned, is that you do what you believe is right, that you follow your conscience.

Hardly! Something else is important, truly, objectively important: the real world of real values. But if the error of relativism is so obvious, why mention it? The reason is that for all its falseness, relativism is a popular moral approach. Consider these two groups of relativists.

First, there are teenagers. Adolescents are often very relativistic in their approach to life. "Love means never having to say you're sorry." "If we're sincere, it will work out." "We are good guys, and we pray before each game. So we will surely win the championship." Somehow the intoxication of self-discovery that occurs during adolescence is so profound that the objectivity of the real world often seems forgotten. Teenagers overlook the fact that good guys sometimes finish last, that sincerity does not guarantee success, that you can mean well and still bring about disaster.

But teenaged relativism has one positive thing going for it: It is temporary. Sooner or later, the uncontrollable reality of life reasserts itself. Sometimes the world asserts its claims tragically: an auto accident, an unplanned pregnancy, an addiction to drugs. Other times life is gentler: a flunked test, rejection as a boyfriend or girlfriend, the final game lost in the closing seconds. And in such cases relativism dies in the process. The fact that values are real, even when they are overlooked: This fact is itself rediscovered. And teenaged relativism, the relativism of naivete, comes abruptly to an end.

There is another group given to relativism: the middle aged. We have in mind employees who wonder if all that Christmas money they are given is really gifts; or parents who wonder if the high school that "everyone" is going to really inculcates the life vision they espouse for their children; or religious leaders who know they ought to try to think out the ethical dilemmas of our day. But they all flee that daunting task.

These persons see the question, but they are overwhelmed by the complexity of life. They despair of figuring out what is really right. They are anxious about the demands they might face if certain conclusions emerged. So they settle for something else; they settle for "being nice." They will not be aggressively evil, but neither will they make prophetic waves. They will go with the flow. They will "mean no harm." They will be relativists, believing it is enough to live out of a certain superficial conformity, floating on a sea of uncritical conventionality.

But life is not so cooperative; it has a reality beyond intention. The employees receive a subpoena. The parents see their children turn into strangers. The ministers are shocked to discover the rage of the poor, the disenfranchised, the victims of violence. With luck, they eventually rediscover the truth that values are real, whether we like it or not. Without luck, they remain blind, and we all pay the price of unnecessary suffering in the world. Because even in the presence of sincerity, harm happens.

Middle-aged relativism is the more troublesome, for it expresses not naivete but despair. The despair is understandable, of course. Dealing with the moral challenges of the day is indeed difficult. But the wisdom of the Catholic tradition is that the difficulties of my moral thinking are no consolation to the victims of my oversight. Even when it is inconvenient, the world is real. It must be taken seriously. The goal of moral judging is not just to make a sincere judgment. It is also, and even more ultimately, to do the truly right, truly helpful, constructive, life-giving thing.[4]

Legalism

The second counterfeit moral approach is *legalism*. This is an approach asserting that what is really central to moral living is obedience to the law. The neighbor who is in need may be the *occasion* for my moral decision. The neighbor may even be the *topic*. But the essence of the moral event is my decision to conform myself to the pertinent law, my act of obedience to the demand placed on me.

Think once again, if you will, of the moral judgment in your life that you retrieved at the beginning of this chapter. What role did obedience play in that judgment? Was the challenge one of finding the law and obeying it? Or was the challenge one of finding the truly helpful, constructive act and doing it? To say that values are real is to choose the latter alternative. Morality is not an enterprise of obedience,[5] it is an enterprise of wise and caring action. But if that is so obviously the case, why even mention legalism? Is it really a viable alternative? Do we really need to fear legalism, or legalists? It seems that we do. Consider these three sorts of legalism: civil, ecclesiastical, and divine.

There are some whose behavior implies that being moral requires nothing more (or less) than obeying the laws of the civil authority. "If it's legal, it's moral." Abortion. Racial discrimination. Deceiving the buyer of my secondhand car. Filling a hospital informed-consent form with so much detail that no ordinary person can understand it. "What ought to be done? Check with the attorneys! If it's legal, it's moral!"

There was a time when, in some locales within the United States, Catholics could not receive exemption from military service on grounds of conscientious objection because, it was claimed, Catholics were always obliged to obey "legitimate authority." One paradoxical by-product of the decision of the U.S. Supreme Court legalizing abortion is that this claim is now proven obviously false. Just because something is legal, it does not follow that it is moral. Similarly, we have come to realize that just because something is illegal, it does not follow that it is always prohibited. There is such a thing as an unjust law, and civil disobedience may sometimes be required. The goal of moral judgment is not obedience; it is wise and caring action.[6]

Good citizenship requires cooperation in common life, of course. And that indicates a general readiness to abide by the laws of the land. But this readiness is not ultimate; this obedience is not blind. And that is the difference between being law abiding and being a civil legalist.

Another form of legalism may be more insidious, especially for those who were formed by the Catholic tradition. There are many who think, for example, that only Catholics are prohibited from getting divorced and that the reason why they cannot get divorced is simply that "the Church forbids it." One hears the claim that "the Church prohibits active euthanasia/test-tube fertilization/capital punishment/nuclear war/ etc." And the implication of the claim is that we are dealing here with a *rule* and that the Christian's act of response is essentially an act of obedience.

This is a distortion. The Catholic tradition's involvement in moral questions is not essentially a matter of rules, but of *teachings*. It is a matter of wisdom acquired, wisdom claimed, about how human persons can best serve one another. It is a matter of insight into what forms of behavior truly humanize life and allow persons to flourish, and what forms do not. And it is a matter of sharing that wisdom, out of care for and commitment to the persons who are involved.[7]

There is no denying that Catholic leadership speaks forcefully about the values it sees and the behaviors it believes to be appropriate. Just as a friend who sees that you are about to walk into a wall will shout: "Look out!" so religious leaders often speak about values in imperative language. To do so is quite human, and to obey such "commands" is quite reasonable. The point here is that the fundamental *reason* that the act is wrong is not that it is prohibited, but that it is destructive. And moral "commands" are therefore not really acts of authority, but rather acts of emphatic instruction.

Let us put this one more way. Because human persons love one another, they often say: "Do this!" or "Don't do that!" If the recipient of this "command" is an adult, he or she will often respond: "Why?" If the speaker communicates the reason, then we have a successful example of moral conversation, moral teaching. But if the speaker answers: "Because!" (that is: "because I say so!" or "because it's the law!"), then legalism is born. For legalism is the moral approach claiming that obedience is the essence of morality, rather than wisdom. And ecclesiastical legalism claims that what makes actions right or wrong is the fact that they are either commanded or prohibited by the Church. The Catholic natural law tradition, on the other hand, claims that what makes actions right or wrong is the actual, objective fact that they are either helpful or harmful to persons. For values, in the end, are real.

There is a last, subtle form of legalism that we should note. Is abortion wrong? Or capital punishment? Or active euthanasia? Or nuclear war? And if they are, why? One sometimes hears it said that such acts are wrong because "they are against the Fifth Commandment," because "they violate the law of God," because "they are against the moral law." And such phrases sound so innocuous, so unassailable.

But in fact such phrases severely distort the reality of Christian morality, for they suggest that there is something arbitrary about the wrongness of these acts. It's as if God *happened* to prohibit the acts, whereas God might equally have chosen to require them. Such phrasings suggest that the essence of moral living is to find out what God *happens* to have required or prohibited and then to obey these positive or negative commands. And in so suggesting, such phrases in a very profound sense insult both God and the human person and grossly distort the meaning of morality. They imply that God's "commands," rather than growing from the ground of God's love for humankind and expressing what is truly in humankind's best interest (as a beautiful Jewish legalism would assert), are nothing more than expressions of arbitrary authority.

Catholic tradition, on the contrary, has said that, to the extent that natural law can rightly be called law at all, it is a law promulgated in the very act of creation. It is a law much more like the law of gravity than like the laws of inheritance. That is, the will of God is expressed not in some additional, presumably optional law, but in the way things actually are. Given the sort of world this is, what is right has to be right, what is wrong has to be wrong. So the fundamental reason for rightness and wrongness is not the will of God – if that will is understood as over and above the truth of the real world. Rather, the reason is that values are real, that this is the way things are. Divine legalism, then, is just as much a distortion as ecclesiastical or civil legalism. In every case, morality is viewed as blind obedience when in fact it is wise and caring action.

So the first, absolutely fundamental thing to be said about the values that we confront in our moral decisions is that they are real. But it is not the only thing to be said. Three other qualities can also be noted. And it will be important for us to give attention to each.[8]

Conflict

When moral judgments are made in the real world, they always end up dealing with a conflict of values. Consider the cases listed at the beginning of this chapter. If I give the money to charity, I cannot spend it on myself. Indeed, I cannot even give it to another charity. Disciplining the child will cause him or her pain, to say nothing of myself! Sexual intimacy? If I act without commitment, I enter a risky business, for nakedness inevitably tends toward vulnerability, and vulnerability in the absence of respect is the recipe for hurt;[9] if I act with commitment, I foreclose other possible relationships. Revealing a confidence may help someone avoid harm, but it also undermines trust. And joining a community group means that a certain amount of time and energy will no longer be available for recreation, for rest, even for other altruistic activities.

And consider that moral judgment of your own, the judgment that has been your touchstone for this chapter. The same truth will reveal itself: In the human world, everything costs. The philosopher Leibniz is quoted as saying: "All things are possible but all things are not compossible."[10] That is, perhaps one can do anything, but one most certainly cannot do everything. Life is a matter of choices, of tradeoffs. So also moral judgments. They are not simply choices of the good that consequently involve rejections of the bad. They are choices of a good that involve exclusions of other goods. No solution is a perfect solution, no act is a perfect act. Consequently, all moral judgments are judgments "in a bind," judgments among the less-than-ideal, judgments of, and choices among, relative (not absolute) goods.[11]

That this is so is simply a datum of our experience. But *why* is it so? The reason, simply put, is finitude, the finitude of the world and the finitude of the human person. Human beings are finite, are creatures. This limitedness is the reason why compossibility, to put it in Leibniz's term, is impossible. I really would like to do all good things. At a very mundane level, I would like to attend every party, listen to every concert, participate in every conversation, see every movie. But I cannot! Not only is there the limitation of money and other physical resources. More profoundly, there is the limitation of time and of energy. I may not like it (indeed, perhaps one of the evidences for original sin is our discomfort about it), but I am finite. And because of this finitude, all my choices are choices among goods.[12]

Let us add one further point. Saying that all choices are choices *among* goods may seem implausible. If I choose between participating in Sunday worship and burning down the church building, it is hard to imagine the latter choice as good. But in some senses it is. At the very least, the choice is good inasmuch as it exists. Medieval philosophy pointed out that goodness is coextensive with being; that is, mere existence is a value. Hence whatever exists is good precisely because it exists. But beyond that, most if not all things are also "good for something." That is, they are realities that, in addition, are truly *suited* for something. Hence their goodness is not only metaphysical (that is, rooted in their mere existence), but also functional (that is, rooted in their usefulness). This would be the case if (implausible though it be) burning the church were found to be the only way to destroy a life-threatening germ lodged within it. Thus, most if not all choices are also choices among truly useful goods, where even the "wrong" choice is nonetheless good in its way.

This insight has a very practical application. Sometimes, when individuals hear the Christian teaching that a certain act is immoral, they will refute the teaching by claiming that there most certainly is something good about the act. That is, they will presume that Christians oppose the act on the grounds that it is a totally evil thing; and quite obviously the act is not totally evil. But of course, the presumption is wrong. To assert that an act is immoral is not to assert that it is totally evil. Rather, it is to assert that the act, though good in many ways, is ill suited to the fulfillment of human persons, at least in this circumstance. The act is insufficiently good, or it is decisively less good than possible alternative acts, or its goodness is overwhelmed by destructiveness, or its goodness nonetheless coexists with something else about the act that makes it inevitably incompatible with human fulfillment.

Thus Christians willingly acknowledge, for example, that genital action has real goodness, in whatever situation. They just claim that in some situations (namely, those lacking the context of abiding commitment) this good thing simply will not fulfill its potential and, indeed, will prove destructive to human persons. Christians willingly acknowledge that capital punishment disposes of malefactors, may tend to give a feeling of reestablished social balance, may even serve as a deterrent to future crime. But they, or at least many of them, also claim that these goods are overwhelmed by the assault on human dignity, not the dignity one earns through behavior but the dignity one owns through creation, that is inevitably involved.

As mentioned earlier, this insight is important because, in its absence, ethical assertions appear implausible. Indeed, they appear silly, and thus are easily rejected by the very people they are intended to serve. And that, when it happens, is really tragic. For values are real. And even innocently incorrect judgments have the effect of harming the human persons whom we love.

Change

Another characteristic of these worldly values that we seek to serve is that they change. Or at least that their relative importance is subject to change. Perhaps it is morally right for me to give this money to the charity I have chosen. But suppose that a loved one of mine becomes ill. Suddenly what was once moral will become immoral. Perhaps my proposed sexual intimacy is immoral, for we are not committed to each other. But our relationship grows, we become committed and, in the end, celebrate that commitment in marriage. The intimacies now become moral, not because they have suddenly become legal in some way, but because they have suddenly become true, they have found the context in which their goodness can truly flourish. Perhaps it is morally right for me to join this community group. But then my employer informs me that, to keep my job and therefore to support my family, I will need to stay late or take home work on a regular basis. Suddenly what was moral will become immoral.

Again, consider the moral judgment that has been your tool of comparison through this chapter. No doubt you can imagine circumstances that would materially alter the case, that would tend to require another judgment. Even if what you chose was the right thing (because it was the better thing), it certainly was not the absolutely best thing, or the only thing. And new circumstances can really change matters so that what was right can become wrong, what was wrong can become right.

As in the case of value conflict, we assert this potential for change because it is a datum of our experience. But why is it so? In the language of philosophy, the reason is human historicity. That is, human beings live in time, as we said earlier in this book. This historicity (or temporality) means that change is itself one of the constitutive elements of human life. Individuals change, so that what was wrong in adolescence may become right in mature adulthood, what was right in the single state may become wrong in the presence of the responsibilities of marriage, what was not necessary for the participant may become obligatory for the elected leader, and so on. And society as a whole changes, so that what was right in a rural setting may be wrong in the midst of the city, what was wrong in a barter economy may become right in the world of modern finance, what was right in a time of limited weaponry may become wrong in the nuclear age.

This point is, like the issue of value conflict, important for us. It sometimes happens that those who note this potential for change are accused of relativism. They are accused of abandoning the firm ground of objective morality and slipping into the swamp of moral indifferentism. It should be clear that this is not the case.

Relativism, as we saw, holds that the only thing that counts is inner sincerity. In contrast to relativism, the natural law tradition holds that values are objective and real, that they exist and exercise their influence whether or not we intend them. But in asserting the objectivity of values, the natural law tradition does not necessarily assert their immutability. That is, just because something is objectively true, it does not follow that it is forever true, that it is exempt from the law of worldly change. For example, to assert that I am at this moment at my typewriter is not to assert that I will be here forever. It is not to assert that

I am still at my typewriter as you read these words. It simply asserts that really, truly, objectively I am/was at the typewriter at the moment when I wrote them.[13]

So the natural law vision does not claim the immutability of worldly values. Quite the contrary, it asserts the historicity of worldly values. That is, it asserts the objective reality of values in an objectively changing world. Hence the vision also does not assert that moral judgments are unchanging. Quite the contrary, inasmuch as the priority of values is subject to change, so also the bottom-line moral judgment is subject to change. And far from being a flight from objectivity into relativism, this recognition of the potential for change is an act of fidelity to the historical reality of the world in which we are called to life.[14]

Grounded

The values we have been considering have one last characteristic to be noted. And it is a particularly important characteristic, since it indicates the overall frame or context within which the values exist. For us to understand clearly the claim that these values are "grounded," it will help to proceed through a series of questions.

We have claimed that values in the human world are real, but that they exist in tension with one another and in a historical setting that makes their interrelation susceptible to change. The fact that they are in tension means that the correct act in one setting may not be the correct act in another setting, since the competing values may differ in the various settings. And the fact that their interrelation is susceptible to change means that the correct act at one time may not continue to be the correct act at another time, since new values may appear. But if this is true, one faces a troubling question: Is *any* action always right or always wrong? Is *any* behavioral option always the correct or incorrect choice, in any circumstance whatsoever, at any time before or yet to come?

We will answer these questions in the affirmative: There are such acts, such behavioral options. Well, if so, then two follow-up questions immediately arise: What are these acts? And why is it that they have this exceptionless character? Let us take the second question first.

Why is it that some actions are always right or wrong? This question has three possible answers. First, it could be because these actions are either commanded or prohibited by legitimate authority. That is, one could argue that because some proper authority has, for example, commanded us to remain within a single monogamous marriage or forbidden us to have genital relations with persons of the same gender, for that reason these moral assessments are unassailable and unchangeable.

But from everything that has been said thus far in this chapter, it is clear that this answer is simply a return to legalism. There is no doubt about the important role of moral teaching in the illumination of moral truth. Nor is there doubt about the appropriateness of attempting to coerce conformity to moral truth (at least in some cases, where the common good is at stake) through legislation. But if one asserts (as the preceding statement does) that moral legislation actually *creates* the value, so that the command is the *reason* the act is right and the prohibition is the *reason* it is wrong, then one is asserting legalism in just the sense that was discussed earlier in the chapter. And as we said then, the error of legalism is serious precisely because in the attempt to support moral values, it actually insults both God and the human person, making of morality an arbitrary and ultimately trivial exercise in obedience.

A second explanation for the fact that a given action alternative is always right or always wrong could be that it will always be the most constructive or destructive of the available options. That is, given that the radical moral challenge is to engage in wise and caring action through the pursuit of real values and given that the pursuit of these values finds them always in conflict with one another in a finite world, it is clear that any action alternative that would always be the best of the available options would always be morally obligatory, and any alternative that would always be the worst, most destructive option would always be morally wrong.

So this explanation is plausible. But it is also problematic. For we can never *know* whether there are any such acts. Since the number of possible configurations of values is indefinite, we can never know if we have thought out all the possible choice settings. And since the future is precisely that, we can never know if some not-yet-imagined situation may offer an action alternative better – or worse – than the one we are considering. So although it is logically possible that a class of acts such as this could exist, there is no way to describe the class concretely. Thus, to put it a bit differently, it could be that the reason some acts are always right or wrong is because they are always the best or the worst of the options. And if such acts exist, it is clear that they are always right or wrong. But it is not clear whether such acts exist. So this reason, plausible though it be, cannot be the reason we are using in claiming that some acts are, indeed, always right or wrong.[15]

We come now to a third possible reason.[16] If some action alternatives are either integral to or antithetical to the very essence of morality, if some action alternatives are such that, in and of themselves and regardless of what other action alternatives may be simultaneously present, they either are required that morality may be actualized or are utterly incompatible with the actualization of morality, then such actions will be either obligatory or forbidden for just that reason.

Well, that makes sense. But once again we face the question: Are there any acts that can be shown to be such? It seems so.

First, there is a class of acts internal to a person. As shown in the chapters of part II of this book, the willingness to do good and avoid evil, the commitment to loving God, oneself, one's neighbor, is the very essence of morality. Thus it is, at least as an abiding internal life direction, always obligatory. Conversely, to choose to do what one believes to be wrong, to violate one's conscience and thereby commit actual sin, is the very essence of immorality. Thus it is always forbidden. Analogously, an internal attitude of worship toward God on the one hand and of blasphemy on the other, presuming that one has a genuine appreciative awareness of God, present themselves as exceptionless demands/prohibitions.

Second, there is a group of external and interpersonal acts that fit into this category, namely, unprovoked attacks on human persons. What we have in mind is the group of acts that the moral tradition gathered under the claim that the direct killing of the innocent is always immoral – indeed, that it is "intrinsically evil." In the next three chapters we will explore in much more detail this dense and pregnant statement. Obviously, the two limiting terms "direct" and "innocent" need to be clarified carefully. But for now, to start that analysis, we will simply develop one line of thought.

We are claiming that a certain sort of death-dealing act is always wrong. Once again, we return to our perennial question: What is the *reason* it is wrong? And the argument just outlined gives the answer. This sort of act is wrong because in any circumstance whatever it represents an affront to the very enterprise of morality. It is not an act made *within* the context of moral obligation and as a possible expression of it. Rather, it is a rejection of morality itself. For morality, after all, is nothing else than the responsibility that follows from the intrinsic dignity of human persons, the responsibility of human persons to be caretakers to themselves and one another. Therefore, to "dispose" of a human person is to cut the very legs out from under the moral enterprise, it is to "bail out" on the central challenge of morality. Or, to put this another way, human persons are not objects next to other objects, to be relatively compared in the process of resolving value conflicts. Rather, human persons are subjects, on whom the very existence of the moral enterprise is built.[17]

In a finite world, it is no doubt impossible to do *all* things on behalf of human persons. And thus it is surely impossible to prevent the death of all persons (and this, as we shall see, is the force of the limiting word "direct"). And in a world trapped by original sin it may even be necessary to defend oneself against others who unjustly attack one's life, perhaps even to the point of killing lest one be killed (this, again, is the force of the limiting word "innocent"). But what is surely never right, because it is a simple assault on the very essence of morality, is that action alternative which involves killing (not merely permitting the death of) innocent (i.e., nonaggressing) human life.

This class of actions, then, constitutes the irreducible "bottom line" of natural law morality. It names the behavioral limits beyond which it is always wrong to go. And it establishes the grounding on which all other moral judgments, as resolutions of conflict in a changeable world, firmly rest.

Conclusion

How shall we understand the Christian natural law tradition? We shall understand it as the pursuit of values, realizing that values are real, in conflict, susceptible to change, and firmly grounded. Much more needs to be said about this. We need to amplify this vision by the presentation of current theological vocabulary (chapter 15), to connect it with the historic roots of the Catholic tradition (chapter 16), and to address a strenuous current theological debate (chapter 17).

But at least a context has now been established, an overall vision of the natural law has been put in place.

Chapter 15

MORALITY: VALUES AND NORMS

In the last chapter, by reflecting on concrete moral decisions that confront us, we affirmed the centrality of *values*. And then we isolated four characteristics that these values have: They are real, in conflict, susceptible to change, and firmly grounded.

That last characteristic, however – that the values are firmly grounded – deserves more extended attention.

Our question, you'll recall, was whether any behavioral alternatives are always right or always wrong. And our answer was that, on the one hand, all sorts of internal human acts – love, hate, worship, blasphemy, and the like – are always right or wrong. In addition, we answered that one category of external act – the direct killing of the innocent – is always wrong, and demonstrably so.

In giving this answer, however, we were taking a position in an intense ongoing debate about *intrinsically evil acts*, as they are called. The debate is extremely important because of the implications it offers for all of Catholic morality. It is also quite high profile at the present time, so that the simple goal of being educated demands familiarity with it. For both these reasons, then, we now need to become more conscious about that debate, about the various positions that have been taken over the centuries and about the state of the question today. We need to enter in an intense and responsible way into the ongoing conversation. That will be the goal of the next three chapters.

But to enter an ongoing conversation has one problem. The conversationalists have already said some things; they have defined a vocabulary, they have found ways to name the issues, they have provided the terms within which the subject should be pursued. If we are to join the conversation, we have to learn the language. Hence the next three chapters will also have the purpose of educating us to the way in which these questions are raised. Thus, at one and the same time we will struggle with some important questions and become knowledgeable about some important conversations.

The first thing we must do is clarify some terminology that is constantly present in discussions about this question and make some basic but critical distinctions. And to begin we must return to the idea of *values*, and to note that this word is used to describe two quite different realities.

Premoral Values

"There is a real world out there." That is the basic presupposition of the natural law vision of life. It is a world that exists on its own terms, a world that operates according to its own laws. What is more, it is a world of values, of "goods" and "bads" that simply are. It is a world of life and death, prosperity and poverty; a world of truth and error, knowledge and ignorance, understanding and confusion; a world of harmony and friction, union and alienation, companionship and loneliness; a world of health and sickness, comfort and discomfort, fertility and sterility; a world of possession and loss; a world of beauty and ugliness. In these ways, and in many more besides, it is a world of values and disvalues.

And it is a world where these values and disvalues compete. Just listing so many of these goods and bads should make it clear that no one can attain them all. In fact, in the process of concretely "doing" our lives, the decision to reach for one value can often mean forsaking another. It may even mean attacking another. So, for example, telling the truth may turn two friends apart. Bearing children may lead to relative poverty. Finishing an important job may make the worker sick. And, as the cliché points out: "That's life!"

So even though these concrete values, these "doing values," are real and important, it may not be altogether accurate to call them *moral* values. If, for example, giving money to charity were called a *moral* value, then not giving money to charity would have to be termed *immoral*. And we saw that this is not the case. Giving money to charity is a good thing, but it is not always an obligatory thing. And causing a child pain is a bad thing. But it is not a "moral disvalue" (i.e., immoral). For, as we saw, it is not always the wrong thing: There is such a thing as disciplining a child. So causing a child pain is a bad thing, but it is not always a wrong thing.

So these values are important. But achieving them is not absolutely essential to the project of being a moral human being. In fact, achieving them may in some cases be proof that a person is quite immoral. Thus, if a woman stays awake through the night to care for her ailing child, we would hardly brand her a bad mother or a bad person. The most we would say is that her fatigue is "too bad" in the sense that it is unfortunate, regrettable. It is hardly a good thing in and of itself, but in this case it is far better than the alternative of getting her rest and neglecting her child. So, in a way that may be paradoxical but is also quite commonplace, doing a bad thing is often necessary in order to be a good person.

Thus, we might speak of the values described here as *nonmoral*, except that this is not altogether accurate, either. For one cannot completely ignore these values; they are not morally irrelevant. If the mother were staying up most of the night on a regular basis, and only because she loved the late movies, and if this practice were making her sick or unable to fulfill her other responsibilities, then surely we would claim that there was a moral issue. So even though all those "doing values" we listed are not moral in the sense of being absolutely essential to the living of a virtuous life, still they are morally relevant. Or, in the terminology preferred today, they are *premoral* values.[1]

The exact reason for this terminology will become evident as we proceed. For now, it is not particularly important; what is important is how it expresses the underlying insight that we developed in the last chapter: We live in a value-laden world. We cannot realize all the values in our experience simultaneously. But we must at least attend to those values, take them into consideration. The virtuous person is the person who realizes those values as much as possible while neglecting or attacking them as little as necessary. That is, morality is a matter of maximizing the premoral goods that we encounter and of minimizing the premoral evils. And premoral values, simply defined, are the concrete good things that ought, to the extent possible, to be done. They are the real values of our world, values to which we must always attend even though they cannot always be realized.

This underlying insight, moreover, is something most people intuitively realize. Married people will talk about the difficulty of deciding how much time to spend with their families, how much on community affairs, and how much on outside personal interests. Business people point out the tension between their responsibilities to stockholders, to employees, and to consumers. Doctors often experience conflict between the value of getting their patients home as soon as possible and the value of doing tests that may lead to discoveries that will help others. All these people intuitively know that living as one ought, being moral, entails the proper balancing of these premoral goods and evils. All we are doing is raising this intuition to consciousness, giving it some clarity, and pointing out that it truly summarizes the strategy of moral living.

Moral Values

The objective of all our moral judgments is to do the good or, more precisely, to do what is right. And, as we said before, that rightness is constituted by doing as much good as possible and as little evil as necessary. It is not a matter of doing what one feels like. It is not even a matter of being sincere. Good and sincere people regularly do things that injure themselves and those around them. And though we may appreciate their sincerity of intention, we still offer a judgment on the behavior they perform. So, without denying the dignity of human persons, the rights of personal conscience, or the importance of inner sincerity, it is still appropriate to speak of moral success and failure. In any situation, in fact, some action is the right action, some action really does maximize the premoral good and minimize the premoral evil. Other actions, no matter how well intentioned, are objective failures of the moral enterprise. Indeed, perhaps the fact that people argue so forcefully about ethical issues proves they know how true this is.

So it is not surprising that, in addition to everything we have discussed so far, there also exists a whole language of moral success and failure, a language of human ideals. We speak of honesty, of justice, of chastity, of reverence for life. And on the other side, we speak of cruelty, of lust, of disrespect, of injustice. We speak of those qualities that characterize the person who is both sincere and objectively correct, or who is not. We speak of the virtues and the vices they oppose.

The qualities we have listed here are, of course, good or bad things. They are important in themselves, valuable in their own right, so it is certainly appropriate to call them values. But they are also clearly values of a different sort.

On the one hand, they are values we consider truly essential to proper human living. If a person fails to get a good night's sleep, that is bad (in the sense of "unfortunate"), but it is not necessarily wrong (that is, immoral). On the other hand, if a person fails to be honest, that is not only bad; it is also always wrong. These values, then, do not just describe things we should attend to in our daily living. They describe things we should, indeed must, possess. They are really alternative ways of describing moral living itself. And so they are called "moral values."

On the other hand, these values differ from those we saw earlier in that they do not so much point "out there" as "in here." They do not name aspects of a specific situation that should be noted and taken into account. Rather, they describe qualities of moral persons themselves as they confront and correctly deal with their situations. They describe the kind of persons they should be. If we name these values by using adjectives (fair, honest, just, chaste, etc.), then the adjectives are most appropriately modifiers of moral agents themselves. They describe their way of being, they report their success and failure in maximizing the premoral good and minimizing the premoral evil in a particular area of life. For this reason, again, they are called "moral values."[2]

It should be clear that the reality we're looking at now is identical with one of the classes of always-wrong acts we discussed in the last chapter. We spoke of those *inner* actions of a person, acts like loving one's neighbor, committing a sin, worship, blasphemy. And we asserted that these acts are always right or wrong, always moral or immoral, as the case may be. Now, it should be obvious why this is so. These acts include, in their very definition, the element of propriety or impropriety. For they are, really, nothing else than redefinitions of, specifications of, the very challenge of morality: authentic and responsible personhood.

Thus we find in our experience two sorts of values: not only premoral "doing values," but also moral "being values." And as we compare these two, we find that, paradoxically, moral values are both more and less than premoral values. They are more in that they point at qualities that are absolutely essential for proper human living. They are less in that they are so obvious and sometimes so lacking in specific content, really little more than synonyms for goodness itself.

This fact, that they are both more and less, is precisely what explains their existence. We know that the goal of human living is to be both sincere and correct in our moral judgments. So it is the most natural thing in the world that we should create a vocabulary to describe this goal. Inasmuch as this goal must be sought in a variety of different dimensions of our lives, it is utterly natural that we should create terms to describe the goal in each. In the area of interpersonal communications, we call it honesty. In the area of mutual rights and duties, we call it justice. In the area of sexual behavior, we call it chastity. And even though these terms do not wrestle with the total complexity of the various situations, they do articulate the ideal that should always be sought.

Norms

Several times we have noted the role of norms in morality. Just because we reject legalism, it does not follow that we wish to be normless. Norms are based on values, of course, and not vice versa. Still, norms have an important function. They spotlight our value insights and value convictions, so that we can communicate these to our neighbors more effectively. Because human persons are social, we try to share the things we value. We can do this through wordy, ponderous descriptions of all the values involved in a particular situation. Or we can do this through the pithy language of norms. "Don't cross the street!" is not dehumanizing legalism; it is a loving assertion of the esteem we have for the person we are addressing. It is a shorthand way of saying: "I consider you important; and there are dangers in crossing the street that, at your age, make it too risky for you to cross the street alone."

So norms are important, even in a value-oriented morality. We will want to say more about norms. But as we join the contemporary conversation, we will find that, parallel to the two sorts of values, ethicists customarily distinguish two sorts of norms.

Material Norms

It is obvious that in order to implement the Christian strategy of doing as much good as possible and as little harm as necessary, we have to assess properly the importance of the various premoral values we encounter. And often enough that is no simple thing. Of course, if the two competing values are fatigue and the health of one's child, then the priority is clear. But the cases of the married people, the business people, and the doctors exemplify that priorities are often not clear. Hence the assessment of specific concrete premoral values has always been a major concern. It is a concern of people in general, and it is a concern of moral theology as a science.[3]

As that assessment process is completed, the results are quite commonly summarized in pithy form. They are articulated in a way that is easily communicable, readily accessible to others.

"Do not kill." "Get eight hours of sleep." "Do not take another's possessions." "Tell the truth." "Repay your loans." All these are norms. They are formulated in different ways, but they have the common characteristic of articulating values in terms of how we should behave. They tell us what, if possible, we ought to do. They point at a specific, concrete human situation, and they tell us where the values reside in that situation – or at least where one of the values resides, for there could be others. If I am starving, I do not repay my loans. If I am asked an intruding question about a client of mine, I do not tell the truth. If I am accosted by a deranged knifewielder, I may kill. But still the norms do point to values. And they remind us not to take them lightly.

Norms like these, norms that point at the premoral values to be found in our world, are commonly called "material norms." That is, they seek to be quite specific, to describe concretely the material of human situations, and they try to name and assess the premoral values that reside there. They try to inform us about those values so that we can correctly and insightfully proceed to the judgment we must make. Indeed, they attempt (whether successfully or not) to make that judgment for us. We know we must maximize the premoral good and minimize the premoral evil. Material norms call our attention to the various values we must take into account in doing precisely that. And in naming those values, material norms attempt to write a very specific script for the living of our human lives. They bluntly announce precisely what ought to be done.

Such norms may not be exceptionless, of course. As we have seen, there may be times when I encroach on another's property rights, when I should withhold the truth, when I may have to kill. There are, in other words, times when the script may have to be revised. But such norms are nonetheless very useful. For they give us some concrete input. In fact, their very concreteness militates against their being exceptionless. One cannot have it both ways. Either a norm remains very general, describing the sort of people we should be, and in its generality is obviously exceptionless; or it becomes quite specific, describing the actions we should do, and in its specificity risks being susceptible to exception. Either I say, "Do what's right!" and speak in easy absolutes, or I say, "Do your homework!" and live with the possibility that there will be exceptions. And material norms, forced to choose between specificity and absoluteness, serve us by pursuing the first.[4]

Formal Norms

Moral values, too, are often proclaimed in normative language: "Be honest." "Respect life." "Give to all their due." "Honor your father and mother." But they are obviously norms of a different sort, not at all in the nature of a behavioral script. They are so vague, so lacking in content, that they hardly seem to deserve being called norms at all. If we are going to consider them norms, then they will have to have a special name. Theologians today refer to them as "formal norms," for they describe the form, the style, the shape that one's life should have in a particular area of ethical concern. Although material norms try to grapple with the concreteness of the situation, with its material, in order to assess the various values, formal norms try to point out, in a specific area of moral choice, the character, the form, the successful moral agent will possess. Or to put this in other ways, whereas material norms seek to write a useful, albeit tentative, script for action, formal norms proclaim the goal to which every script ought to conform, the dream that every script ought to incarnate. Or again, although material norms tell us what we should do, formal norms tell us who we should be.

The reader may have noticed that the examples of formal norms used here were all affirmative in character. Are there no formal norms that are prohibitions? There are, but we avoided them at first because they are a bit problematic: "Do not murder." "Do not lie." "Do not steal." Are these norms formal or material? That is, do they describe the form or shape that one's life should take in a particular area of ethical concern, or do they describe a specific item of premoral material and point out its value or disvalue? In answering these questions, one might well be tempted to view these prohibitions as material norms. They are, after all, more specific than the affirmative commands with which we began this section. They are more like a script, and less like a goal, than the others. There seems to be a world of difference between "Respect life" and "Do not murder." But is there really?

Take the case mentioned earlier, where I am accosted by a deranged man on a rampage with a knife. In self-defense I kill the man. Have I murdered him? Most people would say no. They would say that I had committed a justified homicide. In fact, even the civil courts would say that. Well, then, what is murder? Perhaps it can be defined as unjustified killing. But if that is the case, then the norm we are considering really declares: "Do not kill without justification." It points out quite literally that wrong killing is wrong.

In other words, this norm really does not give us any information, it is not oriented toward the material of a given situation. Rather, it too, in its own way, spotlights the form or style that moral living should have. It too proclaims the sort of person we should be. Despite the apparent differences between "Respect life" and "Do not murder," they are really exactly the same sort of norm. They are both formal norms.

This sort of analysis could be pursued with the other prohibitions. Lying is precisely those violations of the truth that are unjustified. Promiscuity is irresponsible sexual behavior. Stealing occurs when one takes another's possession without a proportionate reason.[5] In all these cases, the norm does not actually give any information about the real premoral values of a situation. It does not really attempt to write a script for our lives, to tell us what to do. Rather, it denominates the posture of moral agents who successfully deal with the values that confront them in their lives. It tells us who to be. It proclaims the nonnegotiable goal that applies to every situation.

Implications

So there are such things as formal norms. But having said this, and having defined what formal norms are, two further questions arise. One simply asks why formal norms have been created at all. The other asks why it is so important to distinguish them from material norms. We ask both these questions because our objective is a strategy for living the Christian life. We are not interested in idle distinctions, and so we legitimately ask: What difference does it make?

So, to the first question. It may well have occurred to the reader by this time that formal norms are really tautologies. That is, they repeat themselves and somehow involve circular logic. We found that "Do not murder" really means "Wrong killings are wrong."[6] Since this is so, one wonders why we should have such norms. There is no doubt that we do. This entire discussion of values and norms has merely described what people do and how they talk. We have created nothing, we have merely noticed what is. But still, it may be worth inquiring why people think and talk this way. Why do people make such statements?

The answer, and it is a very significant answer, involves returning to an insight discussed much earlier in this book. In chapter 5 we discussed the difference between speculative and evaluative knowledge. We discovered how important evaluative knowledge is, but also how neglected it can be in our technological culture. The distinction comes to mind once again in this context. For if one's goal is solely and precisely to get information about what one ought to do, then clearly formal norms are of little use. But is information the only need of the human moral agent? Is it really true that my only moral problem is to discern what I ought to do, that once I have that information I always obey it? By no means.

At least as important as information for the moral enterprise is motivation. I do not only need the data, I also need encouragement. I need formulations of my own values, formulations that in their conciseness and directness help me to remain faithful to those values. And here is the specific (and very important) function of formal norms. They take the meaning of humanity, with its challenge of intellect and freedom. They further specify that meaning to a particular area of human life (for example, property rights). And they declare, in pithy form, what I already know but tend to forget or neglect: Do not steal. By presenting me with that challenge, almost in aphoristic style, formal norms serve me in those moments of human weakness and temptation that are so much a part of our sin-affected situation.[7]

Formal norms, especially, are the homiletics of the Christian moral life.[8] Indeed, it is no accident that much preaching as well as much of the writing in Church documents is cast in the language of formal norms, challenging people to responsibility, urging them to fidelity, calling them to generosity. And it could hardly be otherwise. Preachers and those who write for large and diverse audiences cannot get into the minutiae of the unique situations that confront their people. They cannot make people's decisions for them. They cannot conclude the comparative evaluation of the various premoral values for them (though in many cases they can assist in that process). So such moral leaders speak the only language that is applicable to all, the only language that is general enough to apply in all situations. They speak the language of formal norms.[9]

So formal norms exist because ethical discourse has not one function but two. That is the simple answer to our first question. The second question asks why it is so important for us to distinguish formal and material norms in our analysis. Again the answer is simple. Indeed, it has already been implied, but it should be said clearly. The distinction is important for us because only formal norms are self-evidently exceptionless.

Inasmuch as formal norms specify styles of living that are characteristic of the moral person, they speak without fear of contradiction. It is always right to be honest; it is never right to be promiscuous. But inasmuch as material norms point at concrete values that reside in the moral situation, and inasmuch as those values coexist with others that might arguably have to take precedence, such norms are necessarily susceptible to exception. Generally one should not kill, but sometimes it may be necessary. Generally one should speak the truth, but sometimes deception must occur.

This does not mean that there will necessarily be exceptions to all material norms. It is precisely the purpose of the debate about intrinsically evil acts to raise that question. And the last chapter revealed the conviction of this author that at least one material norm – that prohibiting the direct killing of the innocent – can be proven exceptionless. What it does mean is that the debate must, indeed, take place. For the exceptionless character of any material norm will have to be proven. It cannot be presumed.

In some cases, a certain sort of exceptionlessness may, in fact, be proven rather easily. After all, the very nature of material norms makes clear that any given norm will be more or less applicable as it includes more or fewer of the relevant considerations. If I say: "Tell the complete, unvarnished truth." I am probably expressing a norm for which there will be many exceptions. If I say: "Tell the truth to on-duty policemen investigating crimes," I am coming much closer to a norm without exceptions. And the more specific conditions that are added to the norm itself, the closer to being exceptionless it will be. Thus, we may have occasion to speak of "virtually exceptionless material norms," "practical absolutes," if you will. That is, we may very well be able to formulate norms that, although we can imagine an exception that is theoretically possible, present themselves as without exception in the ordinary run of life.

Still, if I wish to find a material norm that is *absolutely* exceptionless, and if, realizing what was said earlier, I wish to accept the challenge to *prove* this exceptionless character, then I will need a very specific sort of argument. For, as we saw briefly at the end of chapter 14, the grounds for asserting that a material norm is exceptionless cannot be that the forbidden act will always be the most destructive of the available options, that its consequences are evidently and always unduly harmful. For to make that assertion, one would have to be able to read the future, to envision that indefinite number of potential conflicting premoral values, and to demonstrate that in every conceivable case this alternative is worse than all other available options. And that, of course, is by definition an impossible task.

So our reflection on the character of material norms, although it does not exclude altogether the possibility of an exceptionless norm, does make clear that some other ground for that certainty will have to be found. And that ground, as indicated in the last chapter and as we shall see again, is the intrinsic incompatibility of some acts with the very existence of morality itself.

Thus, a reason for the importance of drawing the distinction between formal norms that describe qualities of the moral person and material norms that specify values in the moral situation is that only in this way can we keep clear the issues and the elements in the debate about intrinsically evil acts. And that, of course, is most important as we seek to develop a strategy for Christian living.

Conclusion

We can now bring together what has been said in this chapter and thereby enrich the overall vision of moral living that was developed in chapter 14.

As human persons, and all the more as Christians who understand something of the dignity and destiny of our world, we are called to goodness and responsibility. We experience ourselves as accountable, as challenged by ourselves and our world, as worthy of praise or blame depending on how we respond. Whether this phenomenon is viewed as conscience/1, as Heideggerian located being, or as von Hildebrand's experience of importance, it is a central aspect of existence.

This call to be moral, moreover, makes itself heard across the length and breadth of our lives. No matter what the situation, no matter what the concrete issue, we experience ourselves as called and challenged by the real. We must do what is right. We must find and pursue the good. We must cultivate and nurture existence, we must be agents of creation and not of destruction. This is what it means to be moral, and these images describe the most fundamental of all moral values.

But we can be a bit more concrete. We can speak of the sort of people we should be in particular areas. We can talk about honesty and justice, about chastity and temperance, about love and respect, about generosity and concern. These, too, are moral values, for they are good things and, indeed, good things without which one is really a failure as a human being. They are virtues, and the virtuous person should be the end product of human living.

So we can speak of these values. And having found them for ourselves, we can proclaim them to one another. We can cast them in the language of norms. Such norms are formal, of course. They are general and abstract. They do not tell us precisely what to do. They do not really give us any new information about our specific situation. In fact, they give us no information at all; they tell us nothing we did not already know. But they are important nonetheless, for they focus the goal of our endeavors, they challenge and motivate us, they urge us to carry on. And, in describing the kind of people we should be, they are utterly absolute.

Still the question returns: "What should I do?" And the answer is very clear: "There is a real world out there. Deal with it." And as we do, we find that it is a world of values, of "goods" and "bads." We find that these values are real, but we also find that they are in competition with one another. We find that we cannot realize all of them, that sometimes we must even do something harmful that good may result. But for all that, we cannot ignore them.

We find, in other words, that it is a world of premoral values and disvalues. And we sense that the term "premoral" introduces both a negative and a positive tone. There is a negative tone, for the term reminds us that these values are less than moral. Their achievement may not be utterly essential to being a good person. And in some cases it may be expressive of a bad moral person, as in the case of the person who acquires wealth without attention to its effects on others. But there is also a positive tone. For the term "premoral" reminds us that these values are the input for our moral lives, they are the content with which we deal, the reality to which we respond. They lead to the moral judgment.

These values, too, are something we talk to each other about. They are something we seek to communicate, especially since such values can often be overlooked. In a society where elective abortion is increasingly common, someone must speak out regarding the value of fetal life. In a world where women are often denied opportunities for the expression of their talents and gifts, the central truth of human dignity, with its quite specific implications regarding full participation, must be trumpeted. In a time of sexual confusion, the meaning and value of physical intimacy must be rearticulated. In a situation where technological skill can outrun human control, specific values and disvalues in medicine, in scientific research, in cybernetics must be isolated and proclaimed. In all these areas, precisely because they are so important, we must at least attempt to write a script. We must at least attempt to say concretely what we ought to do.

When we formulate this script, we have material norms. Concrete, informational, instructive; but also debatable, often tentative, open to the possibility of exceptions. Such norms may not settle personal or social issues. Rather, they point to values. They shed light on the situation. And in so doing, they specify for moral agents at least some of the factors they must take into account in reaching their final judgment.

For that is what agents must do. They must deal with that world, with its values and disvalues. To be moral persons, they must maximize the goods and minimize the evils, for only in that way can they fulfill themselves and their world. If they are sincere, then their life as a religious enterprise is safeguarded. But for moral persons, precisely because they are sincere, sincerity is not enough. They yearn also to be correct. And this not in order to be self-righteous but that good may truly flourish, that they and their neighbors may be treated as they deserve, that values may be protected and disvalues avoided, that the situations they encounter may be better as a result of their presence.

That is the strategy for the moral life. For there is a real world out there. And it is the world that God has made.[10]

Chapter 16

TRADITIONAL MORAL MAXIMS

W̲e continue our efforts to understand objective morality and, in particular, the reality of *intrinsically evil acts*. In the last chapter we equipped ourselves with the perspectives and the vocabulary of the contemporary discussion. Now we need to familiarize ourselves with that discussion's historical roots.

For the discussion of intrinsically evil acts, of the question about whether any concrete external behavioral alternatives are always the morally right or morally wrong action, is not new. It has been part of the Catholic tradition for at least five hundred years.[1] So the purpose of this chapter will be to review and retrieve that tradition, studying first the specific concept of intrinsically evil acts and then two related traditional concepts: the three-font principle and the principle of the double effect. At the same time, the purpose will also be to enrich that tradition with some contemporary reflections, assessments, and enhancements.

Intrinsice Malum

One of the notions most identified in the popular mind with the moral theology of the manuals is that of "intrinsically evil acts" (Latin *intrinsice malum*). The question is whether there are any specific external acts that a Christian person ought never, under any circumstance, to do. Are there any acts that, if freely done in any situation, always constitute moral wrong? The answer, at least for many theological authors, was that there are.

What are those acts? The first thing that is interesting about the answer to this question is that very few acts were usually proposed. For most of the areas of our lives, it turns out, the kind of division between moral and premoral values that we have seen was affirmed. That is, particular concrete acts were seen as good or bad, and therefore generally to be done or avoided. But it was recognized that there were exceptions.

that the case might arise where one value would have to yield to another, more important value.

In certain areas, however, this was not the case. In certain areas specific, concrete, material acts were viewed as intrinsically evil and therefore never to be done. So again we ask: What were those acts? Anywhere from three to five categories of acts were named in the traditional texts.

A first such category was lying. The purpose of the human faculty of speech is to communicate truth. It may not always be possible – or even right – to pursue that purpose actively. Secrets may need to be kept, confidences respected. Consequently, people may, for a greater good, need to be left in ignorance, or even in error. But, it was asserted, it is never right to do the opposite, to contribute actively to either error or ignorance. Lying is always wrong. It is intrinsically evil.

A second was committing suicide. It is true that one is not necessarily obliged to pursue all avenues to preserve life. And the sacrifice of one's life in the process of caring for others can even be virtuous. Still, human life is a gift from God. Human persons have the "use" of human life, but not control over it. To take one's life is therefore an act of presumption, a taking over of a divine prerogative. And thus the prohibition of suicide, though a material norm, is nonetheless an exceptionless norm. The act is intrinsically evil, in the sense that it is always wrong and for no reason justifiable.

A third was destroying the marriage contract. In the view of traditional Catholic theology, the prohibition against divorce and remarriage was absolute. At least in the case of sacramental and consummated marriages, remarriage was absolutely prohibited. Or to put this another way, the prohibition against divorce and remarriage in these cases, despite the fact that it was a material norm, was nonetheless viewed as an exceptionless norm.

A fourth area was sexual morality. The free exercise of the sexual faculty, apart from normal sexual intercourse within a marriage relationship, and indeed intercourse essentially open to the possibility of procreation, was prohibited, no matter what the intention or the situation. So, again, we have a material, but exceptionless, norm; we have a description of a material act that is nonetheless viewed as *intrinsice malum*, intrinsically evil.

A fifth area was the direct taking of innocent life. It was recognized that one sometimes has to take such life indirectly. For example, the cancerous uterus of a pregnant woman might have to be surgically removed even though the fetus would consequently die. Or a wartime pilot might have to drop bombs knowing that some noncombatants would also be killed. But to take such lives directly was forbidden. Putting this in our terminology once again, the prohibition of the direct taking of innocent life was seen to be a material norm, describing a quality of the situation, that was nonetheless exceptionless.

Now, the obvious question revolves around the grounds for these assertions. For only if we understand the reason these positions were taken can we determine if they are valid. An understanding of these reasons is difficult to achieve, however, because different explanations were given by different authors. What is more, the reasons for the absolute prohibitions seem to have varied with each of the five cases. But we can offer at least a brief summary of the typical presentation.[2]

Lying

In the case of lying, as intimated already, the argument was based on the "nature and purpose of the faculty." That is, it is clear what the function of the faculty of speech is: to communicate. Hence to use this faculty in such a way as to frustrate – indeed, to attack – that purpose is unnatural. It is an attack on the very meaning of humanity. And for that reason the act is immoral.

Now, as far as it went, that argument is quite plausible. But does it go far enough? As mentioned earlier, there are clearly times when we must withhold the truth. So silence is sometimes moral. But what of times when the only way to protect a "private" truth is to speak a "falsehood"? For instance, the classic, if homely, example of the door-to-door salesman who asks: "Is your mother home?" Some authors solved such a case by asserting that, although speaking falsehood is never right, since it violates the nature of the faculty of speech, it is not always necessary to protect others from "misunderstandings." Hence if I can speak an answer that is literally true but that will be misunderstood, then that is permissible. For the faculty of speech has not been contravened, and the private truth has remained protected. So, in our example one might respond, "No!" meaning "Mother is not home *to you*." Or one might respond, "I'm not sure," thinking that it is always just possible that in the last five seconds she has stepped out the back door and therefore is not, in the literal sense, "at home."

This style of analyzing the morality of truth telling, then, permitted the use of *mental reservations*, that is, internal editing of one's answer so that the answer, though literally true, would nonetheless have the effect of deceiving.

There are obvious objections to this approach. For one thing, it seems to make a game of the really quite serious obligation of truthful interpersonal communication. For another, it seems to require that one be quick on one's feet and, indeed, a bit duplicitous, in order to protect a secret virtuously. For another, it seems to focus with inappropriate and unnecessary passion on the "faculty of speech" when it should pay attention to the overall reality of communication, intended to build up community but with the potential to divide and harm.

For all these reasons, the trend in ethical reflection has, in recent years, been toward another approach. This approach makes a distinction between a *mendacium*, literally a lie, and a *falsiloquium*, a falsehood. That is, moral reflection has asserted the true obligation to respect the truth and to share the truth with others when it is needed or deserved. But it has accepted the fact that in some circumstances, where communication of the truth is not needed and deserved, service of the moral good can require the speaking of a falsehood.

We can put this another way, contemporary ethical reflection has come to understand the word "lie" as a formal, not a material, term. That is, it is a term designating inappropriately or unnecessarily false communication, rather than simply designating any communication that is not literally true. In sum, then, there would be little support today for the assertion that the prohibition of lying, to the extent that it is understood as a material norm, is absolute and exceptionless, for the assertion that the material act of lying is intrinsically evil.

Suicide

The case of suicide is quite different. As we indicated, the traditional argument for asserting that it is intrinsically evil was not that it was "unnatural" but that it was "presumptuous," that it went beyond the rights of the human person.

Once again, this is an interesting argument. It is not, however, altogether compelling, since there is no utterly decisive proof for the assertion that the human person does not have the right of free self-disposition. But more to the point, anyone involved in ordinary pastoral life must be struck by the insensitivity of considering suicide a "moral problem," as if people choose to end their lives the way people choose to write a bad check, violate a marital commitment, or procure an abortion. Suicide, after all, is a poignant, tragic psychological issue. It is a case not of freely chosen evil-doing but of inescapable personal despair. The agent of suicide is not a perpetrator, he or she is a victim. And thus the entire project of ethically evaluating suicide seems misguided.

There is, admittedly, one small "subspecies" of suicide that may be an apt candidate for ethical analysis. We have in mind the case, so popular in romantic novels and high school religion classes, of the spy or prisoner of war who faces the prospect of revealing state secrets to the detriment of millions. Can a person in this setting commit suicide?

Though the case is certainly not "common," it is useful as a way to test our theory. So perhaps a few words are appropriate. It seems that contemporary theology proposes various answers to the question. Some would argue, along with the tradition, that this suicide is an unjustified assumption of personal control over the gift of human life. Others would argue that we have here not suicide in the ordinary sense, but a variety of self-sacrifice, that the true analogue of this case is that of a soldier bravely marching into battle, that the detail that the death is self-inflicted is immaterial. Still others would argue that the case is closely related to that we shall consider shortly: the direct killing of the innocent.

In any case, it seems clear that how one ethically assesses this rare sort of suicide depends mainly on which broader category one puts it in. There is not a great deal of debate about the ethical status of each of the various categories, just about which category this case belongs in. So perhaps we should simply accept the ambiguity of the case, and thus the ambiguity of the assertion that suicide is an intrinsically evil act.

Remarriage

The argumentation in case of divorce and remarriage is different yet again. Indeed, it is quite different. Here two justifications are possible for the assertion that it is intrinsically evil, and both have been offered at one time or another. In fact, as E. Schillebeeckx has shown, the history of this prohibition is extremely complicated.[3] On the one hand, it can be argued that divorce and remarriage is prohibited because it violates the natural law, because it is intrinsically opposed to the meaning of human life properly lived. But if this is true, then it is hard to understand the Catholic practice of granting divorces "in favor of the faith." (This is the so-called Pauline Privilege, based on 1 Cor 7:12–15.)

In fact, if one is willing to argue that the tenets of the natural law should be understood here as in the other situations we have seen in these pages – namely, as premoral, as expressing real but relative values – then the practice of the Church (and the words of Paul) do make sense. The survival of a marriage truly is a value. But it is not an ultimate value, and it is not the only value. It must sometimes yield to other values, for not all values can be simultaneously served in a finite human world.

If one follows this line of thought, however, then the next question is why such a practice is not also permitted in the case of sacramental and consummated marriages. In answering this question, the second ground for the absolute prohibition emerges. What is that ground? It is the meaning of the Sacrament of Matrimony, the real and ontological bond that exists between the partners in such a marriage, which not even the Church can contravene.

Is such an assertion valid? Here this present writer must exercise some humility and say that he simply does not know. It must be left to sacramental theologians to determine whether this is an appropriate way to understand the Sacrament of Matrimony, and to biblical theologians to determine whether this is appropriately concluded from the often quoted words of Jesus prohibiting divorce (Mt 5:31f; Mk 10:1–12; Lk 16:18). All we can say here, as we have already said, is that there is no apparent reason why the objective, material fact of divorce and remarriage should be understood any differently than the general run of moral issues. Whether the reality of Christian life as prophetic, whether Christian marriage – not only as a natural fact but as a religious symbol, as a sign of the relationship of Christ and the Church (Eph 5:22–33) – demands this utter and exceptionless fidelity, we cannot here decide. But that it is not forbidden in such an absolute way by the natural law, that it is not a material disvalue so evil that no other good could ever justify it, we can and must affirm.[4]

Sexual Acts

Next we come to the area of sexual morality. Here, of course, the tradition judged to be intrinsically evil not just a single sort of act, but rather every sort of act except one. The ideal of genital behavior was described as the complete act of sexual intercourse, open to procreation, consummated between a man and a woman who are married to each other. Any other actuation of the genital faculty was judged to be wrong. Not just bad in the sense of "less than ideal," of "involving some negative aspects," but truly unjustifiable, morally wrong, intrinsically evil.

What were the grounds for this assertion? They bore a certain similarity to the arguments used in the case of lying. Observation, it was said, could teach us the true meaning and function of sexuality. The sexual organs have their purpose. The underlying human sexual faculty has its purpose. This purpose is presented to us not just as fact, but also as obligation. As this purpose is the "nature" of sexuality, so the demand of the "natural law" is to conform. Consequently, any other use of the sexual faculty is "unnatural" and therefore, no matter what the circumstances, results, or intention, morally wrong, intrinsically evil.

There is no denying that the basic claim that all nonideal expressions of genital sexuality are morally wrong is challenged today. And the challenge does not come merely from some secular, un-Christian source. Rather, it is evident that many believing Catholic Christians do not find this basic claim convincing. Still, it is not the purpose of this chapter – or even this whole book – to address that question. That is another important project that must await another time. Our purpose is to become clear about moral methodology, to establish an overarching vision of Christian morality and, in this case, of the reality of objective morality. So we can only ask a more modest question: What about the traditional *argument* for the intrinsically evil nature of all nonideal genital behavior?

It seems clear that the argument has at least two weak links. First, contemporary science has made clear that the allegedly obvious "purpose" of the sexual faculty is not so obvious, after all. Or perhaps it would be better to say that it is not obvious that there is only one purpose, or even that the various purposes interact in any single specific way. There may be many purposes to the sexual faculty, and the purposes may interact in varying ways. On the contrary, the traditional analysis owed perhaps even more to the specific historical and cultural context in which it was formulated than to any compelling and abiding philosophical logic. Second, even if these traditionally asserted "facts" of sexuality are true, it is not evident why they present themselves to us also as exceptionless obligation. Why is it inappropriate for human persons to use their intelligence, and the tools of technology, to modify those facts and to channel them more effectively toward the end of humanizing and fulfilling human behavior? In sum, is it really true that nonideal genital behaviors are "unnatural"? And even if it is in some sense true, why does that fact compel particular ways of behaving?

So it is not at all clear that the traditional argument for the status of nonideal genital behavior as intrinsically evil holds. Still, as mentioned earlier, the weakness of this argument does not mean that the conclusion is false. There may be other grounds for holding the conclusion. And even if one cannot prove that these behaviors are intrinsically evil in the technical sense, it may nonetheless be the fact that they have proven themselves so consistently destructive that on the grounds of the moral general natural law argumentation (pursuit of real human values in a world of conflict and change), they ought always to be avoided.

Direct Killing of the Innocent

Finally, we come to the case of the direct killing of the innocent. Here our analysis must proceed in a somewhat different fashion. For, as argued in chapter 14, it seems that this category of acts is, indeed, demonstrably intrinsically evil. Still, let us begin with the question that we have posed four times already: What were the grounds on which the tradition claimed that this category of acts is intrinsically evil?

Pursuing this question, we note that the grounds often offered in the Catholic tradition were those discussed when we considered suicide, namely, the absence of the right to act. The argument was that human persons are given human life as a gift, for their stewardship. But they are not the rulers of this life, and they have no right to dispose of it.

There is something to be said for this argument. You will recall that our problem, in the case of suicide, was that even in the rare case of will-ful suicide (e.g., military action) it wasn't clear that the act belonged in this category. We wondered if it belonged rather in the category of altruistic self-sacrifice. But the category itself remained plausible, and it remains so here.

It is also worth noting that this traditional argument was also extraor-dinarily nuanced. After all, we are talking about the *direct* killing of the *innocent*, two conditions that greatly limit the category. The tradition, in considering whether there was a kind of act that deserved to be called intrinsically evil, eliminated many kinds of killing from consideration. First, they eliminated killings that occur as a by-product of some other act. The classic example of this is the ending of fetal life in the course of a surgical intervention directly focused on saving the life of the mother. Second, they eliminated killings that occur in the process of defending oneself against attack. Again, a classic example was that of military action in war. Third, they eliminated killings that occur as an act of legitimate authority, supervising life in community, that is, capital punishment.[5]

Please note, the tradition did not necessarily judge that these acts are morally right. It simply did not take the positive step of asserting that they are intrinsically evil. It was only the direct killing of innocent (i.e., both nonaggressing and inculpable) human life that was so judged. And the grounds seem to have been that, at least in these cases, human persons have the duty of stewardship, not the right of disposition.

So this argument has something to commend it. On the other hand, it is not absolutely compelling. Precisely how do we know that we lack the right of disposition over human life? One could argue, after all, that, especially in an age when technology gives us an almost unnatural capacity to prolong life and an increasing capacity to create and modify it, human persons are challenged precisely by the right – and duty – to dispose of life in a responsible way. And if this is so, then the question is precisely what acts of death dealing might be really responsible exer-cises of this right. What, for example, of active euthanasia in the case of a person who surely will die of AIDS? What of abortion in the case where it is known that the fetus is severely handicapped and will die shortly after birth? Is there really no *right* to act in these cases? Even if the acts are wrong, is this the reason? Or is the reason rather that they are demonstrably irresponsible exercises of a right that human persons have nonetheless?

So the traditional argument, though intriguing, is not compelling. But, as we have said in other cases, weaknesses in the argument do not prove the fallacy of the conclusion. And in this case that is particularly true. For, as we saw in chapter 14, this category of acts does indeed present itself as intrinsically evil, though for a somewhat different reason.

As we saw before, the direct killing of the innocent can be demonstrated to be intrinsically evil because it is a radical attack on the very meaning of morality. Since morality is the task of responsible interpersonal care and is based on the fact of inherent human dignity, the disposal of nonthreatening human life is an attack not only on that individual life but also on the enterprise of morality. This sort of death dealing implies a rejection not only of the rights of the victim, but also the rights of all human persons. It asserts, by unavoidable implication, that human persons are not possessed of inherent rights, that they are essentially "components" of a project oriented toward the achievement of other ends. But if that is the case, then morality as a whole has no reason to exist. Indeed, the premise for the very existence of morality is the inherent dignity of human persons.

There is no denying that persons of goodwill – indeed, committed members of the Catholic church – sometimes challenge even this argument, for some tragic and heart-rending situations raise serious questions. Perhaps most poignant is the case of the terminally ill. Must we stand by as those we love are trapped in suffering? Is it not a sort of kindness to "put them out of their misery"? We claim that it is not. And we note that the Catholic tradition customarily used the distinction between direct and indirect in responding to this sort of objection.

The tradition would assert that it is our right (and duty) to intervene with persons in this situation, providing them with the kind of medical help that will ease their suffering and the kind of love that will support them in their ordeal. The medical help may, in fact, have the effect of shortening their life, and that is a "risk" of some pain medications. But that is all right. We are not obliged to maintain life at all costs. Indeed, the effort to maintain life is always no more than a temporary success in any case, since all human persons eventually die. If it happens that such a medication results in death, that is an "indirect" killing, the byproduct of the sincere attempt to be a caretaker to the living. And as such it is far from being an intrinsically evil act. Indeed, it could be a morally obligatory act.

What is intrinsically evil, by contrast, is the act of death dealing as such, the act whose true goal is (for whatever reason) to end the life. And active euthanasia, no matter how "well intentioned," is an example of just this reality. This sort of killing is intrinsically evil, then, for a very profound reason. It not only fails the patient, it fails ourselves. It runs away from our identity as lovers of persons and as faithful fellow-travelers on the road of life and death.

One further note should be offered to this argument. When we say that the direct killing of the innocent is intrinsically evil because it is a direct attack on the very meaning of morality, a treating of the human subject, possessed of inherent and inalienable rights, as merely an object, a quantity to be calculated against other finite goods, we are enunciating an argument that applies *only* to this case. We are saying that the direct killing of the innocent, and this act alone, is intrinsically evil for this reason. If there are other intrinsically evil acts, they must be intrinsically evil for some other reason. For this reason can apply only to the case of the ultimate disposing of the human person as such and as a whole.

In conclusion, then, we can answer our opening questions: What is this notion of *intrinsice malum*? What does it mean? How has it been defended – and how can it be?

Are there any concrete external action alternatives that it is always wrong to choose? We have seen that several sorts of acts have been proposed for this category. Some sorts may indeed always be wrong, for it is possible that they may be always the most destructive of the available alternatives. But we are not able to prove this in advance. And one sort, the direct killing of the innocent, clearly is always wrong, for it is not only the most destructive alternative for the victim, it is also intrinsically and decisively self-destructive for the agent and for morality as a whole.

And thus, radical respect for life, what is called the consistent ethic of life,[6] in the end presents itself to us not only as an interesting ethical focus, but also as the fundamental basis for Christian morality, indeed, as nothing else than a more specific formulation of the very identity of the ethical task.[7]

Three-Font Principle

We now move on to two other traditional principles, principles that, each in its own way, help to clarify our understanding of the reality of intrinsically evil acts.

The first of these cognate ideas speaks of the "three fonts of morality." We discussed this principle briefly in chapter 8. And the remarks that must be made here are really just an extension and completion of what was said there. But first we must summarize the principle again. It pointed out that human action involves three components: the deed itself, the relevant circumstances, and the motive of the agent. It asserted that to evaluate a human action morally one must evaluate each of these components. One must judge whether the deed itself is morally good, bad, or indifferent. One must consider whether any of the circumstances alter the moral quality of the act. Then one must judge whether the agent's motive is moral. And this maxim declared that an action is truly moral only if all three of the components are moral. If any one of them is not, then the action is immoral. (The trenchant Latin read: *Bonum ex integra causa, malum ex quocumque defectu.*)

Now, this traditional principle is impressive for its clarity, and often it is a helpful tool in dealing with the ambiguity of human life. But, as we saw in chapter 8, the dictum also contributes some ambiguity of its own. So at this point in our reflections it must be subjected to critical scrutiny.

First, as we saw in that earlier discussion, the principle combines the worlds of subjective and objective morality. This is, on balance, a good thing to do, since persons and their actions do always go together. But it is also important to keep the two realms distinct, as we have done in these pages.

If one is focusing on the subjective realm, on the realities of sanctity and actual sin, then it is clear that motive is the one and only font of morality. For salvation, as we have seen, is ultimately dependent on the genuineness of one's commitment and the sincerity of one's efforts to do the good. And that, after all, is what we mean by motive. And that is why the assessment of motive must always come first. For it is foundational within the vision of Christian morality.

But motive is not everything. (That would be relativism, as we have seen.) So it is also possible, and important, to focus on the objective realm, on the question of whether a specific action is objectively moral. But when we do that, it is the deed and the circumstances that demand our attention. For our question is precisely whether this deed in these circumstances is morally right or wrong. In this regard, two points need to be made, however.

The first is that deeds and circumstances are always assessed *in light of* the motive. That is, the first question to be asked of any action is whether it is, in fact, an apt way to achieve the goal expressed in the agent's motive. If not, then no matter the sincerity of the agent, we will claim that the action is objectively immoral. So, for example, two subjectively good and sincere persons who are unable to make an abiding commitment to each other may intend to express love and care in a genital action. The wisdom of the Christian tradition, however, is that this action, in these circumstances, is not apt for their goal. In the absence of commitment, that sort of intimacy is destructive.

Second, in many if not all cases, we do not know whether the action is objectively moral until we have assessed the deed and the circumstances taken together. Taken separately, these action elements are more likely to be premoral values or disvalues. For example, if the deed itself is taking money without permission, we know well enough that this is a disvalue. But we are not yet in a position to say whether it is immoral. Only when we add the circumstance that the money is being taken from a pauper by one who has sufficient funds himself or herself are we in a position to make the moral judgment: This is wrong.

Principle of the Double Effect

The third traditional formulation that deserves our attention at this point is the well-known principle of the double effect. This principle stated that, when confronted by a prospective action that will have two effects, one good and the other evil, I may do the action only if four conditions are satisfied: (1) the action itself must be good or indifferent, (2) my motive (intention) must be to achieve the good effect, (3) the good effect must not occur by means of the bad effect (for otherwise I truly intend the evil, however begrudgingly), and (4) there must be a proportionate reason for tolerating the evil effect.

Once again, we should freely acknowledge the pragmatic usefulness of this principle. It did give the sincere moral agent a way to sort out and analyze the complexities of the human situation. But that usefulness did not remove the substantial theoretical problems inherent here.

Consider the first condition. It speaks of the central action as being either good or indifferent. That is, the action must not be evil. Now, obviously the word "evil" in this context does not just mean "nonideal." It does not even mean "partially destructive." The point is that the action should not be morally evil, that is, intrinsically evil. But as we have seen, in only one case can we speak confidently of acts that are intrinsically evil irrespective of their circumstances. (And even then one might consider the victim's status as "innocent" to be a circumstance rather than part of the deed.) In all other cases, acts, apart from their circumstances, do not yet have any clearly defined moral status at all.

And consider the third condition. Human experience teaches that often we allow evil to function as the means for the achievement of good, and in a way that seems quite moral, even obligatory. Parents stay awake all night and deprive themselves of sleep to be available for their sick children. Doctors remove cancerous organs to save the patient's life. Christian ascetics do penance to become focused on the transcendent mystery of God. In our ordinary experience we judge as moral an action whose prevailing direction is toward the good, an action where the good outweighs the evil. Whether the evil arises as a coeffect or whether it is the means to the good is not pivotal.[8] The predominance of good is what counts.

Finally, and as a summary of the last two comments, we have come to see that every human action involves both good and bad effects, that this "grey" quality is an inevitable by-product of the finite nature of the human person. Indeed, in real life we are confronted not with "double effects," but with "multiple effects" that demand our attention as responsible moral agents. So, whereas the principle implies that it is responding to a specific subset of human choices, we see that it is really describing the essence of all human choices. Of course, some might object that the principle of the double effect did not have in mind just ordinary bad effects but rather morally bad effects. But again, as we have seen, effects taken by themselves are, as a general rule, neither moral nor immoral; they are premorally good or bad. Effects provide the input for a moral evaluation. They do not constitute that evaluation.[9]

So the principle of the double effect, as it was traditionally taught, had best be avoided. That does not mean that all the wisdom it contained is now to be jettisoned. Quite the contrary, the second condition of the principle remains important. Even though motive, as we have seen, does not immediately contribute to our evaluation of the objective morality of an action, it is nonetheless central to the actual pursuit of the Christian life. So its inclusion in a practical maxim is quite understandable and commendable. Similarly, the fourth condition is to be maintained. Indeed, the notion of proportionate reason lies at the very core of the vision of natural law that these chapters have developed. Rather than being one of four conditions, we now see proportionate reason, the living out of the virtue of prudence, as central to moral behavior. It is the proportional prevalence of premoral good over premoral evil that in fact characterizes the reality of moral action for the Christian person.

One last point. The principle of the double effect is often articulated through a more colloquial formulation: "The end does not justify the means." This formulation, precisely because of its familiarity, deserves a bit of analysis. The problem here is the ambiguity of the word "end." This term can be understood to refer either to motive ("I did it to help you"–*finis operantis*) or to result ("The action is the sort that will help you"–*finis operis*). But, as we have repeatedly seen, motive and result are very different things. Likewise, this maxim means very different things depending on how "end" is understood.

If we mean that one's motive does not justify the means, then the maxim is altogether true. Indeed, to justify means on the grounds of one's motive is the very definition of that relativism which we rejected in chapter 14. In contrast to this, experience teaches that good people, guided by good intentions, are forever doing objective injury to one another. So a good motive in no way provides an objective justification for the means (or, for that matter, for any other element of the total action). The action is objectively justified only by the fact that it really, truly does contribute to the good of the neighbor and the self.

But if the maxim means that the results do not justify the means, then it must be rejected. For it is precisely the results, where they are predominantly positive and premorally valuable, that do justify the means. Nothing else.[10] And this for all the reasons that have been developed through the last several chapters.

Several years ago a newspaper editorial provided an analysis of the American tragedy involved in the Watergate affair. The author asserted, in the course of his wide-ranging critique, that Watergate was the inevitable result of a naive and self-serving ethic willing to believe that "the end justifies the means." If the author is correct, then this is a telling objection to all that has been presented here. But is he?

Consider for the moment the deceptions perpetrated by those involved with Watergate, and compare them to the deceptions of Dietrich Bonhoeffer and his coconspirators in their attempt to assassinate Adolf Hitler. What is the difference? Is it that the latter group had noble intentions, whereas the former did not? Perhaps. But it is risky business to base objective moral judgments on the alleged quality of the agent's motives. Our criticism of Watergate dares not base itself only on the insincerity of the participants. Rather, we must (and certainly do) complain that what they did was objectively wrong. So again we ask: What is the difference between the two groups? Is it that the Germans did not use means that are evil (at least premorally evil)? This is patently not the case. Both groups indulged in deception. The difference, we would assert, is precisely a difference in the envisioned, intended, and actual results, and this in light of grossly different circumstances. The difference is that in the case of Watergate these ends (results) did not justify these means, whereas in the other case they did.

So we find that the editorial author, though no doubt working out of a valid intuition about the moral climate of Nixonian Washington, did not isolate the real enemy. The evil of Watergate was not the result of asserting that the end justifies the means. Rather, the evil was the result of a profound failure in judgment, a failure to realize that, precisely because only the end justifies the means, the proposed action should have been unequivocally condemned.[11]

Conclusion

The core of the ongoing exercise of Christian moral living is precisely the pursuit of realistic thinking, in a world where values conflict and can change. That is what Thomas Aquinas sensed in his encomium to prudence, as we shall see in chapter 17. That is what traditional moral theology intuited in its repeated emphasis on proportionate reason. And that is what contemporary ethical thinking is reasserting more forcefully than ever with its focus on, and distinguishing of, moral and premoral values, formal and material norms.

In developing a vision of the natural law, we emphasized the way in which real values conflict and are susceptible to change. In developing a strategy for living the Christian moral life, we saw that this realistic assessment of worldly complications was central. And now, having reflected on these traditional moral maxims, we find our earlier insight reaffirmed.

The traditional maxims were admirable creations in that they tried to specify the implications of prudence in a practical way. But they were regrettable in that this effort led to new confusions and even some errors. Perhaps there is a lesson here, namely, that it is impossible to eliminate the process of prudential judgment by which the moral person reaches concrete conclusions. Assistance can be provided, insight can be offered, the significance of the premoral values that comprise the situation can be highlighted. But the moral judgment can never be so sanitized and packaged that it frees the individual from her or his burden.

And if this is true, then the challenge of moral education is clearer than ever. In chapter 6 we talked about the development of Christian character. It now becomes powerfully evident how central that character is and how critically important is its development. The real search is not for values or norms, it is not for maxims or principles. The real search is for the prudent woman or man. For only that prudent person will have the skill to enflesh sincerity in the accurate assessment of the complex choices of daily life.

Chapter 17

THE CURRENT DEBATE

Through the last three chapters we have developed an understanding of objective morality, of why actions are right or wrong in themselves and irrespective of both subjective intention and extrinsic legislation. The overall vision of objective morality that was presented in chapter 14, though in certain respects unique to this writer, was largely representative of current thinking among Catholics. Chapter 15 shared some additional insights and clarified the terminology with which these ideas are discussed today. And chapter 16 went back into the history of Catholic moral thought to locate the roots of this contemporary vision, to see how fundamentally traditional this vision is and, at the same time, to be clear about the ways in which it is innovative.

Now a final project remains. This contemporary vision of objective morality has been the subject of some controversy. Indeed, one could argue that the most heated debate within Catholic theology through the last twenty years has been the one concerning the existence of absolute material norms, and the question of whether there are any intrinsically evil acts. And the discussion of this question has, more deeply, been a discussion about moral methodology, about the overall vision.

To some extent the debate has been caused – or fueled – by misunderstandings. But in other respects it has been a genuine disagreement about matters of substance. This present writer has been part of that debate; the first edition of this book is often cited among the last decade's contributions to the debate. And the insights offered by those many contributors to the debate have resulted in the substantial modifications of the moral vision that are found in this new edition, particularly in chapters 14 and 16.

Because the debate is about important theological matters, because the reader of this book is seeking to be an educated and intelligent participant in the discussions of the day, because the debate has had a significant impact on the overall life of the Catholic church, and because the presentation that has been made in these pages has, one hopes, moved the debate a step farther in providing a synthesis that can be the basis for future discussions, it is important that the debate itself receive our focused attention.

Proportionalism

The roots of the contemporary debate lie in an attempt by Catholic theologians to move beyond the constricted and often thoughtless style of the moral theology of the nineteenth- and twentieth-century manuals.[1] Although attempts to move beyond that tradition can be found in the early decades of the twentieth century, this particular advance, on the question of absolute material norms, is often dated from 1967 and the publication of a landmark article by theologian Peter Knauer.[2] It is interesting that the article focused not on intrinsically evil acts, but on the principle of the double effect. Still, chapter 16 has made clear how closely interlocked those two ideas are. So the choice of entry point, though interesting, is not critical.

The development of these ideas was the work of several European theologians, especially Josef Fuchs and Bruno Schuller.[3] But it was also given considerable attention in the United States, to the point that it could be argued that the United States became the center of the development. The work of Richard McCormick is most significant here, both because of his own astute contributions and because his famous annual summary of ethical discussions, "Notes on Moral Theology," facilitated the ongoing international conversation.[4]

The key elements of these developments are easy to summarize and, to a large degree, have been presented already in these pages. To be faithful to the Catholic tradition is to reject relativism and to acknowledge that behaviors have ethical significance before and apart from intention. At the same time, however, there is a need to avoid that extrinsicism which would settle ethical discussions with the simple assertion that the act is prohibited. For as the natural law tradition had always said, acts are forbidden because they are wrong, not wrong because they are forbidden. So legalism must equally be rejected.

But if actions are to be judged not on the basis merely of subjective intention nor because of the extrinsic accident of legislation, what alternative is there? The answer, of course, is that actions are judged on the basis of their actual effects on human persons and on the living of human life. Or, to put this another way, actions are judged on their consequences. And that, indeed, is the term often found in the literature, so much so that in some quarters this renewed approach to natural law came to be known as Consequentialism.[5] The term has some difficulties, however. Particularly troublesome is the tendency to associate this idea with utilitarianism, in the classic philosophical sense of John Stuart Mill, with its narrow, this-worldly goal of "the greatest happiness of the greatest number."

This association was often resisted, of course. Some argued that consequentialism is attentive to a much broader, richer, humanistic vision of fulfillment.[6] Others asserted that, unlike utilitarianism, consequentialism assesses actions against the consciously affirmed backdrop of Christian destiny, resurrected and endless life beyond the grave.[7] The potential for confusion, however, was serious enough that, little by little, the term has fallen into disfavor.

Still, the central concept, that actions are to be assessed in light of how they actually contribute to or detract from human fulfillment, remained central to this line of theological development. And attention to that concept led to a further insight: that, in fact, actions always *both* contribute to and detract from human fulfillment, that actions always have *both* good and bad effects.[8] It follows, then, that actions are adjudged to be moral not because they are perfect or ideal, but because of the proportionately positive value they evidence. And conversely, actions are adjudged to be immoral not because they are diabolical, but because they are disproportionately destructive. It is a matter of proportion.[9]

And that is the term which, in preference to consequentialism, came to be favored: proportionalism. But before we can give this approach a comprehensive definition, one last idea must be added.

This renewed vision of the natural law asserted clearly that the moral assessment of actions must be based on the actual function of the acts in human life, that to judge an act morally, one must look at the act itself. When one looks at human acts, however, one must look at them in the context of the reality of the world. And as contemporary philosophy and anthropology have made clear, the world is a reality in the midst of change. The study of history is, after all, the science built on the premise that things change, that the future is capable of being really different.[10] Along similar lines, it has often been pointed out that the Hebrew vision of time, as linear and open ended, was quite different from the Greek cyclic vision. Fidelity to that biblical vision, then, requires that we remind ourselves of the radical openness of the human process.[11]

But if this is true, and if it is also true that moral assessment is impossible apart from direct consideration of acts as they really function in human life, then we risk a radical ethical agnosticism, at least as regards exceptionless norms. Just because an action has always been unnecessarily, and therefore unjustifiably, destructive in the past, we cannot conclude that it will always be so. And therefore we cannot – by the very nature of reality and of morality – take the further step of making definitive concrete moral assertions about the future. We cannot know. We can only "wait and see." Therefore, it follows that the notion of absolute material norms, of concrete acts that are known to be intrinsically evil, is untenable. The very nature of natural law morality, the pursuit of objective value in a genuinely historical world, makes it impossible. Or to put this the other way around, this understanding of natural law makes clear that claims on behalf of intrinsically evil acts and of absolute material norms are, in actuality, nothing but disguised versions of legalism, subtle regressions into that distorted natural law tradition of recent centuries.

The contributors to this recent renewal, of course, wanted no part of that legalistic, extrinsicist heritage. And so they rejected, along with it, the idea of intrinsically evil acts. They preferred a courageous fidelity to the logic of intrinsicist natural law, pursued in the world of history. They preferred fidelity to the proportionalist methodology, pursued with respect for the perennial possibility of change.

That, then, is the definition of proportionalism.[12] It is an approach to morality that affirms intrinsic value in a world of conflict and change, that consequently describes moral decision making as the process of assessing the proportion of value and disvalue in specific acts, and that concludes to the radical impossibility of absolute material norms and to the contradictoriness of the idea of discoverable intrinsically evil external acts.[13]

Basic Goods Theory

Alongside this effort to renew Catholic natural law theory has been another, the product of a group of Catholic moral philosophers.[14] This second approach deserves our attention on its own merits, as will be obvious later. But it also demands attention because, in recent years, proportionalism and this second effort have entered into conflict to the point that they can be viewed accurately as alternative and competing methodologies within the natural law tradition. So we are challenged to judge between them or else, as is really the case, to go beyond them to a vision that incorporates the best of both. In fact, key elements of this second approach have already manifested themselves in these pages, particularly in the overview presented in chapter 14. For that reason, this perspective, like the first, can be summarized fairly briefly.

The primary architect of this second approach is Germain Grisez, an American, who presented a formulation of his ideas as far back as 1964.[15] The ideas have been communicated by a group of Grisez's colleagues in the United States, including Joseph Boyle and William E. May.[16] And within the last ten years the insights have been given their most substantial presentation – and have been significantly developed – by John Finnis, an Australian now at Oxford, England.[17]

The ethical argument presented by these authors has two elements. One is a critique of proportionalism as an argument that it is at best unusable and at worst contradictory. The second is the assertion that another approach is better because it is both reasonable and usable.[18] Lest this alternative approach be viewed simply as a reaction and not also as the positive contribution that it is, let us begin with the second element.

The key idea of this vision is that life presents the human person with certain *basic goods* that demand recognition and respect. These goods are essentially connected to human life as valuable, so that to attack these goods is, by the very nature of things, to act inhumanely and therefore immorally. It is not always possible to cultivate these goods actively, for human persons are, after all, finite. And therefore any reasonable selection of one or another good for particular attention is morally acceptable. But it is never right to attack the goods.

What is more, since all the basic goods are essential to the meaning of being human, since they are diverse and therefore incommensurable in the way that apples and oranges are incommensurable (or perhaps better, apples and insights!), there is no reasonable grounds for sacrificing one good to another. Instead, they must all be accepted in their plural reality and respected in the person's concrete choices.

Therefore, in response to the question, Are there any intrinsically evil acts? this approach would respond affirmatively. Acts that attack any of the basic goods or that sacrifice one good to another are intrinsically evil. For in attacking these goods they attack the reality of human persons as valuable and therefore attack the central meaning of the moral enterprise as such.

What are these basic goods? Finnis lists seven: life, knowledge, play, aesthetic experience, sociability (friendship), practical reasonableness, and religion.[19] Grisez offers substantially the same list, adding one additional good, personal integration (interior harmony), and in a recent listing combines knowledge and aesthetic experience into the pursuit of truth and beauty.[20]

How do we know that these are the basic goods, that all the items belong in the list and that there are no others? The response to these questions is twofold.

First, inasmuch as these basic goods present themselves to us as truly basic, it may not be appropriate to ask for "proof" of their status. After all, by definition there is nothing more basic in terms of which such a proof could be developed. Rather, what is proposed is a sort of convincing reflection. That is, reflection on one's own life reveals that certain activities are pursued for their own sakes, certain realities are, in fact, considered valuable in themselves.[21] This modest sort of proof is not insignificant, of course. Indeed, it was just this sort of phenomenological reflection that we pursued with von Hildebrand in chapter 11. So in response to the question, Are these goods basic? the answer is: Our experiences and reflection reveal that they are.

Second, if one asks whether other goods ought also to be included on the list, the response is simply to acknowledge the possibility. After all, the power of this moral approach does not lie in the precise naming of all the goods. Rather, it lies in the central assertion that there is a multiplicity of basic goods, all of which, even when they cannot be actively pursued, require the irreducible minimum of respect.[22] Thus, if the reader can think of yet another basic good, so much the better. For we do want to achieve as accurate a list as possible. At the same time, the developers of this approach, having reflected on the matter for years and having heard many proposals for additions to the list, find that this enumeration seems to exhaust the realistic possibilities.[23]

So there are several basic goods. All are essentially linked to human flourishing. Therefore all place a nonnegotiable claim on us as we proceed with the conduct of our lives. It follows from this that although neglect of one or another of these basic goods may be unavoidable in a world of finitude, direct attack on them is never justifiable. Indeed, it is fair to say that any act that constitutes such an attack on one or another basic good is, in and of itself, intrinsically morally evil. This is the essential core of the basic goods approach.

As mentioned earlier, the authors of this perspective place considerable emphasis on the fact that their proposal is an alternative to proportionalism and that the development of such an alternative is very important. For, in their view, proportionalism is a fatally flawed vision, a vision that ought not to be affirmed by those who wish to discuss Christian moral living. What arguments are offered in support of this opposition to proportionalism? There are two. First, because values are incommensurable, proportionalism is impossible. Second, if values are not incommensurable but rather commensurable (as proportionalism seems to require), proportionalism is literally absurd. Let us follow each of these lines of argument.

First, the critics of proportionalism argue that it is impossible because values are incommensurable. We saw that the values present themselves to us as truly *basic*, as individual and important in such a way that they are not to be rendered subordinate to one another. It follows that they *ought* not to be compared or measured against one another. We also saw that these basic values present themselves as truly *various*, as unique in such a way that they are like apples and oranges. From this it follows that they *cannot* be compared or measured against one another. From this dual insight, then, we can conclude that any theory that calls for comparing or measuring those values, any theory that claims that morality is constituted by doing as *much* good as possible, as if the various goods could and should be measured against each other, is proposing something that is wrong and indeed impossible. For it is calling for the comparing of things that should not and cannot be compared, that are literally incommensurable.

Second, the critics of proportionalism argue that this theory is absurd inasmuch as it presumes commensurability. This is a somewhat different and intriguing argument. Its starting point is morality as *free*. After all, the entire moral enterprise has no meaning if human persons are not free. Why bother with the struggle to choose rightly if I am not able to choose at all? Apart from that freedom, there is no such thing as morality.

But what happens if (as proportionalism apparently presumes) values are truly commensurable? What happens is that we have values neatly listed on some mythical hierarchy of values (the "most good," the "better value," etc.). But if the moral agent is confronted by just this sort of clear hierarchy of values, then the choice of anything less than the best choice (the right choice) is not only wrong, it is also incomprehensible. Why would anyone take two dollars when there are five dollars on the table? Such an alternative is ridiculous, indeed existentially impossible. In such a case there simply is no freedom to choose anything except the greater good. For that greater good, inasmuch as it is commensurable with the lesser goods, includes them and absorbs them so that they no longer remain plausible alternatives in their own right. Therefore, in a real sense I no longer have freedom to choose in such a circumstance. The right choice is, in fact, the only choice – which, to that extent, is no choice at all.

Paradoxically, then, the possibility of real choice only exists where, and to the extent that, alternatives are truly incommensurable. And consequently, if an action alternative is wrong, it is not wrong because the good chosen isn't really "better" than the good rejected. Rather, the reason for the immorality, if that is the case, is because the good rejected ought not, on its own merits, to have been rejected in that way.

And that, of course, is not what proportionalism says. Proportionalism calls for comparative selection. And that presumes commensurability. But if there is commensurability, then free choice, the essential prerequisite for any morality at all, is impossible. Therefore, since proportionalism as a moral system calls for free choice on the basis of conditions (commensurability) that render free choice impossible, it is, as a moral system, absurd. Not just wrong, not just impossible, but internally and intrinsically absurd.[24]

A Third Alternative

Thus far we have given a systematic presentation of proportionalism and the basic goods vision. What can be said about this? It is this writer's judgment that both approaches include assertions that are quite true, indeed that both approaches represent essential components of a comprehensive Christian vision of objective morality. What is needed is not some simplistic choice between the two alternatives, then, but a thoughtful combination of them.

In the overall presentation of objective morality in chapter 14 we have already seen such a synthesis. This chapter, then, does not need to repeat it. But several other things are needed. First, we need to see precisely how the synthesis is faithful to both approaches and responds to the objections of each. Second, we need to see why the two approaches are not, themselves, adequate accounts of objective morality.[25]

The Contribution of Basic Goods

In the synthetic presentation in chapter 14, our ending point was the neuralgic question of whether "intrinsically evil acts" exist. That is, are there specific external acts that, irrespective of intention, ought to be judged to be always wrong and, therefore, never to be intended by human persons? And our answer, you'll recall, is that at least one such act exists: the direct killing of the innocent.

Around this issue, as we saw, proportionalism is not able to make a positive answer. Given the core assertion that moral judgments are always judgments made among alternatives, that is, judgments made in a context of conflict and within history, a decisive affirmative answer to the question of intrinsically evil acts is impossible. We just don't know what conflicts the future may bring. Therefore, if it is true that this act is intrinsically evil (as this author claims), then a basic goods approach is needed. For only a basic goods approach explains the immorality of the act, in that it highlights the internal incoherence of some acts with the very project of morality, which is to act responsibly toward the end of human fulfillment. And, of course, we saw that life itself was always listed as one of the basic goods.

As a matter of fact, our explanation of the immorality of the direct killing of the innocent is not dependent solely on the tenets of the basic goods approach. It is also greatly enriched by the insights of Paul

Ramsey, who, though sympathetic to the perspectives of that approach, can hardly be considered a member of the "basic goods school." It was Ramsey who pointed out that human persons are not themselves mere premoral goods to be comparatively evaluated. Indeed, they are not even moral goods, if by that one means "objects" in the moral world. Rather, human persons are the *subjects* of the whole moral enterprise. It is, after all, the central thrust of morality to guide us in caring for human persons. Therefore, to kill the innocent directly is not to judge incorrectly *within* morality. Rather, it is to attack the very existence and meaning *of* morality.[26]

The basic goods approach proceeds, of course, to speak of other "intrinsically evil acts." Indeed, it is the core of this vision that there are several basic goods, all of which must be respected at all times, at least to the extent of not directly attacking them. And this certainly makes sense. Inasmuch as the other basic goods, such things as religion, knowledge, interpersonal communion, and the like, are inextricably connected to the flourishing of human persons, to attack these goods directly is to attack directly the person who, as Ramsey puts it, is the subject of morality itself.

But there is something different about these other basic goods. They are not *material* realities in the way that life itself is. Rather, they are *formal*, that is, they are aspects of human being that can result from any number of specific acts and, in a particular context, might be attacked by the very act that otherwise would nurture them. If a man shoots his terminally ill brother, we know that we have a direct killing of the innocent. And we may conclude that no matter how good the subjective intention of the agent, the action is morally wrong. But if a man refuses to go on vacation with his brother, we do not know whether this act constitutes a direct attack on the basic good of friendship (or for that matter, of play) or not. The act is, in itself, premoral, and its morality (the assessment of whether it constitutes a direct attack on a basic good) remains to be judged.

So even though the norm, "Do not directly kill the innocent," is a material, though moral, norm, the norm, "Do not directly attack the basic good of friendship," is a formal, and thus moral, norm. But that, of course, is a position with which all contemporary moral theologians, including proportionalists, are in complete agreement, as we saw in chapter 15. So there is no special contribution made at this point by the proponents of the basic goods approach. Indeed, it may be quite the opposite. For the obvious question is: How shall we assess whether a particular act constitutes a direct attack on these formal basic goods? And the proponents of this approach say relatively little on this matter.

The Contribution of Proportionalism

The proportionalists, on the other hand, make the answer to this question their primary agenda. They emphasize that the concrete selection of acts in pursuit of these formal basic goods takes place within a world of conflict and change, where not all good acts are compossible and where the relative constructiveness of particular acts may vary across time and space. They conclude from this that the heart of daily moral decision making is the selection of specific acts from among the available alternatives, that the summary moral challenge is therefore, "Do as much good as possible and as little harm as necessary," and consequently that, as Aquinas taught, the central moral virtue is prudence, the developed skill of concrete judgment within the world. On the basis of all this, then, proportionalists succeed in articulating a very helpful strategy for moral living.

But can this be? The critique of proportionalism by the proponents of a basic goods approach rejects the comparative assessment that lies at the heart of this strategy. They claim that inasmuch as basic goods are incommensurable, it is wrong to make comparisons, for this act of comparing sacrifices one good to another inappropriately. What is more, they argue that if the goods are in any sense really commensurable, moral judgment is impossible because we are no longer free. What can be said of this? Several points must be made.

First, there is the simple fact that human persons do, indeed, make just these sorts of judgments and that they experience them as morally significant. We struggle regularly with questions of how to spend our money, where to put our time, how to handle the competing demands of our lives, and the like. We say: "I think I should stay home and study for this test, not go to the movie. To do otherwise would be irresponsible (immoral)." It may not be clear how we can theoretically explain this activity. But it does take place. So whatever else we may say, let us not be led to deny our experience just because our theory is weak.[27]

Second, this human practice has long been recognized and, indeed, celebrated by the Catholic moral tradition. We have seen that "proportionate reason" is a criterion often put forward by the tradition in assessing the morality of specific acts. The principle of the double effect as well as a number of other traditional maxims such as the principle of totality, the just war theory, and the criteria for material cooperation in the moral evil of others all included the requirement that there be a proportionate reason for the harm that the act would involve. Similarly, Thomas Aquinas was forceful in claiming that the central moral virtue was prudence. That is, although love, as the "heart of all the virtues," must be present as the underlying motive for moral action, the essence of the moral judgment itself is astute and wise judgment among the alternatives presented by the concrete world. And since the alternatives presented are so complex, wise judgment is itself a skill, indeed a moral skill or virtue – the virtue called prudence. And, of course, the exercise of this virtue is the very act that we have described as conscience/2 and that the tradition termed "moral science." So, in highlighting the challenge of selecting among alternatives in a world where not all good things can be done, proportionalists are doing nothing more than restating a long-standing claim of our tradition.

Third, though this may seem surprising, even the proponents of a basic goods approach affirm the practice of proportionate reasoning. They do not give it great attention, which, after all, is the reason that the proportionalists are more helpful at the level of concrete moral strategy. Also, proponents of a basic goods approach take great pains to point out that proportionate reasoning is not the final or sufficient ground for moral rectitude, which, of course, is the point already made here as well. But they do affirm it.[28] This is all the more curious given their strong assertion that basic goods, as incommensurable, are strictly incomparable.

Which brings us to a fourth observation. We can understand the human practice, exercised by all, of indulging in these comparisons if we make a simple distinction between incommensurability, as the proponents of the basic goods approach define it, and *comparability*. Once again, it is Protestant theologian Paul Ramsey who suggests the essential idea.

Ramsey begins by acknowledging that

the distinction between the *directly voluntary* and the *indirectly voluntary* has functioned to recognize a sort of ambiguity that cannot be eliminated from moral choice. It calls our attention to the unavoidable ambiguity which arises when we confront incommensurate goods or evils.[29]

And yet Ramsey believes that even in these situations, where one is confronted by various basic (and therefore incommensurable) goods,

it may still be that values are in some sense *comparable*, that some are higher than others. Values may be comparable qualitatively. . . . Higher and lower values, more worthy and less worthy goods, may be known to us while still there may be gaps – incommensurability – in the scale, or perhaps there may be no clear single scale on which to measure the lesser or greater good or evil.[30]

Indeed, for Ramsey, the phenomenon of strict commensurability is relatively less common. It "deals with only a limited number of similarities or differences in the comparison of goods or evils."[31] On the contrary, moral comparisons among values that are, strictly speaking, incommensurable are not only possible, they are relatively more common. "Such indeterminate decisions are frequent in human experience."[32]

Ramsey goes on to make several important related points. "Judgments of comparative overall similarity or dissimilarity are exceedingly difficult to execute or to account for in moral reasoning."[33] That is, first, although the phenomenon of incommensurability does not mean that we don't make these comparisons (experience manifests that we do), it does mean that they are exceedingly difficult, even slippery. (An argument, one would think, for rigorous moral conversation among those who seek to love their neighbor well.) And second, this comparison among incommensurables, though part of our everyday experience, is difficult to explain theoretically. But, as his own presentation exemplifies, our difficulties at the level of theory should not tempt us to deny the data of our experience. All the more is this true if, as Ramsey asserts in his third point, the tradition has long acknowledged the rightness of comparisons of incommensurables. For "the term *proportionate* has traditionally been used in the totality of the rule of double effect to refer also to what I now call indeterminate decisions and not for commensurate decisions alone."[34]

These quotations from Ramsey reveal a vision considerably more complex and subtle than that proposed by the supporters of the basic goods approach. They had argued that specific values are either commensurable or they are not. If they are, then proportionality is absurd, since no one ever chooses the measurably less when the measurably more is available. If they are not, then proportionality is impossible. Ramsey's analysis, on the contrary, affirms common experience by acknowledging the possibility of comparison with or without commensurability. There are purely technical comparisons, cases of strict commensurability. And it is true that, in such cases, it is ridiculous to imagine that one would knowingly select the lesser. But much more common are comparisons among incommensurables. In this case, says Ramsey, there nonetheless remains enough similarity (qualitative, as he calls it) that comparison remains possible, even if they are "exceedingly difficult to execute or account for." Such comparisons are indeterminate, but they are not impossible. Ambiguity is, in the end, different than *absolute* incommensurability.

Conclusion

So, if the special strength of the basic goods approach is that it explains clearly and cogently the foundation of moral action for human persons and the inner dynamic of human responsibility that characterizes Christian morality, the strength of proportionalism is that it clarifies the strategy of everyday decision making that Christians must pursue. For as proportionalists make clear (and as proponents of the basic goods approach agree), respect for the basic goods still and also demands the exercise of prudence within a world of conflict and change.

Proportionalism is not, in the end, an adequate system for the understanding of objective morality. For that task we need a broader vision of who the human person is and what the radical challenges of the moral task are. Something like a basic goods approach is more helpful here. At the very least it helps us to understand the radicality of the obligation to respect life, to maintain a consistent ethic of life, and never to solve the real problems of life by simply eliminating the persons who have or cause those problems.

Proportionalism, on the other hand, is a useful tool for the development of moral strategy. For it articulates with clarity the concrete task that faces the moral person in the process of trying to live a life of reverence, respect, and compassion. Indeed, to this extent, proportionalism is the contemporary articulation of the perennial vision of the Christian task, presented to all the followers of Jesus from Jerusalem to our home town.

But if it is thus clear that both of these approaches offer complementary strengths, it is equally true that both are, by themselves, incomplete. It is time to move beyond the polarities of these approaches in seeking a sufficient and comprehensive description of objective morality as understood in the Catholic Christian tradition. The presentation developed in chapter 14, amplified in chapters 15 and 16, and precisely located in this chapter intends to do just that.

Chapter 18

THE KNOWABILITY
OF NATURAL LAW

In discussing the natural law, theologian Karl Rahner declares that "the mutability or immutability of this law and the possibility of knowing it are an important theme in Greek and Christian philosophy."[1] In the last several chapters we have dealt primarily with the first aspect of this theme while somewhat ignoring the second. In technical language, we have pursued metaphysical questions while avoiding epistemological ones. But that imbalance must now be rectified.

For Rahner is right. If our fundamental question is, "What should I do in living the Christian life, and how can I discover what I should do?" then the answer requires two investigations. On the one hand, it must be asked what in the nature of human persons and their world affects that answer. And this we have done. But on the other hand, it must also be asked what in ourselves as knowers affects that answer. And this we have not done.

So we devote one more chapter to the topic of natural law. In so doing, we will not be entering absolutely new areas of concern. For the knower and the known always go together. Rather, we will be looking again at topics that have already concerned us, but we will be approaching these topics from a new point of view. We will be tinting the picture already developed with the color of the way we human persons know.

Specifically, we will summarize some insights from the scholastic tradition. Then we will introduce three facts about ourselves as knowers, facts that must always be kept in mind as we seek to know the natural law. We will investigate those facts and try to appreciate their significance for our Christian lives.

Scholastics

The question is, "Can we know the natural law?" And the interesting thing about the scholastic answer is that even this tradition, which is sometimes accused of "naive realism," gave a guarded response. They answered, "Yes and no." Let us specify their response.

The manuals of moral theology began their discussions of the knowability of natural law by distinguishing three levels of that law. First, there are the most general and universal dictates of the natural law: "Do good and avoid evil." "Give to everyone their due." Norms such as these, dictates that are little more than definitions of the natural law itself, were judged by the scholastics to be absolutely knowable. Everyone knows that these norms express truth. And everyone feels obliged to obey them. We ought not to find this surprising, since these very universal norms are little else than alternative formulations of that basic dictate of conscience, the demand of conscience/1, which we considered in chapter 9. To be a human person is to be aware that one is accountable. Formulations of that fundamental accountability are what we mean by the first level of natural law.

The second level of natural law is comprised of norms that are more concrete than those considered earlier, but that are nevertheless still somewhat general. These are the norms on which people of goodwill generally agree, norms that function as basic rules of behavior in most situations. Scholastics suggested that the Ten Commandments of the Old Testament provide us with a typical list of such second-level natural law norms: "Adultery is wrong." "One ought to tell the truth." "Thou shalt not steal." These are second-level norms; and they, like the norms of the first level, were knowable by all, in the Scholastics' view. It is possible for people to deny these norms, particularly in the absence of good will. Nonetheless, most people know them and affirm them, even when they fail to obey them.[2]

The third level of natural law contains all the extremely concrete and detailed applications of the more universal norms. They are the conclusions drawn by individuals or by communities, conclusions that make explicit what ought to be done or not done in a particular case. The case may be an utterly unique situation never to be repeated, or it may be common and widely shared. But either way, the norms describing the morality of the case are third-level norms, for they attempt to express rightness or wrongness in specific, detailed, and concrete terms. Such norms, said the Scholastics, are by no means universally known. Indeed, the attempt to formulate third-level norms is a task involving considerable risk and significant possibility of error. Why is this?

The reason lies in the intricacy of human reality. The fact of the matter is that life is complex, comprised of myriad significant factors, all of which must be taken into consideration in formulating the norms. It is extremely difficult to include all these factors and to evaluate them accurately. Consequently, even for the Scholastics, human attempts to formulate concrete moral norms are clumsy, risky, and difficult. Moreover, even when such norms are accurately formulated, their ability to be communicated to others, to be shared in a convincing way, is problematic. To use a contemporary example, the vast majority of Catholic theologians as well as many Protestant theologians currently share the opinion that most (if not all) abortions are immoral. But it is a painful fact of our current culture that these theologians and religious leaders have been notably unable to convince much of the general public of this moral judgment. This would not surprise members of the scholastic tradition, for they understood that all concrete norms, norms at the third level of the natural law, share this difficulty of certitude and communication.[3]

But if scholastic writers frankly admitted this difficulty, contemporary theologians confess even greater difficulty. And the three topics that explain this difficulty now demand our attention.

Weakness of Formulations

We begin our investigation of current insights by distinguishing very strongly between understandings of the natural law and the formulation of those understandings. It is one thing to say that I know something; it is quite another to articulate and verbalize that knowledge. Indeed, many things in our experience we know quite surely but cannot adequately express. Thus it is extremely important in the matter of the natural law, as in other matters, to distinguish between understandings and formulations.

The moral history of humankind is cluttered with the corpses of moral norms, formulations of the natural law that failed to express accurately the reality beneath. Consider an example we have used before, the usual text of the Fifth Commandment: "Thou shall not kill." What is the meaning of this formulation? How adequate is it? Experience and common wisdom immediately respond that the norm is by no means adequate. There is the sad but recurring necessity of war that generated the Catholic just war theory. There is the widely (but by no means universally) accepted right of governments to employ capital punishment, when and if it is in the best interests of society. There is the right of persons to defend themselves against unjust aggressors, criminals or irresponsible people who would do them harm. And all these cases must be taken into account. It is clear that human beings possess some sort of moral obligation to respect the sanctity of life. But it is equally clear that the norm as expressed in the Fifth Commandment does not precisely define that moral obligation.

Thus, through the centuries people of wisdom and common sense have felt themselves obliged to nuance and clarify that general statement. In so doing they have exemplified what we now see as a basic fact of life, namely, that formulations never succeed in capturing all the intricacies and complexities of our moral obligations.[4]

There is a very clear reason that this is so. If we think about it, we realize that formulations, and indeed all human words, are clumsy and indelicate tools for the expressing of reality. Reality is subtle and fluid; words are static and rigid. Reality is individual and at least partly unique; words are abstract and universal. Reality, existing in time, always retains the possibility of change; words exist in a timeless and static death.[5] We cannot avoid the use of words, of course. They are the main way at our disposal for the expression of our insights into moral obligation. Indeed, as we saw in chapter 13, they are one of the two characteristic ways at the disposal of human, physical persons for the achievement of their life goal, the goal of spirit, which is communion in knowledge and love.

But for all that, words are never genuinely adequate to their task of communion. And they are most definitely clumsy, if unavoidable, instruments of moral communication. As long as people exist, they will express their moral convictions in formulations. But for the same period of time they will also continue to add subordinate clauses to those formulations in the vain but understandable attempt to achieve utter accuracy.

Therefore, we must be careful to distinguish our understanding of natural law from the formulations of that natural law.[6] Indeed, we must be careful to do so not only because the difference between these two is factual, but also because failure to be conscious of it can lead to unfortunate conclusions.

For example, one will occasionally hear the argument that natural law must not exist, since, if it did, people would surely agree on its formulations and we would not have all the moral disagreements and debates that we do. But in light of what has been said here, we can see how fallacious this reasoning is. Just because women and men of good will cannot agree on the formulation of the natural law, it does not follow that they lack genuine insight into its nature. Even more, it certainly does not follow that this law is nonexistent. As we saw in our earlier discussion of evaluative knowledge, many things in life are real that cannot be put into accurate words.

Thus this insight reminds us to be humble about our own formulations, to anticipate the fact that they will not communicate our thoughts with perfect accuracy. It reminds us to be thoughtful and questioning with regard to the formulations of others; not to presume too quickly that real communication has taken place.[7] And it reminds us always to protect our understandings by recognizing that they are different from the language in which they are clothed. For only in this way can we grant the weakness and inadequacy of much religious and ethical language and at the same time continue to affirm the reality of moral obligation.

Partiality of Understandings

But if our question, "Can we know the natural law?" is taken to mean, "Can we understand the natural law?" how shall we answer? To respond to this query, it will be necessary for us to make use of several insights derived from fields other than theology. The first of these insights comes from sociology. Sociology, of course, is the science of groups. It studies groups, their causes, their activities, and their effects. As its major premise, sociology presumes the "social construction of reality." That is, sociology presumes that groups have an effect on individuals, that to a greater or lesser extent groups influence and determine the individuals within.

Beginning about 1850, and continuing until recent years, sociologists have spent considerable time discussing *ideology* as a factor in group process. What is ideology? In its simplest terms, ideology is the distortion of reality for the sake of one's own interests. It is the denial of the facts of the case; it is the substitution of one's own desires. The witty cliché, "My mind's made up, don't confuse me with the facts," is a classic statement of ideology.

Karl Marx made much of ideology in his analysis of nineteenth-century Europe. The bourgeoisie, he asserted, did not recognize the true facts of their situation, their exploitation of the proletariat and their subjugation of the powerless, precisely because it was not in their best interests to do so. The bourgeoisie were affected by ideology, and that ideology prevented them from seeing the truth. Religion, for Marx, was an example of ideology, as was also the idealistic philosophy of his time. Marx judged all these groups to be guilty of "tunnel vision," a distortion and denial of reality out of self-interest. He accused them of ideology.[8]

For many years, then, it was common to distinguish ideology from objectivity. There are those who deny reality and those who accept it, those who distort and those who see the truth. And these two groups comprise all of humankind. In recent decades, however, sociologists have denied this clear dualism. In so doing, they have developed a new subscience within the field of sociology: the sociology of knowledge. This new science offers a contribution of major importance for theology and ethics. According to the sociologists of knowledge, there is a third possibility in addition to the two previously suggested: accurate but partial knowledge. Just because we see what is there, avoiding ideology and affirming reality, it does not follow that we see everything that lies before us. Indeed, it is impossible for us to see everything.[9]

For example, an artist and a botanist may contemplate the same tree. They are not guilty of ideology, of distorting its reality. Rather, they are open to that reality. But this does not mean that they "see" the same tree. They do not. For the artist the tree is a shape, a color, a combination of light and shadow. In a word, it is a thing of beauty. For the botanist the tree is a specimen of a particular species, having certain characteristics, capable of growing to a certain height at a certain rate. The artist and the botanist could each provide us with descriptions of what they see, but those descriptions would be quite different. Each of them has seen the tree, the truth. But their "in-sights" are by no means the same. What they see is determined, at least in part, by the perspective from which they look. It is determined by their identity as they approach the tree; it is determined by their position in the group. Their knowledge has, to some extent at least, a sociological explanation. Intellectually speaking, they "stand in different places," and thus they see the tree in quite different ways.

But what if two viewers share common vision? What if their approach is similar? Will they necessarily see the same thing? It depends. Where are they standing? If two artists view the same tree, but from opposite sides, they will not see the same thing. They will both see the tree; what they say about the tree will be true. But it will not be all truth, truth from all perspectives. It will be partial truth, in this case determined not by their intellectual position but by their geographical position. But the same point obtains: They see in a partial, limited, finite way. Though they speak the truth, they speak the truth from a distinct point of view.

The sociology of knowledge, then, asserts that all human knowledge is influenced by one's placement. Such placement can be intellectual, social, economic, geographical, or otherwise. But it is real, and it affects knowledge. When we escape ideology, we touch the truth. But we never conquer the truth; we never capture it totally. Reality is bigger than our understanding. Of course, the knower can move from one placement to another. We can educate ourselves to other ways of understanding; we can move from one location to another. The one thing we cannot do, however, is see reality from all points of view at once. We always stand somewhere, and the place where we stand determines what we see. Human knowledge, then, is never totally objective, in the sense of exhaustive, inclusive, neutral. It is always partial, always limited. Or to put this another way, in jargon that is commonly used: Human knowledge is always, and essentially, perspectival. It is knowledge from a particular, nonexhaustive perspective. "Men were usually right in what they affirmed and wrong in what they denied."[10] That was true in the past and remains true today. Just because we know the truth, it does not follow that we know all truth. Reality is bigger than our understandings, and it will always be so.

The implications of these insights from the sociology of knowledge for our study of natural law are evident. In the past, perhaps, we have been entirely too sanguine about our ability to touch, comprehend, grasp, and conquer the reality of our world. We have presumed that we could know the nature of human beings, that we could know it thoroughly, and that we could know it exhaustively. And that was very foolish.

There is no doubt that we do have some sense of reality, some understanding of our world and ourselves. So we are by no means prepared to say we know nothing. Indeed, thinkers of the past also wanted to avoid that admission at all costs. We can appreciate how, confronted with only the two choices of being labeled ideologists or else asserting total objectivity and total comprehension, they would choose for the latter. But with the development of the field of sociology of knowledge, thinkers, and Christians generally, are provided with another option.

To avoid admitting that our understandings are nothing but ideology, it is not necessary to go to the other extreme. What is more, it is not permissible to go to that extreme, not rational to do so. Do we know the natural law? Yes, no doubt we do. But do we know it comprehensively, exhaustively? No. Does our knowledge absolve us from the continuing task of searching out and pursuing the meaning of ourselves? By no means.

And again, when we know the natural law, do we know it in a neutral, simply "human" way? Again, by no means. As we have seen before, our ethic is not simply a human ethic, for all its commitment to the idea of a natural law. It is a profoundly Christian ethic. It is Christian because in the actual living of it, we are grounded in profoundly Christian motivations. But it is also Christian because, even when we look at the "world," at the objective reality of the natural law, we look with our own eyes, from our own perspective. And that perspective is Christian. And so, although it is true that what we see is objectively true (and therefore communicable to others – even, though with some effort, to those who do not share our initial perspective), it is also partial. It is a Christian view we have; and the world we see, the natural law we affirm, is tinged by that Christian "color" to which we are attuned.[11]

Knowledge, then, is much more a task than an accomplishment. It is something that is real, but it is also something partial. A little humility is going to have to be an increasingly prominent characteristic of theological reflections and discussions. And the topic of natural law is no exception.

Tentativeness of Understandings

We have been asking whether we can know the natural law. And we began our answer by coming to grips with the weakness of all human formulations. Beyond that, we also discovered that our underlying understandings are at best partial. Now we wish to make clear that our understandings are also tentative. For, as we shall see, it is always possible that a characteristic of the human person that we consider to be intrinsic, to be part of human nature as such, may actually be nothing more than an accident of historical, cultural, social, or psychological conditioning. It is always possible that though human beings "have always been thus," it is not necessary that they be thus. Consequently, when we set out to describe the nature of humans (and thus the natural law), our descriptions will always be characterized by a certain hesitancy, a certain tentativeness. But why is this so? The following observations may help to answer that question.[12]

What do we mean by human nature? Do we mean people as they now actually exist? That cannot be. For one thing, historical research makes very clear the fact that we have greatly evolved over the eons. We have changed, we do change, and we presumably will continue to change. Thus the status quo is by no means the benchmark of nature. But surely certain characteristics are common to all people throughout the centuries. Are not these characteristics the content of "human nature"? Perhaps not. For many theologians hold the opinion that God could have created the human species without the supernatural destiny that is, in fact, ours. And if we had been thus created, we would still have been humans. We would have been different from those people throughout the centuries, but not for all that any less human. What is more, the Christian belief in the resurrection of the body leads us to affirm that human existence will continue after death. Persons will still be persons. But will they be like the people of our experience? We have no way to tell.

Human nature, then, is not identical with the people who are part of our experience. In fact, in a certain sense, human nature does not exist. Persons exist. Persons possess human nature but are not identical with it. Existing persons, in the language of the Scholastics, are the composite of essence (nature) and accidents (all those qualities and attributes and characteristics of people that are but need not be). Thus human nature as such is the underlying structure to which all those accidents are connected, is that which is common to all people who have existed or could exist.

Human nature, then, is not an existential reality. Rather, it is a metaphysical concept. It is not "that which exists." Rather, it is "that by which we exist." It is a principle of being rather than an existing being (an *id quo* rather than an *id quod*). Human nature is a philosophical concept (*Begriff* in German), a concept grounded in reality, a thoroughly justified concept, but a concept nonetheless.

But how do we arrive at that concept? Perhaps it is not all that difficult to understand why there must be such a thing as human nature. But how do we decide what comprises human nature? In discussing the various historical differences, as well as the theological differences, among people, we have already implied the answer to that question. We discover the content of human nature through a process of subtraction. We look at human persons as they exist, as they have existed in the past, and as we imagine they might exist in the future. Under the light of faith we remind ourselves of the possible alternative modes of human existence: merely natural persons, fallen persons, redeemed persons, resurrected persons. And from this selection of existential varieties we subtract out all the variables. Whatever is true of only one sort of person cannot be human nature itself. So we eliminate it from our understanding. And just as the process of subtraction in arithmetic yields a remainder, our philosophical subtraction yields a "remainder concept" (*Restbegriff* in German). That remainder concept is, presumably, identical with the content of human nature.[13]

But is it? Or more precisely, can we be sure that it is? Clearly not. For we are historical beings, we have a future. And that future is open, since we are capable of change. We cannot be certain that the person of the past and the present will be the person of the future. Perhaps something that we now consider essential will someday reveal itself as merely accidental. For example, are humans essentially sexual, gendered beings? One would think so. It is more than likely. But can we be absolutely certain? No. It is at least conceivable that sexuality is merely a characteristic of people as they have existed, not as they must exist. Thus, precisely because our understanding of human nature, our concept of human nature, is a *Restbegriff*, that understanding will always have a certain tentativeness.

This point should not be overemphasized. There are some things about ourselves that we spontaneously judge to be essential. If we were not free, or at least called to freedom, would we still be human? If we were not rational, or capable of rationality, would we be human? If we were not physical, what then? Or (as we discovered in chapter 14 when we isolated that single dependable moral absolute which provides the grounding for the entire moral enterprise), if we were not accountable beings, beings with a "vocation to morality," would we still be human? Still, if we can sketch the broad outlines of human nature with some confidence, we must also be conscious that the details are far less certain.

One further point should be made here. And it can be brought out through the following example. Until recent years, it had been the practice of architects to design buildings in such a way as to hide the skeletal structure under surface decoration. Most of our homes were built in this way, as were many public buildings. One could look at such a building and know very well that a superstructure indeed existed; otherwise the building would not stand. But where is that superstructure? Which walls support the roof, and which are merely dividers? One could not always be sure. In some cases, one could be quite certain that a particular wall or façade or doorway was a nonessential addition (an accident). It could be removed and the building would still stand. In other cases, one could be relatively certain that a post or pillar was essential. But in many cases, perhaps most, one could not be certain. Of course there was a way to find out. One could remove the wall in question and see what happened. If the building still stood, it was nonessential. If the building collapsed, it was necessary. But in either case, absolute certitude could be achieved only at the risk of destruction.

The same is true of the nature of human beings. As we move through history, we do, in fact, change. To an increasing extent, that change is under our own control. We can plan and design that change; we can experiment. And some of those changes will no doubt indicate more precisely the perimeters of human nature. But experiments on humans, like all experiments, involve risk. And the risk in this case is the risk of self-destruction. We have the power to change ourselves and the power to destroy ourselves. The search for human nature is a search that can result in the destruction of human nature. Thus the only road to absolute certainty about the nature of the human is the road of self-destruction.[14]

For all these reasons, then, our understanding of our own nature will always be tentative. The concept of human nature is a remainder concept, a *Restbegriff*. And it will always be thus.

Conclusion

Can we know human nature and the natural law? We can finally summarize our threefold answer. First, if we are talking about the formulations of our understanding, we must acknowledge that formulations are often inadequate. Second, if we are referring to understandings themselves, we must be conscious that such understandings are always partial; they are subject to the sociology of knowledge. And third, such understandings are also tentative; they never possess apodictic certitude. We know much about ourselves, but we do not know everything. And what we do know is not always thoroughly certain.

Nonetheless, this knowledge is the basis for our moral judgments. And it must be so. For we are obligated, accountable, responsible beings. We are moral beings (seen from the subjective side as conscience/1 and from the objective side as the first principles of the natural law, the grounded character of that law). And so we must take what knowledge we have and use it to shape our life. We must do the best we can. For the Christian, this is what God expects – and it is all God expects.

Chapter 19

THE THEOLOGY OF HUMAN LAW

This author once had occasion to organize a program on the nature of human law. We wanted to include some discussion of the philosophy of human law, and our presumption was that we should hire a lawyer to speak to this topic. But we were quickly corrected. As a colleague said: "Lawyers are trained to be pragmatists. Their job is to know and use the law, whatever the law may be. The demands of their duties directly militate against a lawyer's temptation to step back and ask what the law should be. For your project you may want a political scientist, but you most certainly do not want a lawyer."

Perhaps the same comment could be made regarding the theology of human law. Whether one's focus is primarily civil law or the law of the Church, lawyers are not the ideal spokespersons for the understanding and interpretations that we seek. From the point of view of the civil or canon lawyer, and perhaps also of an administrator of state or Church, the law no doubt appears to be an "ultimate." The law dictates what is or is not to be done, and that is that. But such people view law as an ultimate only because they view it from within, so to speak. They see law only in terms of itself, and there is no denying that from that perspective law presents itself as an ultimate. For viewed thus, law presents itself as an exercise in power, and power is indeed a certain sort of ultimate. The law does what the law can get away with doing.

But power and true authority are very different things, as the sad history of many nations teaches. In the words of the cliché: "Might does not make right." Consider this example: If I am driving a sick friend to the hospital late at night and violate the speed limits, there is no denying that I can be ticketed and fined. I have violated the law, and the state is quite capable of punishing me. That is the prerogative of power. But for all that, it does not necessarily follow that I was wrong in speeding. One might well be able to make a case for the claim that I had a clear moral obligation to do exactly what I did and that I would have been wrong to obey the law in this case. The fact that authority is able to ignore this claim and to use its power to punish me does not change things in the slightest.

So it is important, in the context of a discussion of the principles of Catholic morality, to ask broad questions about the nature, purposes, and limits of human law. Our pursuit of these questions will have four parts. First, we shall see, in sketchy form, an outline of the traditional scholastic understanding of human law. We do this because that understanding offers us several worthwhile insights. Second, we shall consider in detail two alternative approaches to the question of whether, why, and how human laws impose moral obligation on us. This in turn will lead us to a series of related observations. Some conclusions will comprise the fourth part.

Traditional Understanding

Thomas Aquinas begins his entire treatise on law by developing a definition. Although this definition can in some ways be applied to any law, its most obvious relevance is to the category of human, positive law. Aquinas says that law is a "reasonable decision promulgated by competent authority for the common good" (I-II, 90, 4). This definition, which has been taken over and preserved in almost all scholastic writings, contains four separable elements, and each is very important.

Law is a reasonable decision. It is an exercise of human intelligence, not arbitrary and capricious but prudent and purposeful. It is a decision that is promulgated. That is, it is imposed on its subjects only after sufficient notice and, therefore, with due respect for their rights and dignity. It is created by competent authority, by the person or persons who legitimately exercise this function in a particular community and over particular matters. Finally, law is created for the common good. For all human law has as its general function the direction of social life among human persons. It is not primarily oriented toward the welfare of the isolated individual but rather concerns itself with the welfare of society itself.

This, then, is the generic definition of law. And in a special way it is the definition of human, positive law, those laws of Church and state. But behind the definition are a number of further points made by the Scholastics. These points are of interest to us both because of their content and because of the life vision that they implied.

For example, by further reflection on the notion of "common good," the Scholastics succeeded in specifying much more completely the proper functions of human law. They isolated two such functions.

First, it is common experience that many laws are actually human ratifications of precepts of the natural law. That is, a law of the Church or the state may repeat a dictate that is fundamentally moral (e.g., do not murder) and, by exercise of authority, urge its acceptance by the general populace. The justification for this function, though, must always lie in the common good. That is, it is not appropriate for human law to attempt to compel the inner reality of conscience. But inasmuch as the violation of the moral law has a real effect on the quality of human life (as we saw in analyzing the natural law), it is often necessary and appropriate for human law to attempt to coerce compliance where a particular citizen might not be personally inclined to do the good.[1]

Second, human law often functions as a means of particularizing and specifying the natural law. For example, it is clear that the natural law requires in justice that human persons give one another what is their due. But what is their due? In many subtle areas of economics, property rights, distribution of inherited property, and the like, the answer to that question is not at all clear. In such cases people properly reach determinations that, though they do not contradict the natural law, go beyond that law in precision and clarity. And these determinations quite appropriately assume the force of human law.

Or again, the natural moral law makes clear that people driving cars must take due care to avoid threatening the lives or property of others. But in order to achieve this goal someone must stipulate which side of the street to drive on, the meaning of various signs and signals, the speed at which one is permitted to travel, and numberless other details. It is one of the functions of human law to make decisions about these details in order to structure the common life of citizens so that they can, to the greatest extent possible, live together in peace and harmony.[2]

These, then, are the two traditional functions of human law, functions isolated by reflecting on the reality of the common good, which was mentioned in the definition of that law. Another component of the definition that received particular attention from the manual theologians was the idea of "competent authority." Interestingly enough, their reflections on this notion had the effect of establishing stringent limits to the development of human law. It was as if these theologians intuitively knew that we also need as much freedom as can reasonably be ours. Thus they were taking some pains to be sure law did not overburden the citizen in any way.

To this end, the Scholastics asserted that authorities, to be competent, must possess both jurisdiction and power. "Jurisdiction" means that they must be legislating for those *people* who truly are their responsibility. The governor of Illinois has jurisdiction over the citizens of Illinois but not those of Indiana. And "power" means that they must be legislating on a topic that is legitimate for them. An academic dean ought not to attempt to control academically irrelevant aspects of his or her teachers' lives. In the judgment of the scholastic tradition, then, human law is only justifiable when it arises from the decision of an authority possessing both jurisdiction and power.[3]

Finally, the manualists also took a closer look at the notion of "reasonable decision." Even granted that a particular law comes from a legitimate authority, it does not follow that the law is legitimate. In their opinion, for that latter situation to prevail the law itself must have four characteristics: First, it must be moral, not commanding its subjects to do something immoral. Second, it must be fair, treating all alike in those matters relevant to their welfare – and this precisely because the general purpose of law is the common good, and arbitrarily discriminatory law can never fulfill that purpose. Third, it must be possible. To command the impossible or the unreasonably difficult is to attack the welfare of society, not to serve it. Finally, for the same reasons, it must be useful. Useless law is, indeed, worse than useless; it is harmful. Thus, for the Scholastics, useless law is not at all binding on those who are its subjects.[4]

The truly interesting feature about these four characteristics of law, as about the distinctions made before, is the sensitivity and wisdom they imply. Even though the highly structured thinking of a scholastic synthesis may not completely mesh with contemporary styles, it is clear that the scholastic intention was perennially valid. It represents a concern for the commonweal, and for the maximum development of human persons, that is admirably human and thoroughly Christian in its inner dynamic.

Binding Force

Given this overall understanding of human law, however, the Scholastics were not without their differences of opinion. In particular, these revolved around the question of the precise binding force of law. This is a terribly important issue, both because of its specific details and because the two positions taken represent differing general understandings of human life. For the position one takes on this question tends to reflect a fundamental commitment on the question of whether human persons, as individuals, are worthy of unconditional respect, whether they are, in the end, trustworthy. The resolution of this question, which we will now pursue, consequently has immense implications for life in the Church and in the civil order in our own day.

Historically, the two approaches to the question of the binding force of human law are identified with the great theologians Francis Suarez and Thomas Aquinas.[5] Let us briefly outline the position held by each. Suarez, who died in 1617, was a theologian greatly influenced by the nominalistic and positivistic perspectives of that period. Thus, his basic understanding of law was a voluntaristic one. That is, he fundamentally conceived of law as an exercise of the *will* of legislators by which they ruled over subjects. The validity of the law was primarily a function of the legitimacy of the legislator. For the legislator was the source and repository of authority. Or, to put this another way, for Suarez, "authority" referred to a person and, indeed, was identified with that person.

This did not mean, of course, that a ruler could do absolutely anything. Suarez was familiar with the four-part definition of law that came from Thomas, and he accepted it. But it did mean that the definition was understood in a particular way. Two elements, "reasonable dictate" and "common good," were interpreted very broadly. It was presumed that whatever was proposed by the legitimate authority had those two characteristics, unless the opposite was very evident indeed. By the same token, the other two elements, "competent authority" and "promulgated," were interpreted rather strictly. Since authority was viewed as identified with the person of the ruler, it was of high importance that the legitimacy of his or her rule be clearly established.

One further point will help to "enflesh" this Suarezian vision even more. Traditional Catholic theology has long spoken of *epikeia* as an important factor in handling human law. *Epikeia* is a term describing the way in which a Christian ought to deal with what appears to be a conflict between the letter of the law and the spirit of the law. Thus, to return to an earlier example, if I violate speed limits in order to get a sick friend to the hospital, it is *epikeia* that justifies my doing so. But how shall we understand this thing called *epikeia*? Suarez had an answer.

Since law is essentially an exercise of the will of the legislator and achieves its validity by that will, *epikeia* can only be understood as the "benign interpretation of the legislator's will." That is, in an intuitive way I judge that if the legislator were with me in my car at 3:00 A.M., he or she would not want me to obey the speed limits. Rather, the legislator would want me to exercise due caution for the lives of others and then move to the hospital at the maximum possible speed. Since I judge that the legislator's will no longer stands behind this law, but rather supports just the opposite (or would if the facts were known), I am perfectly justified in violating the law in this instance.

All of this, however, was understood quite differently by Thomas Aquinas. Indeed, as recent scholarly rediscoveries have made clear, he could hardly have disagreed with this synthesis more. So let us try to sketch out the Thomistic vision on this question.

In the first place, the Thomistic view of law was in no way voluntaristic. Quite the contrary, like all of Thomas's theology, his conception of law was determined by the notion of finality. Classic philosophy had asserted that one knew something if one knew its four causes: material, formal, efficient, and final. And for Aquinas, the final cause was pivotal. A thing is justified by its purpose and by the fact that it truly achieves that purpose. It is the actual functionality of a thing that constitutes its *raison d'être*. Thus, far from being a voluntarist, Thomas was a thoroughgoing functionalist when it came to the question of human law.

Since this is the case, Thomas also held understandings of a number of specific points that differed greatly from those of Suarez. For example, Aquinas viewed law not primarily as an exercise of the will of the legislator, but as an exercise of the *intellect*. That is, law is the tool by which the legislator intelligently orders individual components of society so that the proper ends of society can be more easily achieved. Following from this, Thomas also avoided closely identifying human law with the person of the legislator. To the extent that a law is indeed an intelligent and functional servant of the common good, the law is self-justifying. It does not derive its force from the person of the legislator, but rather from its own evident utility.

This theory of law, moreover, led Thomas to understand "authority" in a special way. For him this term does not refer to a person; it refers to a function. One does not say that a person *is* the authority; one says a person *has* authority. That changes things substantially, for it tends to separate the law from the lawgiver and to make consideration of the law itself more important than consideration of the way the law was made. Thus, the Thomistic understanding, while accepting the same basic definition of law, handled it very differently. Those following Aquinas dealt very carefully with the two elements focused on the law, namely, the ideas of "reasonable dictate" and "common good." The elements oriented toward the lawgiver, on the other hand, were interpreted more broadly. There was less concern about whether the source of this self-validating law really was competent authority or whether all the niceties of promulgation had been observed.[6]

Finally, and following from all this, Thomas's general vision of law led him to a much richer understanding of the reality of *epikeia*. He would argue in this way: Since law is essentially the intelligent ordering of means to an end, *epikeia* must be understood as the "correct interpretation of the intention of the law." Every human law is an attempt to concretize in the letter of the law the intention of the spirit of the law. But inasmuch as everyday life is complex and constantly shifting, it is to be expected that the letter of the law will not always succeed in serving the spirit of the law. That, we could surmise, is the case in our example of the rush to the hospital. The real intent of the law is to protect lives. In this case, however, observing the speed limits will not protect lives.

Quite the contrary, it will threaten lives. That being the case, the Christian's duty is to the spirit of the law, to the intended end that is the common good. If the letter of the law does not in fact function in service to that end, the Christian must forsake it.

Further Observations

This Thomistic understanding of human law is rich in its relevance to our contemporary situation. Several further points will help to make that clear. First, note that we say Christians must forsake the letter of the law if it does not actually serve the common good in a particular case. It is not a matter of being permitted to violate the law. One is morally obligated to do so because the basic moral obligation is to seek the good. If a human law does not actually serve that good, Christians must do whatever will serve that good. Thus the notion of *epikeia* is not (as is often thought) a matter of replacing duty with un-Christian license. No, it is a matter of replacing one apparent duty (to the letter of the law) with another, more fundamental duty (to the spirit of the law, to its true function of serving the common good).

Second, since *epikeia* is here understood as a quality by which Christians pursue their moral obligation to the good, it is thoroughly understandable that Thomas asserts it to be a virtue (II-II, 120, 1 and 2). Just as justice, fairness, and chastity are virtues, so also is *epikeia*. *Epikeia* is the virtue (power, skill, habit) by which Christian persons discern the inner meaning of any human law so as to obey it intelligently in the majority of cases and to violate it reasonably in the properly exceptional case. *Epikeia* is the virtue by which Christians deal humanely with the reality of human law. They respect law for what it is, but they do not ask it to be what it is not. They recognize that no humanly formulated law can be expected to cover all possible contingencies (as we saw in chapter 18), so they accept their proper responsibility and deal with those contingencies when they arise. They do not hide out in the law. They use the law, respect it, and willingly go beyond it when they must.

Third, this understanding of law and of the virtue of *epikeia* makes clear that the opinion of the legislator is not, of itself, particularly relevant. In the Suarezian conception of *epikeia* as the benign interpretation of the legislator's will, it was quite possible that *epikeia* could be rendered useless by some announcement of the legislator. The ruler could simply proclaim: "What you view as my will is not my will. I now know your situation and nonetheless expect you to follow the letter of the law." And such a declaration would dispose of any appeal to *epikeia*. Not so in the Thomistic understanding. Christians could hear the legislator speak in this way and nonetheless continue to judge that in this case the letter of the law does not truly function in service of the common good. And if they so judge, Christians could (indeed, should) opt for some other behavior that they believe to achieve the spirit of the law more completely.

Of course, the legislator retains his or her ability to punish persons choosing to do this. Here we see again the difference between power and authority that was raised earlier. The fact that a legislator is not truly exercising functional authority in a given case does not, in this imperfect, sinful world, guarantee that he or she will not use dominative power to coerce and to punish. But "might does not make right." So Christians may in the end have to tolerate that punishment rather than do what they honestly believe to be "not good." Deciding this will take wisdom and prudence; the use of "proportionate reason," as we have seen, has long been recognized as central to the living of the Christian life. But it is a possibility that cannot be ignored.[7]

Fourth, it should be obvious that this Thomistic vision is highly consistent with our theory of the natural law. Like that theory, it presumes that values are real but subject to conflict and change. In the best sense of the word, this Thomistic view is pragmatic. It looks not to appearances and formalistic legitimacy; it looks to the facts and to actual utility. Indeed, this is perhaps the central difference between Suarezian and Thomistic concepts of human law. And it is painfully germane in our time.

For example, should a German citizen have obeyed the laws of Hitler's government? The Suarezian would tend to answer in the affirmative. Until it becomes overwhelmingly evident that these laws violate the more basic dictates of the natural law, one ought to obey. For Hitler's rise to power was altogether legitimate; he had the appearance of rightful authority, and obedience was therefore both justified and expected. Thomists, on the other hand, would not be unduly concerned about these niceties. They would attempt to judge the objective value of the laws, and on the basis of that judgment they would obey or they would not. In either case they would seek consistently to serve the spirit of the law so that the common good might truly be achieved.

But take another case: Should a Cuban citizen obey the laws of Castro's regime? Once again, the two theories would offer contradictory judgments. Suarezians would tend to say no. Inasmuch as Castro took power by violent and illegal means, his authority is not legitimate. Therefore, any law he might propose, even if it is a consummately intelligent means to the common good, does not of itself demand obedience. It is not truly binding human law. Thomists, of course, would say the opposite. Cuban citizens have the fundamental moral obligation to cooperate with any law that actually functions for the common good. It is not particularly important who formulated the law or by what means it was promulgated. The law's justification lies not in the legislator but in itself. And thus obedience is altogether required.

Finally, a third example. A celebrated political conflict within the Catholic church some years ago involved Cardinal Josef Mindszenty of Hungary and Pope Paul VI. Cardinal Mindszenty had been in voluntary captivity in the U.S. Embassy in Budapest for years. He refused to leave the country and thereby concede some victory to the Communists. Therefore, since he would not be permitted to return to his previous post and situation, he chose to remain in the embassy. After years of this "no-win" situation, however, Pope Paul VI arranged for (commanded?) Cardinal Mindszenty to leave his homeland and come to Rome. He did so, with considerable obvious displeasure.

Though it is dangerous to apply general labels to complex historical events, it seems that a good case could be made for viewing this episode as the result of a conflict between Suarezian and Thomistic theories of human law. There is no doubt that, at the beginning, Cardinal Mindszenty was unjustly hounded from his post by the Communists. So his decision to seek asylum and to remain in the country was likely a prudent, even astute, thing to do. But as time went along, things changed. And Mindszenty's view did not. He viewed the Communist party in Hungary as his eternal enemy. They had grasped power through violent means. They were illegitimate rulers. They professed to be atheists, and so their dictates could hardly fulfill the scholastic requirement that human law be moral. Thus he felt justified in altogether rejecting or ignoring the regime and all its works.

Pope Paul apparently interpreted the situation in a different way—we would say, a Thomistic way. The undeniable fact is that this regime does rule Hungary today. How they came to power becomes less and less relevant as time goes on. What is relevant is the question of what will best serve the common good here and now. It appeared that the Communist regime was enacting many laws that well served the people of Hungary. What is more, it was judged likely that, with the departure of Cardinal Mindszenty, greater freedom for the Church and for religious people in Hungary could yet be achieved. In other words, a tenuous, uncertain (typically human) judgment was made that the common good would best be served by some sort of rapprochement with the ruling regime. That rapprochement, with the calling of Cardinal Mindszenty to Rome as one of its components, was therefore pursued.

If newspaper accounts can be believed, it seems that Cardinal Mindszenty never fully understood or approved of this Vatican decision. And this is no surprise. From the Suarezian perspective of his own seminary training it was indefensible. The decision could only be defended from a quite different Thomistic point of view. The theology of human law, as it has retrieved its deeper Catholic roots, has been profoundly renewed in recent decades. And that shift of perspective no doubt added in its own sad way to the pain of the entire episode.

Conclusion

This brings us to a final observation, or complex of observations, that will also serve to conclude this chapter. We refer to the fact that the difference between these two understandings of human law, and of the way that law should be handled, is correlative to a differing understanding of the individual in relation to the group, which in turn is based on one's fundamental view of the trustworthiness of the human person.

There is no denying that the Thomistic conception of human law is highly respectful of individual Christians. It freely acknowledges their dignity, it emphasizes their right (and duty) to make independent judgments. In focusing itself in this way, of course, the Thomistic understanding runs the risk of encouraging anarchy. When legislators object to this theory on the ground that it makes their job more difficult, they are quite right. They no longer have the ability to command and to be obeyed simply because they have commanded. Within a Thomistic framework the legislator is obeyed only because the law serves, and is seen to serve, the common good. And all citizens reserve the right (and duty) to judge for themselves whether this is the case. So it is quite true that since the theory of human law that traces itself to Aquinas is undeniably grounded in a trust of the individual, there exists the consequent threat of disorder in the group at large.

But that threat must be tolerated. Why do we say this? There are two important reasons. First of all, Suarezian theories of human law are not without their own dangers. Whereas the Thomistic perspective risks anarchy in society, Suarezian visions risk tyranny.[8] By placing such high emphasis on the person of the legislator and on the obligation of obeying this individual, by effectively denying that individuals deserve to be trusted to make their own judgments, these theories are in constant danger of violating both the integrity of the individual citizen and the humanity of the legislator. They are in danger, paradoxically, of giving both too little credit to the citizen and too much to the ruler.

On the one hand, to deny individuals their right (and duty) to make personal judgments and decisions is to deny them a central component of their human dignity. And that is not only wrong, it is ultimately futile. For, against this first tendency, human persons inevitably and ultimately seek to reassert the reality of their dignity and the obligation of others to respect it. This has been the dynamic direction of human history over the last several hundred years. But the only way to resist it is tyranny, denying those rights and seeking to coerce compliance. Suarezian views are constantly tempted to such tyranny.

On the other hand, to focus authority on the person of the ruler is to make him or her a member of some "privileged order" of being. It is to deny the limitations of their creatureliness and, instead, to presume that by birth, appointment, ordination, or whatever, they have inevitably acquired the skills needed to guide wisely the conduct of public life – a "divine right of kings" myth of some sort. And that is, to say the least, a dubious supposition. But it is a necessary supposition, for without it the Suarezian view is internally contradictory. After all, the view tells us to obey the legislator because individual human persons cannot be trusted to make their own judgments. But if the myth is false, the legislator is, alas, an individual human person and therefore not worthy of trust! So once again, to avoid this contradiction the myth that the authority is superhuman must be maintained.

But this maneuver, too, is futile. For many reasons, not least the reality of instant communications in the modern world, it is utterly evident to ordinary people that their leaders are similarly ordinary. They have mothers and fathers, strengths and weaknesses. They engage in both work and leisure, have preferences and tastes. To invoke the homely dictum, they put their pants on one leg at a time, just like everyone else. And television and the print media make this ordinariness crashingly clear. This being the case, then, the myth must die. And a study of history reveals that it is dying.

Indeed, one can fairly characterize the series of political shifts in the last 300 years, both in secular and ecclesiastical structures, as the death throes of medieval monarchy. Not the death of authority, of course, even less the death of leadership – both these are perennial needs in the human community – but the death of a view that endows the person of the leader with qualities that remove him or her from the fellowship of ordinary human life. Indeed, the only way to prevent the death, to maintain the myth, or at least to maintain behaviors such as the myth used to motivate, is by tyranny. Suarezian views, then, are constantly tempted to tyranny.

So the first reason for tolerating the risks involved in a Thomistic understanding of human law is the dangers that the alternative theory itself entails. A second reason focuses on the "cosmological mood" implied by the two perspectives. What we have in mind is the fundamental optimism about the human person that is suggested by the Thomistic vision. In its willingness to tolerate the risk of anarchy, this theory is in effect asserting that anarchy is not likely to occur. It is claiming that people are not likely to take untoward advantage of their freedom, to exercise their alleged independence in a socially destructive way. At base, this theory is asserting that people are basically good, that they are inclined as human persons toward doing the good, and that good is far more likely to result from this expression of respect for them than is evil.

This optimism about people and their nature is no mean thing. It is characteristic of all of Thomas Aquinas's theology. Thomas recognized the reality of original sin, of course. But he was careful to point out that it has not altogether undermined the goodness of human nature, that nature is wounded but not destroyed. Aquinas acknowledged the reality of personal sin. But he was strong in asserting that sin is an act against the grain of human nature, that for the human person good is actually more attractive than evil, that one has to go against the very fiber of one's nature to choose selfishness and isolation and cruelty. And Thomas affirmed the central role that the community plays in the development of the morally upright human person. We are not meant to be isolated individuals, and the affirmation of human dignity is not a call to naive individualism. Rather, as humans we are essentially "located" beings. Still, Thomas affirmed that human persons, both in their individual natures and in their drives toward community and communication, retain a fundamental thrust toward the good. As we have seen in many places in this book, an anthropological optimism is one of the foremost characteristics of the writing of Thomas Aquinas and, even more profoundly, of the incarnational vision that is Catholic Christianity.

If many people do not accept this optimism today, and if, therefore, they are far more comfortable with the pessimism of a Suarezian theory of human law, then perhaps that is one of our problems. A well-known Catholic preacher once asserted that much of the evil that confronts us today is caused by the acceptance of the expression, "I gotta be me," as a principle of life. Of course, there is no doubt that this phrase, like any aphorism, is ambiguous. It can be interpreted in such a way that it represents an utterly selfish and, indeed, naive life program, an individualistic view that resists the complex of mutual responsibilities that constitute life in community. But such aberrations need not be the case. The fact of the matter is that I do "gotta be me." My own personhood is what I have been given by God as the challenge and the arena for the pursuit of my Christian life.

As we saw at the conclusion of the first half of this book, this personhood of mine is unique and communal. This last characteristic, essential as it is, provides the very grounding for the necessity of human law. At the same time, it is *my* life that has these characteristics. And the theology of conscience reminds us of the irreducible reality of personal responsibility and dignity, the very grounding of absolute natural law obligations, that is at the heart of a Christian morality.

All this can be asserted, then, in a way that is not negatively selfish precisely because we presume that "me" is, in all our individual cases, and even more when we come together in community, someone good, a being of dignity and beauty, a creature loved by God and blessed with life and grace. Because we, along with Thomas Aquinas and many great saints throughout the ages, stand in awful appreciation for the dignity of the person, we can celebrate and accept this Thomistic theory of human law.

We appreciate the need for law, on the one hand, because we appreciate the facts of life in our human, finite, partly sinful, and honestly weak world and, on the other, because we celebrate the communal nature of the human person. But we also recognize and clearly affirm the limitedness of law. Law is not the ultimate norm of life; it is not an ultimate in any sense. Law is a tool that we use. It serves us, we do not serve it. When it meets our needs and the needs of others, we obey it. Indeed, we obey it with joy and a cooperative spirit.

But when law fails to meet those lofty goals, we are neither distressed nor distracted. We are not distressed, for it is no surprise that law sometimes fails to express the truly good. It is, after all, only a human construct in the hands of human agents. More than that, it is static words seeking to capture a rather fluid reality. So it does not bother us that the law must at times be transcended. And we are not distracted, either. That is, we do not remove our attention from its proper object: the good. If the law guides us to the good, so much the better. But if it does not, then the law must be forsaken, it must be violated, it must be ignored. The good must be sought, always and in all things.

For the good, after all, is where God is finally to be found.

PART IV

Concluding Essays

Chapter 20

"CHRISTIAN" MORALITY

Throughout the chapters of this book we have presumably been seeking to understand Christian morality. Yet it must be admitted that our attention to explicitly religious concepts and sources has been sporadic. For much of the time, the discussion has been more philosophical and phenomenological.

This, of course, was no accident. In chapter 3 we presented an explicitly theological justification for this approach. But now, as we come to the end of our investigation, it may be useful to return to this topic and to reflect on it a bit more deeply. If we truly wish to hold and celebrate a Christian morality, as we do, what shall we mean by this term? What are the characteristics of such a morality? These are the questions that concern us in this present chapter.

If this Christian, Catholic ethic really is different, the difference could come from four angles: There could be different obligations, different sources of wisdom, a different vision, or different motives. Our position will be that Christian morality possesses all four of these differences, but in specific, limited senses.[1] And with regard to the first two differences, a very specific aberration will need to be rejected in order to clarify the positive understanding. Let take each in turn.

Different Obligations

Do Christians have specifically different obligations? Does a Catholic understanding of morality such as we are presenting here envision such obligations? Our answer is yes and no.

Yes, there are different obligations, for several reasons. First and most obviously, each and every human person has different obligations. This follows from the uniqueness that we discussed in chapter 10. For all our emphasis on "human morality," there is no such thing as simple, undifferentiated human morality. Each person's morality is to some extent unique, not in a relativistic sense where objective morality is replaced by solipsism, but in the sense that the objective uniqueness of a person generates objective uniqueness of obligation. Thus a person who has embraced the Christian Gospel and accepted the call to discipleship will, by that very fact, be bound to different obligations – not the least of which is the obligation to cultivate that radical commitment.

What is more, various groups have diverse moralities as a result of their diverse identities and circumstances. This follows from the understanding of natural law that we developed in chapter 14. The demands of objective morality present themselves in a world of diversity and change. There is your morality and mine, the morality of now and of then, the morality of here and of there. Thus different moralities are the norm, not the exception. It follows from this that Christian persons, too, inasmuch as they affiliate with religious communities and undertake religious activities, will find themselves confronted by obligations that are quite specific and at the same time quite different from those who have not made these commitments. Their worldly "locale," just as everyone else's, will generate obligations that should not be avoided. And religious duties, in particular, will emerge from this kind of personal and communal "situation."

Still, if there is a correct sense in which one should speak of the specifically different obligations of Christians, there is an incorrect sense as well. Indeed, a not uncommon tendency understands Christian morality in narrowly sectarian terms. Though this sectarianism has typical Protestant forms, let us focus here on its Catholic version.

This author remembers a grammar school student's comment that he didn't like being a Catholic because "it's wrong for me to play around with girls whereas it's all right for the public schoolers." What sort of distorted pedagogy would lead a Catholic to that notion? And yet it is common. Many Catholics, one suspects, believe that divorce is wrong simply because they are Catholics. Indeed, it is often forgotten that the Catholic church holds a marriage between two baptized Protestants, once consummated, to be sacramental and just as indissoluble as any Catholic marriage.

We already referred to this distortion under the title of ecclesiastical legalism in chapter 14. Here we simply remind ourselves that in light of the overall theory of natural law presented in these pages, Christians are called to do the humanly good thing and that consequently their moral obligations are generally synonymous with those of all people. Whatever we hold and teach to be right or wrong we so describe because the action is judged to be harmful to human persons. Therefore, moral assertions are assertions that the action in question should not be done by any person in a similar situation. With regard to the "worldly" duties of their everyday lives, Catholics do not have unique or specific moral obligations. Rather, they participate in the moral life that is the task and challenge of the entire human community.

What is more, to hold this material identity of Christian ethics and human ethics is not to say anything new. Even though it has not been particularly emphasized in recent centuries (for all the reasons that we saw in chapter 2), still the idea is very much part of our Catholic tradition. Indeed, it is one of the glories of the incarnational vision that is Catholic theology. For example, Thomas Aquinas, having analyzed the natural law, asks whether the law of the Old Testament added anything new from a moral point of view. His answer is that it really did not. His discussion makes clear that he sees the contribution of the Old Law as one of clarification and reinforcement. And Aquinas believes these are necessary, given human weakness due to original sin. But the law did not, in his view, introduce any materially new moral precepts (I-II, 99, 2).

Further on, Aquinas asks whether the law of the New Testament, the law of Christ, introduced any innovations. With one exception, his answer is the same. Having asserted that the essence of the New Law is the internal grace of the Holy Spirit, Aquinas goes on to claim that

the New Law had to make such prescriptions or prohibitions alone as are essential for the reception or right use of grace. . . . Hence Christ of himself instituted the Sacraments whereby we attain grace. . . . But the right use of grace is by means of works of charity. These, in so far as they are essential to virtue, pertain to the moral precepts which also formed part of the Old Law. Hence, in this respect, the New Law had nothing to add as regards external action. (I-II, 108, 2)

So, except for the sacraments, insofar as these can be viewed as "commands," there is no new moral dictate in the New Law, as there was none in the Old Law. The inescapable conclusion, then, is that for Aquinas there is really no such thing as a materially specific Christian ethic. And this very traditional position of his is what is emphatically espoused today and has been developed here.

Different Sources

But if Catholics do not have special ethical obligations, do they at least have special ethical sources? Is the distinguishing characteristic of Christian ethics the fonts from which its wisdom is derived? Once again, we will answer yes and no. There is a sense in which Catholic moral theology affirms both the Scriptures and the teachings of the Church as distinctive ethical sources. But there is also a sense in which this is not the case, a sense in which affirming the uniqueness of Christian ethical sources represents the aberration known as fundamentalism.

Repeatedly in these pages we have spoken of the dangerous temptation to reduce the moral obligations of the Christian to one sort of legalism or another, to suggest that certain actions are wrong because they are forbidden by the law. The error of this understanding is evident when one focuses on human law as an ethical source, and most particularly evident when one focuses on human civil law. And, as we saw, appeal to ecclesiastical law, or even to the law of God, is just as erroneous. Whether we consider the pronouncements of the ecclesial magisterium or the pages of sacred Scripture, it is clear that they cannot be considered a special source of ethical wisdom in the sense that their judgments make things right or wrong.

But what if we avoid this legalism? What if we assert that these sources do not create moral value but that they do articulate it in a special, privileged, and completely dependable way? Several responses are in order here.

First, we would have to assert, logically, that such ethical insights are also, in principle, available to all people through the use of human reason. That is, we would have to hold that ethical pronouncements of Scripture or magisterium are at most a species of confirmatory data. They reaffirm facts of human experience that have been, or can be, discerned and validated independently. Seen in this way, such pronouncements would be accepted as gift, as helpful illuminations of human experience, and not as a sort of burden imposed on the Christian as law. This, after all, is fundamentally the position exposed by Aquinas.

But what sort of dependability could such pronouncements have? That is, what would one do if such pronouncements of Scripture or magisterium appeared to conflict with the data of experience regarding the value of certain actions? It is surely naive to presume that this experience, particularly if it is limited to personal observations, is *prima facie* to be preferred. If anything, one could well argue that, given the presence of the Spirit in the Church, one should presume that the sacred sources are more trustworthy. If those sources present a unified commitment, even more if they claim to be quite certain, then giving them the presumption of the truth is quite reasonable. But is that the case? What, precisely, do we find in those sources? That is our next question.

With regard to Scripture, it must honestly be acknowledged that we rarely find either unanimity or independence of judgment. Rather, what we find are quite diverse judgments, judgments that often enough are rooted in various secular sources. As one Scripture scholar puts it,

There is an eclecticism that characterizes the New Testament ethic. The sayings of the sages, the ethics of the Stoic philosophers, contemporary ethical standards, the teaching of the rabbis, the Jewish catechism, the texts of the Bible, and the good sense of the New Testament authors each contribute to the content of New Testament ethics. The result is that there is both an openness and a pluralism in New Testament ethics. Consequently, it is not easy to, nor is it legitimate to reduce the ethical teachings of the New Testament to a single ethical view.[2]

Beyond this, it must also be admitted that some concrete moral judgments of the Bible can in no way be supported today. One thinks, for example, of Paul's dictates regarding slavery and the place of women. On the other hand, many of the more important ethical issues of our time (e.g., concrete questions of economic justice or medical and scientific procedures) receive no attention at all.

There is no doubt that the New Testament at least presents a relatively clear vision of the sort of person a Christian should be, a person of generosity and love, a person empowered by the Spirit, a person of prayer and good works.[3] But when it comes to the crucial question of whether particular actions are consistent with that personhood or not, the simple fact is that one cannot give the biblical texts implicit and uncritical trust. As one theologian put it,

the biblical renewal has emphasized the historical and cultural limitations of the Scriptures so that one cannot just apply the Scriptures in a somewhat timeless manner to problems existing in different historical circumstances.[4]

Indeed, this view that one cannot depend on the Scriptures to provide specific moral instruction has been affirmed even by the bishops of the Catholic church. In 1977, a somewhat controversial book presenting Christian reflections on human sexuality was published.[5] Subsequently, a rather critical response to the book was issued by the Committee on Doctrine of the U.S. National Conference of Catholic Bishops. And one of their complaints concerned the ways biblical texts were used in the book. One would expect that the bishops would have objected on the grounds that the authors had watered down the scriptural testimony, had failed to use a rigorous exegesis that would have supported traditional prohibitions. But quite the contrary is the case:

The Committee on Doctrine regrets to find in the report a rather impoverished concept of the role the word of God must play as a foundation for theology. While critical exegesis contributes to the church's understanding of the sacred texts, it cannot be considered the source of their meaning. God's word is proclaimed in the living reality of the church which by its teaching, its liturgy and the witness of its saints continues to reveal the riches of this word.[6]

This is a really remarkable statement. The bishops are, in effect, saying that the fundamental meaning of biblical texts is not necessarily the meaning intended by the original author, the meaning sought by the science of exegesis. Rather, they are saying, if you want to know what a scriptural text means, find out how the community has used the text in proclaiming its faith, find out how the text has been employed in worship, find out what holy people think the text means. For that is what it truly means. Just as the text was originally composed within a community of faith, to express that community's experience of God, so the text continues to abide in the community. And it is the community that continually interprets the text and rediscovers in the text the faith that it already lives.[7]

Hence, in the pursuit of the moral life, the primary function of biblical testimony is to assist the community in noticing and embracing its values, to challenge and stimulate the community. Anything more, any more definitive role for Scripture, is simply fundamentalism, a sort of biblical idolatry.

But if these reflections prompt a modesty in our expectations of Scripture, they may seem to imply just the opposite in the case of Church teaching. They may seem to suggest, indeed, that the really special source for moral knowledge is that body of ecclesiastical pronouncements. But that is not the case.

Indeed, similar observations, leading to a similar modesty, can be made with regard to the magisterium of the Church. We saw as much when we discussed this topic in detail in chapter 9. Here we need only supplement that discussion with a few additional comments. It is true that the First Vatican Council held that "the Roman Pontiff, when he speaks ex cathedra . . . possesses the infallibility with which the divine Redeemer willed his Church to be endowed in defining doctrine concerning faith or morals" (DS1839). But it is also true that, whatever the exact meaning of this declaration, it appears never to have been exercised in moral matters. Indeed, in the entire history of the Roman Catholic church there has never been a clearly infallible pronouncement by either pope or council on an ethical issue. All the teaching that has taken place has been of the sort known as "ordinary magisterium," teaching that does not pretend to be protected from the possibility of error.[8]

What is more, there has not even been a great deal of this sort of teaching. When concrete ethical questions have been submitted to the Vatican for discernment and judgment, quite commonly the response has been *videantur auctores probati* (consult the approved authors). In other words, the magisterium seems to have been sensitive to the complexity and ambiguity of such moral questions. It has preferred to allow the slow process of analysis and interpretation to continue rather than abort that process by premature declaration.[9]

The theory of natural law that has been developed in these pages, of course, makes us see the wisdom of this practice. To the extent that morally right action is precisely constituted by the maximization of premoral good over premoral evil, only one who is thoroughly aware of the various situational factors can dare to risk a definitive judgment. And there is no guarantee that such a judgment will continue to have validity in some new situation. Therefore the only case in which one can, with absolute confidence, articulate a perennial moral judgment is the case where the specific action is internally contradictory to the very living of the Christian life. And specific actions fitting this definition are, obviously, few and far between. So it is with good wisdom, and a very Christian sort of prudence, that the magisterium has generally chosen to avoid very specific ethical judgments. Indeed, to expect otherwise of the Church is to indulge in another form of fundamentalism, an ecclesial idolatry.[10]

Still, this effort to reject fundamentalism does not mean that Scripture and the teachings of the Church have no positive role. Quite the contrary.

In the case of the biblical materials, we have not only discussed this important role in these pages, we have seen it in action. Repeatedly we have gone to the Scriptures, not to find facile answers to the complex questions of life but to hear a challenge, to gain a perspective, to experience a context, to embrace a vision. We have experienced the truly absolute character of Scripture, not an absoluteness that escapes the incarnational reality of human experience, including the experience that the Holy Spirit guided in the development of these texts. Rather, we have experienced an absoluteness that affirms the presence of the divine precisely through and in the decisively human, and therefore limited and enculturated, reality of those pages.

In the case of Church teachings, the same point must be made, and perhaps even more forcefully inasmuch as the Church is more primordial. For it was the people of the Church who, under the guidance of the Spirit, created the Bible, and it is in the Church (as we saw in the statement of the American bishops' Doctrinal Committee) that the Bible continues to live. So we want to affirm in an emphatic manner the important, nonfundamentalistic role of Church teaching.

Once again, attention should be drawn to the remarks in chapter 9, where we pointed out three reasons for affirming the role of moral leadership in the Church. Here we simply add that the exercise of just this sort of leadership has always characterized the ministry of bishop (*episcopos*) in the Church. This moral leadership, moreover, has included both homiletic support for the ongoing project of Christian discipleship and pointed proclamation of concrete value insights of the community. But this leadership, particularly in the latter case, is "teaching" of a very unusual sort.[11] It is not so much an educational project, sharing wisdom and the reasons behind it (*cognitio per causas*, knowledge based on an understanding of the causes). Rather, it is more a form of prophetic initiative, a profoundly pastoral activity challenging deeper thinking on the part of all and more radical commitment to Christian values in a contemporary context.[12]

This activity, then, is quite appropriate within the Church. Indeed, given the human capacity for self-deception and weakness, it is critically necessary. The world, even that portion of the world that seeks to follow the way of Jesus with generous love, is badly in need of just that sort of moral leadership.

Different Vision

In the third place, we ask whether Christian morality is distinctively different by virtue of a particular vision of life. And here we need not answer yes and no. Indeed, we emphatically answer yes.

In discussing just now the proper role of Scripture as an ethical source, we began to see the importance of this vision. For, as believers and as followers of Christ we are gifted with a profoundly Christian view of the meaning of the world. This worldview functions as a basis and context for all our concrete moral judgments. In particular, it contributes two things: a deeper understanding of the human person's dignity and a clearer sense of her or his destiny.

We have already discussed the first of these items in chapter 10. The point is that, with our understanding of the mysterious reality of grace, we are in a position to grasp much more fully and more perfectly the real being and situation of human persons. Inasmuch as we know humankind to be supernatural, to be called by God in the depths of their hearts, to be, in essence, responders to revelation, we know the human mystery in ways no philosopher or social scientist can touch. We have, in Karl Rahner's phrase, a theological anthropology, a vision of the human that is shaped and guided by our theological commitments. And this vision of personal dignity contributes to our ethical judgments in offering us a benchmark in terms of which to judge the concrete good.

Similarly, the Christian vision of the world's meaning deeply affects our ethical thinking insofar as it speaks of the destiny of the human race. Our human hopes are not to be dashed. The human drive for interpersonal union, for life shared in love, is not to be frustrated. Indeed, these very human urges are but glimmers of the wonder God has in store for us. Thus there is great reason for us to accept and cooperate with the call to human growth, to fidelity and generosity and honor, that we hear within ourselves. Of course, it is not a matter of doing the "unpleasant good" in order to be rewarded at the end. Rather, it is a matter of knowing that the call to the good, a call that we sense as part of our human composition, is not the prelude to absurdity. It is not an invitation to develop ourselves only to be crushed into nothingness in the end. There is meaning to the best that is human. The world is ultimately benign and not perversely malignant.[13] The Christian life is not a cosmic joke but rather a joyous cosmic gift. Thus human beings have a dignity and destiny that give the Christian a very special sense of the meaning of the world.

Theologian Charles Curran has powerfully described precisely how the central doctrines of the Christian faith shape our vision of the world and thereby serve as a basis for a distinctive approach to morality.[14] As Curran sees it, there are five such doctrines. First, there is the doctrine of the goodness of creation, that grand truth proclaimed in the first chapters of Genesis. Second, there is the sad truth of sin also announced in Genesis, that potential for destructiveness that hides in the web of the human world. Paralleling these two doctrines of the Jewish Scriptures are two distinctively Christian doctrines. On an optimistic note, there is the doctrine of the Incarnation about which so much has been said in these pages. And there is the doctrine of the cross, that salvation came only at the cost of Jesus' life, that when God became human we put him to death.[15] Still, it is hope that energizes the living of the Christian life. So, as Curran views it, the doctrine of the resurrection, with its promise of a future of fulfillment, is what ultimately grounds the Christian vision of moral living.

Different Motives

Hearing this description of the Christian vision, and of the doctrinal commitments that shape it, it is not difficult to imagine their power to energize behavior. So it hardly seems a separate point to note that there is a Christian ethic in the sense of being characteristically Christian motivations for the actions people undertake and the commitments they maintain. Still, the insight should be emphasized. For no matter that our behavior is materially oriented toward the human good, in actuality it is existentially generated by a whole complex of peculiarly Christian motives.

If it is asked why the good should be done, no doubt one can properly answer that it should be done simply because it is the good. That is, a thoroughly human rationale can (and probably should) be offered for the behaviors that are encouraged or proscribed. That, after all, is what natural law means: that one's value commitments are in principle communicable in human, this-worldly categories. But if it is asked why I do the good, the answer would probably be quite different. It might be that the personal experience of Jesus Christ, the Savior who has personal love for each of us, motivates my altruistic behavior. It might be that the Church asks for this behavior, and the Church has gifted me with the experience of Christian community. It might be that I sense this behavior to be more in accord with the vision and ideals of Scripture. All these are most legitimate motives. Indeed, they are common if not universal motives. And to the extent that behavior is only well understood in the context of motivation, these motives rightly lead us to speak of a "Christian ethic."

This is no small thing to say. As we saw in our discussion of the sociology of knowledge in chapter 18, how one views a reality has tremendous reverberations on what one does about it. Indeed, in some ways "seeing makes it so"; vision is a fountainhead of behavior. For example, Christians may be doing the very same good deeds as their nonreligious neighbors, but Christians interpret their behavior very differently. They see it as a sign of love for the loving God, as a response to the gifts of Christ. They see their behavior as profoundly religious. And because they see it thus, it is thus.

To put this another way, the life of Christians may be materially identical to the life of other people. But it has a radically different formality. The Christian life is a life of Eucharist, of thanksgiving, of response to divine initiative. And this is so precisely because and to the extent that we see it to be so.

This point has been powerfully developed by the Protestant ethicist James Gustafson, and his thoughts deserve a bit of attention. Though granting the possibility of a theoretical (metaphysical) identity of Christian ethics and human ethics in the ideal, Gustafson reminds us that they are existentially quite different.

It might be interesting to find out whether historically the moral teachings of the Christian community have been distinguishably different from the moral teachings of other communities. . . . My suspicion is that most historians of cultures are likely to claim some distinctiveness.[16]

This is all the more true if one focuses on the contemporary scene.

It is almost ironic to ask this, for while the ablest moral theologians in the Catholic Church are working assiduously to indicate that Catholic ethics . . . are not radically distinguishable from general human ethics, most politicians, scientists, and physicians in North America would answer the question . . . with a resounding affirmative. My conjecture is that many persons would observe that the most distinctive moral community (with regard to its teachings) in North America is the Catholic Church.[17]

Why is this so? Gustafson makes a most significant contribution to our reflections when he states that "there are affective aspects to be accounted for. . . . I would in addition suggest that moral teachings . . . emerge out of historic human experience, and not simply out of a rational apprehension."[18] Having highlighted both the affective and the historical influences on the living of the Christian life, Gustafson concludes:

If the affective and the historical are not merely accidental, or merely a source of error, some things follow. . . . One need not be so apologetic about the distinctiveness of Catholic . . . or any other ethics. . . . To make my point in a dramatic way, we are not going to get ethics unqualified until we get rational minds unqualified by affectivity, or persons unqualified by particular histories; or knowledge of a moral order unqualified by historical and embodied experience.[19]

We have, of course, seen many of these ideas before. Recall the discussion of the centrality of Jesus in moral living in chapter 4, of evaluative knowledge in chapter 5, of the Christian life as communal in chapter 10, of the historical and contextual character of the natural law in chapter 14, and of the role of the sociology of knowledge in chapter 18. Now, however, they come together in this affirmation of a specifically Christian vision and vitality, of meanings and motivations that make the Christian moral life, as lived, distinctively different. And, as Gustafson's comments make clear, the difference is highly significant.

In the end, then, what we have developed in the pages of this book is a human ethic that is at the same time a profoundly Christian ethic. We have developed a Christian humanism, a vision that is in accord both with experience and with faith, and that is accountable to both these sources. We have been articulating a vision that recognizes the interpenetration of the divine and the human in the lives we lead, and that reflects that interpenetration.[20]

Christ and Natural Law

All this can be put another way, and a very important way. We have been developing an "incarnational" vision. And this vision has acknowledged that essentially and ultimately the natural law and the law of Christ are one and the same thing. Just as (and because) the divine and the human were conjoined in the person of Jesus, the Christ, so they are conjoined in the reality of this ethic.

This is no small thing. One often hears people speak of the law of Christ as if it were something quite different from the natural law, as if it were some additional or supererogatory ethic. It is not, as we have seen. So it may be helpful to conclude this reflection on the question of a specifically Christian ethic by noting the four ways in which these two laws are really and profoundly one.

First, the natural law is, properly understood, nothing else than the law of Christ "ontologically." As we saw in chapter 3, Christ is in no way the historical afterthought of creation. Rather, he stands at the very head of creation. He is its exemplary cause, the model on which its reality is based. Thus Christ is the ground of all things, and all things are potential sacraments of Christ. The result of this ontological connection is that any good action is a potential avenue of relationship with the divine. "The good leads to God." The similarity of these two terms is not merely a matter of spelling; it is also ontological. And this because of the central function of the Logos, the Son of the Father, the exemplary cause of creation.

Second, the natural law and the law of Christ are identical "existentially." By this term we mean to take note of the fact that humans have always possessed a supernatural destiny. Our existence, as it has actually been lived, has always been a supernaturally oriented and supernaturally shaped existence. We may assert (and indeed we must) that the supernatural gifts we affirm in faith are not owed strictly to us. They are truly gifts, undeserved and radically unrequired. But to say this is not to say that they have ever been withheld. Quite the contrary, the perspective of Christian history is that God has always been involved in the world, has always intended more for us than we deserve. Even if we may speak of "pure nature," metaphysical nature viewed apart from any supernatural additions, such a nature has never actually existed. It is a mental fiction. The humanity that has existed is supernaturally endowed humanity, Christian humanity. Thus the natural law is existentially identical with the law that is Christ himself.

Third, and following from the preceding, these two laws are synonymous "operationally." We saw in chapter 10 that it is only with the aid of grace that we are able to adopt a fundamental direction that is positive and oriented toward the good. It is only grace that makes us able to be all that we should be. Paradoxically, therefore, it is only by means of grace that we are capable of becoming and remaining fully human. If this is true, then it follows that only grace, the grace that comes through and because of Christ, makes us able to respond to the natural law, to perceive and obey the demands of our being and our world. It is grace that empowers, therefore, the achievement of even that natural morality which appears to be an utterly human thing. Without grace we are less than human, with grace we are more than human. There is no in between. Thus, as the natural law operates in my life, calling me, challenging me, and guiding my response, it is really the law of Christ that lies hidden within.

Finally, the natural law and the law of Christ are united "historically." For it was in the historical event of the Incarnation that all the foregoing became apparent. Indeed, more than that, it was only in relation to the Incarnation that all the foregoing became real. When God became human, the humanity of God, the Christ, ratified the human. He certified its dignity. He revealed and manifested its oneness with the divine. He showed, as we have said before, that God does this saving thing "on our turf." Consequently, he made clear that the path to God is the path of this human world, that fidelity to the human is the sure promise of the presence of the divine. Thus Christ, in the Incarnation, made apparent the fact that there is no other law of Christ than the law of our own being.[21]

Conclusion

"To thine own self be true," said Shakespeare. The words are more accurate than is usually suspected. For what are Christians called to do, as they live their human lives? They are called to do the good, as best they can. That is the natural law. But the natural law is, in the end, also the law of Christ. If we are true to our selves, if we are faithful to the selves that we understand and interpret in the light of the Gospel proclamation of human destiny, then we are true to the law of Christ.

At a much deeper level than is often surmised, then, we have been discussing a Christian ethic throughout the pages of this book. Not an ethic with sectarian demands, not a specifically Christian ethic in that sense, but a human ethic rooted in and shaped by the Christian vision that is our theological heritage, an ethic that properly locates specifically Christian obligations in a profoundly Christian identity. Not an ethic predicated on a fundamentalistic use of our scriptural and magisterial sources, but a rational ethic suffused and illumined by a vision of humans and their world that is deeply biblical and strongly, proudly traditional.

We have been discussing a human ethic, but a human ethic for Christian persons in an ultimately Christian world. And so we have been discussing a Christian ethic in the deepest and most exciting sense possible.

Chapter 21

CATHOLIC MORALITY:
TODAY AND TOMORROW

$\mathbf{A}$s we come to the end of this enterprise, it is reasonable to ask two questions. What have we done? Where will it lead? In this brief concluding chapter, we wish to respond to these questions.[1]

What Have We Done?

The simple answer to this question is: Not everything, but something. In general, we have been attempting to develop a theology and philosophy of the Christian life. But to apply this rubric is really to overstate the project in which we have been involved. For the study of the Christian life involves three distinct tasks, and we have only been pursuing one of these. Christian living clearly involves the challenge to behave ethically and to develop an ethical commitment and sensitivity in one's life. But it also involves the development of an inner spirituality by which to nourish that life, and the participation in a liturgical community by which to express the posture of worship-response. Thus the "science" of the Christian life involves not only moral theology, but also spirituality and liturgy.[2]

We have neglected the latter two aspects. And the result is that our perspective has been only partial. We have, for example, spoken very little about the ascetical realities of the Christian life. We have neglected the profound truth that sacrifice of self is not merely an external religious command; it is also an inevitable, profoundly human, and potentially enriching correlate of commitment to the service of others. We have not spoken, therefore, of a most potent theme: the ascesis of love, which must surely play a role in the successful living of the Christian life.[3] Similarly, we have not dealt at length with the important reality of corporate living and worship. We have made brief references to this issue, for example when speaking of the Christian life as communal in chapter 10, becoming conscious of the sociology of knowledge in chapter 18, and noting the significance of Christian motivations in chapter 20. But it has not been given nearly the attention it deserves. For liturgical worship-response functions, in the real world, as a most profound component in the living of the Christian life.[4]

So we have not done everything. It is important to say this, not only because it is true but also because unreasonable expectations can lead to unjustified criticisms. It is a rather common characteristic of students that they criticize a course, book, or lecture on the grounds that it does not deal with everything, that it does not solve all problems. And the only response to this criticism, of course, is agreement. But perhaps such objections can be forestalled by a free admission from the start. Moral theology is not everything. Indeed, from any truly Christian non-Pelagian point of view, it is not even the most important thing. It is at most one good thing.

Similarly, in this book we have not done everything, but we have done something. At least we have attempted to do something. We have taken a point of view, we have stood somewhere. Specifically, we have used as our starting point and our ongoing point of reference the moral person, the Christian seeking to respond to the gift and call of the Lord. From this point of view we have attempted to look everywhere. Though we have not tried to describe exhaustively how the Christian life can and should be lived, we have tried to express what goes on in the living of that life. We have tried to look in all the important directions, to ask all the important questions, and to formulate responsible answers. Specifically, we have attempted to move from this consciously chosen individual and existential starting point to an internally coherent and experientially adequate theory of the moral life.[5] And we have tried to develop this theory in a way that maintains the linkage with the best of the Christian and Catholic tradition.

But doing this has presented problems of its own. Not least among these is the fact that as a comprehensive theory the argument of this book belongs to this author alone. Because of our decision to "stand someplace," to view things in a certain way, we have ended up disagreeing with just about everyone else in some particular or other. We have reserved our strong criticism for those who would trivialize God, the Christian person, or the Christian life. But inasmuch as these pages have been a sort of dialogue with others who take all the same issues seriously, whether they be members of the Catholic magisterium, fellow theologians, or Christian individuals, inevitable points of disagreement have emerged. And this raises the very serious question of theological diversity today.

Where Will It Lead?

Given the fact of this diversity, our second question naturally arises: Where does this particular synthesis lead? And where does the fact that it cannot represent a universally held position lead?

Of the fact that diversity exists there can be no doubt. Even prior to the personal and therefore unique synthesis that is this book, Catholic moral theology has been marked by substantial amounts of diversity.[6] And this book will not eliminate that diversity. Though we believe that this synthesis largely represents a collection of widely held convictions and we hope that bringing these convictions together in this way will facilitate communication and the search for agreement, still it is surely true that no one will agree with absolutely everything. And some will probably find themselves in disagreement with most of what has been said here.

In one sense this diversity is regrettable. Certainly the vision of the Church as a people one in mind and heart, as a place not only of common commitment but also of common conviction, is an ideal fondly to be hoped for. Indeed, it is a goal to be striven for.[7] Conversely, when a community that sincerely seeks this goal is nonetheless confronted with substantial areas of disagreement and contradictory diversity, a certain amount of pain is to be expected. At the same time, this phenomenon can be seen as good in that it reveals three things: honesty, sincerity, and humility.

For one thing, it is a manifestation that honesty is alive in the Church. Theology is an exercise of intellect, not of will; it is an effort to discern, not to command. And if the fact is that people see things differently, then the admission of these differences is a powerful proof of the honesty of all the participants. The one truly tragic thing would be to claim or exhibit unanimity before it is actually discovered, to accept common ways of speaking before they are truly understood, to proclaim common convictions before they are really affirmed. That God's people should always be an honest people, that the Church should be a "zone of truth," is something that must never be sacrificed.[8]

In the second place, this diversity is a good thing in that it demonstrates the sincerity of the members of the Church. It is one thing to speak privately about one's personal opinions, to express disagreement or complaint in the safe environment of personal conversation. It is quite another to articulate these things in a formal and public way, to state one's position and to present one's reasons, to exhibit one's convictions before the eyes of all who would see. To do this is to invite response, to permit others to disagree in turn, and to allow for the possibility of being found wanting or proved wrong. No human being takes such a risk lightly. Thus the fact that such risks are being taken in the Church today is *prima facie* proof of the sincerity and dedication of all who join in the theological debates of our time.

Third, this diversity is an example, and a sacrament, of humility. If the central convictions of the Christian faith mean anything, they mean that God is in charge. As human persons, we are beings of great dignity, but we are also distinctly finite beings. Our perspectives are limited, our understandings are partial, our capacity for error is unremitting. Even as a Church, we do not escape this finitude, with all the dangers that are consequent. We are finite, and there is no avoiding that.

What is more, the Christian faith asserts not only that we are finite, but also that we *may* be finite. It is not necessary for us to find all the answers, to resolve all the doubts, to conquer all the ambiguities of life. God is in charge, and the one who is larger than our thoughts and transcends our theories will care for us with a love that we cannot describe or predict.

Indeed, we *must* be finite. Despite all that has been said earlier, the fact is that the human mind yearns for truth. It seeks understanding and clarity of insight. It is unsatisfied with incomplete answers and unresolved questions. It is, in Augustine's term, restless. This desire for perfection is no doubt good, since it was put in us by God. But it can also be a temptation, since it can lead us to be dissatisfied with the being that is ours. In the extreme case, it can lead us to dream of being God; it can even deceive us into thinking we are God. But we are not. The truth for which we yearn is Truth itself. The life we would like to envision for ourselves is Life itself. And the way we really should walk is that Way that is the Lord's own self. Augustine surely was speaking truth when he described our hearts as restless; he was deeply wise when he completed his thought: "Our hearts are restless till they rest in Thee."[9]

We are powerfully, even painfully, reminded of all this by the theological diversity of our day. We do not have all the answers, and we never will. Often enough we do not even know how to formulate the questions properly. We must search, to be sure. We cannot turn off our minds. But we must at least not be surprised when our efforts bear less than perfect fruit. We must in the end be humble.

Conclusion

So again we ask: Where will all this lead? We do not know. This author fondly hopes that the insights of this book will be a real service to all those men and women who constitute the Church. He hopes that it represents a step forward, a move not toward greater division but toward deeper oneness of heart and mind. But he is under no illusion about the complete achievement of that goal. Diversity exists, and it will continue to exist. It may be a pain-causing reality. It may occasion a certain amount of embarrassment. Not confronted, it can even lead to rancor. But at the same time, and in a strangely paradoxical way, it is also a proper insignia to adorn the Christian uniform, an ultimate admission that God is God, that we are merely human and that such a situation is finally very good.

There is a sentence penned by St. Irenaeus in the second century, a sentence usually interpreted as high praise for human beings. And it is that, for it proclaims that we are very important to God. But the sentence is also, in a subtle way, an expression of this humility we have been considering. It says we are important, but it affirms that we are finite. It says that we are powerful, but it acknowledges that we are dependent. It says that we are humans and not animals, but it admits that we are humans and not God.

That sentence is central to the perspective of this book. It is the keystone of Christian morality as we understand it. Its realization in our minds and its achievement in our hearts is also central to the motivation of this book. And so, more than a hope, it is a prayer that brings this book to a conclusion.

May all the followers of Jesus Christ, and in a special way those followers who find their roots and meaning in the Catholic tradition of Christianity, more and more come to appreciate and celebrate and live the truth of the Incarnation proclaimed by Irenaeus: "The glory of God is the human person – fully alive."[10]

NOTES

For full data on books and articles cited in the notes, see the bibliography.

CHAPTER 1

1. See e.g., B. Lonergan, *Method in Theology*; and D. Tracy, *Blessed Rage for Order.*

2. J. Daniélou, "Christian and non-Christian Religions," p. 91–92.

3. It is interesting that Aquinas parallels Paul's understanding when he speaks of a "pastoral magisterium," the bishops, and a "teaching magisterium," the theologians. Cf. *Quodlibet* 3, Q.4, art. 1; as reported in A. Dulles, "The Theologian and the Magisterium," p. 242.

4. This notion of theology as bridging revelation and culture is richly developed by P. Tillich, *Theology of Culture*, esp. pp. 40–51.

5. Some authors offer precise distinctions between the terms "moral theology" and "Christian ethics." I have found it impossible to control ordinary usage, where the two are treated as equivalent. In this work, therefore, the terms will be considered synonymous.

6. Both of these subsciences are, in turn, dependent on and accountable to Scripture and tradition. Consequently, as theological sciences, they are served by the cognate disciplines of scripture study and history. That explains why, as we proceed, biblical and historical materials will play a large part. More about the exact role of biblical and historical data will be said later in this chapter as well as in chapters 9 and 20.

7. The German language offers an interesting example of the relationship of these two moments, even linguistically connecting them: *Gabe*, "gift"; *Aufgabe*, "task."

8. D. Maguire presents a fascinating listing of resources not for moral theology as such, but for moral judgment. Cf. *The Moral Choice*, esp. p. 115, where the various sources he describes are schematically presented.

CHAPTER 2

1. In the first edition of this book, completed in 1978, a note at this point explained a major difficulty in composing the chapter: the absence of a book-length history of Catholic moral theology. At that point the available resources consisted of brief historical summaries, not unlike this chapter, and monographs on very narrow questions and specific periods. There was no book-length discussion of this history. The wish was expressed that "this lacuna will soon be filled." It is a pleasure to note that a significant step toward the elimination of this difficulty has been taken with the publication of J. Mahoney's *The Making of Moral Theology*. For a far more comprehensive discussion of the evolution of this discipline, the reader is referred to this book.

   In developing the points that comprise this historical overview, we have primarily followed the lead of Bernard Häring, *Law of Christ*, 1:3–33. This has been supplemented by material from articles in the *New Catholic Encyclopedia*, from T. Deman, *Aux origines de la théologie moral*, F. Murphy, *Moral Teaching in the Primitive Church*.

2. Quoted in Häring, p. 7.

3. These two figures offer an interesting example of theologian David Tracy's distinction between analogical and dialectical thinking in theology. Cf. his "Presidential Address."

4. For example, Häring, p. 8; G. Regan, *New Trends in Moral Theology*, p. 23.

5. For example, A. Kosnik et al., *Human Sexuality*, p. 37.

6. In one other particular Augustine stands as significant for modern theology, and that is in his roots in Platonic philosophy. There is no doubt that Platonism is a philosophy that risks dualistic excesses, and some would probably say that Augustine himself is a contributor to such excesses. But in my view it need not be so. Platonism also offers the possibility of grounding a richer, more poetic and mystical approach to theology. Indeed, it seems to have done so in our time. So if it is true that much modern theology is Platonic in the best sense of the word, and if Augustine in a major representative of this theological approach, he is on that account particularly deserving of our attention. Cf. T. O'Connell, "Old Priest, New Theology: A Dilemma."

7. For example, even the outstanding volumes of Bernard Häring, *The Law of Christ*, carry the subtitle: *Moral Theology for Priests and Laity*, feeling the need to be explicit about the intention to address others than priests.

8. From his *Prologue to the Commentary on the Book of Sentences*; quoted by Häring, p. 11.

9. This same line of argument is used by John Courtney Murray to show that the American political vision logically requires a commitment to natural law, to the objectivity and discernibility of value. Cf. *We Hold These Truths*.

10. It was not only in moral theology that this permutation took place; similar changes can be discerned in liturgical theology. From a science with clearly dogmatic roots and with implications for spirituality, it became a science of the correct, of the valid and licit, of rubrical propriety. Liturgy, too, developed an affiliation with canon law. Again, this was a development that has lasted to our day. Even today the Gregorian University in Rome publishes two journals: *Gregorianum*, a journal of theology, and *Periodica de re morali, canonica et liturgica*, a journal of moral, canonical, and liturgical matters.

11. The focus on the German sources for twentieth-century renewed moral theology may be influenced by the major roles of Häring and Fuchs. A broader perspective might note the major importance also of renewed theology in nineteenth-century France, the *nouvelle théologie*, with its connections to seminary education through the Sulpicians. It is obvious that the intellectual forces shaping the Second Vatican Council were rooted in the intellectual ferment in both these countries and that recent developments in moral theology are, partly through the council, also notably dependent on them.

CHAPTER 3

1. J. Fitzmyer, "Pauline Ecclesiology and Ethics," sec. 166.

2. E. Schillebeeckx, *Christ the Sacrament of the Encounter with God*.

3. On the vision of Christ developed here, cf. J. Fuchs, "The Law of Christ," in *Human Values and Christian Morality*, pp. 76–91; and K. Rahner, "On the Theology of the Incarnation."

4. Rahner, p. 115.

5. Ibid., p. 116.

6. This is not to say that "sacred space" is unimportant, of course. It is simply to say that its importance is psychological rather than directly theological (though, needless to say, human psychology is itself theologically significant). The function of sacred space is precisely to highlight and make explicit the presence of God that is to be found throughout creation. Thus the church building is *our* building, not God's. Or perhaps better: It is God's house *because* it is ours.

7. To describe this dependence upon the wisdom of the community and upon tradition is to affirm the critical role of "magisterium," of ecclesial leadership in its task of articulating that patrimony. Although a full treatise on the theology of magisterium is beyond the project of this book, more will be said about it in various places as we proceed.

CHAPTER 4

1 This chapter represents a relatively significant refocusing of material that appeared in the first edition under the title: "Elements of a Biblical Morality." Indeed, the very fact of the refocusing is significant. In using the first edition for teaching purposes, the author would often ask students to address themselves to the question: "What is the relationship of Christ to morality?" He expected the answer to incorporate the sorts of themes found in the previous chapter. Instead, students would regularly respond: "The place of Jesus in my moral life is. . . ." Note both the move from Christ to Jesus and the move from morality to *my* moral life. It eventually became clear that what was actually happening was also a move from "high" ontological Christology to "low" historical Christology. And most centrally, I think, it was a move from systematic theology to spirituality. Even though I believed – and still do – that the themes of the previous chapter are important, I also became convinced that the students were sensing a serious lacuna. The new arrangement is intended to respond.

2. In addition to the refocusing mentioned in note 1, the material from the first edition has also been expanded here. In the original composition a major source, as indicated in note 8, was R. Schnackenburg, *Ethics in the New Testament*. In revising the material for this new edition, special attention has been given to T. Ogletree, *The Use of the Bible in Christian Ethics*. Though Ogletree's analysis does not radically diverge from earlier research (not surprisingly), he does offer fresh perspectives that have prompted some modifications of content and emphasis.

3. Lisa Sowle Cahill organizes biblical references to ethical matters into three categories: texts that address specific questions, such as divorce; texts that do not consider the exact dilemmas faced today but do address closely related questions, such as those celebrating parenthood (used to illuminate the question of contraception); and texts that address the overall style/quality/tone/approach which Christian morality should evidence. Cahill suggests that this third category, often treated trivially by fundamentalists, is actually the most useful for the conduct of moral theology; cf. "Moral Methodology: A Case Study." Obviously, this third category of texts will be the focus of this chapter.

4. In the course of this book we shall have other occasions to explore the biblical sources. Indeed, some of the biblical themes to be considered later are extremely prominent ones: for example, *law, sin, conscience, obedience*. The goal now is more specific: to explore some biblical themes that serve to ground that spirituality which energizes the moral living of Christians. For a full view of the biblical approach to morality, on the contrary, this chapter, chapter 3, and these other sections yet to come should be read in concert.

5. That this overall vision and sense of "Christian character" is the most significant contribution of the Bible to Christian morality is well argued in B. C. Birch and L. L. Rasmussen, *Bible and Ethics in the Christian Life*.

6. This theme is richly described by Ogletree, pp. 49–53.

7. The significance of the idea of covenant for Christian moral theology has often been pointed out. Among others, it has been extensively used by theologian Enda McDonagh; cf., for example, *Invitation and Response*, pp. 43–47.

8. R. Schnackenburg, p. 13. Much of the following material is based on Schnackenburg's excellent research.

9. The central significance of "reversal," not only in specifically ethical contexts but also in the parables, is highlighted in J. Crossan, *In Parables*.

10. Indeed, Ogletree differs from Schnackenburg in asserting that "in the Synoptic Gospels discipleship emerges as the central category for setting forth the moral life" (p. 92). Actually, the difference may be semantic, since discipleship is a way of describing "kingdom as lived." In any case, Ogletree's exposition of discipleship is illuminating; cf. esp. pp. 92–97.

11. The ways in which the traditional concept of law were incorporated in each of the Gospels is helpfully detailed by Ogletree, pp. 97–116.

12. As a Jew, of course, Jesus carried with him a profound reverence for the Torah, the law of Moses. And consequently "obedience" for him would have been not a venal and subservient posture but a highly religious one. Consequently, both law and obedience, within this Jewish perspective, carried an energy of love far distant from legalistic styles with which contemporary Christian religion is familiar.

13. R. Bultmann, *Jesus*, (1951), p. 79, quoted in Schnackenburg, p. 76.

14. A theme beautifully developed by R. McCormick, "Human Significance and Christian Significance," pp. 234–235.

15. See, e.g., J. T. Sanders, *Ethics in the New Testament*, pp. 91–100.

16. Ogletree, *op. cit.*, p. 87.

17. p. 89.

18. pp. 88–89.

19. Schnackenburg, pp. 15–16.

CHAPTER 5

1. All the ideas sketched here will be considered again in these pages. For now, they are mentioned simply by way of introducing the present topic.

2. For example, H. Davis, *Moral and Pastoral Theology*, 1:11. The entire presentation of this chapter is representative of Davis and other manuals such as J. Fuchs, *Theologia Moralis Generalis*, 2:1–43; and H. Noldin, *Summa Theologiae Moralis*, 1:15–100.

3. It is interesting to note that the distinction between human acts and acts of man is not only a datum of common experience, it is also a principle of law. Criminal trials often spend considerable effort determining the freedom and responsibility of the defendant at the time of the crime. The question of whether negligence was involved is raised. The legal distinction between murder and manslaughter is carefully protected. All these examples are expressions of this same fundamental insight: Not everything that a person does is her or his responsibility.

4. This last caveat is important: arguing against the Stoic idea that the ideal human being is totally "apathetic," untouched by emotion. For an outstanding description of the way in which feeling grounds all moral decision, cf. D. Maguire, *The Moral Choice.*

5. A. Maslow, *Toward a Psychology of Being*, esp. pp. 21–70.

6. Indeed, from quite a different point of view they are extremely positive. Here we are following the scholastic tradition in dissecting an individual moral choice. From this perspective knowledge and freedom are high values. But there is another tradition, much developed today, that seeks to understand the dynamics of a successful moral life, viewed in its totality. Such a life is called "virtuous." But a virue is defined in the scholastic tradition as a "moral habit." Does this make it "less than human"? Quite the contrary, it is a human achievement. For it is an integrated human skill, painfully developed over time, of such excellence that wise and prudent judgments are achieved "automatically." Thus it is "more than human." Perhaps the most articulate spokesperson for this perspective is S. Hauerwas, who speaks of "Christian character"; cf. his *A Community of Character.*

7. Cf. J. Fuchs, 1:155f.

8. Much of what follows is dependent on the brilliant presentation found in D. Maguire's *The Moral Choice*. I have reshaped these ideas considerably, however, so they may no longer be completely faithful to his thought. In particular, I have joined Maguire's insights with those of Stanley Hauerwas and John Shea. Also extremely helpful was an issue of *Chicago Studies* devoted to this subject: G. Dyer, ed., *Communicating Moral Values*, pp. 229–336.

9. An excellent discussion of the role of experience in the development of moral values is found in Michael Place, "Philosophical Foundations for Value Transmission." Maguire also addresses the question in *The Moral Choice*, pp. 309–342.

10. Cf. Maguire, *The Moral Choice*, pp. 189–217.

11. Maguire strikingly discusses the role of comedy and tragedy in moral formation in *The Moral Choice*, pp. 343–369.

12. Perhaps the clearest explanation of the role of story is W. Bausch, *Storytelling: Imagination and Faith*. The importance of story is both elucidated and exemplified in the wonderful books of John Shea: *Stories of God, The Challenge of Jesus, An Experience Named Spirit,* and *The Spirit Master.* Also very useful is an issue of *Chicago Studies* devoted to these questions: G. Dyer, ed., *Storytelling and Christian Faith*, pp. 3–103.

13. *A Community of Character*, p. 9. The entire book develops these themes of the role of story in community and of the specific nature of the Christian community and its story.

14. Hauerwas develops an encompassing narrative vision of Christian ethics in his *The Peaceable Kingdom.*

CHAPTER 6

1. It is an interesting curiosity that the development of this three-dimensional view of the human person was spearheaded in Germany. Among many reasons for this fact, one might deserve comment here. The German language, allowing the creation of new words through combination of old words, encouraged this development. For it made rejection of the past less necessary. Did the tradition speak of knowledge (*Erkenntnis*) and freedom (*Freiheit*) as central to human action? Fine! Let us simply call attention to the depth (*Grund*) dimension by referring also to *Grunderkenntnis* and *Grundfreiheit*.

2. In chapter 14 we shall see that moral choice always involves choosing *among* goods, that doing good always also involves paying a price: the good left undone. There is always an element of conflict and compromise, then, in moral choice. This discussion of categorical freedom explains why this is so.

3. In German this exemplified the type of changes discussed in note 1, for the term was *Grundentscheidung*, literally "basic choice." The term "fundamental option" seems to have been coined by a translator rendering Karl Rahner's reference to *Grundentscheidung* into French as *option fondamentale*.

4. The general understanding of fundamental option, though not the precise term, can be traced as far back as 1922. Cf. D. von Hildebrand, "Sittlichkeit und ethische Werterkenntnis." It entered the manual tradition in J. Fuchs, *Theologia Moralis Generalis*, 2:4. In a broader sense, of course, its roots go back as far as Kant, and perhaps Descartes. It is no accident that scholars such as Rahner and Lonergan are called "transcendental Thomists" for their efforts to combine the wisdom of Thomas with the peculiarly modern questions of the Kantian tradition. And central among those questions is the meaning of personhood and especially of interiority.

    Both the concept and the term "fundamental option" have been implicitly affirmed by the magisterium of the Roman Catholic church in the "Declaration on Certain Questions Concerning Sexual Ethics" of the Sacred Congregation for the Doctrine of the Faith (December 29, 1975), no. 10. The document criticizes certain distorted understandings of fundamental option, but in so doing it also indicates an appropriate understanding substantially the same as that presented here.

5. Cf. K. Rahner, "Guilt and Its Remission: The Borderland Between Theology and Psychotherapy," pp. 269–271.

6. J. Fuchs, 2:147. This insight into the tentativeness of human fundamental options has led some authors also to posit the existence of a "final option" made at the moment of death. This option, in contrast to all the others, is definitive and irrevocable. Cf. R. Troisfontaines, *I Do Not Die*, pp. 160–188.

7. This attentiveness to the depth dimension of human life has roots in philosophy, of course. The "turn to the interior" that began with Descartes and was so profoundly influenced by Kant makes this tendency obvious. On this philosophical basis – and in recognition of cultural experience in the modern world – moral theology has, as we have seen here, similarly developed. In the literature of moral theology, there are many excellent presentations of this overall view of the human person. Among the best of the sources in English are: J. Fuchs, "Basic Freedom and Morality," in his *Human Values and Christian Morality*, pp. 92–111; id., "Sin and Conversion"; J. Glaser, "Transition Between Grace and Sin: Fresh Perspectives"; R. McCormick, "The Moral Theology of Vatican II"; K. Rahner, "Some Thoughts on a 'Good Intention'"; id., "Theology of Freedom"; id.,

"Guilt-Responsibility-Punishment Within the View of Catholic Theology"; F. Podimattam, "What Is Mortal Sin?"; R. Tapia, "When Is Sin Sin?"; N. Rigali, "The Moral Act"; R. Modras, "Implications of Rahner's Anthropology for Fundamental Theology."

8. This emphasis on the fourth dimension has philosophical roots, as did the focus upon the third. In this case one thinks of the emphases of twentieth-century process thinkers such as Whitehead, Hartshorne, and others. Contemporary moral theology, as we are seeing here, also takes time seriously. We will also make reference to this reality in chapter 8 and again in chapter 14. Both here and in those contexts we are greatly dependent on the insights of B. Lonergan, "The Transition from a Classicist World-View to Historical-Mindedness"; also J. Walgrave, "Is Morality Static or Dynamic?"; and B. Häring, "Dynamism and Continuity in a Personalistic Approach to Natural Law."

9. S. Hauerwas, *Character and the Christian Life*, p. 11. Cf. also his *Vision and Virtue*. In both these works Hauerwas admirably develops the theme of "character" as central to the Christian ethics.

CHAPTER 7

1. Indeed, it makes no sense to us either. This author was once asked by a teenager: "If I don't believe in God, is it still a sin to miss Mass?" Paradoxically, actual sin is only possible to those who believe in God. Sin presumes faith at the very moment that it attacks fidelity. Atheists can engage in sincere and thoughtful discussions of ethics – and they do. But "sin" will not enter the conversation. In such a setting it is, literally, absurd.

2. This linking of the "horizontal" and "vertical" dimensions of sin occasions some interesting reflections on the practice of the Sacrament of Reconciliation in the Catholic church. The point has often been made, with some justification, that past practice focused almost exclusively on sin as an offense against God; the neighbor was largely overlooked. Recent renewal, both in practice and in catechesis, has attempted to remedy this imbalance. But in some cases it has seemed to move to the opposite extreme. This writer had occasion once to talk with a group of high school students who asserted that if their neighbor was the one they had offended by their sins, they should apologize to the neighbor rather than "go to confession." At first I was tempted to accuse the students of oversimplification. But then I realized they were right. If only the neighbor has been injured, then only the relationship with the neighbor requires reconciliation, and the sacrament serves no purpose. Only if we experience the reality of covenantal love relationships with *both* our neighbor and our God, and only if we experience these two as inextricably intertwined, does a sacramental ritual of reconciliation truly have meaning.

3. I am told that more recent medical practice involves tickling the baby – that is, irritating it in a gentler, more subtle fashion. I am inclined to view this as simply a more duplicitous pursuit of the same goal!

4. Dylan Thomas's line comes to mind: "Do not go gentle into that good night."

5. As C. S. Lewis suggests, the Christian doctrine that is easy to prove out of experience is not the doctrine of God's goodness but the doctrine of original sin. "If the universe is so bad or even half so bad, how on earth did human beings ever come to attribute it to the activity of a wise and good creator? . . . The spectacle

of the universe as revealed by experience can never have been the ground of religion." (*The Problem of Pain*, p. 3).

A similar observation was offered by theologian Morton Kelsey in a public lecture February 1, 1989. "Any honest theology," said Kelsey, "is a theology of catastrophe."

6. Shortly before the second edition of this book went to press, a most extraordinary article appeared: S. Duffy, "Our Hearts of Darkness: Original Sin Revisited." Through Duffy's broad historical review and his own "deconstruction and reconstruction of the doctrine of original sin," he leads us to essentially the vision presented here.

7. One objection to this overall understanding of sin has been lodged on occasion: namely, that the emphasis upon sin as a fact may lead to an abandonment of personal responsibility, that seeing oneself as a victim of (original) sin may discourage one from energetic resistance to (actual) sin. That objection is, I think, decisively answered in Patrick McCormick's outstanding book, *Sin As Addiction*.

McCormick points out that the very same objection was lodged against Alcoholics Anonymous in its early days: that allowing alcoholics to see themselves as sick would encourage them to evade responsibility for their drinking. The facts, as we know, have proven to be just the opposite. Acknowledging the degree to which one is victim of one's past, and not an intrinsically bad person, mobilizes one for committed effort in the future. McCormick concludes from these reflections that there is a place for a "sickness" model of sin as an alternative to the "juridical guilt" model that we inherit from Augustine. I believe that my synthetic presentation comes to much the same conclusion.

Indeed, in view of the central place for the ministry of healing in the New Testament, one might well argue that this "sickness" model is more attuned to the mission and message of Jesus than is its alternative that, for itself, seems more concerned with assigning blame than with mediating salvation.

CHAPTER 8

1. This seems to be the position of Thomas Aquinas, as well; cf. *De. Ver.* 27, 1 ad 9.

2. This idea that we do not achieve complete certitude regarding our moral state is well developed in K. Rahner, "Guilt–Responsibility–Punishment Within the View of Catholic Theology," p. 204f.

3. This is beautifully expressed in J. Fuchs, "Sin and Conversion." This theory of fundamental (and final) option also gives a much more plausible justification to the theological concept of hell, namely, the power of human freedom must include even the utterly perverse capacity to elect forever a living-in-isolation that frustrates and negates the person. Not to acknowledge this power is to undermine the significance of human freedom. And, similarly, hell is to be understood not as something God does to us, but as something we are frighteningly capable of doing to ourselves. Cf. K. Rahner, "Guilt–Responsibility–Punishment Within the View of Catholic Theology," p. 215.

4. Cf. K. Rahner, "The Theological Concept of Concupiscentia."

5. A line of argument usefully pursued by C. Curran, "Masturbation and Objectively Grave Matter," in *A New Look at Christian Morality*, pp. 201–232.

6. Some authors prefer to distinguish mortal sin, venial sin, and "serious sin" to deal with the very issue addressed in this paragraph. For them, serious sin is

grave matter that has not yet functioned as the occasion for a fundamental option but that, because of its seriousness, may very well be a preamble to such an option. The distinction may well have some pastoral utility, but we have avoided it because it blurs the anthropological and theological differentiation between acts that mediate a fundamental option and acts that do not. Clarity on this differentiation seems to us the highest priority, particularly when the phenomenon of "venial sins with grave matter" can be explained as simply as it has been here.

7. Sometimes the term "objective sin" is used in this connection. The tendency of this term to lead to misunderstanding, implying that a person could destroy the relationship with God "accidentally," is the reason it has been avoided here. But the term will probably continue to be used, and is even legitimate if it is carefully and properly understood.

8. Many of the ideas developed in this chapter, and the one before, are also considered in T. O'Connell, "The Point of Moral Theology."

CHAPTER 9

1. The role of experience in the shaping of moral affections was discussed in chapter 5, building on the insights of D. Maguire in *The Moral Choice*. Maguire also indicates the proper role of intellectual reflection, as such, namely, as the source of a distanced critique on those experience-engendered feelings and, consequently, as prescriber of additional experiences that can occasion refined feelings.

2. This interpretation of posterior conscience is well presented by E. M. Pattison, "The Development of Moral Values in Children." Cf. also K. Rahner, "Guilt and Its Remission."

3. For example, J. Fuchs, *Theologia Moralis Generalis*, 1:152–55. Other authors speak of two sorts of conscience, *synderesis* and *syneidesis*, and understand moral science as the methodical application of *synderesis*: e.g., H. Noldin. *Summa Theologiae Moralis*, 1:197–198.

4. B. Häring, *The Law of Christ*, 1:151.

5. J. Rudin, "A Catholic View of Conscience," p. 110. The reference is to IV Sent., Disp. 38, Q. II, Art. 4, Expos. Text.

6. National Conference of Catholic Bishops, *Human Life in Our Day*, p. 14.

7. Ibid., pp. 14–15.

8. J. Fuchs, 1:176.

9. A point recognized also by Protestant theologians. Cf. J. Gustafson, "Is There a Catholic and/or Christian Ethic? – A Response," and L. Gilkey, *Catholicism Confronts Modernity*.

10. This expression of the matter is, of course, at variance with much recent writing, which speaks instead of a Catholic's obligation to give "religious and internal assent of mind and will" even to noninfallible teachings. But as a number of authors have shown, recent practice has presumed a narrow, highly juridical conception of magisterium that is of recent origin and not consonant with the bulk of Catholic tradition. Thus this presentation seeks to reclaim and restate that broad tradition. Cf. Y. Congar, "Pour une histoire sémantique du terme 'magisterium'" and "Bref historique des formes du 'magistere' et de ses relations

avec les docteurs"; id., "The Magisterium and Theologians – A Short History"; A. Dulles, "The Theologian and the Magisterium"; R. McCormick, "Notes on Moral Theology – Theologians and the Magisterium," 1977, pp. 74–100 (where additional citations are offered).

11. In the recent, somewhat caustic debate about the morality of artificial contraception, a small group of authors has asserted that the prohibition has been so widely and consistently taught by the magisterium that it falls in this category, i.e., is infallible by way of ordinary magisterium (i.e., J. Ford and G. Grisez, "Contraception and the Infallibility of the Ordinary Magisterium"). Their opinion has not, however, received widespread support in the scholarly community (cf., e.g., J. Komonchak, "*Humanae vitae* and Its Reception: Ecclesiological Reflections"; also cf. an exchange of articles leading up to G. Hallett, "Infallibility and Contraception: The Debate Continues," as well as numerous references in "Notes in Moral Theology" in *Theological Studies*). Indeed, I think it is fair to say that the opinion is generally regarded as extreme, if not eccentric.

12. We will return to this notion of historicity, and explain it more fully, in chapter 14.

13. We should also note that the word "teach" is here used in an analogous, probably ambiguous, and possibly equivocal sense. The journal *Chicago Studies* published an outstanding series of articles detailing the history of "magisterium" in the Catholic Church. Several conclusions were obvious from the historical data: (1) The Church has always included the function of *supervision* or *leadership*, and it was quickly identified with the role of bishop. (2) The Church has always included the function of illuminating *instruction*, but this has been seen as a charism, exercised by whoever had the knowledge and skill. (3) The role of leadership included supervision of instruction/teaching, so that in that sense office was held above charism. But supervision, for all that, was not the same as teaching. (4) Around the beginning of the nineteenth century, some theologians began adding to the traditional two roles of the bishop (to rule and sanctify) a third, to teach, and came to understand this as "authoritative teaching." But in the ordinary sense of the words this was not so much real teaching, the sharing of wisdom and the invitation to understanding, as it was the declaration of official policy. Cf. G. Dyer, ed., *Magisterium*.

There is reason to believe that the pre-nineteenth-century Catholic usage is more helpful for illuminating the complementary roles of bishop and theologian and for describing how the appropriation of faith and insight into moral values actually occurs in the lives of Catholics. That traditional usage is implied in this presentation.

14. Cf. G. Hughes, "Infallibility in Morals"; also cf. his more recent *Authority in Morals*, in which these ideas are developed yet more fully.

15. This is not to deny that the Church, like any human institution, may need to protect its identity and effectiveness through the exercise of external discipline, all the more so in that values are, as this book repeatedly argues, fragile. They, too, need care and protection. Thus there is a place for such a thing as excommunication. But if such a practice is plausible, it should also be rare, invoked only when the very life or mission of the community is at stake.

CHAPTER 10

1. The uniqueness of the individual Christian life, and therefore also of some moral obligations, is particularly developed by K. Rahner. Cf. esp. "On the Question of a Formal Existential Ethics."

2. Increased emphasis on the essentially social nature of the human person and, consequently, on the critical importance of the community, is one of the marks of the new edition of this book. These themes were present in the first edition. But passing years – and perhaps changed conditions in the American scene – have convinced me that they require significantly greater emphasis.

3. For example, G. Gutierrez, *A Theology of Liberation*; the various works of J. Segundo and L. Boff; and G. Baum, *Religion and Alienation*.

4. For example, P. Lehmann, *Ethics in a Christian Context*; and J. Gustafson, *The Church as Moral Decision Maker*.

5. The work being done at the National Opinion Research Center at the University of Chicago is particularly notable in this regard. One also thinks of the mammoth study of the American parish undertaken by a group based at Notre Dame University and of the work of Dean Hoge at Catholic University of America. Cf. D. Hoge, *Future of Catholic Leadership*.

6. For example, the clinical task of child psychology is in many places giving way to "family counseling." The special needs of adult children of alcoholics (ACOA) are being noted and dealt with. In general, the impact of dysfunctional families is being appreciated more fully. Indeed, a focus on "systems" is developing as a fundamentally different way of conceptualizing diagnosis and therapy. For it is being recognized increasingly that healthy individual growth can only take place in a healthy family unit.

7. R. Bellah et al., *Habits of the Heart: Individualism and Commitment in American Life*.

8. This line of thought, which has a long history going back at least to Augustine, is presented here in dependence on C. Meyer, *A Contemporary Theology of Grace*, and R. Gleason, *Grace*. For a related presentation, cf. T. O'Connell, "Grace, Relationship and Transactional Analysis."

9. Indeed, the theological concept of fundamental option was at least partly developed by dogmatic theologians seeking to understand the mystery of grace more profoundly. Cf., for example, S. Dianich, "La corruzione della natura e la grazia nella opzioni fondamentali"; M. Flick and Z. Alszeghy, *Il Vangelo Della Grazia*, esp. pp. 141–167, 192f; P. Fransen, "Towards a Psychology of Divine Grace"; and H. Rondet, *The Grace of Christ*.

CHAPTER 11

1. M. Heidegger, *Being and Time*; cf. also L. Binswanger, *Being in the World*; May, Angel, Ellenberger, eds. *Existence*.

2. D. von Hildebrand, *Ethics*.

3. It is no accident that we are describing values in terms similar to those we used in chapter 5 in discussing evaluative knowledge. The similarity of these two notions is more than semantic. Speaking ontologically, evaluative knowledge is the way by which the human person perceives the values of our world. And speaking historically, the two notions were developed by the same group of scholars as aspects of the same essential insight. Note, for example, that J. Fuchs cites von Hildebrand in his discussion of "cognitio aestimativa" (*Theologia Moralis Generalis*, I: 156). The approach is characteristic of a school of moral philosophy, *Wertethik* (value ethics), whose central figure is Max Scheler. Cf. also A. Deekken, *Process and Permanence in Ethics: Max Scheler's Moral Philosophy*.

4. This presentation is typical of that found in the manuals. Cf., for example, H. Noldin, *Summa Theologiae Moralis*, 1:104–129; and H. Davis, *Moral and Pastoral Theology*, 1:117–158.

5. A number of these questions are discussed in depth in J. Fuchs, *Natural Law: A Theological Investigation*. This book includes some very noteworthy advances over the typical manual; it is, however, still fundamentally within that tradition.

6. An example of the first position would be H. Noldin, p. 111. The second position was adopted by H. Davis, p. 127.

7. This idea of three levels of natural law will serve as the starting point for our own consideration of the "knowability" of the natural law in chapter 18.

CHAPTER 12

1. The formulation of these various types of law exhibits distinguishable varieties, too. According to a widely held distinction generally associated with exegete Albrecht Alt, there are apodeictic and casuistic laws. The former are clearly proclaimed, universal prohibitions; they are deductive laws, as it were. The latter work inductively, from cases to a principle. Casuistic laws are much more common in nonbiblical literature (cf., for example, S. Freyne, "The Bible and Christian Morality"). Another distinction, particularly applied to the Christian Scriptures, is that which differentiates parenetic from explanatory discourse. The former has a homiletic quality, not meant to be taken literally and not intended to be really exceptionless. The latter is literal and technical. Thus, "Thou shalt not kill" is an example of parenetic discourse, since people have always recognized that it is sometimes sadly necessary to kill. Cf., for example, R. McCormick, "Notes on Moral Theology," (1976), pp. 72–74, where he uses this distinction in a very helpful way to respond to an article of this author.

2. The relationship of law and covenant is beautifully developed by T. Ogletree, *The Use of the Bible in Christian Ethics*, pp. 47–86. This source, appearing after the publication of the first edition of this book, adds many helpful nuances. In addition, it is exhaustively footnoted, so that its citations are themselves a valuable resource. Thus Ogletree's volume is a primary tool for anyone wanting an in-depth presentation of biblical morality.

3. This may be the place to note that a quite different line of thought about law also is present in the Jewish Scriptures. This is the approach found in the wisdom literature: a practical, down-to-earth discernment of the sorts of human interactions that really fulfill persons. Actually, the sayings of the wisdom books are, in many ways, more directly akin to the vision of the natural law. But for some reason they remained peripheral to the vision of Israel. No matter how much the style of the wisdom books might be imitated in the Talmudic sayings of the rabbis, the heritage of Israel continued to be known as the "Law and the Prophets." This explains why the wisdom literature is relatively neglected in the presentation of this chapter.

4. M. O'Connell, "Some Aspects of Commandment in the Old Testament," pp. 12–13.

5. J. Michener's novel, *Source*, beautifully captures the flavor of this love-motivated legalism.

6. J. J. Stamm and M. E. Andrews, *The Ten Commandments in Recent Literature*, pp. 68–70.

7. Thus people should not be surprised, as they aften are, to notice that the biblical text of the Decalogue (unlike the version learned in school) includes a statement of the First Commandment so extended that it is almost as long as the other nine put together. Indeed, the Fourth through Tenth Commandments, the more "practical" dictates, occupy less than a third of the text!

8. On these topics I am primarily dependent on Stamm and Andrews, *The Ten Commandments in Recent Literature*, cf. also E. Nielsen, *The Ten Comandments in New Perspective*. I cannot resist one further comment. Recent catechetical practice in Catholicism has tended to avoid teaching the Ten Commandments to children. The hope, I suppose, was that by avoiding these texts a more positive and loving approach to ethics might be developed. But on the basis of the understanding presented here, I would suggest that the Decalogue should be taught – not as if it could function as a sufficient ethical framework for life, nor as divine commands that the good Catholic docilely accepts and blindly follows, but rather as a sacred poem, as a collection of wisdom and love, that, following the inspiration of the Holy Spirit, "our people" have been reciting and proclaiming for three thousand years.

9. T. Ogletree, op. cit., does an excellent job of summarizing overall Gospel visions of law. His chapter titles even present a helpful characterization of each of the Synoptics in this regard: "Mark: the Primacy of the Moral Law" (pp. 97–99), "Luke: The Continuing Authority of the Mosaic Law" (pp. 99–104), "Matthew: Law as the Perfection of Love" (pp. 104–116).

10. R. Schnackenburg, *The Moral Teaching of the New Testament*, p. 95. This last point Schnackenburg distills from the Lukan version of this event. For there Jesus moves right from the proclamation of the two great commandments into the story of the Good Samaritan.

11. *In Epistolam Joannis*, tract. 7, cap. 4, PL 35, 2044.

12. This relativizing of the reality of law in Paul is discussed by T. Ogletree, pp. 135–174.

13. I have not attempted to discuss all the many, quite specific moral dictates to be found in Paul's writings. Almost all of the Epistles include a section dealing with how the Christian should behave, and Paul was not above getting into considerable detail. I have avoided discussing these for several reasons. First, a comprehensive consideration would be far beyond what could be attempted here. Second, to assess these norms fairly at this point in the book would require the development of a theology of revelation and inspiration that is, again, beyond the scope of what is possible. The brief references to that area of theology that have already appeared and that will appear as we proceed will have to suffice. And third, in due course we shall establish the proper way to understand *all* specific moral dictates, whether found in the Bible or elsewhere.

14. There are many fine sources available on the topic of the biblical understanding of law and commandment. In addition to those cited in the course of this chapter, the following should be noted: J. Blank, "Does the New Testament Provide Principles for Modern Moral Theology?"; K. Berger, "Law"; J. Fitzmyer, "Pauline Ecclesiology and Ethics," secs. 157–166; G. Schneider, "The Biblical Grounding of the Ethical Norms"; R. Collins, "Scripture and the Christian Ethic"; and responses to Collins by J. Dedek and V. Peter in *Proceedings*, pp. 243–246 and 247–254.

CHAPTER 13

1. The fact that the prevailing understanding of natural law is at least in part a function of the character of the wider cultural scene is noted and exemplified by B. Häring, *Morality Is For Persons*, pp. 146–158.

2. *De Republica*, lib. iii, c. xxii, 33; as cited in C. Ryan, "The Traditional Concept of Natural Law: An Interpretation," p. 15. Ryan contrasts this view with the more passive understanding of the Stoics.

3. The fact that natural law can have these two meanings, that the historical debate has involved them, and that one must eventually choose to emphasize either the world as obligatory fact or as right reason has often been noted. For example, P. Delhaye, "'Droit naturel' et théologie morale," p. 140, speaks of the opposition between the visions of natural law as *cosmos* and as *logos*. R. Troisfontaines, "L'insémination artificialle: Problèmes ethiques," distinguishes natural law as conformity to nature and as communion of persons. And K. Rahner, "The Experiment with Man," p. 215f, establishes that how one answers this natural law question will determine what one considers permissible in the area of biological and genetic manipulations. C. Ryan, p. 15, also points out what he calls "two possible strands in the concept of natural law."

4. Our own answers to these questions will be developed in the next chapters.

5. C. Curran, "Natural Law and Contemporary Moral Theology," in *Contemporary Problems in Moral Theology*, p. 106. For much of the data summarized in this historical survey we are dependent on Curran's work. Cf. also his "Absolute Norms in Moral Theology," in *A New Look at Christian Morality*, pp. 75–84; J. Arntz, "Natural Law and Its History"; and G. Watson, "Pagan Philosophy and Christian Ethics."

6. In the elucidation of these two diverse conceptualizations of the human person and the demonstration that the latter is to be found in Thomas, I am dependent on philosopher Richard Westley. Westley has often presented these ideas in a lecture format. A summary of them appears in his *A Theology of Presence*, pp. 11–15.

7. A fact noted by M. Crowe, "Natural Law Theory Today."

8. Cf. T. O'Connell, "Grace, Relationship and Transactional Analysis."

9. L. Bernstein, *The Unanswered Question*.

10. It is interesting, if not amusing, that the great chronicler of our culture, *Time* magazine, devoted a major article to the "rebirth" of natural law: "The Rediscovery of Human Nature," April 2, 1973, pp. 79–81. The article was part of a series entitled, "Second Thoughts About Man."

CHAPTER 14

1. The terms I have chosen here are not the only ones that might be appropriate. The first quality might equally be noted by describing values as "intrinsic" or "objective."

2. Paradoxically, they are also, in another sense, not at all real. For example, the value "peace" is real in the sense that its importance is not a creation of the subject; it has objective status. At the same time, it is precisely the absence of peace, the fact that it is not now real in the world, that motivates us to pursue it. I am grateful to theologian Edward Vacek, S. J., for highlighting this paradox.

3. This might also be termed "subjectivism." I have avoided that term because all morality is subjectivist in the (quite limited) sense that human subjects are the ones who implement it. On the other hand, one could argue that all morality is also relativistic in the (quite limited) sense that rightness and wrongness are relative to the facts of the case. No matter which term one elects, I have found, it still must be given a precise definition.

4. This rejection of relativism has been articulated by the Roman Catholic magisterium when it rejected that situation ethics whose authors hold "the decisive and ultimate norm of action to be not the right objective order . . . but a sort of intimate judgment and illumination of the mind and of the unique individual" (DS3918).

5. Obedience has a positive role, of course, which was highlighted in chapter 12.

6. Cf. chapter 19, where the proper role of civil law will be clarified.

7. The Church does, of course, also have rules, for it is a human community that, like any human community, needs to structure itself and provide order to its life. We will discuss the right and necessary function of these rules (and the complementary obligation of obedience) in chapter 19. The point here is that these rules (positive law) must not be confused with the much more central reality of moral teachings (which seek to express the natural law).

8. In the first edition of this book, the fact that values are real was developed into two other characteristics: that they are experiential and consequential. I remain convinced that the central insights of that presentation remain true. But experience has taught that the terminology was more distracting than helpful. For example, great effort was needed to distinguish values as experiential from the philosophical position of empiricism. Similarly, the precise sort of consequentialism being espoused (what was called "macroconsequentialism") had to be distinguished from a naive and narrowly pragmatic "microconsequentialism." In the end, it became clear that these discussions were neither essential nor worth the effort. It will suffice for our purposes to recognize that values are real, incarnated in the fabric of God's creation, and not merely creatures of fantasy, on the one hand, or the result of legal stipulation, on the other. Nonetheless, this philosophical and theological discussion is interesting. In addition to the literature that will be reviewed in chapter 17, the reader may wish to consult the sources identified in the notes to chapter 14 of the first edition of this book, sources that remain listed in the bibliography of this second edition.

9. This writer once heard a man explain that he rarely dated the same woman twice because "if you spend too much time with her, you start to care about her." An insightful comment, even if used to explain a perverse lifestyle!

10. Quoted by John Dedek, *Titius and Bertha Ride Again*, p. 104.

11. In the first edition of this book, this quality of values was discussed under the title "proportional." The term has been much discussed in recent theological literature, and those who hold it as *the* central and decisive quality of values have come to be called proportionalists. It will become clear in chapter 17 that I reject proportionalism as a fundamental moral methodology. Indeed, the concluding remarks of this present chapter will indicate how my judgment diverges from classic proportionalism. Hence it seems best not to introduce a term that will later need to be redefined in a way that varies greatly from current usage. Still, human finitude does have the effect that moral judgments are made in the context of competing interests, needs, and opportunities. This discussion of *conflict* is simply intended to make us conscious of that fact.

12. This same truth about human experience was noted in chapter 6, when we discussed categorical, as opposed to transcendental, freedom. Categorical freedom is always, in a paradoxical sense, a limiting freedom, for selecting one good always involves the foregoing of others.

13. Gerard Hughes had developed this line of thought in a most helpful way: *Authority in Morals*. The key ideas, particularly as they relate to the truth of moral teaching, were first presented in "Infallibility in Morals." This was subjected to critique by B. Tierney, "Infallibility in Morals: A Response," and the result was the revised version found in the book. The book has, in turn, been challenged by J. Finnis, "Reflections on an Essay in Christian Ethics Part I: Authority in Morals," and "Reflections on an Essay in Christian Ethics Part II: Morals and Method."

14. In addition to the book by Hughes, the concept of historicity is admirably developed in the following sources: B. Lonergan, "The Transition from a Classicist World-View to Historical-Mindedness"; J. C. Murray, "The Declaration on Religious Freedom"; B. Häring, "Dynamism and Continuity in a Personalistic Approach to Natural Law"; C. Curran, "Natural Law and Contemporary Moral Theology," in *Contemporary Problems in Moral Theology*, pp. 97–158; J. Walgrave, "Is Morality Static or Dynamic?"; M. Crowe, "Human Nature: Immutable or Mutable," and K. Rahner, "The Experiment with Man."

15. G. Hallett has argued that, from a logical point of view, it is possible that there is a "worst of all possible options in all possible circumstances" *and* that, at least in principle, it is possible that this option could be known. For example, one could perhaps make a compelling case that annihilating the entire human community through nuclear holocaust is the worst imaginable action alternative; it would therefore never be justifiable. Apart from the question of logic that this argument raises, it is not particularly helpful. The point remains that, for practical purposes, the comparative measuring of action alternatives cannot provide the basis for firmly grounded and perduring exceptionless norms. G. Hallett, *Christian Moral Reasoning*.

16. In the first edition of this book, the question of the existence of exceptionless norms was answered in the negative. The reason was that only these first two possible reasons for absoluteness were considered. The following paragraphs will make clear the significance of this third alternative, and the discussion in chapter 17 will amplify the reasons for modifying the earlier position.

17. For this insight I am dependent on P. Ramsey, "Incommensurability and Indeterminancy in Moral Choice," in McCormick and Ramsey, eds. *Doing Evil To Achieve Good*, especially pp. 93–95, although I am developing the idea in a way that may go beyond his point.

CHAPTER 15

1. This term comes from J. Fuchs, "Absoluteness of Moral Terms." Others express the same insight in alternative vocabularies. L. Janssens speaks of "Ontic Evil and Moral Evil," in an article of that title. P. Knauer distinguishes moral evil and physical evil in his "The Hermeneutic Function of the Principle of Double Effect." And D. von Hildebrand, *Ethics*, pp. 265–281, discusses moral values and morally relevant values.

2. We do speak of a "just wage," a "fair deal," an "honest statement." But in so doing we use the terms analogously and with a conscious narrowing of our focus. And

even in these usages we can apply the value terms only because persons are involved. A just wage, for example, is a wage appropriate to the dignity and the contribution of a person. Still, this loose, analogous usage can be confusing.

3. That, indeed, is the function of Special Moral Theology. As this book pursues General Moral Theology in trying to develop appropriate principles, so Special Moral Theology seeks to assess accurately the ethical importance of the various specific premoral values of our world.

4. Paradoxically, one could argue that the ultimately specific, concrete, detailed material norm is the most exceptionless, precisely because it more exhaustively includes all of the relevant circumstances. But it is exceptionless only in its application to this ultimately specific (and rather exceptional) constellation of circumstances! This point will be highlighted later in this chapter.

5. Some may find the example of stealing a bit difficult. I have found that for some people "stealing" is a term used to describe taking another's possession with or without a good reason. Thus some would argue that "Do not steal" is a material norm. This is a perfectly acceptable understanding as long as one is clear about the implications. If stealing is understood in this material way, then a distinction would have to be made between justified and unjustified stealing. The norm would have to be understood as probably admitting exceptions, as indicating a premoral value to be attended to, not as proclaiming an evident absolute to be always observed. But if there is this sort of clarity, then the difference is merely semantic. And with consistent definition it should cause no problem. Still, most moral theologians would doubtless prefer to use the term as I have in the text.

6. At least in their negative formulations. It is clear that "Do not murder" is a tautology. "Respect life" is arguably a "synthetic" norm about an inner attitude. But inasmuch as it still does not specify what behaviors constitute the external expression of that respect, it is a "near-tautology." That is, irrespective of the details of our taxonomy of norms, there are those norms that describe behaviors and assess them and those norms that articulate an ideal to be achieved in the selection of one's behaviors. This is the distinction served by contemporary use of terms such as "moral and premoral values," "material and formal norms."

7. Cf. T. O'Connell, "The Question of Moral Norms." I am grateful for the critique of this article in R. McCormick, "Notes on Moral Theology" (1976), pp. 72–74. Although I cannot althogether agree with McCormick, his insightful comments have led to a somewhat different formulation of the matter here.

8. Actually, a principal function of *all* norms is exhortation. We saw as much in the last chapter when we distinguished legalism from the legitimate use of "Stop that car!"

9. The danger, or course, is that preachers, and others in similar roles, can settle for empty platitudes that evade the real issues of people's lives. So there is need to speak the language of material norms, too. In certain instances preachers may need to point out the evil of refusing to sell one's house to another purely on the basis of race, of the proliferation of pornography, of allowing young people to wander about at all hours of the night, and so on. But rarely if ever can preachers draw concrete behavioral conclusions for their audiences. They cannot determine how these premoral disvalues will interact with other factors in the lives of specific members of the congregation. That judgment only the individual persons can make—and not so much because it is "their right" as because in the ordinary case they alone are in the best position to know fully all the pertinent specifics.

10. In addition to the sources cited in this chapter, and those that will be mentioned in the next two chapters, these ideas are also deeply pursued by R. McCormick in the various editions of his "Notes on Moral Theology" in *Theological Studies*. Cf., especially, 32 (1971), 33 (1972), 36 (1975), 37 (1976), and 38 (1977). In these pages McCormick both presents his own views and summarizes most of the significant contributions of others. Also very helpful is McCormick's monograph *Ambiguity in Moral Choice*. For a very interesting, consistent, and thoughtful application of the theory developed in these chapters, cf. P. Keane, *Sexual Morality: A Catholic Perspective*. Keane employs Janssens's terminology, which distinguishes moral evil from ontic evil. And he works out all his specific judgments in the area of sexual morality by asking, first, what the ontic evils present might be and, second, in what situations these evil might be outweighed by the goods (with the result that the action would be morally right) or not outweighed (so that the action would be morally wrong). Keane also presents an excellent brief summary of the ideas we have been considering throughout this book, though with some specific differences, in his chapter 3: "Some Pertinent Themes in Fundamental Moral Theology," pp. 35–56.

CHAPTER 16

1. The entrance of the term into the tradition of Catholic ethical reflection has been identified in a landmark series of articles by J. Dedek. The last of the four articles cites and summarizes the earlier three and then locates to emergence of the doctrine of intrinsically evil acts in the fourteenth century: "Intrinsically Evil Acts: The Emergence of a Doctrine."

2. This summary of the reasons will, in most cases, reveal the inadequacy of the arguments. This does not, of course, prove that these acts are *not* intrinsically evil. It simply proves that the traditional arguments are inadequate. Indeed, in one case I will offer an alternative argument that I do find compelling.

3. E. Schillebeeckx, *Marriage: Human Reality and Saving Mystery*

4. These sacramental and dogmatic issues continue to be pursued by theologians, though no clear resolution has yet appeared. Cf. W. Bassett and P. Huizing, eds., *The Future of Christian Marriage*; L. G. Wrenn, ed., *Divorce and Remarriage in the Catholic Church*; the entire issue of *The Jurist* 30 (January 1970); D. Doherty, *Divorce and Remarriage: Resolving a Catholic Dilemma*; C. Curran, "Divorce: Catholic Theory and Practice in the United States," in *New Perspectives in Moral Theology*, pp. 212–276, and "Divorce in the Light of a Revised Moral Theology," in *Ongoing Revision*, pp. 66–106 (the two articles by Curran also review a good deal of the other literature on this topic); T. Mackin, *What Is Marriage?* and *Divorce and Remarriage*; and M. Lawler, *Secular Marriage, Christian Sacrament*.

5. Interesting discussions of the precise meaning of "innocent" in the tradition have appeared recently. Cf. Lisa Sowle Cahil, "A Natural Law Reconsideration of Euthanasia."

6. The term, of course, is identified with the reflections developed by Cardinal Joseph Bernardin. For a collection of those writings and a variety of commentaries on them, cf. his *Consistent Ethic of Life*

7. It should be noted that this entire section, as well as the discussion of intrinsically evil acts in chapter 14, is oriented toward assessing the notion that there are acts that are intrinsically *morally* evil (or better: morally wrong). In contrast to

this, the assertion that there are acts that are intrinsically premorally evil is quite correct. Indeed, it is the correlate to the assertion that value is *real* and that relativism is a counterfeit moral understanding. Stealing, for example, always involves a premoral disvalue, namely, the loss of possessions by the victim and the placing of the agent in a role that is at least socially disruptive. So stealing is intrinsically evil in the premoral sense. The question is whether it is also intrinsically morally evil in every case. And this we question.

8. The point is sometimes made that there is a difference between means and coeffects, namely, that the one who wills the effect wills the means but may not (in the same sense) will the coeffect. This logic strikes me as cogent. But it leaves untouched the key question: Is it wrong to will the means? It can be wrong only if the means is, itself, intrinsically evil. And that, of course, is the question we have already addressed.

9. This analysis was first developed by P. Knauer, "The Hermeneutic Function of the Principle of the Double Effect." My presentation differs from that of Knauer in several particulars, but it is nevertheless indebted to him. Also very worthwhile is C. Curran, "The Principle of Double Effect," in *Ongoing Revision*, pp. 173–209.

10. Even in the case of the direct killing of the innocent, that demonstrably intrinsically evil act, this is somewhat true. For it is one "result" of the act that we, as agents, deny, undermine, and evacuate the very essence of the moral enterprise, care for human persons. The inevitability of that "result" is the reason, indeed, that the act is always wrong.

11. After composing the preceding paragraphs I discovered a somewhat similar analysis of Watergate in J. Fletcher, "Situation Ethics, Law, and Watergate." I point this out while also asserting that the analysis in these pages in no way matches the "situation ethics" for which Fletcher is famous. Indeed, his theory is actually a relativism grounded in nominalist philosphy – and we have rejected both relativism and nominalism.

CHAPTER 17

1. C. Curran has, in many of his writings, made clear the inadequacies of that tradition, e.g., "Natural Law and Contemporary Moral Theology," pp. 97–158, in *Contemporary Problems in Moral Theology*. This assessment seems to be shared by G. Grisez, e.g., *The Way of the Lord Jesus*, pp. 103–106, 146–147.

2. P. Knauer, "The Hermeneutic Function of the Principle of Double Effect."

3. Their key articles, along with most of the other seminal contributions, are most easily found in Curran and McCormick, eds., *Readings in Moral Theology No. 1: Moral Norms and Catholic Tradition*.

4. McCormick's earlier contributions, originally published in *Theological Studies*, have been collected in book form: *Notes on Moral Theology 1965–1980*. His later editions are found annually in the spring number of that journal. McCormick's more direct contribution to the discussion was a lecture delivered in 1973. The lecture was subsequently published in a volume that joined it to several critiques from other theologians and a concluding response from McCormick, with the result that this volume is itself one of the central sources for those wishing to trace the discussion: McCormick and P. Ramsey, eds., *Doing Evil to Achieve Good: Moral Choice in Conflict Situations*. Cf. also B. Hoose, *Proportionalism: The American Debate and Its European Roots*

5. The term, as well as the general idea, was prominent in the first edition of this book, especially pp. 146–149. The reason it has been avoided here will be clear from what follows.

6. The first edition attempted this. Cf. pp. 148–149 and note 7, p. 222, with their discussion of "macroconsequentialism."

7. Cf., for example, L. Cahill, "Teleology, Utilitarianism, and Christian Ethics," esp. pp. 624–629.

8. This explains the key insight of Knauer's article as well as the reason he chose the principle of double effect as his entry point.

9. That quality was also highlighted in the first edition of this book. Cf. pp. 152–154. The reason that it is no longer isolated for individual attention, and even less is proposed as an adequate moral theory, will become clear later.

10. For that reason the landmark article by Bernard Lonergan was often cited by moral theologians participating in this development: "The Transition from a Classicist World-View to Historical-Mindedness."

11. So much that Josef Fuchs could comment that "mutability belongs to man's immutable essence": "Absoluteness of Moral Terms," in Curran and McCormick, eds., *Readings in Moral Theology No. 1*, p. 107.

12. This summary definition can be nuanced, and helpfully so. Cf. especially J. Walter, "Proportionate Reason and Its Three Levels of Inquiry: Structuring the Ongoing Debate," and E. Vacek, "Proportionalism: One View of the Debate."

13. This is, of course, the precise position espoused in the first edition of this book. That it is no longer my position, and the exact reasons for the change will become clear later.

14. A number of theologians, most notably John Connery, have also offered critiques of proportionalism. But the creators of this substantive alternative vision have been philosophers. William E. May, ed., *Principles of Catholic Moral Life*, includes contributions by most of the theological critics of proportionalism, as well as by the philosophers we will be discussing later. That volume and the conference on which it was based were obviously designed to respond to proportionalism. Indeed, they appear to be intended as a direct response to the first edition of this book. Note, for example, the similarity of titles. I appreciate, and have found helpful, this intensive consideration.

15. *Contraception and the Natural Law.*

16. Boyle has primarily worked in collaboration with Grisez, e.g., *Life and Death with Liberty and Justice: A Contribution to the Euthanasia Debate.* May has provided a popular book-length summary of Grisez's approach: *Becoming Human.*

17. Cf. his two important books, *Natural Law and Natural Right* and *Fundamentals of Ethics.*

18. The order in which these points are pursued varies. In *The Way of the Lord Jesus* Grisez first presents his approach, then critiques proportionalism. So does Finnis in *Fundamentals of Ethics.* In *Life and Death with Liberty and Justice* and *Abortion: The Myths, the Realities, and the Arguments,* however, Grisez places the critique first, then follows with his exposition.

19 *Fundamentals of Ethics,* p. 51. The same list is presented and discussed in *Natural Law and Natural Rights,* pp. 85–90.

20. Cf. *Abortion: The Myths, Realities and the Arguments* (1970), pp. 312–313; *Life and Death with Liberty and Justice* (1979), pp. 359–360; *The Way of the Lord Jesus* (1983), p. 124.

21. Cf., Finnis, *Natural Law and Natural Right*, pp. 85–86, *Fundamentals of Ethics*, p. 51. Also cf. Grisez, *The Way of the Lord Jesus*, p. 145, where he points out that proportionalism also cannot really "prove" itself and that his critique of proportionalism will therefore not be based on the absence of such a proof

22. Cf., for example, Grisez, *Life and Death with Liberty and Justice*, pp. 360–361.

23. Cf., for example, Grisez, *The Way of the Lord Jesus*, p. 124; Finnis, *Natural Law and Natural Right*, pp. 90–91.

24. Cf. Finnis, *Fundamentals of Ethics*, pp. 89–90; Grisez, *Way of the Lord Jesus*, pp. 153–154.

25. The two approaches detailed here, and the authors associated with them, are clearly the main contributors to contemporary Catholic moral theory. But they are not the only contributors. The synthesis offered in chapter 14 and developed later is enriched also by two other perspectives, neither of which can be facilely identified with either "camp": G. Hallett, *Christian Moral Reasoning*, and P. Ramsey, "Incommensurability and Indeterminancy in Moral Choice," in McCormick and Ramsey, eds., *Doing Evil to Achieve Good*, pp. 69–144.

26. Cf. "Incommensurability and Indeterminancy in Moral Choice," op. cit., especially pp. 93–95.

27. This is an important point. If there is a fundamental difference between the way theologians and philosophers approach issues, it may be this. Because of their radical commitment to the presence of the Spirit in the Church, theologians are inclined to trust the "truth of experience," even when theory has not yet developed to the point of explaining it adequately. Philosophers, on the other hand, (or at least those of a certain ilk) are radically committed to rational and cogent thought. For them, then, the weakness of a theory is a decisive weakness, utterly precluding the adoption of that point of view. It is somewhat like the case of the empirical sciences, where, it is said, theories do not yield to contradictory data but only to new theories. In the absence of a new, more adequate theory, the old theory stands, even if some data remain unexplained. Philosophers, quite rightly, adopt a similar stance. It is not, however, the stance of theologians, who faithfully affirm experience while continuing the search for theory.

28. In most cases, the affirmation appears begrudging, even accidental. So, for example, G. Grisez, *Way of the Lord Jesus*, p. 147: "Suppose, for instance, a pregnant woman has been told she must have an abortion, lest she and her unborn child both die. She can reject the calculus and refuse the abortion; in doing so, she can hold against proportionalism that purposely destroying her baby would be an act of unfaithfulness to it, and *as such a greater evil* than accepting the risk of a natural disaster in which she and the baby will both die" (emphasis added).

This sort of case involves special difficulties. For one thing, is the child really "innocent," as the tradition used that term? The child is, after all, a threat to the mother's life. So it is not clear that the tradition would prohibit a medical intervention to remove the fetus, in any case. For another thing, one need not espouse a thoroughgoing basic goods approach to judge the abortion to be morally wrong. The presentation in this book has itself already asserted that direct killing of the innocent is wrong, and on other than proportionalist grounds.

Still, particularly significant in this context is the fact that Grisez himself resorts to a comparative statement (italicized here). This implies that the other alternative also involves evil (and good) and therefore also affirms, indeed exemplifies, the possiblity of just such comparative judgments as his approach rejects. In other words, pursuing his own line of argument, Grisez could as plausibly have said that the woman agrees with proportionalism and since, given her vision of life, she judges unfaithfulness to her identity of mother/lifegiver to be a greater evil than physical death, she refuses to do it. Thus, his argument does not prove the uselessness of a proportionalist methodology and may indeed have accidentally demonstrated its inevitable role in moral judgment.

A more forthright acknowledgment of the role of proportionate reason is given in J. Finnis, *Natural Law and Natural Rights*, pp. 111–118. Even here, the energy of the presentation is focused on the inadequacy of consequences, as he calls them, to provide an ultimate basis for morality. Still, the presentation begins and ends with a positive assertion of their place

29. P. Ramsey, "Incommensurability and Indeterminancy in Moral Choice," in McCormick and Ramsey, eds., *Doing Evil to Achieve Good*, p. 69. All italics in this and the following quotations are Ramsey's.

30. Ibid., 71.

31. Ibid., 72.

32. Ibid.

33. Ibid.

34. Ibid., 74.

CHAPTER 18

1. In K. Rahner and H. Vorgrimler, *Theological Dictionary*, p. 305.

2. The examples given in this paragraph include both formal and material norms This may confuse things. But the fact of the matter is that the manuals did not clearly distinguish these two, so in our summary of their thought neither shall we. And if this does raise some questions, perhaps that will just prove again how important the distinction is.

3. For typical manualist presentations of these three levels of the natural laws, cf H. Noldin, *Summa Theologiae Moralis*, 1:113; and J. Fuchs, *Natural Law*, pp. 117, 151.

4. A point made and impressively developed by P. Ramsey in "The Case of the Curious Exception."

5. Words can take on new meanings, of course. But that only adds to the confusion. For it results in the possibility that we may grossly misinterpret the actual meaning of formulations from an earlier, different era. Hence the need for hermeneutics, a science whose very existence testifies to the difference between formulations and understandings.

6. An insight somewhat appreciated in more recent scholastic writings, e.g., J. Fuchs, *Theologiae Moralis Generalis*, 1:81ff, where the author asserts that the very term "natural law" refers primarily to an inner reality and only secondarily to formulations.

7. The occasion of the preparation of the second edition of this book prompts some humbling meditations along this line. This author certainly thought he had been "crashingly clear" in composing the first edition. Regarding some points, as we have seen, his intellectual position has changed. Such is the human condition.

More humbling are the cases where he came to realize that his position had simply not been well expressed. The challenge was not to find new ideas, but to find clearer words. It is one thing to experience this fact; it is another to find the explanation for it in one's own writings!

8 Cf., for example, Marx's *Critique of Hegel's Philosophy of Right*

9. Cf., for example, W. Stark, *The Sociology of Knowledge.*

10. J. S. Mill, as quoted by H. R. Niebuhr, *Christ and Culture*, p. 238

11. Theologian Stanley Hauerwas must be credited for challenging spokespersons for a natural law morality such as myself to be more attentive to this perspectival character of all human knowledge. I happily acknowledge how much I have learned from him since the publication of the first edition of this book. Cf. his *A Community of Character* and *The Peaceable Kingdom*. We will return to these ideas in chapter 20.

12. In many ways, the following reflections constitute a return to the insight presented in chapter 14, when we named as one of the characteristics of the natural law that it is subject to change. What is different here is the perspective (making this an example of the just previous point of this chapter!). Before, the focus was the natural law itself (metaphysics). Now the focus is our understandings (epistemology).

13. On the idea of human nature as a *Restbegriff*, cf. K. Rahner, "Concerning the Relationship Between Nature and Grace," p. 313f; J. Fuchs, *Natural Law*, p. 45; E. McDonagh, *Invitation and Response*, p. 34.

14. A point made by K. Rahner, "The Experiment with Man," pp. 218–219

CHAPTER 19

1. These are points very well argued by J. C. Murray, "Should There Be a Law? The Question of Censorship," in *We Hold These Truths*, pp. 155–174.

2. Cf. J. Fuchs, *Theologia Moralis Generalis*, 1:113.

3. Cf. H. Noldin, *Summa Theologiae Moralis*, 1:123–124.

4. Cf. J. Fuchs, pp. 117–120; H. Noldin, pp. 132–136.

5. This entire section is dependent on the work of J. Fuchs, "Auctoritas Dei in Auctoritate Civili." A general understanding of Fuchs's argument can be derived from the digest of this article, "The Authority of God in Civil Authority." His understanding of human law is exhaustively reported in O'Connell, *Changing Roman Catholic Moral Theology: A Study in Josef Fuchs*, pp. 121–178.

6. That the common good and not "legitimate source" justifies positive law is emphasized by K. Rahner, "The Dignity and Freedom of Man," p. 256.

7. Thus fidelity to one's judgment in the face of continued enforcement of the letter of the law can lead to tragedy. This point is acknowledged and discussed by K. Rahner, p. 252.

8. On the twin risks of anarchy and tyranny (totalitarianism), and the tensions that these cause in human living, cf. K. Rahner, pp. 235–264.

CHAPTER 20

1. This is a change from the emphasis present in this chapter in the first edition At several previous points I have noted the shift in my thinking from more

individually oriented categories to those more communally sensitive and from more static, essentialistic conceptions to those more aware of the role of historical and social context. I have also noted before the degree to which this development is beholden to the insights of Stanley Hauerwas. His influence will be apparent in the revised formulations of this chapter.

2. R. Collins, "Scripture and the Christian Ethic," p. 240.

3. And it is particularly to this overall vision that one refers in, quite rightly, affirming the existence of "absolute moral norms" in Scripture. In addition to the other sources mentioned here, these insights are dependent upon Lisa Sowle Cahill's "Moral Methodology: A Case Study."

4 C. Curran, "Dialogue with the Scriptures: The Role and Function of the Scriptures in Moral Theology," in *Catholic Moral Theology in Dialogue*, pp. 23-64. This article includes considerable additional bibliography on this topic.

5. A. Kosnik et al., *Human Sexuality*.

6. Committee on Doctrine, "Bishops' Doctrinal Committee Responds," p. 376.

7. That is why, in the end, the Catholic tradition consistently places its faith not so much in the God of the Book as in the God of the Gathering.

8. A point made by, among others, D. Maquire, "Moral Absolutes and the Magisterium," p. 80.

9. The fact that this approach has changed somewhat in the last hundred years and the reasons for the change are discussed by Y. Congar, "The Magisterium and Theologians – A Short History."

10. How this understanding is to be reconciled with the declaration of the First Vatican Council is a serious question. I am impressed by the suggestion of G. Hughes. Cf. his *Authority in Morals*, where he also reports on objections raised against earlier forms of his proposal and responds to them.

11. Indeed, even the use of the term "teaching" to characterize this episcopal function is of relatively recent vintage, having entered Catholic usage around 1800. Cf. M. Place, "Theologians and Magisterium from the Council of Trent to the First Vatican Council," in G. Dyer, ed., *Magisterium*, pp. 225-241. Given the recentness of this term and the cloudy circumstances under which it entered the theological vocabulary, it might be better to return to the earlier usage, seeing the episcopal role, with its twin aspects of jurisdiction and orders, as a ministry of leadership and recognizing that leadership includes oversight, even oversight of theological conversation.

12. A splendid example of just this sort of moral leadership is to be found in the preparation and promulgation of the two recent pastoral letters of the U.S. National Conference of Catholic Bishops, that on War and Peace and that on the Economy. The fact that the process in both cases involved successive drafts and widespread consultation is intelligible only on two conditions: (1) that at the beginning of the process the bishops did *not* know the answer, the truths they were destined to teach, and (2) that they clearly saw it as a duty of their leadership office to initiate, stimulate, and facilitate the process of communal discernment from which genuine wisdom could emerge. In so doing the two letters were benchmark incarnations of a profoundly traditional understanding of magisterium.

13. A very apt phrase I once heard sociologist and theologian Andrew Greeley use

14. C. Curran, "The Stance of Moral Theology," *New Perspectives in Moral Theology*,

pp. 47–86. I have nuanced these ideas in a manner slightly different than Curran's. But I do not believe I have tampered with his central insight.

15. Andrew Greeley and Mary Greeley Durkin have astutely noted that emphasis on either the two optimistic or the two pessimistic doctrines is characteristic of the Catholic and Protestant traditions, respectively. Cf. their *How to Save The Catholic Church*, esp. pp. 51–73.

16. J. Gustafson, "Is There a Catholic and/or Christian Ethic?–A Response," p. 155.

17. Ibid., p. 156.

18. Ibid., p. 158.

19. Ibid., pp. 158–159.

20. In addition to the sources cited thus far, this topic has been helpfully pursued by the following: J. Fuchs, "Human, Humanist and Christian Morality," in *Human Values and Christian Morality*, pp. 112–147; id., "Gibt es eine specifisch christliche Moral?" which is summarized in "Is There a Specifically Christian Ethic?"; C. Curran, "Dialogue with Humanism: Is There a Distinctively Christian Ethic?" in *Catholic Moral Theology in Dialogue*, pp. 1–23; J. Gustafson, *Can Ethics Be Christian?*

21. This fourfold identity of the natural law and the Law of Christ is derived from a similar presentation by J. Fuchs, *Theologia Moralis Generalis*, 1:100–109.

CHAPTER 21

1. In preparing the second edition of this book, I was briefly tempted to draft an entirely new final chapter. All the more was this attractive since I think some may find its optimism rather quaint. I have chosen not to do so for two reasons. First, the motivations described here continue to drive my theological work. And second, when the psalmist declared: "My soul waits for the Lord more than sentinels wait for the dawn" (Ps 130:6), he was reflecting on not only the hoped-for dawn but also the painfully long night. This point seems to me worth remembering.

2. In a Catholic context it is also sometimes seen to include the study of canon law. The justification for this is that the Christian life is lived socially, that society needs structuring, and that canon law is the means by which the Catholic community structures itself in order to facilitate the living of that life.

3. Moral theology, because it is a limited thing, often neglects this theme. One author who has attempted to address it is G. Gilleman, *The Primacy of Charity in Moral Theology*.

4. One author who has attempted to address this truth is E. McDonagh, "Liturgy and Christian Life," in *Invitation and Response*, pp. 96–108.

5. These two ideas, internal coherence and external adequacy, are seen as the two characteristics of any successfuol theory by J. Macmurray, *The Self as Agent*, p. 25.

6. Cf. C. Curran, "Moral Theology: The Present State of the Discipline."

7. A point made in an otherwise unhelpful article: T. Dubay, "The State of Moral Theology: A Critical Appraisal." Here Dubay responds to the article of Curran cited in note 6. Their discussion in print has continued, an interesting example because it is a disagreement about disagreement.

8. The phrase comes from Charles Davis, *A Question of Conscience*, pp. 64–77.
9. *Confessions*, p. 1.
10. Irenaeus, *Adversus Haereses*, book IV, chap. 20, section 7.

BIBLIOGRAPHY

NOTE: Some books listed may no longer be in print. All should be easily available through libraries, however.

BOOKS

Bassett, William, and Huizing, Peter, eds. *The Future of Christian Marriage (Concilium 87)*. New York: Seabury, 1974.

Baum, Gregory. *Man Becoming*. New York: Herder and Herder, 1970.

_____. *Religion and Alienation: A Theological Reading of Sociology*. New York: Paulist, 1975.

Binswanger, Ludwig. *Being in the World*. New York: Harper Torchbooks, 1968.

Birch, Bruce C., and Rasmussen, Larry L. *Bible and Ethics in the Christian Life*. Minneapolis: Augsburg, 1976.

Böckle, Franz. *Law and Conscience*. New York: Sheed & Ward, 1966.

Crossan, John. *In Parables*. New York: Harper & Row, 1973.

Curran, Charles. *A New Look at Christian Morality*. Notre Dame: Fides, 1968.

_____. *Catholic Moral Theology in Dialogue*. Notre Dame: Fides, 1972.

_____. *Contemporary Problems in Moral Theology*. Notre Dame: Fides, 1970.

_____. *New Perspectives in Moral Theology*. Notre Dame: Fides, 1974.

_____. *Ongoing Revision*. Notre Dame: Fides, 1975.

_____. *Themes in Fundamental Moral Theology*. Notre Dame: University of Notre Dame Press, 1977.

Davis, Henry. *Moral and Pastoral Theology*. 4 vols. 7th ed. New York: Sheed and Ward, 1958. Vol. 1, *Human Acts, Law, Sin, Virtue*.

Dedek, John. *Contemporary Medical Ethics*. New York: Sheed & Ward, 1975.

_____. *Contemporary Sexual Morality*. New York: Sheed & Ward, 1971.

_____. *Human Life*. New York: Sheed & Ward, 1972.

_____. *Titius and Bertha Ride Again: Contemporary Moral Cases*. New York: Sheed & Ward, 1974.

Deekken, Alfons. *Process and Permanence in Ethics: Max Scheler's Moral Philosophy*. New York: Paulist, 1974.

Delhaye, Philippe. *The Christian Conscience*. New York: Desclée, 1968.

Deman, Thomas. *Aux origines de la théologie morale*. Montreal: Institut d'Études Médiévales, 1951.

Doherty, Dennis. *Divorce and Remarriage: Resolving a Catholic Dilemma*. St. Meinrad, Ind.: Abbey Press, 1974.

Flick, Maurizio, and Alszeghy, Zoltan. *Il Vangelo Della Grazia*. Rome: Lib., Editrice Fiorentina, 1964.

Fransen, Peter. *Divine Grace and Man*. New York: Mentor–Omega, 1965.

Fuchs, Josef. *Human Values and Christian Morality*. Dublin: Gill & Macmillan, 1970.

———. *Natural Law: A Theological Investigation.* New York: Sheed & Ward, 1965.

———. *Theologia Moralis Generalis.* 2 vols. Rome: Gregorian University Press, 1963 and 1967.

Gilkey, Langdon. *Catholicism Confronts Modernity.* New York: Seabury, 1973.

Gilleman, Gerard. *The Primacy of Charity in Moral Theology.* Westminster, Md.: Newman, 1959.

Gleason, Robert. *Grace.* New York: Sheed & Ward, 1962.

Guindon, André. *The Sexual Language.* Ottawa: University of Ottawa Press, 1976.

Gustafson, James M. *Can Ethics Be Christian?* Chicago: University of Chicago Press, 1975.

———. *Protestant and Roman Catholic Ethics: Prospects for Rapprochement.* Chicago: University of Chicago Press, 1978.

———. *Christ and the Moral Life.* Chicago: University of Chicago Press, 1976.

———. *The Church as Moral Decision Maker.* Philadelphia: Pilgrim, 1970.

Gutierrez, Gustavo. *A Theology of Liberation.* Maryknoll, N.Y.: Orbis, 1973.

Häring, Bernard. *The Law of Christ.* 3 vols. Westminster, Md.: Newman, 1961–1966. Vol. 1, *General Moral Theology.*

———. *Morality Is for Persons.* New York: Farrar, Straus & Giroux, 1971.

Hauerwas, Stanley. *Character and the Christian Life.* San Antonio: Trinity University Press, 1975.

———. *Vision and Virtue.* Notre Dame: Fides, 1974.

Keane, Philip. *Sexual Morality: A Catholic Perspective.* New York: Paulist, 1977.

Kosnik, Anthony, et al. *Human Sexuality.* New York: Paulist, 1977.

Lehmann, Paul. *Ethics in a Christian Context.* New York: Harper & Row, 1963.

Lonergan, Bernard. *Method in Theology.* New York: Herder and Herder, 1972.

Macmurray, John. *The Self as Agent.* New York: Humanities, 1978.

———. *Persons in Relation.* New York: Humanities, 1979.

Macquarrie, John. *Three Issues in Ethics.* New York: Harper & Row, 1970.

Maly, Eugene H. *Sin: Biblical Perspectives.* Dayton: Pflaum, 1973.

May, Rollo; Angel, Ernest; and Ellenberger, Henri; eds. *Existence.* New York: Simon & Schuster, 1967.

McCormick, Richard A. *Ambiguity in Moral Choice.* Milwaukee: Marquette University, 1977.

McDonagh, Enda. *Gift and Call.* St. Meinrad, Ind.: Abbey Press, 1975.

———. *Invitation and Response.* New York: Sheed & Ward, 1972.

Meyer, Charles R. *A Contemporary Theology of Grace.* Staten Island: Alba House, 1971.

———. *The Touch of God.* Staten Island: Alba House, 1972.

Milhaven, John G. *Toward a New Catholic Morality.* Garden City, N.Y.: Doubleday, 1970.

Murphy, Francis. *Moral Teaching in the Primitive Church.* New York: Paulist, 1968.

Murray, John Courtney. *We Hold These Truths.* New York: Sheed & Ward, 1985.

National Conference of Catholic Bishops. *Human Life in Our Day.* Washington: U.S. Catholic Conference, 1968.

———. *To Live in Christ Jesus.* Washington: U.S. Catholic Conference, 1976.

Niebuhr, H. Richard. *Christ and Culture.* New York: Harper Torchbooks, 1956.
———. *The Responsible Self.* New York: Harper & Row, 1978.
Nielsen, E. *The Ten Commandments in New Perspective.* Naperville, Ill.: Allenson, 1968.
Noldin, Hieronymous. *Summa Theologiae Moralis.* 3 vols. Innsbruck: Rauch, 1957–1960. Vol. 1, *De principiis, de poenis ecclesiasticis, de castitate.*
O'Connell, Timothy. *Changing Roman Catholic Moral Theology: A Study in Josef Fuchs.* Ann Arbor: University Microfilms, 1974.
———. *A Contemporary Meditation on Personal Holiness.* Chicago: Thomas More, 1975.
———. *What a Modern Catholic Believes About Suffering and Evil.* Chicago: Thomas More, 1972.
Regan, George M. *New Trends in Moral Theology.* New York: Newman, 1971.
Rondet, Henri. *Original Sin.* Staten Island: Alba House, 1972.
———. *The Grace of Christ.* Westminster, Md.: Newman, 1967.
Salm, C. Luke. *Readings in Biblical Morality.* Englewood Cliffs, N.J.: Prentice-Hall, 1967.
Sanders, Jack T. *Ethics in the New Testament.* Philadelphia: Fortress, 1975.
Schelke, Karl. *Theology of the New Testament.* 4 vols. Vol. 3, *Morality.* Collegeville, Minn.: Liturgical Press, 1973.
Schillebeeckx, Edward. *Christ the Sacrament of the Encounter with God.* New York: Sheed & Ward, 1987.
———. *Marriage: Human Reality and Saving Mystery.* New York: Sheed & Ward, 1965.
Schnackenburg, Rudolf. *Christian Existence in the New Testament.* 2 vols. Notre Dame: University of Notre Dame Press, 1968 and 1969.
———. *The Moral Teaching of the New Testament.* New York: Crossroads, 1989.
Schoonenberg, Piet. *Man and Sin.* Notre Dame: University of Notre Dame Press, 1965.
Shea, John. *What a Modern Catholic Believes About Sin.* Chicago: Thomas More, 1971.
Stamm, J. J., and Andrews, M. E. *The Ten Commandments in Recent Literature.* Naperville, Ill.: Allenson, 1967.
Stark, Werner. *The Sociology of Knowledge.* London: Routledge and Kegan Paul, 1967.
Tracy, David. *Blessed Rage for Order.* New York: Harper & Row, 1979.
Troisfontaines, Roger. *I Do Not Die.* New York: Desclée, 1963.
Van der Marck, W. H. *Toward a Christian Ethic.* New York: Newman, 1967.
Van der Poel, Cornelius J. *The Search for Human Values.* New York: Paulist, 1973.
Von Hildebrand, Dietrich. *Ethics.* Chicago: Franciscan Herald Press, 1953.
Wrenn, Lawrence G., ed. *Divorce and Remarriage in the Catholic Church.* New York: Newman, 1973.

ARTICLES

Arntz, Joseph. "Natural Law and Its History." *Concilium* 5 (1965): 39–57. New York: Paulist.
Berger, Klaus. "Law." In *Encyclopedia of Theology*, edited by K. Rahner, pp. 822–830. New York: Seabury, 1975.

Blank, Josef. "Does the New Testament Provide Principles for Modern Moral Theology." *Concilium* 25 (1967): 9–22. New York: Paulist.

Collins, Raymond. "Scripture and the Christian Ethic." *Proceedings of the Catholic Theological Society of America* 29 (1974): 215–241.

Congar, Yves. "Pour une histoire sémantique du terme 'magisterium'" and "Bref historique des formes du 'magistere' et de ses relations avec les docteurs." *Revue des sciences philosophiques et theologiques* 60 (1976): 85–112.

——. "The Magisterium and Theologians – A Short History." *Theology Digest* 25 (1977): 15–20.

Connery, John. "Morality of Consequences: A Critical Appraisal." *Theological Studies* 34 (1973): 396–414.

Crowe, Michael. "Natural Law Theory Today." In R. McCormick et al., *The Future of Ethics and Moral Theology*, pp. 78–105. Chicago: Argus, 1968.

——. "Human Nature: Immutable or Mutable." *Irish Theology Quarterly* 30 (1963): 204–231.

Curran, Charles. "Moral Theology: The Present State of the Discipline." *Theological Studies* 34 (1973): 446–467.

Daniélou, Jean. "Christianity and non-Christian Religions." In *The Word in History*, ed. T. P. Burke, pp. 86–101. New York: Sheed & Ward, 1966.

Dedek, John. "Scripture and the Christian Ethic: A Response." *Proceedings of the Catholic Theological Society of America* 29 (1974): 243–246.

Delhaye, P. "'Droit naturel' et théologie morale." *Revue théologique de Louvain* 6 (1975): 137–164.

Dianich, Severino. "La corruzione della natura e la grazia nella opzioni fondamentali." *Scuola Cattolica* 92 (1964): 203–220.

Dubay, Thomas. "The State of Moral Theology: A Critical Appraisal." *Theological Studies* 35 (1974): 482–506.

Dulles, Avery. "The Theologian and the Magisterium." *Proceedings of the Catholic Theological Society of America* 31 (1976): 235–246.

Fitzmyer, Joseph. "Pauline Ecclesiology and Ethics," *Jerome Biblical Commentary*, 79:157–166. Englewood Cliffs, N.J.: Prentice-Hall, 1968.

Fletcher, Joseph. "Situation Ethics, Law, and Watergate." *Cumberland Law Review* 6 (1975): 35–60.

Fransen, Peter. "Towards a Psychology of Divine Grace." *Lumen Vitae* 12 (1957): 203–232.

Freyne, Seán. "The Bible and Christian Morality." In *Morals, Law and Authority*, ed. J. P. Mackey, pp. 1–38. Dayton: Pflaum, 1969.

Fuchs, Josef. "Absoluteness of Moral Terms." *Gregorianum* 52 (1971): 415–458.

——. "Auctoritas Dei in Auctoritate Civili." *Periodica de Re Morali, Cononica, Liturgica* 52 (1963): 3–18.

——. "Gibt es eine specifisch christliche Moral?" *Stimmen der Zeit* 185 (1970): 99–112.

——. "Is There a Specifically Christian Ethic?" *Theology Digest* 19 (1971): 39–45.

——. "Sin and Conversion." *Theology Digest* 14 (1966): 292–301.

——. "The Authority of God in Civil Authority." *Theology Digest* 12 (1964): 104–109.

Glaser, John. "Transition Between Grace and Sin: Fresh Perspectives." *Theological Studies* 29 (1968): 260–274.

Gustafson, James M. "Is There a Catholic and/or Christian Ethic?–A Response." *Proceedings of the Catholic Theological Society of America* 29 (1974): 155–160.

——. "Context vs. Principles: The Misplaced Debate in Christian Ethics." In *New Theology 3*, ed. M. E. Marty and D. G. Peerman, pp. 69–102. New York: Macmillan, 1966.

Häring, Bernard. "Dynamism and Continuity in a Personalistic Approach to Natural Law." In *Norm and Context in Christian Ethics*, edited by G. H. Outka and P. Ramsey, pp. 119–218. New York: Scribner, 1968.

Hughes, Gerard. "Infallibility in Morals." *Theological Studies* 34 (1973)· 415–428.

Janssens, Louis. "Ontic Evil and Moral Evil." *Louvain Studies* 4 (1972). 115–156.

Knauer, Peter. "The Hermeneutic Function of the Principle of Double Effect." *Natural Law Forum* 12 (1967): 132–162.

Lonergan, Bernard. "The Transition from a Classicist World-View to Historical-Mindedness." In *Law for Liberty*, ed. J. E. Biechler, pp. 126–133. Baltimore: Helicon, 1967.

Maguire, Daniel. "Moral Absolutes and the Magisterium." In *Absolutes in Moral Theology?* ed. C. Curran, pp. 57–107. Washington, D.C.: Corpus, 1968.

Malloy, Edward. "Natural Law Theory and Catholic Moral Theology." *American Ecclesiastical Review* 169 (1975): 456–469.

McCormick, Richard. "Human Significance and Christian Significance." In *Norm and Context in Christian Ethics*, ed. G. H. Outka and P. Ramsey, pp. 233–264. New York: Scribner, 1968.

——. "Notes on Moral Theology." *Theological Studies* 32 (1971): 80–97; 33 (1972): 68–90; 36 (1975): 85–100; 37 (1976): 71–87; 38 (1977): 70–100.

——. "The Moral Theology of Vatican II." In R. McCormick et al., *The Future of Ethics and Moral Theology*, pp. 7–18. Chicago: Argus, 1968.

Millhaven, John G. "Towards an Epistemology of Ethics." *Theological Studies* 27 (1966): 228–241.

——. "Objective Moral Evaluation of Consequences." *Theological Studies* 32 (1971): 407–430.

Murray, John Courtney. "The Declaration on Religious Freedom." *Concilium* 15 (1966): 3–16. New York: Paulist.

O'Connell, Matthew. "Some Aspects of Commandment in the Old Testament." In *Reading in Biblical Morality*, ed. C. L. Salm, pp. 9–29. Englewood Cliffs, N.J.: Prentice-Hall, 1967.

O'Connell, Timothy. "Grace, Relationship and Transactional Analysis." *Thought* 48 (1973) 360–385.

——. "Identification of Sin." *Reconciliation Background Papers.* Chicago: Liturgy Training Program, 1976.

——. "Old Priest, New Theology: A Dilemma." *American Ecclesiastical Review* 167 (1973): 236–251.

——. "Sin and Reconciliation." *Reconciliation Resources II.* Chicago: Liturgy Training Program, 1975.

——. "The Point of Moral Theology." *Chicago Studies* 14 (1975): 49–66.

——. "The Question of Moral Norms." *American Ecclesiastical Review* 169 (1975): 377–388.

Pattison, E. Mansell, M.D. "The Development of Moral Values in Children." In *Conscience: Theological and Psychological Perspectives,* ed. C. Nelson, pp. 238–262. New York: Newman, 1973.

Peter, Val. "Scripture and the Christian Ethic: A Response." *Proceedings of the Catholic Theological Society of America* 29 (1974): 247–253.

Podimattam, Felix. "What Is Mortal Sin?" *Clergy Monthly* 36 (1972): 57–67.

Quay, Paul. "Morality by Calculation of Values." *Theology Digest* 23 (1975): 347–364.

Rahner, Karl. "Concerning the Relationship Between Nature and Grace." *Theological Investigations I,* pp. 297–318. Baltimore: Helicon, 1961.

——. "Evolution and Original Sin." *Concilium* 26 (1967): 61–73. New York: Paulist.

——. "Guilt and Its Remission: The Borderline Between Theology and Psychotherapy." *Theological Investigations II,* pp. 265–282. Baltimore: Helicon, 1963,

——. "Guilt-Responsibility-Punishment Within the View of Catholic Theology." *Theological Investigations VI,* pp. 197–217. Baltimore: Helicon, 1969.

——. "On the Question of a Formal Existential Ethics." *Theological Investigations II,* pp. 217–234. Baltimore: Helicon, 1963.

——. "On the Theology of the Incarnation." *Theological Investigations IV,* pp. 105–120. Baltimore: Helicon, 1966.

——. "Some Thoughts on a 'Good Intention.'" *Theological Investigations III,* pp. 105–128. Baltimore: Helicon, 1967.

——. "The Dignity and Freedom of Man." *Theological Investigations II,* pp. 235–264. Baltimore: Helicon, 1963.

——. "The Experiment with Man." *Theological Investigations IX,* pp. 205–224. New York: Herder and Herder, 1972.

——. "The Sin of Adam." *Theological Investigations XI,* pp. 247–262. New York: Seabury, 1974.

——. "The Theological Concept of Consupiscentia." *Theological Investigations I,* pp. 347–382. Baltimore: Helicon, 1961.

——. "The Two Basic Types of Christology." *Theological Investigations XIII,* pp. 213–223. New York: Seabury, 1975.

——. "Theological Reflexions on Monogenism." *Theological Investigations I,* pp. 229–296. Baltimore: Helicon, 1961.

——. "Theology of Freedom." *Theological Investigations VI,* pp. 178–196. Baltimore: Helicon, 1969.

Ramsey, Paul. "The Case of the Curious Exception." In *Norm and Context in Christian Ehtics,* ed. G. H. Outka and P. Ramsey, pp. 67–135. New York: Scribner, 1968.

Ryan, Columba. "The Traditional Concept of Natural Law: An Interpretation." In *Light on the Natural Law,* ed. I. Evans, pp. 13–37. Baltimore: Helicon, 1965.

Schneider, Gerhard. "The Biblical Grounding of Ethical Norms." *Theology Digest* 22 (1974): 117–120.

Schüller, Bruno. "Neuere Beiträge zum Thema 'Bergründung sittlicher Normen.'" *Theologische Berichte* 4: 109–181. Einsiedeln: Benziger, 1974.

———. "What Ethical Principles Are Universally Valid?" *Theology Digest* 19 (1971): 23–28.

Tapia, Ralph. "When Is Sin Sin?" *Thought* 47 (1972): 211–224.

Tierney, Brian. "Infallibility in Morals: A Response." *Theological Studies* 35 (1974): 507–517.

Tracy, David. "Presidential Address." *Proceedings of the Catholic Theological Society of America* 32 (1977): 234–244.

Troisfontaines, Rogers. "L'insémination artificielle: Problèmes éthiques." *Nouvelle Revue Théologique* 95 (1973): 764–778.

von Hildebrand, Dietrich. "Sittlichkeit und ethische Werterkenntnis." *Jahrbuch für Philosophie und phänomenologische Forschung* 5 (1922): 463–602.

Walgrave, Jan. "Is Morality Static or Dynamic?" *Concilium* 5 (1965): 22–38. London: Burns & Oates; New York: Paulist.

Watson, Gerard. "Pagan Philosophy and Christian Ethics." In *Morals, Law and Authority*, ed. J. P. Mackey, pp. 39–57. Dayton: Pflaum, 1969.

ADDITIONAL BIBLIOGRAPHY:
1978–1988

BOOKS

Augustine. *Confessions*, trans. F. Sheed. New York: Sheed and Ward, 1944.

Battaglia, Anthony. *Toward a Reformulation of Natural Law*. New York: Seabury, 1981.

Bausch, William. *Storytelling: Imagination and Faith*. Mystic, Conn.: Twenty-Third Publications, 1984.

Bellah, Robert, et al. *Habits of the Heart: Individualism and Commitment in American Life*. Berkeley: University of California Press, 1985.

Bernardin, Joseph. *Consistent Ethic of Life*. Kansas City: Sheed & Ward, 1988.

Bernstein, Leonard. *The Unanswered Question*. Cambridge: Harvard University Press, 1975.

Böckle, Franz. *Fundamental Moral Theology*. New York: Pueblo, 1980.

Curran, Charles and McCormick, Richard, eds. *Readings in Moral Theology No. 1: Moral Norms and Catholic Tradition*. New York: Paulist, 1979.

——. *Readings in Moral Theology No. 2: The Distinctiveness of Christian Ethics*. New York: Paulist, 1980.

——. *Readings in Moral Theology No. 3: The Magisterium and Morality*. New York: Paulist, 1982.

——. *Readings in Moral Theology No. 4: The Use of Scripture in Moral Theology*. New York: Paulist, 1984.

——. *Readings in Moral Theology No. 5: Official Catholic Social Teaching*. New York: Paulist, 1986.

——. *Readings in Moral Theology No. 6: Dissent in the Church*. New York: Paulist, 1988.

Davis, Charles. *A Question of Conscience*. New York: Harper & Row, 1967.

Dyer, George, ed. *Communicating Moral Values*. An issue of *Chicago Studies* 19 (1980): 229–336.

——. *Magisterium*. An issue of *Chicago Studies* 17 (1978): 144–310.

——. *Storytelling and Christian Faith*. An issue of *Chicago Studies* 21 (1982): 3–103.

Finnis, John. *Fundamentals of Ethics*. Washington, D.C.: Georgetown University Press, 1983.

——. *Natural Law and Natural Rights*. Oxford: Clarendon Press, 1984 (corrected version).

——. Boyle, Joseph and Grisez, Germain. *Nuclear Deterrence, Morality and Realism*. New York: Oxford University Press, 1987.

Fuchs, Josef. *Christian Ethics in a Secular Arena*. Washington, D.C.: Georgetown University Press, 1984.

――――. *Personal Responsibility and Christian Morality.* Washington, D.C.: Georgetown University Press, 1983.

Greeley, Andrew and Durkin, Mary Greeley. *How to Save the Catholic Church.* New York: Viking Press, 1984.

Grisez, Germain. *Abortion: The Myths, the Realities and the Arguments.* New York: Corpus Books, 1970.

――――. *Contraception and the Natural Law.* Milwaukee: Bruce, 1964.

――――. *The Way of the Lord Jesus.* Chicago: Franciscan Herald Press, 1983.

―――― and Boyle, Joseph. *Life and Death with Liberty and Justice: A Contribution to the Euthanasia Debate.* Notre Dame: University of Notre Dame Press, 1979.

Gula, Richard. *What Are They Saying About Moral Norms?* New York: Paulist, 1982.

Gustafson, James. *Ethics from a Theocentric Perspective.* Chicago: University of Chicago Press, 1981.

Hallett, Garth. *Christian Moral Reasoning.* Notre Dame: University of Notre Dame Press, 1983.

Häring, Bernard. *Free and Faithful in Christ.* 3 vols. New York: Seabury, 1978–1981. Vol. 1: *General Moral Theology.*

Hauerwas, Stanley. *A Community of Character.* Notre Dame: University of Notre Dame Press, 1981.

――――. *The Peaceable Kingdom.* Notre Dame: University of Notre Dame Press, 1983.

Heidegger, Martin. *Being and Time.* New York: Harper & Row, 1962.

Hoge, Dean. *Future of Catholic Leadership.* Kansas City: Sheed & Ward, 1987.

Hoose, B. *Proportionalism: The American Debate and Its European Roots.* Washington, D.C.: Georgetown University Press, 1987.

Hughes, Gerard. *Authority in Morals.* Washington, D.C.: Georgetown University Press, 1978.

Lawler, Michael. *Secular Marriage, Christian Sacrament.* Mystic, Conn.: Twenty-Third Publications, 1988.

Lewis, C. S. *The Problem of Pain.* New York: Macmillan, 1945.

Mackin, Theodore. *Divorce and Remarriage.* New York: Paulist, 1984.

――――. *What Is Marriage?* New York: Paulist, 1982.

Maguire, Daniel. *The Moral Choice.* Garden City, N.Y.: Doubleday, 1978.

Mahoney, John. *The Making of Moral Theology.* Oxford: Clarendon Press, 1987.

Marx, Karl. *Critique of Hegel's Philosophy of Right.* Cambridge: Cambridge University Press, 1970.

Maslow, Abraham. *Toward a Psychology of Being.* Princeton, N.J.: Van Nostrand, 1968.

May, William E. *Becoming Human.* Dayton: Pflaum, 1975.

McCormick, Patrick. *Sin as Addiction.* New York: Paulist, 1989.

McCormick, Richard. *Notes on Moral Theology 1965 Through 1980.* Washington, D.C.: University Press of America, 1981.

――――. "Notes on Moral Theology – Theologians and the Magisterium." *Theological Studies* 38 (1977): 74–100.

McCormick, Richard and Ramsey, Paul. *Doing Evil to Achieve Good: Moral Choice in Conflict Situations.* Chicago: Loyola University Press, 1978.

Michener, James. *Source.* New York: Random House, 1965.

Ogletree, Thomas. *The Use of the Bible in Christian Ethics*. Philadelphia: Fortress Press, 1983.

Rahner, K. and Vorgremler, M. *Theological Dictionary*. New York: Herder & Herder, 1965.

Schuller, Bruno. *Wholly Human: Essays on the Theory and Language of Morality*. Washington, D.C.: Georgetown University Press, 1986.

Shea, John. *An Experience Named Spirit*. Chicago: Thomas More, 1983.

——. *The Challenge of Jesus*. Chicago: Thomas More, 1975, 1984.

——. *The Spirit Master*. Chicago: Thomas More, 1987.

——. *Stories of God*. Chicago: Thomas More, 1978.

Tillich, Paul. *Theology of Culture*. New York: Oxford University Press, 1959.

Westley, R. *A Theology of Presence*. Mystic, Conn.: Twenty-Third Publications, 1988.

ARTICLES

Cahill, Lisa Sowle. "Teleology, Utilitarianism, and Christian Ethics." *Theological Studies* 42 (1981): 601–629.

——. "Contemporary Challenges to Exceptionless Moral Norms." *Moral Theology Today: Certitudes and Doubts*, pp. 121–135. St. Louis: Pope John XXIII Center, 1984.

——. "A 'Natural Law' Reconsideration of Euthanasia." *Linacre Quarterly* 44 (1977): 47–63.

——. "Moral Methodology: A Case Study." *Chicago Studies* 19 (1980): 171–188.

Committee on Doctrine, U.S. National Conference of Catholic Bishops. "Bishops' Doctrinal Committee Responds to Book on Sexuality," *Origins* 7, #24 (December 1, 1977): 376–378.

Dedek, John. "Moral Absolutes in the Predecessors of St. Thomas." *Theological Studies* 38 (1977): 654–680.

——. "Intrinsically Evil Acts: An Historical Study of the Mind of St. Thomas." *The Thomist* 43 (1979): 385–413.

——. "Premarital Sex: The Theological Argument from Peter Lombard to Durand." *Theological Studies* 41 (1980): 643–667.

——. "Intrinsically Evil Acts: The Emergence of a Doctrine." *Recherches de Théologie Ancienne et Medievale* 50 (1983): 191–226.

Duffy, Stephen. "Our Hearts of Darkness: Original Sin Revisited." *Theological Studies* 49 (1988): 597–622.

Finnis, John. "Reflections on an Essay in Christian Ethics: Part I: Authority in Morals." *Clergy Review* 65 (1980): 51–57.

——. "Reflections on an Essay in Christian Ethics: Part II: Morals and Method." *Clergy Review* 65 (1980): 87–93.

Ford, J. and Grisez, G. "Contraception and the Infallibility of the Ordinary Magisterium." *Theological Studies* 39 (1978): 258–312.

Hallett, G. "Infallibility and Contraception: The Debate Continues." *Theological Studies* 49 (1988): 517–528.

Keane, Philip. "The Objective Moral Order: Reflections on Recent Research." *Theological Studies* 43 (1982): 260–278.

Komonchak, J. "*Humanae vitae* and Its Reception: Ecclesiological Reflections." *Theological Studies* 39 (1978): 221–257.

McCormick, Patrick. "Human Sinfulness: Models for a Developing Moral Theology." *Studia Moralia* 26 (1988): 61-100.

McCormick, Richard. "Notes on Moral Theology." *Theological Studies* 42 (1981): 74-121.

———. "Notes on Moral Theology." *Theological Studies* 43 (1982): 69-124.

———. "Notes on Moral Theology." *Theological Studies* 44 (1983): 71-122.

———. "Notes on Moral Theology." *Theological Studies* 45 (1984): 80-138.

McCormick, Richard, et al. "Notes on Moral Theology." *Theological Studies* 46 (1985): 50-114.

———. "Notes on Moral Theology." *Theological Studies* 47 (1986): 69-133.

———. "Notes on Moral Theology." *Theological Studies* 48 (1987): 87-156.

Modras, Ronald. "Implications of Rahner's Anthropology for Fundamental Theology." *Horizons* 12 (1985): 70-90.

O'Connell, Timothy. "Sexuality and the Procreative Norm." *Contemporary Ethical Issues in the Jewish and Christian Traditions*, pp. 81-110. Hoboken: Ktav, 1986.

Philibert, Paul. "Addressing the Crisis in Moral Theology: Clues from Aquinas and Gilligan." *Theology Digest* 34 (1987): 103-113.

Place, Michael. "Philosophical Foundations for Value Transmission." *Chicago Studies* 19 (1980): 305-334.

Rigali, Norbert. "The Moral Act." *Horizons* 10 (1983): 252-266.

Rudin, Josef. "A Catholic View of Conscience." *Conscience*, ed. Nelson. New York: Newman, 1973.

Vacek, Edward. "Popular Ethical Subjectivism: Four Preludes to Objectivity." *Horizons* 11 (1984): 42-60.

———. "Proportionalism: One View of the Debate." *Theological Studies* 46 (1985): 287-314.

Walter, James. "Proportionate Reason and Its Three Levels of Inquiry: Structuring the Ongoing Debate." *Louvain Studies* 10 (1984): 30-40.

GENERAL INDEX

SCRIPTURE INDEX